CRUSADING SPIRITUALITY
IN THE HOLY LAND AND IBERIA
c.1095–c.1187

CRUSADING SPIRITUALITY
IN THE HOLY LAND AND IBERIA
c.1095–c.1187

William J. Purkis

THE BOYDELL PRESS

First published 2008
The Boydell Press, Woodbridge
Paperback edition 2014

ISBN 978-1-84383-396-3 hardback
ISBN 978-1-84383-926-2 paperback

The Boydell Press is an imprint of Boydell & Brewer Ltd
PO Box 9, Woodbridge, Suffolk IP12 3DF, UK
and of Boydell & Brewer Inc.
668 Mt Hope Avenue, Rochester, NY 14620-2731, USA
website: www.boydellandbrewer.com

The publisher has no responsibility for the continued existence or accuracy of URLs for external or third-party
internet websites referred to in this book, and does not guarantee that any content on such websites is, or will
remain, accurate or appropriate

A CIP record for this book is available
from the British Library

This publication is printed on acid-free paper

Typeset by Word and Page, Chester

For Nicola and Thomas

CONTENTS

ACKNOWLEDGEMENTS

It is a pleasure for me to acknowledge the financial support that I have received from various sources whilst researching and writing this book. I am grateful to the Arts and Humanities Research Council for providing me with a three-year research studentship; to Emmanuel College, University of Cambridge, for awarding me an external research studentship; and to the Faculty of History, University of Cambridge, for providing me with a Lightfoot Scholarship in Ecclesiastical History. In addition, I have held grants from the British Academy and the Ecclesiastical History Society that enabled me to attend and present my research at a number of international conferences: I thank them both for their assistance. I am also grateful to the British Library for granting permission to reproduce the image of Christ's entry into Jerusalem on the dust jacket of the book. It seems to me that this image, which was produced in the Latin East and is one of a series of miniatures of the life of Christ found in the Melisende Psalter, encapsulates some of the central ideas with which I have been concerned.

This book would not have been possible were it not for the guidance and support I received from my supervisor, Jonathan Riley-Smith. I am pleased to register my gratitude to him for helping me to find direction, for offering constructive criticism of my ideas, and for constantly motivating me to try to do better. My enjoyment of doctoral research was also greatly enhanced by the friendship of my contemporaries in Cambridge; I thank them for their insight, camaraderie and all-round good humour. I am extremely grateful to Norman Housley, Marcus Bull and Bernard Hamilton for reading and commenting on the manuscript of the book at various stages in its development; their advice on content and style has been invaluable. I am also indebted to Colin Morris, who helped me to clarify my thinking on the Cistercian influence on crusading, and to Jonathan Phillips, Sue Edgington and Tom Asbridge, who have been hugely supportive of all aspects of my academic career in recent times. It is highly unlikely that I would have developed a serious interest in the Middle Ages had it not been for the inspirational teaching of Nicholas Wright and Andrew Jotischky: they have been formative influences on my approach to the study of the past, and I offer them my sincere thanks for their kindness and generosity over many years. I am also grateful to Caroline Palmer, Anna Morton and Vanda Andrews at Boydell for their patience and support as the book was being prepared for publication; to Phillip Judge for drawing the map; to Clive Tolley for typesetting the text; and to Helen Barber for designing the dust jacket.

My greatest debts, however, are to my family and friends, who have been such valued sources of encouragement. One individual in particular has been called upon on countless occasions to act as travelling companion, editor, counsellor and critic: thank you, Peter. My parents, grandparents, brother and wider family have given me great moral and material support; their assistance and enthusiasm is deeply appreciated. Most importantly, Nicola and (more recently) Thomas have provided me with the time and the space in which to work, and given me the reassurance and the inspiration to keep going — particularly when things looked bleak. Nicola's uncomplaining commitment to this project (especially when the twelfth century became more prominent in our lives than the twenty-first), and her ability to lift flagging spirits, has been invaluable. I dedicate this book to her and to Thomas in gratitude and with love.

ABBREVIATIONS

BRAH	*Boletín de la Real Academia de la Historia*
CC:CM	*Corpus Christianorum, Continuatio Mediaevalis* (Turnhout, 1966–).
LSJ: CC	*Liber sancti Jacobi: Codex Calixtinus*, ed. K. Herbers and M. Santos Noia (Santiago de Compostela, 1998).
MGH	*Monumenta Germaniae Historica*
MGH SS	*MGH Scriptores in folio et quarto*, ed. G.H. Pertz *et al.* (Hanover and Leipzig, 1826–).
MGH SSRG	*MGH Scriptores rerum Germanicarum in usum scholarum separatim editi* (Hanover and Berlin, 1871–).
OV	Orderic Vitalis, *Historia aecclesiastica*, ed. and trans. M. Chibnall, 6 vols. (Oxford, 1969–80).
PL	*Patrologiae cursus completus. Series Latina*, comp. J.P. Migne, 217 vols. and 4 vols. of indexes (Paris, 1844–64).
RHC	*Recueil des historiens des croisades*, ed. Académie des Inscriptions et Belles-Lettres (Paris, 1841–1906).
RHC Oc.	*RHC Historiens occidentaux*, 5 vols. (Paris, 1844–95).
RHGF	*Recueil des historiens des Gaules et de la France*, ed. M. Bouquet *et al.*, 24 vols. (Paris, 1737–1904).
SBO	*Sancti Bernardi opera*, ed. J. Leclercq, H.-M. Rochais, and C.H. Talbot, 8 vols. (Rome, 1957–77).
SCH	*Studies in Church History*

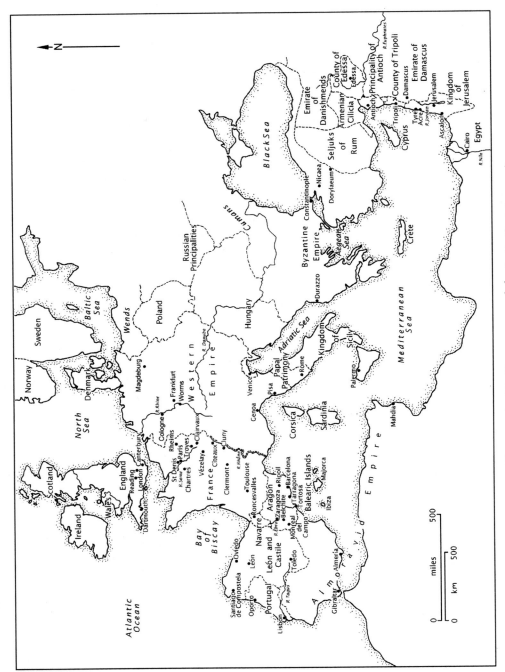

Western Europe, the Mediterranean and the Latin East (c.1145)

Introduction

In his seminal work on the changes in the religious life of the central Middle Ages, *The Reformation of the Twelfth Century*, Giles Constable argued that historians should adopt a new framework for understanding medieval religious experience:

> In looking at twelfth-century religious life, and the movement of reform, it is customary to put in the centre the highly institutionalized types of forms, above all the monks and canons, who led a strict community life, and to see the hermits, recluses, lay brothers, and members of the military orders as peripheral, with pilgrims, penitents, wandering preachers, and crusaders on the margins and all the other various types, if they are considered at all, in a shadowy penumbra. It may be closer to the realities of medieval religious life to think in terms of a different model, putting the individual religious experience at the centre, surrounded by various forms of religious life, of which each was no less important for those involved in them than the more highly organized communities were for their members.[1]

Constable's model suggests that studying the activities and devotions of crusaders ought to be regarded as being as important as analysing those of the Cistercians or Carthusians if a properly nuanced understanding of the religious life of the period is to be reached because, as he put it, in the twelfth century, 'A pilgrimage or a crusade . . . might fill as profound a need in some people as a lifetime reciting the psalms or enclosed in a cell did for others'.[2]

Constable was by no means the first scholar to suggest that the crusades ought to be considered within the broader context of twelfth-century reform.[3] In his study of *The Spirituality of the Middle Ages*, for example, Jean Leclercq began his chapter on 'The New Orders' by considering what he believed to be two related subjects: 'The Crisis of Monasticism' and 'The Crusades and the Pilgrim Spirit'.[4] This important work went on to analyse the wider themes and implications of reform during the eleventh and twelfth centuries, including discussions on the foundation of the military orders, canons regular, Premonstratensians and Carthusians,[5] but it is extraordinary that very little attention has been paid by historians to one of the chapter's opening remarks. In describing

---

[1] G. Constable, *The Reformation of the Twelfth Century* (Cambridge, 1996), p. 86.

[2] *Ibid.*, pp. 86–7.

[3] See also J.S.C. Riley-Smith, 'Death on the First Crusade', *The End of Strife*, ed. D.M. Loades (Edinburgh, 1984), p. 28, who noted that 'the crusade has never been considered . . . [in] recent work on the reform movement'.

[4] J. Leclercq, F. Vandenbroucke and L. Bouyer, *The Spirituality of the Middle Ages* (London, 1968), pp. 127–61.

[5] *Ibid.*, pp. 133–61.

the genesis of crusading, Leclercq wrote that, 'The same spirit lay behind this new kind of *peregrinatio* during that half century [1095–1145] as that which had brought about the monastic crisis and the advent of the wandering hermits'.[6] The present study examines the accuracy of Leclercq's statement by emphasising the importance of pilgrimage to the origins and early development of crusading and, in particular, by considering the influence of two ideals that are more commonly associated with the spirituality of the 'new monasticism': the imitation of Christ and the apostolic life.

Few scholars have approached the roots of crusade ideology in this way.[7] The focus of Carl Erdmann's work on *The Origin of the Idea of Crusade* was on the changes in the Church's attitudes towards war, and although he made important connections with the papal reform movement he did not go so far as to relate the advent of the crusades to many of the equally radical changes in the professed religious life of the period.[8] Similarly, Paul Alphandéry and Alphonse Dupront stressed some of the Christo-mimetic aspects of crusading, particularly insofar as it was understood to be a form of Jerusalem pilgrimage, but their work was more grounded in 'popularism' and in considering the eschatological significance of the Holy Land than it was in the broader context of ecclesiastical reform.[9]

Nevertheless, the intersection between crusading and monasticism has not gone unnoticed by historians.[10] Perhaps most importantly, Jonathan Riley-Smith's study of *The First Crusade and the Idea of Crusading* demonstrated that some contemporaries perceived the crusade to be 'a military monastery on the move',[11] whose 'brethren' were believed to be driven by many of the same ideas that were associated with professed religious.[12] This thesis was given further credence by Marcus Bull, who argued in his examination of the pious practices of arms-bearers from the Limousin and Gascony that 'the fund of

---

[6] *Ibid.*, p. 130.

[7] For a range of overviews, see E.O. Blake, 'The Formation of the "Crusade Idea"', *Journal of Ecclesiastical History*, 21 (1970), pp. 11–31; J.S.C. Riley-Smith, 'The Crusading Movement and Historians', *The Oxford Illustrated History of the Crusades*, ed. J.S.C. Riley-Smith (Oxford, 1995), pp. 1–12; G. Constable, 'The Historiography of the Crusades', *The Crusades from the Perspective of Byzantium and the Muslim World*, ed. A.E. Laiou and R.P. Mottahedeh (Washington, DC, 2001), pp. 1–22.

[8] C. Erdmann, *The Origin of the Idea of Crusade*, trans. M.W. Baldwin and W. Goffart (Princeton, NJ, 1977). See the comments of J.S.C. Riley-Smith, 'Crusading as an Act of Love', *History*, 65 (1980), pp. 191–2. See also É. Delaruelle, 'Essai sur la formation de l'idée de croisade', *Bulletin de littérature ecclésiastique*, 42 (1941), pp. 24–45, 86–103; 45 (1944), pp. 13–46, 73–90; 54 (1953), pp. 226–39; 55 (1954), pp. 50–63.

[9] P. Alphandéry and A. Dupront, *La chrétienté et l'idée de croisade*, 2 vols. (Paris, 1954–9). See also A. Dupront, 'La spiritualité des croisés et des pèlerins d'après les sources de la première croisade', *Pellegrinaggi e culto dei santi in Europa fino alla Ia crociata* (Todi, 1963), pp. 451–83; N. Cohn, *The Pursuit of the Millennium: Revolutionary Millenarians and Mystical Anarchists of the Middle Ages*, revised edition (New York, 1970), pp. 61–70.

[10] See, for example, B. Hamilton, 'Ideals of Holiness: Crusaders, Contemplatives, and Mendicants', *International History Review*, 17 (1995), pp. 693–712; G. Constable, 'The Place of the Crusader in Medieval Society', *Viator*, 29 (1998), pp. 377–403. See also J. Leclercq, 'Monachisme et pérégrination du IXe au XIIe siècle', *Studia monastica*, 3 (1961), pp. 33–52; G. Constable, 'Monachisme et pèlerinage au moyen âge', *Revue historique*, 258 (1977), pp. 3–27.

[11] J.S.C. Riley-Smith, *The First Crusade and the Idea of Crusading* (London, 1986), p. 2.

[12] See below, pp. 21–2.

religious ideas upon which laymen drew when they entered or endowed religious communities was essentially the same as the beliefs which generated crusade enthusiasm'.[13] Both these studies have set important precedents for this book, but the present work is distinctive in two respects. First of all, Riley-Smith's research was concerned with highlighting the influence on crusading of a range of monastic ideas, and tracing their development over a period of around fifteen years (1095–c.1111).[14] Secondly, Bull was more concerned with examining the relationships between the arms-bearers and religious institutions within his particular region of study, analysing the processes by which the two interacted and exchanged religious ideas, and thereby isolating the formative influences on crusade ideology, rather than considering the subsequent development of that ideology itself. In contrast to both these approaches, this book focuses on a narrower range of ideas that were central to early crusading spirituality, and seeks to demonstrate how they developed and changed over a considerably longer period of time. In this respect, the present work can be seen to be approaching a topic that Riley-Smith himself identified in his conclusion to *The First Crusade and the Idea of Crusading*: whether or not 'crusading was becoming markedly less monastic by 1200'.[15]

Whilst the ideals of *imitatio Christi* and *vita apostolica* have not been ignored by historians of the crusades,[16] few scholars have paid close attention to their importance; even fewer have considered them to be worthy of study in their own right, and all too often they have been referred to in imprecise terminology or seen as cliché. This study therefore seeks to offer a detailed analysis of how those ideals manifested themselves in crusading spirituality during the first century of the movement's history. The terminal dates have been chosen for two reasons: first, to enable examination of crusading from its inception in 1095; and second, to conclude that examination at a suitable turning point in the early history of the movement. The year 1187 provides such a juncture because it was after this date that the aim of recovering the earthly Jerusalem once again became the specific focus of crusading activity in the East.[17] The book also considers the repercussions that crusading spirituality had for the development of two associated aspects of twelfth-century religious life: Jerusalem pilgrimage and the Order of the Temple. The historiography of the Jerusalem pilgrimage tradition is vast,[18] but it is striking that scholars working in this field have often been more concerned with the practicalities and legalities of the pilgrim experience rather than with its ideological

---

[13] M. Bull, *Knightly Piety and the Lay Response to the First Crusade: The Limousin and Gascony, c.970–c.1130* (Oxford, 1993), p. 280.

[14] See Riley-Smith, *The First Crusade*, pp. 159–63.

[15] *Ibid.*, p. 155.

[16] See Constable, 'Historiography', pp. 15–16.

[17] See J. Richard, '1187: point de départ pour une nouvelle forme de la croisade', *The Horns of Hattin: Proceedings of the Second Conference of the Society for the Study of the Crusades and the Latin East*, ed. B.Z. Kedar (Jerusalem, 1992), pp. 250–60.

[18] For an overview, see L.K. Davidson and M. Dunn-Wood, *Pilgrimage in the Middle Ages: A Research Guide* (New York and London, 1993), pp. 80–127. See also S. Runciman, 'The Pilgrimages to Palestine before 1095', *A History of the Crusades*, vol. 1, ed. K. Setton (Madison, WI, 1969), pp. 68–78; J. Sumption, *Pilgrimage: An Image of Mediaeval Religion* (London, 1975); D. Webb, *Medieval European Pilgrimage, c.700–c.1500* (Basingstoke, 2002).

foundations.[19] Two recent notable exceptions are the books by Colin Morris[20] and Sylvia Schein,[21] but both these works take significantly broader chronological or thematic approaches than that which is adopted by the present study. Similarly, scholarship on the early history of the Templars has tended to concentrate on the Order's ideological connections with the crusades in terms of meritorious warfare rather than concepts of Christo-mimesis;[22] indeed, it is striking that, like the crusades themselves, the Templars have often been overlooked by historians of ecclesiastical reform.[23] In short, this book attempts to bridge the gap between the study of the spirituality of crusading, pilgrimage and monasticism identified by Giles Constable, and to demonstrate how the history of the crusades ought to be considered to be integral to research into the transformation of the religious life of the eleventh and twelfth centuries.

Before embarking on such a study it is first necessary to offer definitions of two of the most important terms used in this book: 'crusading' and 'spirituality'. Over the past thirty years scholars have become increasingly divided in their understandings and interpretations of the crusading movement in the Middle Ages.[24] Some historians (recently characterised as 'generalists') have argued that the term 'crusading' can be used to describe all forms of Christian holy war; others (the 'traditionalists') have suggested that a crusade was an armed expedition directed to the Near East for the liberation or defence of Jerusalem and the Holy Sepulchre; a smaller number (the 'popularists') understand crusading to be a manifestation of the eschatological concerns of the medieval peasantry; and finally, there are those who believe that crusades were a distinct form of penitential warfare that could be fought in a number of theatres of conflict (the 'pluralists').[25] In addition to these four contrasting approaches, one historian has even recently suggested that the idea of 'crusading' itself – at least for the period covered by the present study – is a later historiographical construct that has been applied to a

[19] See especially E.R. Labande, 'Recherches sur les pèlerins dans l'Europe des XIe et XIIe siècles', *Cahiers de civilisation médiévale*, 1 (1958), pp. 159–69, 339–47; F. Garrisson, 'A propos des pèlerins et de leur condition juridique', *Études d'histoire du droit canonique dédiées à Gabriel le Bras* (Paris, 1965), pp. 1165–89; E.R. Labande, '*Ad limina*: le pèlerin médiéval au terme de sa démarche', *Mélanges offerts à René Crozet*, ed. P. Gallais and Y.-J. Riou, 2 vols. (Poitiers, 1966), vol. 1, pp. 283–91; G.B. Ladner, '*Homo Viator*: Medieval Ideas on Alienation and Order', *Speculum*, 42 (1967), pp. 233–59; A. Graboïs, 'Le concept du "contemptus mundi" dans les pratiques des pèlerins occidentaux en terre sainte à l'époque des croisades', *Mediaevalia Christiana, XIe–XIIe siècles: hommage à Raymond Foreville des ses amis, ses collègues et ses anciens élèves*, ed. C.E. Viola (Paris, 1989), pp. 290–306; D.J. Birch, 'Jacques de Vitry and the Ideology of Pilgrimage', *Pilgrimage Explored*, ed. J. Stopford (Woodbridge, 1999), pp. 79–93.
[20] C. Morris, *The Sepulchre of Christ and the Medieval West: From the Beginning to 1600* (Oxford, 2005).
[21] S. Schein, *Gateway to the Heavenly City: Crusader Jerusalem and the Catholic West (1099–1187)* (Aldershot, 2005).
[22] See, for example, A.J. Forey, 'The Emergence of the Military Order in the Twelfth Century', *Journal of Ecclesiastical History*, 36 (1985), pp. 175–95; M. Barber, *The New Knighthood: A History of the Order of the Temple* (Cambridge, 1994), pp. 38–63.
[23] See the comments of A.J. Forey, *The Military Orders from the Twelfth to the Early Fourteenth Centuries* (Basingstoke, 1992), p. 3. For a revisionist approach, see T. Licence, 'The Military Orders as Monastic Orders', *Crusades*, 5 (2006), pp. 39–53.
[24] For a discussion of the issues surrounding definition, see now N. Housley, *Contesting the Crusades* (Oxford, 2006), pp. 1–23.
[25] For these categorisations, see Constable, 'Historiography', pp. 10–22.

series of events that were altogether more diffuse.[26] Although the conclusions of this latter work are not followed by the present writer, the suggestion that the crusades were retrospectively 'invented' by writers working at a chronological distance from the events that they were describing is a judicious reminder that the crusading movement was evolutionary in nature and was certainly not as coherent or institutionalised in the twelfth century as it was to become in the thirteenth;[27] the implications of this reminder are especially evident in Chapters Five and Six of this book.

The position advocated in the pages that follow might perhaps be best described as a modified form of pluralism. In general terms, this book accepts that the most useful modern definition of a crusade is that offered by Jonathan Riley-Smith, who judged that:

> To contemporaries a crusade was an expedition authorized by the pope on Christ's behalf, the leading participants in which took vows and consequently enjoyed the privileges of protection at home and the indulgence, which, when the campaign was not destined for the East, was equated with that granted to crusaders to the Holy Land.[28]

However, in this book it will be suggested that pluralist historians should be cautious not to underestimate the significance of the idea of Jerusalem pilgrimage to wider contemporary understandings of crusading, at least for the early period of the movement's history.[29] In this respect, the book stresses that the penitential aspects of a crusade were closely associated with ideas of pilgrimage and Christo-mimesis,[30] and that even when crusades were preached in other theatres of war, pilgrimage frameworks continued to be of fundamental importance – indeed, it is argued that it was the primacy of the idea of pilgrimage that initially separated crusading from other forms of penitential warfare, such as the military campaigns that were waged against the political opponents of the papacy in the late eleventh and early twelfth centuries.[31] As a result, the position taken in this book bears comparison with that of 'traditionalists' such as Hans Mayer and Jean Flori, who emphasise the centrality of the Holy Sepulchre in their definitions of the crusade;[32] where it differs, however, is that its resulting focus is not solely on campaigns

---

[26] C. Tyerman, *The Invention of the Crusades* (Basingstoke, 1998).

[27] See also J.S.C. Riley-Smith, *The Crusades: A History*, 2nd edition (London, 2005), who wrote of the birth, adolescence, maturity, old age and death of the crusading movement.

[28] J.S.C. Riley-Smith, *What were the Crusades?*, 3rd edition (Basingstoke, 2002), p. 5.

[29] Cf. Constable, 'Historiography', p. 13, who was 'reluctant . . . to deny that at least a spiritual orientation toward Jerusalem was an essential aspect of crusading'. See also N. Housley, 'Jerusalem and the Development of the Crusade Idea, 1099–1128', *The Horns of Hattin: Proceedings of the Second Conference of the Society for the Study of the Crusades and the Latin East*, ed. B.Z. Kedar (Jerusalem, 1992), pp. 27–40.

[30] For the penitential elements of crusading, see now Riley-Smith, *The Crusades*, pp. 12–16.

[31] See N. Housley, 'Crusades against Christians: Their Origins and Early Development, c.1000–1216', *Crusade and Settlement: Papers Read at the First Conference of the Society for the Study of the Crusades and the Latin East and Presented to R.C. Smail*, ed. P.W. Edbury (Cardiff, 1985), pp. 17–36; J.S.C. Riley-Smith, *The First Crusaders, 1095–1131* (Cambridge, 1997), pp. 51–2; Tyerman, *Invention of the Crusades*, p. 15. See also Riley-Smith, *What were the Crusades?*, p. 87, who concluded that 'A crusade was a penitential war which ranked as, and had many of the attributes of, a pilgrimage.'

[32] See, for example, H.E. Mayer, *The Crusades*, trans. J. Gillingham, 2nd edition (Oxford, 1988), passim; J. Flori, *La guerre sainte: La formation de l'idée de croisade dans l'Occident chrétien* (Paris, 2001),

that were fought in the eastern Mediterranean theatre. As will hopefully become apparent, it is in this way that the book seeks to reconcile some of the tensions between the Jerusalem-centric vision of crusading held by the traditionalists with the broader geographical approach taken by the pluralists.[33]

The emphasis placed on Jerusalem pilgrimage in the pages that follow does, however, give rise to a further problem of definition: how one distinguishes between a crusader and a pilgrim, especially when the term *peregrinus* was used by contemporaries to describe both pilgrims and crusaders alike,[34] and when the adoption of the sign of the cross cannot always be said to have been the preserve of those who had taken the crusade vow.[35] For the present purpose, this book presupposes that where an individual's actions are known to be primarily oratory, he or she was a pilgrim, and where primarily military, a crusader.[36] It is by no means a perfect distinction for it is clear that crusaders would often abandon their weapons upon reaching the Holy Sepulchre, and that pilgrims were not unaccustomed to taking up arms once they had completed their itineraries of the holy places;[37] nevertheless, given the often fragmentary nature of the evidence, it is perhaps the most functional approach to take.

One consequence of this book's acceptance of the pluralist approach to the history of the crusades is that it is not exclusively concerned with military expeditions that engaged Islam in the Holy Land. Although the full range of twelfth-century crusading activity is not considered in the pages that follow,[38] the final third of the book addresses the extension of crusading to another frontier of war: the Iberian peninsula. Until recently, Iberia has often been regarded as playing a formative role in the genesis of crusade ideology but, as will be highlighted in Chapters Five and Six, this position is no longer tenable.[39] Indeed, the idea that 'the reconquest of Spain' gave way to 'the crusade in Spain' must now be regarded as outdated, and Joseph F. O'Callaghan has recently provided a useful description of how concepts of 'crusade' and 'reconquest' ought to be distinguished by historians of the peninsular conflicts between Christians and Muslims:

> The reconquest can best be understood as an ongoing process, which, though often interrupted by truces, remained the ultimate goal toward which Christian rulers directed their efforts over several centuries . . . Unlike the reconquest, the crusade in Spain can be viewed as an event, a specific campaign, resulting from a proclamation by the pope, a council, a papal legate, or a bishop who granted remission of sins to those who would take up arms against the Muslims.[40]

p. 357, wrote 'La croisade est une guerre sainte ayant pour objectif la libération de Jérusalem.'

[33] Cf. Housley, *Contesting the Crusades*, p. 5, who wrote that 'In the strictest sense traditionalism and pluralism are irreconcilable.'

[34] Tyerman, *Invention of the Crusades*, pp. 20–3, 49–55; Riley-Smith, *What were the Crusades?*, p. 2.

[35] See G. Constable, 'Jerusalem and the Sign of the Cross (with Particular Reference to the Cross of Pilgrimage and Crusading in the Twelfth Century)', *Jerusalem: Its Sanctity and Centrality to Judaism, Christianity, and Islam*, ed. L.I. Levine (New York, 1999), pp. 371–81. For an example of this problem, see below, pp. 62–3.

[36] Cf. Riley-Smith, *First Crusaders*, p. 4.

[37] See J.S.C. Riley-Smith, 'An Army on Pilgrimage' (Forthcoming).

[38] See Riley-Smith, *What were the Crusades?*, pp. 12–22.

[39] See below, especially pp. 120–2.

[40] J.F. O'Callaghan, *Reconquest and Crusade in Medieval Spain* (Philadelphia, PA, 2003), pp. 20–1.

It should of course be added that territorial reconquest cannot be proved to have been a priority for all Christian rulers in all periods of medieval Iberian history,[41] and that the ideal of *reconquista* itself was subject to significant change over space and time;[42] indeed, it is clear that significant developments took place as a result of peninsular rulers coming into contact with crusading and crusaders.[43] However, as the present work is specifically focused on the ideology of crusading, it has not been deemed necessary to address the resurgence and revitalisation of ideas of 'reconquest' in the twelfth century, except insofar as they have a direct bearing on crusade ideology itself. Consequently, 'reconquest' is not a term that appears with any great frequency in the discussion of the early development of crusading in Iberia.[44]

A second term used throughout the book to denote the scope of enquiry is 'spirituality'. As has been pointed out elsewhere,[45] 'spirituality' is not a word that would have been employed by medieval writers to describe ideals and impulses associated with the religious life, but it has been used here to encompass a range of themes and concepts more familiar to historians of monasticism than to those of the crusades, most especially the imitation of Christ and the apostolic life.[46] In this respect, works by Brenda Bolton,[47] Caroline Walker Bynum,[48] Christopher N.L. Brooke,[49] M.-D. Chenu,[50] Giles Constable,[51] Herbert Grundmann,[52] Andrew Jotischky,[53] Jean Leclercq,[54] Henrietta Leyser,[55]

---

[41] See, for example, S. Barton, 'Spain in the Eleventh Century', *The New Cambridge Medieval History*, vol. 4.2, ed. D. Luscombe and J.S.C. Riley-Smith (Cambridge, 2004), pp. 154–90.

[42] See, for example, R. McCluskey, 'Malleable Accounts: Views of the Past in Twelfth Century Iberia', *The Perception of the Past in Twelfth-Century Europe*, ed. P. Magdalino (London, 1992), pp. 211–25.

[43] See especially R.A. Fletcher, 'Reconquest and Crusade in Spain, c.1050–1150', *Transactions of the Royal Historical Society*, 5th ser., 37 (1987), pp. 31–47.

[44] I intend to explore the relationship between Iberian crusading and ideas of peninsular reconquest at greater length in future publications.

[45] C.W. Bynum, *Jesus as Mother: Studies in the Spirituality of the High Middle Ages* (Berkeley, Los Angeles and London, 1982), p. 3.

[46] The contemporary significance of these ideals is discussed in more detail below: see pp. 22–7 and 47–8.

[47] B.M. Bolton, '"Paupertas Christi": Old Wealth and New Poverty in the Twelfth Century', *Renaissance and Renewal in Christian History*, ed. D. Baker, *SCH*, 14 (Oxford, 1977), pp. 95–103; B.M. Bolton, *The Medieval Reformation* (London, 1983).

[48] Bynum, *Jesus as Mother*.

[49] C.N.L. Brooke, 'Monk and Canon: Some Patterns in the Religious Life of the Twelfth Century', *Monks, Hermits and the Ascetic Tradition*, ed. W.J. Sheils, *SCH*, 22 (Oxford, 1985), pp. 109–29.

[50] M.-D. Chenu, *Nature, Man and Society in the Twelfth Century: Essays on New Theological Perspectives in the Latin West*, ed. and trans. J. Taylor and L.K. Little (Toronto, 1968).

[51] G. Constable, *Three Studies in Medieval Religious and Social Thought* (Cambridge, 1995); Constable, *Reformation*.

[52] H. Grundmann, *Religious Movements in the Middle Ages*, trans. S. Rowan (Notre Dame, IN, 1995).

[53] A. Jotischky, *The Perfection of Solitude: Hermits and Monks in the Crusader States* (University Park, PA, 1995).

[54] Leclercq *et al.*, *Spirituality of the Middle Ages*.

[55] H. Leyser, *Hermits and the New Monasticism: A Study of Religious Communities in Western Europe, 1000–1150* (New York, 1984).

Lester K. Little,[56] Colin Morris,[57] Sir Richard Southern,[58] Ernest J.Tinsley,[59] and André Vauchez,[60] are of particular value and importance. However, the present study also adopts the broader definition of 'spirituality' suggested by Giles Constable, where the term is understood to refer 'not just to piety and devotion but to the point where faith and action intersect: how a faith is lived and what people do about their religious beliefs'.[61] Consequently, this book should be seen within a broader context of research into the motivations of crusaders, an area that has recently been defined by Norman Housley as an investigation into 'the spectrum of goals, hopes, beliefs and fears that first impelled people to take the cross and later sustained them while they were on crusade'.[62] It is the argument of this book that the ideas of Christo-mimesis that are evident within the sources for twelfth-century crusading should be regarded as fundamental for understanding the ideological frameworks in which men and women from across Europe made their decisions to take the cross.

In conducting the research for this book I have relied on a broad base of primary source material. Because my focus has been on the way crusading spirituality developed over a time span of nearly one hundred years, and on the basis that later writers may have glossed past events erroneously, I have principally used sources that were immediately contemporary with each period under consideration; the terminal dates assigned to each chapter thus give an indication of the years during which the texts discussed therein were composed. Similarly, as my interest is in the ideas of western Europeans, I have concentrated my analysis on Latin sources rather than other contemporary accounts by Arabic, Greek or Jewish writers. Nevertheless, these constraints have not proved to be too limiting. The richness and variety of the epistolary and narrative evidence for the First Crusade has been described in detail elsewhere and it is unnecessary to reiterate the specifics of the early histories of the expedition; suffice to say that much of the available contemporary material has been consulted, most of which is now accessible in modern critical editions.[63] I have not, however, researched extensively into charters,[64]

---

[56] L.K. Little, *Religious Poverty and the Profit Economy in Medieval Europe* (London, 1978).

[57] C. Morris, *The Papal Monarchy: The Western Church from 1050 to 1250* (Oxford, 1989).

[58] R.W. Southern, *Western Society and the Church in the Middle Ages* (Harmondsworth, 1970).

[59] E.J. Tinsley, *The Imitation of God in Christ: An Essay on the Biblical Basis of Christian Spirituality* (London, 1960).

[60] A. Vauchez, *The Laity in the Middle Ages: Religious Belief and Devotional Practices*, ed. D.E. Bornstein (Notre Dame and London, 1993).

[61] Constable, *Reformation*, p. 14.

[62] Housley, *Contesting the Crusades*, p. 77. For a full discussion, see *ibid.*, pp. 75–98. See also J. Flori, 'Ideology and Motivations in the First Crusade', *Palgrave Advances in the Crusades*, ed. H.J. Nicholson (Basingstoke, 2005), pp. 15–36.

[63] See J. France, *Victory in the East: A Military History of the First Crusade* (Cambridge, 1994), pp. 374–82; S.B. Edgington, 'The First Crusade: Reviewing the Evidence', *The First Crusade: Origins and Impact*, ed. J.P. Phillips (Manchester, 1997), pp. 55–77. See also M. Bull, 'Views of Muslims and of Jerusalem in Miracle Stories, c.1000–c.1200: Reflections on the Study of First Crusaders' Motivations', *The Experience of Crusading, Volume One: Western Approaches*, ed. M. Bull and N. Housley (Cambridge, 2003), pp. 13–23.

[64] See G. Constable, 'Medieval Charters as a Source for the History of the Crusades', *Crusade and Settlement*, pp. 73–89; M. Bull, 'The Diplomatic of the First Crusade', *The First Crusade: Origins and Impact*, pp. 35–56.

and where references to such documents are to be found it is on occasion a result of my following in the footsteps of previous scholars.[65] Although the sources for crusading to the East in the first four decades of the twelfth century are fragmentary to say the least, by the time of the Second Crusade there is once again an abundance of narrative and epistolary material.[66] For the period 1150–87, however, I have relied almost exclusively on the texts of letters issued by the papacy and other senior churchmen that appealed for crusades to assist the settlers of the Latin East with only negligible success.[67] Many of the chronicles and documentary sources that pertain to the early history of crusading in Iberia were collated or referred to by José Goñi Gaztambide in his *Historia de la bula de la cruzada en España*,[68] but for this section of the book I have also utilised two types of source that have yet to be fully exploited by crusade historians: miracle stories and foundation legends.[69] A more detailed study of the particular texts that I have used, as well as a review of some parallel studies that have dealt with the use of 'imaginative memory' by writers in the eleventh and twelfth centuries, can be found in Chapter Six. Finally, it should also be stated that for comparative purposes I have referred throughout the book to an array of sources that describe the upheavals in, and spirituality associated with, professed religious life in the eleventh, twelfth and thirteenth centuries. In so doing, I have tried to demonstrate some of the similarities between the language used of crusaders, monks, mendicants and hermits.

In approaching all of these sources, I have been concerned to highlight the frequency and diversity (and sometimes the absence) of references to the ideals of *imitatio Christi* and *vita apostolica*. Some of the most obvious indications of how contemporaries applied these spiritual ideals to crusaders can be detected through quotation from or allusion to certain key scriptural passages, but I have also been careful to consider the implications of other descriptions of the experience of crusading in Christo-mimetic or quasi-apostolic terminology. In this respect, my approach follows the example of Caroline Walker Bynum, who believed that 'the emotional significance of a word or image (even very common words) cannot be inferred from its modern meaning but must be established by a careful study of the other images and phrases among which it occurs in a text',[70] and it is this methodology that has informed my analysis of the changing significance of references to, say, the crusaders' 'unanimity' or their 'taking of the cross'. Furthermore, having established the importance of the idea that crusading was regarded as a Christo-mimetic devotional undertaking, I have looked at how contemporaries understood the crusade to be a form of armed pilgrimage, and have traced how the related concepts of *peregrinatio* and *imitatio* evolved as crusading was extended beyond the Levantine theatre.

As a consequence of the nature of the evidence that I have used and of the approach to the topic that I have taken, many of the arguments presented in this book are more

---

[65] See especially Riley-Smith, *First Crusaders*.

[66] For an overview, see G. Constable, 'The Second Crusade as Seen by Contemporaries', *Traditio*, 9 (1953), pp. 213–79.

[67] For an overview, see J.P. Phillips, *Defenders of the Holy Land: Relations between the Latin East and the West, 1119–1187* (Oxford, 1996), pp. 6–7, 12–13.

[68] J. Goñi Gaztambide, *Historia de la bula de la cruzada en España* (Vitoria, 1958).

[69] Precedents for this approach have been set by M. Bull, *The Miracles of Our Lady of Rocamadour: Analysis and Translation* (Woodbridge, 1999); Bull, 'Views of Muslims and of Jerusalem', pp. 13–38.

[70] Bynum, *Jesus as Mother*, p. 7.

concerned with the spirituality associated with crusading by those who organised, promoted or subsequently wrote narrative accounts of the campaigns rather than by those who took part in the expeditions themselves. The implications of this methodology for the wider study of crusader motivation are considered in more detail in Chapter Two.[71] However, one further issue with the reliance on narrative sources for examining the development of crusading spirituality is that although many of the writers of the texts in question relied on hortatory speeches and sermons in their works, the contents of these reports can never be proved to be wholly reliable; Guibert of Nogent, for example, introduced his report of Urban II's Clermont address by writing that he did not offer an account of the pope's words but of his meaning (*intentio*).[72] Nevertheless, whilst Guibert's account of the pope's words cannot be taken on face value as dependable reportage, his version of events does tell us how *he* interpreted the spirituality of crusading, and it is through comparing his insights with those of his contemporaries that a suitably nuanced model of crusading spirituality can be pieced together.

The book begins by asking why professed religious from across western Europe were moved to respond positively to Pope Urban II's preaching of the First Crusade in 1095–6. By examining a range of contemporary perceptions of what the crusade was, it is suggested that the appeal of crusading to those who had already vowed themselves to a monastic life may have been rooted not only in the idea that the expedition was a form of armed Jerusalem pilgrimage, but also in the fact that it was presented as a strikingly innovative act of *imitatio Christi*. The scriptural origins and eleventh-century perceptions of the ideal of the imitation of Christ are then discussed, and it is stressed that Pope Urban's proclamation of the crusade as a way for Christians to take up Christ's cross and follow him would have been regarded as extremely potent in the context of ideas that were driving monastic reform. In this respect, it is argued that those individuals who abandoned their houses and hermitages to join the armies of the First Crusade ought to be regarded as having undertaken a kind of *transitus*, which was understood to be one of the temptations that the increasingly diverse array of paths of religious observance presented to those who had already taken religious vows.

Having established the broader context for Pope Urban's proclamation of the First Crusade, Chapter Two goes on to analyse in detail how ideas of *imitatio Christi* were manifest in the spirituality of the expedition. The significance of the 'preaching of the cross' is examined, as are some of the unusual responses to that preaching, and the influence of ideas of self-imposed exile, voluntary poverty, Jerusalem pilgrimage and martyrdom as acts of Christo-mimesis is stressed. The second half of the chapter turns to consider the impact upon crusading spirituality of another ideal of contemporary significance: the *vita apostolica*. Representations of the crusaders as living in accordance with the values of the primitive Church and participating in an apostolic activity are described, and the derivation of these concepts is tentatively traced back to the preaching of Pope Urban himself. However, it is concluded that the idea of the crusade as a Christo-mimetic Jerusalem pilgrimage-in-arms must have had a greater resonance for those who set out for the Levant at the turn of the twelfth century.

[71] See below, pp. 57–8.
[72] Guibert of Nogent, 'Dei gesta per Francos', ed. R.B.C. Huygens, *CC:CM* 127 A (Turnhout, 1996), p. 111.

The third and fourth chapters of the book examine the development of ideas associated with crusading and pilgrimage to the East during the eighty-eight-year life of the first Latin kingdom of Jerusalem. It is suggested that the combination of the establishment of a western Christian presence in the Holy Land and Pope Urban's association of ideas of *imitatio Christi* with Jerusalem pilgrimage had important consequences for crusade and pilgrimage piety in the years before 1187, and it is argued that crusading to the East was inextricably linked to the pilgrimage tradition during this period. Nevertheless, it is also stressed that from the Second Crusade onwards there was a discrepancy between the crusading ideas of most western Christians and certain senior churchmen, and through a close reading of the relevant works of Abbot Bernard of Clairvaux it is demonstrated that many of Pope Urban's original ideas of crusading as a Christo-mimetic devotion had been diverted into the spirituality of the Order of the Temple. As a result, the efforts of the Cistercians to institute a new theology of the crusader's cross in the 1140s are described, and their legacy for the preaching of crusades to the East in the period 1150–87 is considered.

Chapters Five and Six of the book see the focus of analysis shift to the Iberian peninsula. The positive response of Spanish arms-bearers to the preaching of the First Crusade is examined, and the initial difficulties that the Church faced in controlling and redirecting the crusade piety of such individuals are highlighted. It is suggested that the reason peninsular penitential warfare proved to be so unappealing in relation to a crusade to the East in the period 1095–c.1120 was because of the primacy of ideas of pilgrimage and Christo-mimesis in early crusading spirituality. Consequently, it is argued that when a crusade was eventually preached in Iberia in the early 1120s, the presence of the idea of opening another route to the Holy Sepulchre via al-Andalus and North Africa was of the utmost importance for the effective propagation of crusading in another theatre of war. Nevertheless, the idea of the *iter per Hispaniam* was soon supplemented by a range of more local crusading ideas, and the efforts of propagandists working in Santiago de Compostela to portray St James the Great as a patron of warfare against Islam and to invent a foundation legend for crusading in Iberia are described. In this respect, it is argued that by the middle of the twelfth century crusading ideology in Iberia was beginning to move away from its roots in the Jerusalem pilgrimage tradition and to develop certain characteristics that were unique to the peninsula. However, it is suggested that the fact that the figure of St James came to reach such prominence in the ideology of crusading in Iberia indicates that some connection between meritorious violence and penitential pilgrimage was maintained, albeit in a modified form.

CHAPTER ONE

The Monastic Response to the First Crusade

Crusading, Pilgrimage and Monasticism

On 7 October 1096 Pope Urban II addressed a letter to the brethren of the congregation of Vallombrosa. He was writing in response to news he had received about the desire of certain members of that congregation to join the armed pilgrims of the First Crusade who were setting out from the West to liberate Jerusalem and the Holy Land from the perceived oppression of Islam. It was Pope Urban's intention to clarify to the Vallombrosans the Church's position on participation in the crusade by those who had already sworn themselves to a monastic life:

> This is, indeed, the right kind of sacrifice, but it is planned by the wrong kind of person, for we were stirring the spirits of knights for this expedition . . . we do not want those who have abandoned the world and have vowed themselves to spiritual warfare either to bear arms or to go on this journey – in fact, we forbid it.

Urban went on to describe the inherent spiritual danger of the crusade for professed religious, before concluding that the full force of papal sanction – the 'sword of apostolic excommunication' – would be used against those who went against his injunction; he also instructed that all the monasteries of the Vallombrosan congregation should be made aware of the contents of his letter.[1]

Pope Urban's letter of October 1096 is not the only evidence to have survived to indicate that he was mindful of the problem of the 'crusading monk'.[2] Less than three weeks earlier he had also written to the people of Bologna with a series of instructions for those who wished to join the crusade, amongst which was a reminder that 'we do not allow either clerics or monks to go unless they have permission from their bishops

---

[1] 'Papsturkunden in Florenz', ed. W. Wiederhold, *Nachrichten von der Gesellschaft der Wissenschaften zu Götingen, Phil.-hist. Kl.* (1901), no. 6, pp. 313–14.

[2] The phrase is borrowed from J. A. Brundage, 'A Transformed Angel (X 3.31.18): The Problem of the Crusading Monk', *Studies in Medieval Cistercian History Presented to Jeremiah F. O'Sullivan*, vol. 1, Cistercian Studies Series, 13 (Spencer, MA, 1971), pp. 55–62. Professor Brundage's study deals with this 'problem' from a juridical perspective, and mostly concentrates on the thirteenth century. See also W. Porges, 'The Clergy, the Poor and the Non-Combatants on the First Crusade', *Speculum*, 21 (1946), pp. 1–23.

or abbots'.[3] Furthermore, in one report of the sermon he had delivered to the Council of Clermont in November 1095 in which he first publicly called for the crusade, Urban was said to have qualified his appeal by stating that 'priests and clerics of any order whatever are forbidden to go without the permission of their bishops'.[4] It is notoriously difficult to reconstruct the actual wording of the Clermont address,[5] but given that this passage appears in the account of Robert of Rheims (who was almost certainly present at the council), and given that the wording of the passage itself is comparable with that of Urban's letters from the autumn of 1096,[6] it seems almost certain that the pope was aware from the outset that his appeal might prove popular with certain religious. Yet although Urban's message to such individuals was far from obtuse, the crusade continued to hold an allure not only for those *bellatores* who were in the world, but also for those *oratores* who were supposed to have renounced it.[7]

It is clear that the Vallombrosans were not the only monastic congregation to have been affected by Pope Urban's preaching for the First Crusade. In a description of the departure of the first crusaders in 1096, the chronicler Bernold of St Blasien recorded that 'there were many apostates in that company who, having abandoned the habit of religion, were setting forth to fight with them'.[8] Similarly, Geoffrey *Grossus* wrote that 'several abbots and monks, and even hermits, were deserting their monasteries and making for Jerusalem',[9] and Baldric of Bourgueil noted that there were 'many hermits, recluses and monks . . . [who] were hastening to go on this journey', not all of whom had received the blessing of their superiors.[10] 'Bishops, abbots, clerics and monks' were amongst those groups that Albert of Aachen identified as responding to the preaching of the crusade by Peter the Hermit (whose epithet itself tells its own story),[11] and Sigebert of Gembloux included a comparable reference in his *Chronica* when he wrote of the 'bishops, clerics and monks' who took the cross in 1096.[12] News of the crusade had also reached England, and in a letter to the bishop of Salisbury, Anselm of Canterbury warned that any monks in his correspondent's diocese who set out to join the crusade would be subject to anathema.[13] Indeed, Anselm's letters also reveal that the papal

---

[3] *Die Kreuzzugsbriefe aus den Jahren 1088–1100*, ed. H. Hagenmeyer (Innsbruck, 1901), no. 3, pp. 137–8.

[4] Robert of Rheims, 'Historia Iherosolimitana', *RHC Oc*. 3, p. 729.

[5] See especially H.E.J. Cowdrey, 'Pope Urban II's Preaching of the First Crusade', *History*, 55 (1970), pp. 177–88.

[6] See also 'Papsturkunden in Florenz', no. 6, p. 313: 'Porro religiosos clericos siue monachos in comitatu hoc proficisci sine episcoporum uel abbatum suorum licentia secundum disciplinam sanctorum canonum interdicimus.' R. Somerville, 'The Council of Clermont and the First Crusade', *Studia Gratiana*, 20 (1976), p. 330, suggested the possibility that such wording was 'an oblique reference to a conciliar canon, perhaps even a Clermont statute, regulating the composition of crusading bands'.

[7] For the social divisions of the Middle Ages, see G. Constable, 'The Orders of Society', *Three Studies in Medieval Religious and Social Thought* (Cambridge, 1995), pp. 249–360.

[8] Bernold of St Blasien, 'Chronicon', *MGH SS* 5, p. 464.

[9] Geoffrey *Grossus*, 'Vita Bernardi Tironiensis', *PL* 172, col. 1378.

[10] Baldric of Bourgueil, 'Historia Jerosolimitana', *RHC Oc*. 4, p. 17.

[11] Albert of Aachen, *Historia Ierosolimitana*, ed. and trans. S.B. Edgington (Oxford, 2007), pp. 2–4.

[12] Sigebert of Gembloux, 'Chronica', *MGH SS* 6, p. 367.

[13] Anselm of Canterbury, 'Epistolae', *S. Anselmi Cantuariensis archiepiscopi opera omnia*, ed. F.S. Schmitt,

prohibition against crusading by monks had been widely disseminated,[14] for at some point in 1096 he wrote the following to a brother of St Martin at Séez:

> I hear, O my dearest friend, that you wish to go to Jerusalem. I say to you in the first place that this longing of yours is not for a good reason, nor is it [good] for the salvation of your soul. It is, indeed, contrary to your profession, in which you have promised stability before God in the monastery in which you have taken the habit of a monk. It is also contrary to the instruction of the pope, who ordered with his great authority that monks should not undertake this journey.[15]

Although Pope Urban's instructions were unequivocal, it seems that his words had little to no effect on the growing numbers of professed religious who wished to set out for the Holy Land. What was it about his message that had stirred the spirit of these individuals in such a way as to leave them intent on abandoning their monasteries and hermitages so that they could join the armies of the First Crusade?

It must be stated from the outset that although the scale on which monks and other religious responded to the preaching of the crusade was undoubtedly considered by contemporaries to be extraordinary and thus worthy of note, the phenomenon of monastic pilgrimage was by no means unprecedented in the 1090s; equally, it is not difficult to identify earlier criticism of such activity.[16] Opposition to pilgrimage in general in the period before the First Crusade had rested first on the premise that the act itself implied a greater reverence for one place over another and, as St Jerome had seen it, 'it is praiseworthy not to have been in Jerusalem, but to have lived well for Jerusalem'.[17] However, as the passage quoted above from the letter of Anselm clearly shows, the more fundamental issue for peregrinating monks was that they had sworn vows of obedience and *stabilitas*, and pilgrimage was seen to be a contradictory excursion into the world that they had previously abandoned. Furthermore, it was deemed by many to be a superfluous spiritual exercise for those who had already committed themselves to a religious way of life; as Bernard of Clairvaux later put it, 'the object of monks is to seek out not the earthly but the heavenly Jerusalem, and this not by proceeding with their feet but by progressing with their feelings'.[18] Bernard also made the striking point that, for Cistercians, the abbey itself *was* Jerusalem. In a letter to the bishop of Lincoln, the abbot described how a Jerusalem pilgrim from the English diocese had fulfilled his vow by becoming a monk at Clairvaux *en route*:

> He crossed over, in this narrow sea, a great and spacious expanse, and, sailing with a

vols. 3–5 (Edinburgh, 1946–51), vol. 4, Ep. 195, pp. 85–6.

[14] See Somerville, 'The Council of Clermont and the First Crusade', pp. 330–1.

[15] Anselm of Canterbury, vol. 5, Ep. 410, p. 355. See also Geoffrey of Vendôme, 'Epistolae', *PL* 157, Ep. 21, cols. 162–3.

[16] For other treatments of this subject, see especially G. Constable, 'Opposition to Pilgrimage in the Middle Ages', *Studia Gratiana*, 19 (1976), pp. 123–46; G. Constable, 'Monachisme et pèlerinage au moyen âge', *Revue historique*, 258 (1977), pp. 3–27; A. Jotischky, *The Perfection of Solitude: Hermits and Monks in the Crusader States* (University Park, PA, 1995), pp. 1–16.

[17] *Sancti Eusebii Hieronymi epistulae*, ed. I. Hilberg, *Corpus scriptorum ecclesiasticorum Latinorum*, 54 (Vienna and Leipzig, 1910), p. 529.

[18] Bernard of Clairvaux, 'Epistolae', *SBO* 8, Ep. 399, pp. 379–80.

favourable wind, he reached the desired shore, and at last came to land at the port of salvation. His feet now stand in the forecourt of Jerusalem . . . And, if you want to know, that Jerusalem is Clairvaux.[19]

Bernard's attitudes towards monastic pilgrimage clearly belong to the twelfth rather than to the eleventh century, but they are indicative of the bases from which earlier critics formed their opinions. In short, if one were to generalise about attitudes towards monastic pilgrimage in the lead-up to the First Crusade, at one extreme (the most liberal), the consensus would be one of theoretical disapproval and, at the other extreme (the most conservative), one of trenchant opposition. The renegade Vallombrosan abbot of St Reparata whom Urban II identified in his letter of 1096 would surely not, therefore, have been without some kind of conceptual framework within which he could have assessed the validity of his decision to start out for Jerusalem.

It is now widely accepted that, from the outset, the First Crusade was conceived as a form of Jerusalem pilgrimage.[20] Pope Urban referred to the holy city as the specific target of the expedition in three of his four surviving letters that relate to the crusade,[21] and if the reports by Robert of Rheims, Baldric of Bourgueil and Guibert of Nogent are to be believed Jerusalem and the Holy Sepulchre were central motifs within the pope's Clermont address.[22] According to Robert, Pope Urban had described the plight faced by Jerusalem, the city that had been sanctified by the life of Christ, and had enjoined his audience to 'take the road to the Holy Sepulchre . . . for the remission of your sins'.[23] Similarly, in Baldric's version, the pope was reported to have given a graphic account of how Jerusalem had been polluted by its heathen overlords and to have stated that it was necessary to launch a campaign for its immediate recovery.[24] Guibert's report, whilst more eschatological in tone, emphasised the importance of Jerusalem to all Christians as the place where 'the blood of the son of God, holier than heaven and earth, poured

[19] *SBO* 7, Ep. 64, pp. 157–8.

[20] See, for example, J.S.C. Riley-Smith, *The First Crusade and the Idea of Crusading* (London, 1986), pp. 22–5; H.E.J. Cowdrey, 'Pope Urban and the Idea of Crusade', *Studi medievali*, 36 (1995), pp. 721–42. H.E. Mayer, *The Crusades*, trans. J. Gillingham, 2nd edition (Oxford, 1988), p. 14, described the crusade as a 'logical extension' of pilgrimage; M. Bull, *Knightly Piety and the Lay Response to the First Crusade: The Limousin and Gascony, c.970–c.1130* (Oxford, 1993), p. 19, referred to the crusade as a 'species' of pilgrimage. But see also J. Flori, 'Ideology and Motivations in the First Crusade', *Palgrave Advances in the Crusades*, ed. H.J. Nicholson (Basingstoke, 2005), p. 21, where it is suggested that 'the expedition's destination allowed it to be *compared* to a pilgrimage' [my italics].

[21] For the letters to Flanders and to Bologna, see *Kreuzzugsbriefe*, nos. 2 and 3, pp. 136–8; to the Vallombrosans, 'Papsturkunden in Florenz', no. 6, pp. 313–14; and to the Catalan counts, *Papsturkunden in Spanien: I. Katalonien*, ed. P. Kehr (Berlin, 1926), no. 23, pp. 287–8.

[22] See especially Cowdrey, 'Preaching of the First Crusade', pp. 177–88; Riley-Smith, *The First Crusade*, pp. 13–30; P.J. Cole, *The Preaching of the Crusades to the Holy Land, 1095–1270* (Cambridge, MA, 1991), pp. 1–36; J.S.C. Riley-Smith, *The First Crusaders, 1095–1131* (Cambridge, 1997), pp. 53–66.

[23] Robert of Rheims, 'Historia', pp. 728–9.

[24] Baldric of Bourgueil, 'Historia', pp. 12–16. See also P.J. Cole, '"O God, the heathen have come into your inheritance" (Ps. 78.1): The Theme of Religious Pollution in Crusade Documents, 1095–1188', *Crusaders and Muslims in Twelfth-Century Syria*, ed. M. Shatzmiller (Leiden and New York, 1993), pp. 84–111.

out, and where his body . . . rested in the Sepulchre', and stressed the urgent need for that place to be liberated.[25] Moreover, in a surviving version of one of the Clermont decrees it was clearly recorded that 'Whosoever for devotion alone, not to gain honour or money, goes to Jerusalem to liberate the Church of God can substitute this journey for all penance'.[26]

The consequence of the fact that Jerusalem was understood to be the goal of the crusade is that contemporary references to the expedition as a pilgrimage are ubiquitous. According to Robert of Rheims, Pope Urban had referred to the crusade as a *sancta peregrinatio*,[27] and this idea can be found in the writings of observers and participants alike. The anonymous author of the *Gesta Francorum* described the crusaders as pilgrims who were taking the *iter sancti Sepulchri*, a *gens mendica* who were able to inflict defeat upon their enemies despite having nothing 'but a bag and a scrip', the traditional accoutrements of the penitential pilgrimage.[28] Fulcher of Chartres also referred to the crusaders as pilgrims (who were following a *sanctum iter*),[29] as did Raymond of Aguilers,[30] Peter Tudebode,[31] and Stephen of Blois.[32] The crusade's other leaders – Bohemond of Taranto, Raymond of St Gilles, Godfrey of Bouillon, Robert of Normandy, Robert of Flanders and Eustace of Boulogne – described themselves as *Hierosolymitani Iesu Christi* in their letter to the pope of September 1098.[33] In addition, there is also substantial charter evidence that demonstrates the extent to which the first crusaders regarded themselves as pilgrims.[34] To cite but one example, in *c.*1096, Nivelo of Fréteval stated in the preamble to his agreement with the monks of the abbey of St Père de Chartres that he was 'going on pilgrimage to Jerusalem (*peregre proficiscenti ad Jerusalem*)'.[35]

Although some historians have attempted to argue otherwise,[36] the application of pilgrimage terminology to the First Crusade by those who took part in it was far more than a convenient rhetorical device. Raymond of Aguilers offered a vivid description of the crusaders' delight upon finally entering Jerusalem in July 1099 – 'it was extraordinary to see the devotion of the pilgrims before the Holy Sepulchre, they were clapping, rejoicing, and singing a new song to the Lord'[37] – and it is revealing that Fulcher of Chartres believed that it was only after he had worshipped at the Holy Sepulchre

[25] Guibert of Nogent, 'Dei gesta per Francos', ed. R.B.C. Huygens, *CC:CM* 127 A (Turnhout, 1996), p. 112.

[26] *Decreta Claromontensia*, ed. R. Somerville, *The Councils of Urban II. I.* (Amsterdam, 1972), p. 74.

[27] Robert of Rheims, 'Historia', p. 729.

[28] *Gesta Francorum et aliorum Hierosolimitanorum*, ed. and trans. R. Hill (Oxford, 1962), pp. 14, 40, 96.

[29] Fulcher of Chartres, *Historia Hierosolymitana (1095–1127)*, ed. H. Hagenmeyer (Heidelberg, 1913), pp. 141, 154.

[30] Raymond of Aguilers, *Liber*, ed. J.H. and L.L. Hill (Paris, 1969), p. 117.

[31] Peter Tudebode, *Historia de Hierosolymitano itinere*, ed. J.H. and L.L. Hill (Paris, 1977), p. 121.

[32] *Kreuzzugsbriefe*, no. 4, p. 138.

[33] *Ibid.*, no. 16, p. 161.

[34] See Riley-Smith, *First Crusaders*, pp. 66–9.

[35] *Cartulaire de l'abbaye de Saint-Père de Chartres*, ed. B.E.C. Guérard, 2 vols. (Paris, 1840), vol. 2, p. 428.

[36] See, for example, J.M. Jensen, '*Peregrinatio sive expeditio*: Why the First Crusade was not a Pilgrimage', *Al-Masaq: Islam and the Medieval Mediterranean*, 15 (2003), pp. 119–37.

[37] Raymond of Aguilers, *Liber*, p. 151.

that his *labor* would be complete.[38] Moreover, Fulcher was not the only eyewitness to record how the crusaders fulfilled the customs of Jerusalem pilgrimage by bathing in the Jordan and gathering palm branches before they began their journeys home,[39] and appended to the author of the *Gesta Francorum*'s account of the expedition was a detailed description of 'the holy places of Jerusalem'.[40]

Those who composed the later narratives of the crusade shared the belief that the expedition had been a pilgrimage. Guibert of Nogent wrote of the hardship that the crusaders had had to endure as pilgrims who were exiled from their homes and families, and he was but one of many writers who believed that the rituals and processions that the crusaders had performed whilst on the march were a necessary part of their penitential exercise.[41] Albert of Aachen described the crusaders as *peregrini et cruce signati*, who followed the *sacra via Iherusalem*, driven by a desire to see the Holy Sepulchre and who, after they had successfully liberated Jerusalem, prepared to return to their native lands 'carrying palms of victory in their hands'.[42] For Ralph of Caen, the crusaders were *Hierosolimipetae*,[43] whilst the term *collegium Jerosolimitanorum* was amongst a range of expressions that was used of the crusaders by Baldric of Bourgueil.[44] Robert of Rheims referred to the expedition as the *via dominici Sepulcri*,[45] and Orderic Vitalis wrote that the crusaders were *peregrini Dei* who had 'set out on pilgrimage for the love of Christ'.[46] Gilo of Paris's anonymous continuator recognised Godfrey of Bouillon as a *peregrinus Christi*, and depicted the crusaders as following the *via sancti Sepulchri*;[47] equally, Caffaro de Caschifelone referred to the crusade as the *iter Iherosolimitanum*, and described how Pope Urban had called upon all the people of Christendom to take 'the way of the Sepulchre for the remission of all sins'.[48]

As far as one can tell, therefore, participants and commentators alike were clear enough about what it was that the crusaders had embarked upon when they had set out

---

[38] Fulcher of Chartres, *Historia*, pp. 331–2.

[39] *Ibid.*, pp. 318–20, 335; Raymond of Aguilers, *Liber*, p. 153. See also Riley-Smith, *First Crusaders*, pp. 144–5.

[40] *Gesta Francorum*, pp. 98–101. It is unclear whether this *descriptio* was written by the author of the *Gesta* himself; see *ibid.*, p. 97, n. 1.

[41] Guibert of Nogent, 'Dei gesta', pp. 275, 276–7. For the development of crusader ritual, see B. McGinn, 'Iter sancti Sepulchri: The Piety of the First Crusaders', *Essays on Medieval Civilization*, ed. B.K. Lackner and K.R. Philp (Austin, TX, and London, 1978), pp. 33–71; see also J.A. Brundage, 'Prostitution, Miscegenation and Sexual Purity in the First Crusade', *Crusade and Settlement: Papers Read at the First Conference of the Society for the Study of the Crusades and the Latin East and Presented to R.C. Smail*, ed. P.W. Edbury (Cardiff, 1985), pp. 57–65.

[42] Albert of Aachen, *Historia*, pp. 50, 164, 386, 474.

[43] Ralph of Caen, 'Gesta Tancredi', *RHC Oc.* 3, p. 681.

[44] Baldric of Bourgueil, 'Historia', pp. 59–60.

[45] Robert of Rheims, 'Historia', p. 739.

[46] OV 5, pp. 142, 32.

[47] Gilo of Paris, *Historie Vie Hierosolimitane*, ed. and trans. C.W. Grocock and J.E. Siberry (Oxford, 1997), pp. 58, 32.

[48] Caffaro, 'De liberatione civitatum orientis', ed. L.T. Belgrano, *Annali genovesi*, 1 (Genoa, 1890), pp. 100, 101. Caffaro was, in fact, an eyewitness to the First Crusade, but did not compose his account until the 1150s. For the date, see R.D. Face, 'Secular History in Twelfth-Century Italy: Caffaro of Genoa', *Journal of Medieval History*, 6 (1980), p. 172.

for the East in 1096. Yet for all that the sources tell us that the origins of the First Crusade lay in the Jerusalem pilgrimage tradition,[49] it is plain that those who travelled to the Holy Land between 1096 and c. 1102 were not simply taking part in another large-scale penitential journey *outremer*, the like of which had been seen on a number of occasions earlier in the eleventh century.[50] The crusade was patently quite different to what had preceded it in two key respects: its participants were not only permitted to bear arms, but they were also required to use them as part of their devotional exercise.[51] In this way, the crusade saw the popular and familiar traditions of the Jerusalem pilgrimage being fused with ideas that were altogether more radical: that certain types of violence could be spiritually meritorious and even regarded as acts of penance.[52]

It is impractical to discuss here in any kind of detail the history of ideas of Christian holy war, and unnecessary to restate the significance of the changes that took place in the eleventh century against the backdrop of papal reform and the military campaigns that ensued from the papacy's ideological programme of *libertas* and, by association, the so-called 'Investiture Controversy'.[53] What is apposite, however, is to refer to three episodes of particular relevance in the development of ideas of penitential warfare in the generation immediately before the proclamation of the First Crusade. In this respect, one of the most fascinating precursors to the crusade idea was Pope Gregory VII's proposed military campaign of 1074 which, had it been enacted, would have seen the papacy leading arms-bearers from the West into Asia Minor to provide the Byzantine Empire with some much-needed assistance against the encroachments of the Seljuk Turks.[54] The importance of this extraordinary plan to the genesis of crusading lies not

---

[49] See also J.A. Brundage, *Medieval Canon Law and the Crusader* (Madison, WI, 1969), pp. 3–18.

[50] See, for example, E. Joranson, 'The Great German Pilgrimage of 1064–1065', *The Crusades and Other Historical Essays Presented to Dana C. Munro by his Former Students*, ed. L.J. Paetow (New York, 1928), pp. 3–43; Riley-Smith, *First Crusaders*, pp. 25–39.

[51] For the prohibition against the bearing of arms by penitents, see Riley-Smith, *First Crusaders*, p. 39; see also H.E.J. Cowdrey, 'Pope Gregory VII and the Bearing of Arms', *Montjoie: Studies in Crusade History in Honour of Hans Eberhard Mayer*, ed. B.Z. Kedar, J.S.C. Riley-Smith and R. Hiestand (Aldershot, 1997), pp. 21–35. For the distinction between crusaders and pilgrims who later took up arms in defence of the Holy Sepulchre, see J.S.C. Riley-Smith, 'An Army on Pilgrimage' (Forthcoming).

[52] For the broader context, see now S. Hamilton, *The Practice of Penance, 900–1050* (Woodbridge, 2001); S. Hamilton, 'Penance in the Age of Gregorian Reform', *Retribution, Repentance and Reconciliation*, ed. K. Cooper and J. Gregory, SCH, 40 (Woodbridge, 2004), pp. 47–73.

[53] See especially C. Erdmann, *The Origin of the Idea of Crusade*, trans. M.W. Baldwin and W. Goffart (Princeton, NJ, 1977); Brundage, *Canon Law*, pp. 19–29; Riley-Smith, *First Crusaders*, pp. 40–52; J. Flori, *La guerre sainte: La formation de l'idée de croisade dans l'Occident chrétien* (Paris, 2001); H.E.J. Cowdrey, 'Christianity and the Morality of Warfare during the First Century of Crusading', *The Experience of Crusading, Volume One: Western Approaches*, ed. M. Bull and N. Housley (Cambridge, 2003), pp. 175–92; J. France, 'Holy War and Holy Men: Erdmann and the Lives of the Saints', *Experience of Crusading, Volume One*, pp. 193–208. For the history of the clashes between empire and papacy, see U.-R. Blumenthal, *The Investiture Controversy: Church and Monarchy from the Ninth to the Twelfth Century* (Philadelphia, PA, 1988); C. Morris, *The Papal Monarchy: The Western Church from 1050 to 1250* (Oxford, 1989), pp. 79–133, 154–73.

[54] See H.E.J. Cowdrey, 'Pope Gregory VII's "Crusading" Plans of 1074', *Outremer: Studies in the History of the Crusading Kingdom of Jerusalem Presented to Joshua Prawer*, ed. B.Z. Kedar, H.E. Mayer and R.C. Smail (Jerusalem, 1982), pp. 27–40; Riley-Smith, *First Crusaders*, p. 50.

only in the fact that participation in the expedition was to have been meritorious, but also in that it was projected that the army was to have marched beyond Byzantine lands and on to the Holy Sepulchre – the parallels with Pope Urban II's intentions in 1095 could hardly be more apparent. Of a comparable significance is the military campaign waged by a contingent of Pisans and Genoese against the Muslim pirates of Mahdia on the north coast of Africa in 1087.[55] Here, those who took part in the attack were understood to have been rewarded with 'the remission of sins', and Hans Mayer has suggested that as the expedition had begun with a pilgrimage to Rome the campaign may have sparked the idea of arming pilgrims in the intellectual circles of the reform papacy.[56] Finally, a relationship between pilgrimage and penitential warfare can also be found in a letter that Pope Urban II addressed to a number of Catalan nobles in 1089. In order to communicate to them the value of military efforts for the episcopal seat of Tarragona, Urban explained that participation in the restoration of the city was equivalent to going on a pilgrimage to Jerusalem.[57] It is evident, therefore, that associations between pilgrimage, warfare and penance – associations that were to become central to early crusading ideology – were not without precedent within the upper echelons of the papal entourage in the final quarter of the eleventh century. Nevertheless, by the time Pope Urban was undertaking his preaching tour of France in 1095–6, the idea of a penitential pilgrimage-in-arms was a revolutionary prospect for Christendom at large.

The crusade's synthesis of penitential pilgrimage and pious violence appears to have been widely comprehended.[58] In Baldric of Bourgueil's *Historia*, Bohemond of Taranto was made to proclaim that 'we are pilgrims for God; we are knights of Christ',[59] whilst Robert of Rheims had Bohemond declare that the crusaders were *peregrini milites sancti Sepulcri*, and 'warriors of God and unfailing pilgrims of the Holy Sepulchre'; Robert himself later wrote of the crusaders as 'our pilgrim knights'.[60] Similarly, for Albert of Aachen and Ekkehard of Aura, the crusaders were an *exercitus peregrinorum*[61] – Ekkehard also referred to them as the *peregrini milites Christi*[62] – and one eyewitness described the visionary, Peter Bartholomew, as 'a pilgrim in our army'.[63] Orderic Vitalis reported a speech in which the crusaders proclaimed that they had 'set out on pilgrimage voluntarily, so that, through the love of Christ, we might throw the pagans into disorder, and set free the Christians'; elsewhere in his *Historia*, he wrote that many of those who joined the third wave of the First Crusade in 1101 'burned with a passion to go on pilgrimage, to see the sepulchre of the Saviour and the holy places, and to prove their military prowess against the Turks'.[64]

---

[55] See H.E.J. Cowdrey, 'The Mahdia Campaign of 1087', *English Historical Review*, 92 (1977), pp. 1–29.

[56] Mayer, *The Crusades*, pp. 18–19.

[57] Urban II, 'Epistolae et privilegia', *PL* 151, no. 20, cols. 302–3. See below, p. 122, for a more detailed consideration of this document.

[58] In addition to the evidence considered here, see Riley-Smith, *First Crusaders*, pp. 67–8.

[59] Baldric of Bourgueil, 'Historia', p. 22.

[60] Robert of Rheims, 'Historia', pp. 746, 747, 844.

[61] Albert of Aachen, *Historia*, p. 62; Ekkehard of Aura, 'Hierosolymita', *RHC Oc.* 5, p. 20.

[62] Ekkehard of Aura, 'Hierosolymita', p. 39.

[63] Peter Tudebode, *Historia*, p. 100.

[64] OV 5, pp. 48, 322. On the 'third wave', see Riley-Smith, *The First Crusade*, pp. 120–34.

The novelty of the idea of crusading was therefore not lost on contemporaries. Indeed, Guibert of Nogent saw the expedition as a 'new pilgrimage' and a 'new penance',[65] an idea that was echoed in Ekkehard of Aura's description of the crusade as a *nova via poenitentiae*.[66] Perhaps most famous of all, however, is Guibert's description of the way in which the crusade presented the pious layman with a new and distinctive path to salvation:

> God has instituted holy wars in our time so that the order of knights and the wandering multitude, who after the example of the ancient pagans were engaged in mutual slaughter, might find a new way of earning salvation. And so they need not abandon the world completely by choosing the monastic life or any other religious profession, as was once customary, for now they can obtain in some measure God's grace while pursuing their own way of life with the freedoms and in the dress to which they are accustomed.[67]

An equally well-known passage is that which Ralph of Caen composed to introduce his biography of Tancred Marchisus, an individual who had been one of the leaders of the First Crusade. Ralph described how, before 1095, Tancred – 'a diligent listener to the precepts of God' – had 'frequently burned with anxiety' because the responsibilities attendant to his position within Christian society meant that he was forced to contravene Christ's prohibitions against violence.[68] However, when Tancred heard the message of the crusade, it brought about a profound change in him:

> After the judgement of Pope Urban granted remission of all their sins to all Christians going out to fight the gentiles, then at last, as if previously asleep, his vigour was aroused, his powers grew, his eyes opened, his courage was born. For before . . . his mind was divided, uncertain whether to follow in the footsteps of the Gospel or the world. But after the call to arms in the service of Christ, the twofold reason for fighting inflamed him beyond belief.[69]

Historians have often used Ralph's words in conjunction with those of Guibert of Nogent's to illustrate the point that in their attempts to get to grips with the originality of crusading, two men perceived independently that the closest analogue to be found was monasticism. It has been highlighted elsewhere that it is remarkable that they should have comprehended crusading in such a similar way,[70] yet perhaps what is more remarkable still is that Ralph and Guibert were not alone in seeing the parallels between crusading and monasticism – Eudes Betevin was but one individual who decided in 1096 that he would 'rather go on pilgrimage to Jerusalem than become a monk'.[71] Indeed, in a similar vein, a number of the chroniclers of the First Crusade ascribed quasi-monastic

---

[65] Guibert of Nogent, 'Dei gesta', pp. 136, 326.
[66] Ekkehard of Aura, 'Hierosolymita', p. 39. Cf. C. Tyerman, *The Invention of the Crusades* (Basingstoke, 1998), pp. 8–29.
[67] Guibert of Nogent, 'Dei gesta', p. 87.
[68] Matthew 5:39–40.
[69] Ralph of Caen, 'Gesta Tancredi', p. 606.
[70] Bull, *Knightly Piety*, p. 4.
[71] *Cartulaire de Marmoutier pour le Dunois*, ed. E. Mabille (Châteaudun, 1874), p. 123. See Riley-Smith, *First Crusaders*, pp. 69–70.

qualities to the subjects of their histories. Guibert of Nogent, for example, wrote that the crusaders had 'very few riches, [and] were living in such thrift and chastity, and in such continuous and severe need, that they were not knights but monks'.[72] Godfrey of Bouillon in particular was singled out as a model of such piety. According to Ralph of Caen, he was someone who 'with his humility, clemency, sobriety, righteousness and extraordinary chastity, was shining with the light of monks rather than as the leader of soldiers'.[73] Similarly, Robert of Rheims wrote that Godfrey was 'more of a monk than a soldier',[74] whilst Guibert described how, because of his remarkable humility and modesty, Godfrey was a worthy exemplar for monks themselves to imitate.[75]

The significance of these equations between crusading and monasticism cannot be overstated.[76] In an age in which there was a near-obsessive fear about the consequences of sinfulness,[77] the perception that the two forms of devotion were almost of an equivalent spiritual value was central to the appeal of the expedition, and one consequence of this was that ideas and rhetoric that had previously been the preserve of organised religion were rapidly transferred to crusading. This remarkable process was considered in detail by Jonathan Riley-Smith, who went so far as to say that some contemporaries perceived the crusade to be 'a military monastery on the move'.[78] Riley-Smith's study of the development and 'theological refinement' of crusading ideology demonstrated how the crusaders, like those who adopted a religious way of life, were seen to be *milites Christi* who adopted poverty and voluntary exile for the love of God, and who strove to reach the heavenly as well as the earthly Jerusalem.[79] But, in a sense, Riley-Smith could have gone further. Although he showed that crusaders, like their monastic counterparts, were following 'a way of the cross',[80] he did not go on to indicate the pervasiveness of this idea, nor did he explore just how fundamental it was to early crusading spirituality.[81] In this respect, the analogy that Ralph of Caen drew between crusading and monasticism is not the only noteworthy feature of the remarks that he made in the introduction

---

[72] Guibert of Nogent, 'Dei gesta', p. 233. See also Raymond of Aguilers, *Liber*, p. 81.

[73] Ralph of Caen, 'Gesta Tancredi', p. 615.

[74] Robert of Rheims, 'Historia', p. 731.

[75] Guibert of Nogent, 'Dei gesta', pp. 317–18.

[76] See also B. Hamilton, 'Ideals of Holiness: Crusaders, Contemplatives, and Mendicants', *International History Review*, 17 (1995), pp. 693–712; G. Constable, 'The Place of the Crusader in Medieval Society', *Viator*, 29 (1998), pp. 377–403.

[77] See M. Bull, 'Origins', *The Oxford Illustrated History of the Crusades*, ed. J.S.C. Riley-Smith (Oxford, 1995), pp. 13–33; Riley-Smith, *First Crusaders*, pp. 26–8, 69–72, 83. For the penitential concerns and activities of the medieval laity, see also Hamilton, *Practice of Penance*, especially pp. 173–206; C.S. Watkins, 'Sin, Penance and Purgatory in the Anglo-Norman Realm: The Evidence of Visions and Ghost Stories', *Past and Present*, 175 (2002), pp. 3–33.

[78] Riley-Smith, *The First Crusade*, p. 2 and *passim*.

[79] *Ibid.*, pp. 118–19, 149–52, 154–5. See also H. Richter, '*Militia Dei*: A Central Concept for the Religious Ideas of the Early Crusades and the German *Rolandslied*', *Journeys toward God: Pilgrimage and Crusade*, ed. B.N. Sargent-Baur (Kalamazoo, MI, 1992), pp. 107–26.

[80] Riley-Smith, *The First Crusade*, pp. 26–7, 113–14, 119, 151, 155. See also Riley-Smith, *First Crusaders*, pp. 62–3.

[81] But see also J.S.C. Riley-Smith, 'Crusading as an Act of Love', *History*, 65 (1980), pp. 178–80; J.S.C. Riley-Smith, 'Death on the First Crusade', *The End of Strife*, ed. D.M. Loades (Edinburgh, 1984), pp. 28–31.

to his *Gesta Tancredi*. Indeed, it is Ralph's reading of the spiritual appeal of crusading that should perhaps be regarded as the most extraordinary aspect of this passage, for when he alluded to the idea that the crusade offered Christians an opportunity to 'follow in the footsteps of the Gospel' within the world rather than without it, he was tapping into the most potent of Christian spiritual ideals: *imitatio Christi*, the imitation of Christ.

The Ideal of the Imitation of Christ

The most cogent consideration of the scriptural foundations for the idea of *imitatio Christi* can be found in Ernest J. Tinsley's *The Imitation of God in Christ*.[82] Tinsley demonstrated that the imitation of Christ was at the heart of the ideology of the primitive Church, with early Christians referring to their faith as 'the Way', after Christ's proclamation *Ego sum via et veritas et vita*.[83] As 'followers of the Way',[84] the earliest believers were devoted to the imitation of Jesus's life, actions and teachings, and hence were engaged in a faith that was Christo-mimetic from its birth – indeed, Christ had enjoined as much upon the Twelve when he had instructed that they should 'follow him'.[85] The idea of being a 'follower' was therefore fundamental to Christ's teachings on discipleship, which focused on the idea that *imitatio* involved suffering and self-sacrifice: 'If anyone comes to me and does not hate his father and mother, his wife and children, his brothers and sisters – yes, even his own life – he cannot be my disciple. And anyone who does not carry his cross and follow me cannot be my disciple';[86] 'If anyone would come after me, he must deny himself and take up his cross and follow me'.[87] The idea of following Christ was also prominent within the Epistles. St Paul instructed the Corinthians to 'Follow my example, as I follow the example of Christ (*imitatores mei estote sicut et ego Christi*)',[88] whilst St Peter sought to encourage Christians who were the victims of persecution by writing that 'To this you were called, because Christ suffered for you, leaving you an example, that you should follow in his steps'.[89] Tinsley therefore concluded that the scriptural basis for *imitatio Christi* lay in the idea that the life of Christ was presented as the model of perfection – 'the ideal man, the pattern humanity [*sic*]'.[90] Christ had shown the believers of the early Church 'the Way' that they should follow, and it was for that reason that his teachings on discipleship were essential to the understanding of what constituted an exemplary existence in subsequent Christian tradition.

A full analysis of the way in which the ideology of the imitation of Christ developed from the early Church to the late eleventh century is beyond the scope of this chapter,[91]

---

[82] E.J. Tinsley, *The Imitation of God in Christ: An Essay on the Biblical Basis of Christian Spirituality* (London, 1960), especially pp. 67–171.

[83] *Ibid.*, p. 67. Citation from John 14:5–6.

[84] For references to 'the Way', see Acts 9:2, 16:17, 18:25, 19:9, 19:23, 22:4, 24:22.

[85] Matthew 4:19, 9:9, 19:21.

[86] Luke 14:26–7.

[87] Matthew 16:24.

[88] 1 Corinthians 11:1.

[89] 1 Peter 2:21.

[90] Tinsley, *Imitation of God in Christ*, p. 106.

[91] On the development of this ideal, see especially G. Constable, 'The Ideal of the Imitation of Christ', *Three Studies*, pp. 143–248.

but it is imperative nevertheless to stress how significant this ideal was for medieval Christians and, more importantly, to illustrate what paths were available for those who wished to become *imitatores Christi* at the turn of the twelfth century. In this respect, the changes that took place in the landscape of religious life around the time of the First Crusade were of critical importance.

Up to *c.*1050 it was generally believed that the coenobitic monastic life offered the surest route to salvation for most Christians,[92] and hence it was cloistered monks who were, as Orderic Vitalis put it so succinctly in the early twelfth century, 'following the Lord in their lives in the habit of religion'.[93] However, by the close of the eleventh century Benedictine monasticism was coming to be regarded as but one among many forms of religious life, and a multiplicity of new models of observance were being established.[94] This transformation, which was once characterised as bringing about a 'crisis of coenobitism',[95] was driven by reformers who sought to recover what they perceived to be a lost purity, whether that be through returning to the strict observance of the Rule of St Benedict, or by living in fulfilment of an ideal that was altogether more abstract and thus open to a range of interpretations, such as the *vita apostolica* of the primitive Church[96] or, more pertinently, the imitation of Christ. Orderic Vitalis's perspective on these changes is obviously that of a conservative Benedictine monk, but his reflections capture some of the sense of what was happening in the early twelfth century:

> See, though evil abounds in the world, the devotion of the faithful in cloisters grows more abundant and bears fruit a hundredfold in the Lord's field. Monasteries are founded everywhere in mountain valleys and plains, observing new rites and wearing different habits; the swarm of cowled monks spreads all over the world . . . In my opinion voluntary poverty, contempt for the world, and true religion inspire many of them, but many hypocrites and plausible counterfeiters are mixed with them, as tares with wheat.[97]

The contemporary reaction to the diverse paths that these reforms took is perhaps best illustrated by the *Libellus de diversis ordinibus et professionibus qui sunt in aecclesia*, a

---

[92] See R. W. Southern, *Western Society and the Church in the Middle Ages* (Harmondsworth, 1970), p. 217.

[93] OV 5, p. 6.

[94] See B. M. Bolton, *The Medieval Reformation* (London, 1983); H. Leyser, *Hermits and the New Monasticism: A Study of Religious Communities in Western Europe, 1000–1150* (New York, 1984); G. Constable, 'The Diversity of Religious Life and Acceptance of Social Pluralism in the Twelfth Century', *History, Society and the Churches: Essays in Honour of Owen Chadwick*, ed. D. Beales and G. Best (Cambridge, 1985), pp. 29–47; G. Constable, *The Reformation of the Twelfth Century* (Cambridge, 1996).

[95] The phrase originated from G. Morin, 'Rainaud l'ermite et Ives de Chartres: un épisode de la crise du cénobitisme aux XIe–XIIe siècle', *Revue bénédictine*, 40 (1928), pp. 99–115. See also N. F. Cantor, 'The Crisis of Western Monasticism, 1050–1130', *American Historical Review*, 66 (1960–1), pp. 47–67; J. Leclercq, 'The Monastic Crisis of the Eleventh and Twelfth Centuries', *Cluniac Monasticism in the Central Middle Ages*, ed. N. Hunt (Glasgow, 1971), pp. 217–37; D. Baker, 'Crossroads and Crises in the Religious Life of the Late Eleventh Century', *The Church in Town and Countryside*, ed. D. Baker, *SCH*, 16 (Oxford, 1979), pp. 137–48; J. van Engen, 'The "Crisis of Cenobitism" Reconsidered: Benedictine Monasticism in the Years 1050–1150', *Speculum*, 61 (1986), pp. 269–304.

[96] See below, pp. 47–8.

[97] OV 4, pp. 310–13.

tract that was written *c.*1140 in the form of a letter,[98] probably by an Augustinian canon from Liège.[99] The anonymous author began by explaining what his purpose in writing was:

> Since different servants of God have arisen from the beginning of the early church, and many kinds of callings have come into being, and, particularly in our day, institutions of monks and canons differing in habit and religious practice are increasing, it is necessary to show, with God's help, how such servants of God differ and what the purposes of the different forms of callings are.[100]

The *Libellus* is an intriguing text, not only because of the way in which its author categorised the variety of forms of religious life (which included hermits, Cluniacs, Cistercians and Premonstratensians) by their relationship to the rest of Christian society, but also because of the way he used Scripture so adroitly to legitimise new religious observances by citing parallels and precedents from both the Old and the New Testaments.[101] As one might anticipate, the Gospel accounts of Christ's life were amongst the principal sources on which the author drew, and it is therefore salutary to examine briefly the way in which the ideal of the imitation of Christ was used in the twelfth century to justify a number of forms of religious life.

It is evident that the author of the *Libellus* believed that each of the religious callings that were under his consideration were models of Christo-mimetic piety in their own right for he began his work by writing that he hoped his correspondent would 'hold well and faithfully to the way of God in which he began', and went on to acknowledge that of those who followed the *via Dei*, 'some walk one way and others another'.[102] Furthermore, his acceptance of religious diversity was obvious from the outset: 'I see that Jesus demonstrated in himself the likeness (*similitudo*) of almost all the callings of the church, which we shall show in their place as well as we can'.[103] Thus his analysis began by demonstrating how the hermit was following Christ's example of fleeing the world for 'the mountain or the desert',[104] and went on to depict the Cistercian convert as someone who, having adopted voluntary poverty, 'followed the poor Christ and bearing His cross entered into the strait and arduous life of monks'.[105] The spirituality of the regular canons 'who establish themselves far from men', such as the Premonstratensians, was described in similar terms:

---

[98] For the broader context, see G. Constable, 'Papal, Imperial and Monastic Propaganda in the Eleventh and Twelfth Centuries', *Prédication et propagande au moyen âge: Islam, Byzance, Occident*, ed. G. Makdisi, D. Sourdel and J. Sourdel-Thomine (Paris, 1983), pp. 179–99.

[99] *Libellus de diversis ordinibus et professionibus qui sunt in aecclesia*, ed. and trans. G. Constable and B.S. Smith, revised edition (Oxford, 2003). For the identity of the author, see *ibid.*, pp. xv–xviii.

[100] *Ibid.*, pp. 2–3.

[101] For an overview, see the 'Table of Biblical Parallels' in the editors' Introduction; *ibid.*, p. xxiii.

[102] *Ibid.*, pp. 2–3.

[103] *Ibid.*, pp. 10–11.

[104] *Ibid.*, pp. 12–13.

[105] *Ibid.*, pp. 42–3. See also G. Constable, '*Nudus nudum Christum sequi* and Parallel Formulas in the Twelfth Century: A Supplementary Dossier', *Continuity and Discontinuity in Church History: Essays Presented to George Hunston Williams on the Occasion of his 65th Birthday*, ed. F. Forrester Church and T. George, *Studies in the History of Christian Thought*, 19 (Leiden, 1979), pp. 83–91.

You therefore who are a canon . . . you wish gradually to take on either the powers of Jesus or the sacraments of the church, as the order of the canonical family urges, to imitate and contemplate my Jesus, not seeking the heights at once but tending gradually thither. Carry your cross with Him and follow Him, and if you are Christ's, crucify your flesh 'with the vices and concupiscences' and going forth 'without the camp' nail yourself wholly to the cross in Calvary, and as if with a completely shaven head, that is having denuded the principal part of your mind of worldly things, rejoice in bearing His reproach.[106]

The *Libellus* also touched on another important contemporary theme within Augustinian spirituality — *docere verbo et exemplo* — when its author described the way in which canons 'who have their houses near the activities of men' should set an example for the laity in the same way that Christ had set an example for his disciples:

So should the canon live, imitating Him who bore all men's wounds so that He might have mercy on all. His disciples also followed Him wishing to go where He went and not being able to as He had foretold to Peter. For as yet they were weak. This also often happens to us, when we do good in the sight of men, so that they may be 'followers of us as we also are of Christ'. They follow us just as the disciples, still weak, followed the Lord, but they cannot follow us in everything.[107]

The *Libellus* is but one source from this period that illustrates the variety of ways in which ideas of *imitatio Christi* were used as 'stimuli to a life of personal reform and withdrawal from the world'.[108] Elsewhere, for example, Orderic Vitalis portrayed Robert of Molesme as being motivated by a desire 'to follow after Christ in the footsteps of the fathers' when he set out to reform the observances of the first of the houses that he had founded;[109] Orderic also described the founder of the congregation of Savigny as an individual who had put aside 'the burdens of worldly cares and riches, to bear the easy yoke of Christ in the footsteps of the apostles'.[110] More striking still is his account of the conversion of the founder of his own house of St Evroul:

While this most holy man was steadfastly living according to a self-imposed rule, and striving with all his might to obey our Lord's commandments, it came to pass that he heard our Lord's summons to his disciples in the Gospel: 'If any man will come after me, let him deny himself and take up his cross and follow me.' The man of God already treasured in his memory and revered what the word of truth promised to those who despise the world, 'Verily I say unto you, that ye which have foresaken all for my sake shall receive an hundredfold and shall inherit eternal life.' Now, encouraged by sure promises, he surpassed his former moderation and, dividing his goods,

---

[106] *Libellus de diversis ordinibus*, pp. 58–9.

[107] *Ibid.*, pp. 76–9. See C.W. Bynum, *Docere verbo et exemplo: An Aspect of Twelfth-Century Spirituality* (Missoula, MT, 1979); C.W. Bynum, 'The Spirituality of Regular Canons in the Twelfth Century', *Jesus as Mother: Studies in the Spirituality of the High Middle Ages* (Berkeley, Los Angeles and London, 1982), pp. 22–58.

[108] Constable, *Reformation*, p. 125.

[109] OV 4, pp. 314–15.

[110] OV 4, pp. 330–1.

gave all that he could to the poor. He gave up to a heavenly spouse the wife that he had taken to perpetuate his father's name, sanctifying her with the veil of religion. He himself hastened to a monastery as one who had escaped from shipwreck. After becoming a monk he remained there for some time, serving God in all humility, whilst love of a holy way of life grew in him more and more.[111]

Similar language was used of religious conversion in the Premonstratensian continuation of the *Chronica* of Sigebert of Gembloux, where it was written of St Norbert of Xanten that 'neglecting the pomp of the world . . . he dressed himself with the tunic of the poor of Christ . . . and carrying his cross, naked, he followed the naked Christ'.[112] And in the seventh book of Otto of Freising's *Chronica*, which contained a *descriptio diversorum ordinum religiosorum* that bears a striking resemblance to the *Libellus de diversis ordinibus* both in its style and its content, it was recorded how at the time Otto was writing (*c.*1143–7) there were 'various bands of saints who, renouncing their desires, their possessions, and even their parents, in accordance with the command of the Gospel, continually bear the cross for the mortification of the flesh and who, filled with a longing for heaven, follow Christ.'[113]

As Giles Constable has shown, one of the most remarkable features of the transformation of religious life between the eleventh and thirteenth centuries was that although reformers sought and found inspiration from many of the same texts and ideals,[114] the foundations that resulted from their labours frequently took dramatically different forms.[115] Indeed, the author of the *Libellus de diversis ordinibus* was aware that the same biblical passages could be interpreted in a number of different ways, for in his analysis of secular canons he wrote that:

> [If] someone says to me: What have you shown of this chapter of the Gospel which is applicable to the canons who live among men? Surely all this can have other meanings and be applied to other servants of God? I reply to that: I know that this has been interpreted differently by other holy expositors of scripture, but there is in these things something suitable for the canons . . .[116]

From this brief but representative sample of sources relating to the eleventh and twelfth centuries it can be seen that the New Testament texts that related to the imitation of Christ were at the heart of many of the reforms and changes in the religious life of the period. The centrality of this spirituality can perhaps be summarised best by the words of the Benedictine monk known as Gilo of Paris, who, at some point before the year 1120, wrote a brief exposition on why the pursuit of *imitatio Christi* equated to a search for Christian perfection:

---

[111] OV 3, pp. 266–7.

[112] 'Sigeberti continuatio Praemonstratensis', *MGH SS* 6, p. 448.

[113] Otto of Freising, *Chronica sive historia de duabus civitatibus*, ed. A. Hofmeister, *MGH SSRG* 45 (Hanover and Leipzig, 1912), p. 369.

[114] Constable, *Reformation*, pp. 125–67.

[115] *Ibid.*, pp. 44–87.

[116] *Libellus de diversis ordinibus*, pp. 102–3.

As the man errs who strives to hold back a wheel set in motion down a slope, when it gains speed, so errs the wretch who will not forsake the unclean world: he is ruined while he pursues what is doomed to ruin. And so let every man shake off hesitation, because the world is ours for but an hour, and seek that which no length of time eats away. Let no man's farm, his fine house, or the world hold him back from seeking the light by taking up his cross. Christ has gone before, and the victory has fallen to Christ: the cross he carried was our healing. Therefore let him who wishes to imitate Christ on equal terms bow his neck and take up the cross in his turn.

The tone of this passage is comparable to that of countless other contemporary texts that describe the imitation of Christ. Its content is all the more striking for the fact that it was used by Gilo to introduce his verse history of the First Crusade.[117]

Conclusion

It is well documented that the impetus that drove ecclesiastical reform in the eleventh and twelfth centuries was the desire to secure salvation by achieving some measure of religious perfection, and that the paradigm of perfection was understood to be Christ himself. In this way, the *imitatio Christi* was one of the ideals that brought a degree of unity to the diversity of new forms of religious observance that proliferated in this period, from Cîteaux to La Grande Chartreuse,[118] and from Prémontré to the Poor Men of Lyons;[119] indeed, it was also the ideal that was the basis for the foundation of the mendicant orders in the thirteenth century.[120]

It is important to note that the increased number of vocations available to those who wished to take up a religious life in the late eleventh and twelfth centuries led, perhaps somewhat inevitably, to a new set of problems. As the letter of Hugh *Peccator* to the Templars in the East (*c.* 1128) demonstrates,[121] religious diversity encouraged an individual to pose questions about which form of observance might suit them best,[122] and consequently there were some professed religious who, despite having vowed to follow one way of life, would leave one congregation or Order for another. The jeopardy of this process, which was known to contemporaries as *transitus*,[123] is illustrated most colourfully by the haranguing that Bernard of Clairvaux directed at his nephew, Robert, after he had abandoned the austerity of a Cistercian abbey for what Bernard perceived to be the comparative luxury of Cluny:

---

[117] Gilo of Paris, *Historia*, pp. 68–71.

[118] See C.H. Lawrence, *Medieval Monasticism: Forms of Religious Life in Western Europe in the Middle Ages*, 3rd edition (Harlow, 2001), pp. 156–60, 172–98.

[119] *Ibid.*, pp. 166–8, 241–2.

[120] *Ibid.*, pp. 238–78.

[121] 'Un document sur les débuts des Templiers', ed. J. Leclercq, *Revue d'histoire ecclésiastique*, 52 (1957), pp. 81–91. See also *Papsturkunden für Templer und Johanniter*, ed. R. Hiestand, 2 vols. (Göttingen, 1972–84), vol. 1, no. 3, p. 207.

[122] See C.W. Bynum, 'Did the Twelfth Century Discover the Individual?', *Jesus as Mother*, pp. 82–109; C.N.L. Brooke, 'Monk and Canon: Some Patterns in the Religious Life of the Twelfth Century', *Monks, Hermits and the Ascetic Tradition*, ed. W.J. Sheils, *SCH*, 22 (Oxford, 1985), pp. 109–29.

[123] See especially D. Roby, '*Stabilitas* and *Transitus*: Understanding Passage from One Religious Order to Another in Twelfth Century Monastic Controversy', unpublished Ph.D. thesis (Yale, 1971).

Let your conscience respond to why you departed from your Order, your brethren, your home . . . If you left for a harder, higher, and more perfect life, you will be secure, because you have not looked back; indeed, you can glory with the Apostle, saying, *Forgetting what I have left behind, intent on what lies ahead, I press on to the palm of glory*. But if it is otherwise, be not high-minded but fearful because – and it is out of kindness that I say this to you – whatever you permit yourself in food, unnecessary clothing, idle words, and licentious and curious travel that is in excess of what you promised when you were here with us, is without any doubt to look back, to transgress, to apostatise.[124]

As was seen at the beginning of this chapter, contemporaries levelled much the same sorts of criticisms at those monks who neglected their vows of *stabilitas* when they took the cross for the First Crusade.

When Pope Urban II wrote to the Vallombrosans in 1096 to inform them that the crusade was an inappropriate undertaking for 'those who have abandoned the world and vowed themselves to spiritual warfare', he began his letter with a phrase that contains a degree of ambiguity: *recta quidem oblatio, sed non recta diuisio*.[125] Clearly, Urban regarded the crusade as 'the right kind of sacrifice', at least in the sense that it was to be an undertaking that would be so gruelling that it would act as a satisfactory penance,[126] but it would not be stretching credulity to read into the pope's words an allusion to a sacrifice of a more spiritual or Christo-mimetic kind.[127] It is impossible to know whether the Vallombrosans believed that denying themselves and taking the cross for an armed pilgrimage to the Holy Land was a 'better' way to imitate Christ,[128] but it does not seem implausible. The Vallombrosan congregation itself was a product of the 'new monasticism' of the age,[129] and it could be argued that its brethren were therefore more likely to be receptive to ideas of religious change[130] and, equally, more susceptible to the temptations of *transitus*. Such an argument would, of course, be conjecture and cannot be proved beyond doubt. However, when one considers the wording of a contemporaneous letter written by Geoffrey of Vendôme, it seems likely that it was the spirituality of *imitatio Christi* that was believed to have inspired at least one crusading monk, the abbot of Marmoutier, to abandon his monastery to join the expedition; Geoffrey stressed to his correspondent that 'it is not necessary for those who carry the

---

[124] *SBO* 7, Ep. 1, pp. 7–8. Citation from Philippians 3:13–14.

[125] 'Papsturkunden in Florenz', no. 6, p. 313.

[126] For the spiritual reward offered to first crusaders, see Riley-Smith, *The First Crusade*, pp. 27–9; Bull, *Knightly Piety*, pp. 166–71.

[127] Leclercq, *Spirituality of the Middle Ages*, p. 132, wrote that 'To go on the Crusade was a way of answering the call of Christ, of taking up one's cross and following him; it was an opportunity to imitate Jesus in his sufferings and death'.

[128] For a contemporary discussion of the idea that one form of religious life might be regarded as *melior* than another, see 'Un document sur les débuts des Templiers', pp. 88–9. See also G. Constable, 'The Interpretation of Mary and Martha', *Three Studies*, pp. 1–141.

[129] See Lawrence, *Medieval Monasticism*, p. 150.

[130] For a consideration of how the Vallombrosans engaged with the programme of the papal reformers, and the surrounding controversy, see K.G. Cushing, *Reform and the Papacy in the Eleventh Century: Spirituality and Social Change* (Manchester, 2005), pp. 130–3.

cross of the Lord and follow the Lord as professed [religious] to seek a pilgrim's tomb'.[131] But Geoffrey of Vendôme, Ralph of Caen and Gilo of Paris were not the only writers to describe the appeal of crusading using the ideals of *imitatio Christi*. The chapter that follows offers an extensive analysis of many of the contemporary sources for the First Crusade, and begins by demonstrating the prevalence of the idea that the first crusaders were imitators of Christ.

[131] Geoffrey of Vendôme, 'Epistolae', Ep. 21, col. 162.

CHAPTER TWO

The Foundations of Crusading Spirituality,

1095–c.1110

The First Crusaders as Imitators of Christ

The anonymous author of the *Gesta Francorum*, who was writing shortly after the liberation of Jerusalem in 1099, began his eyewitness narrative of the First Crusade by describing the reaction to Pope Urban II's proclamation of war in 1095:

> When now that time drew nigh, to which the Lord Jesus points out to his faithful every day, especially in the Gospel where he says *If any man will come after me, let him deny himself and take up his cross and follow me*, there was a great stirring throughout all the regions of Gaul, so that if anyone with a pure heart and mind zealously desired to follow God, and faithfully wished to bear the cross after him, he could make no delay in speedily taking the road to the Holy Sepulchre.[1]

It is unnecessary to subject this passage to a detailed analysis, for the words of the *Gesta*'s author are clear enough: as he saw it, it was the spirituality of *imitatio Christi* and the idea of Jerusalem pilgrimage that inspired the positive response of Christians across Europe to the preaching of the First Crusade. Reference has already been made in the previous chapter to the fact that the crusade's appeal was by no means limited to the laity, and in the light of this passage from the *Gesta Francorum* (which was probably the work of a cleric),[2] the attraction of crusading for a monastic audience is brought into an even sharper focus. If the impact of the crusade message was as profound as the author of the *Gesta* would have us believe, we should not be surprised that certain professed religious from all over western Europe were minded to join the expedition. It was, after all, these

---

[1] *Gesta Francorum et aliorum Hierosolimitanorum*, ed. and trans. R. Hill (Oxford, 1962), p. 1; see also Peter Tudebode, *Historia de Hierosolymitano itinere*, ed. J.H. and L.L. Hill (Paris, 1977), p. 31. It is striking that in his description of the 'taking of the cross', the author of the *Gesta* refers not only to the wording of Matthew 16:24 (*tollere*), but also to that of Luke 14:27 (*baiulare*).

[2] For the authorship of this text, see especially C. Morris, 'The *Gesta Francorum* as Narrative History', *Reading Medieval Studies*, 19 (1993), pp. 55–71; J. Rubenstein, 'What is the *Gesta Francorum* and who was Peter Tudebode?', *Revue Mabillon*, 16 (2005), pp. 179–204. The adept use of scripture highlighted in the footnote above reinforces the argument that the *Gesta Francorum* was the work of an individual from a clerical background.

individuals who were most likely to be disposed to ideas of following Christ and bearing his cross in the first place.

In observing that the appeal of the First Crusade was fundamentally linked with the desire to imitate Christ the author of the *Gesta Francorum* was in unknowing agreement with both Gilo of Paris and Ralph of Caen, whose analyses of the roots of crusader piety were considered in the previous chapter.[3] But whilst this conformity is surely not coincidental, in order to assess how representative of contemporary feeling these three writers actually were it is necessary to broaden the scope of inquiry to include the full range of narrative, epistolary and diplomatic sources that are available to the historian of crusader motivation. It is only by analysing these sources collectively that one can begin to assess how far arms-bearers and clerics alike were believed to have been impelled to crusade out of a yearning to follow Christ. To this end, it is appropriate to begin the analysis by turning to what most contemporaries[4] regarded as the source of crusading impulses: the sermon delivered by Pope Urban II at the Council of Clermont on 27 November 1095, and the message that it contained.[5]

Given the weight of corroborative evidence for Pope Urban's preaching at the Council of Clermont in 1095 there can be no doubt that the crusade was envisioned as a Christo-mimetic activity from the outset. Many of the reports of the Clermont sermon indicate that the pope's appeal centred on ideas of Christian discipleship, and it seems clear enough that reference was made to certain Gospel passages that had previously been inextricably linked with recruitment to the religious life.[6] The most important of these passages were, of course, those that were immediately associated with the practice of the crusader taking the cross.[7] According to the eyewitness testimony of Robert of Rheims, Pope Urban was supposed to have stated that:

---

[3] Gilo of Paris, *Historie Vie Hierosolimitane*, ed. and trans. C.W. Grocock and J.E. Siberry (Oxford, 1997), pp. 68–71; Ralph of Caen, 'Gesta Tancredi', *RHC Oc.* 3, pp. 605–6. See above, pp. 20–2, 26–7.

[4] Albert of Aachen, *Historia Ierosolimitana*, ed. and trans. S.B. Edgington (Oxford, 2007), p. 4, credited Peter the Hermit with being the *primus auctor* of the crusade. On Peter's role, see E.O. Blake and C. Morris, 'A Hermit Goes to War: Peter and the Origins of the First Crusade', *Monks, Hermits and the Ascetic Tradition*, ed. W.J. Sheils, *SCH*, 22 (Oxford, 1985), pp. 79–107; M.D. Coupe, 'Peter the Hermit – A Reassessment', *Nottingham Medieval Studies*, 31 (1987), pp. 37–46; J. Flori, 'Faut-il réhabiliter Pierre l'Ermite? Une réévaluation des sources de la première croisade', *Cahiers de civilisation médiévale*, 38 (1995), pp. 35–54; J. Rubenstein, 'How, or How Much, to Reevaluate Peter the Hermit', *The Medieval Crusade*, ed. S.J. Ridyard (Woodbridge, 2004), pp. 53–69. For Byzantine efforts to stimulate western interest in Jerusalem in the 1090s, see J. Shepard, 'Cross-purposes: Alexius Comnenus and the First Crusade', *The First Crusade: Origins and Impact*, ed. J.P. Phillips (Manchester, 1997), pp. 113–14, 116–21.

[5] For the Clermont sermon as the 'inaugural motif' of a 'constructed narrative' of the First Crusade, see M. Bull, 'Views of Muslims and of Jerusalem in Miracle Stories, c.1000–c.1200: Reflections on the Study of First Crusaders' Motivations', *The Experience of Crusading, Volume One: Western Approaches*, ed. M. Bull and N. Housley (Cambridge, 2003), pp. 21–3.

[6] See above, pp. 22–7.

[7] See J.A. Brundage, '*Cruce Signari*: The Rite for Taking the Cross in England', *Traditio*, 22 (1966), pp. 289–310; J.S.C. Riley-Smith, *The First Crusaders, 1095–1131* (Cambridge, 1997), pp. 81–3; G. Constable, 'Jerusalem and the Sign of the Cross (with Particular Reference to the Cross of Pilgrimage and Crusading in the Twelfth Century)', *Jerusalem: Its Sanctity and Centrality to Judaism, Christianity, and Islam*, ed. L.I. Levine (New York, 1999), pp. 371–81.

Whoever therefore shall carry out this holy pilgrimage shall make a vow to God, and shall offer himself as a living sacrifice . . . and he shall display the sign of the cross of the Lord on his front or on his chest. When, truly, he wishes to return from there having fulfilled his vow, let him place the cross between his shoulders; in fact, by this twofold action they will fulfil that precept of the Lord which he prescribed himself through the Gospel: *He that does not carry his cross and come after me is not worthy of me.*[8]

It is impossible to gauge whether Urban was so explicit about the way in which the crusade badge was to be used; the detailed instructions that Robert reported may actually reflect the text of a lost conciliar decree.[9] What is certain, though, is that the sign of the cross was not only intended to be a symbol of the crusader's vow, and therefore a tangible reminder of his commitment to the expedition: it was also to be a visual encapsulation of the scriptural ideal of *imitatio Christi*. By displaying the sign of the cross on his clothing[10] the crusader was seen to be literally fulfilling Christ's injunction to the faithful that they ought to take up their crosses and follow him. As the author of the *Gesta Ambaziensium dominorum* later put it, at Clermont 'that distinguished pope was proclaiming the Lord to have said to his followers, *If anyone does not carry his cross and come after me, he cannot be my disciple.* "For that reason," he said, "you ought to attach the cross to your clothes."'[11] In this respect, the Clermont sermon was therefore a remarkable feat of pastoral instruction, for by instituting the sign of the cross as the badge of the crusade Pope Urban successfully introduced into the secular world a concept that had previously only been applied to the monastic life. Although the significance of the gesture of taking the cross should certainly be seen within the context of other contemporary penitential practices,[12] Urban's compression of the ideal of *imitatio Christi* into a single, coherent image, and his

---

[8] Robert of Rheims, 'Historia Iherosolimitana', *RHC Oc.* 3, pp. 729–30. Citation from Matthew 10:38.

[9] Cf. 'Historia peregrinorum euntium Jerusolymam', *RHC Oc.* 3, pp. 169–70; *Decreta Claromontensia*, ed. R. Somerville, *The Councils of Urban II. I.* (Amsterdam, 1972), p. 124. See also R. Somerville, 'The Council of Clermont and the First Crusade', *Studia Gratiana*, 20 (1976), pp. 332–4.

[10] An early-twelfth-century representation of the crusade badge can be seen on the sculpture from Belval (now in the Musée historique Lorrain, Nancy). See N. Kenaan-Kedar and B.Z. Kedar, 'The Significance of a Twelfth-Century Sculptural Group: Le retour du croisé', *Dei gesta per Francos: Crusade Studies in Honour of Jean Richard*, ed. M. Balard, B.Z. Kedar and J.S.C. Riley-Smith (Aldershot, 2001), pp. 29–44.

[11] 'Gesta Ambaziensium dominorum', ed. L. Halphen and R. Poupardin, *Chroniques des comtes d'Anjou et des seigneurs d'Amboise* (Paris, 1913), p. 100. Cf. Baldric of Bourgueil, 'Historia Jerosolimitana', *RHC Oc.* 4, p. 16.

[12] See S. Hamilton, *The Practice of Penance, 900–1050* (Woodbridge, 2001), pp. 104–21, who stressed the importance of the penitent's 'body language of humility' in the liturgical rites for Ash Wednesday and Maundy Thursday in the Romano-German pontifical. See also G. Koziol, *Begging Pardon and Favor: Ritual and Political Order in Early Medieval France* (Ithaca and London, 1992), especially pp. 59–76, where it is argued that gestures of supplication and deference were central to delineating and communicating medieval ideas of both earthly and heavenly political and social order. In this context, it is not surprising that the gesture of adopting the sign of the cross was regarded by contemporaries as being as significant as the ceremonial undertakings associated with entry into professed religious life, for which see G. Constable, 'The Ceremonies and Symbolism of Entering Religious Life and Taking the Monastic Habit, from the Fourth to the Twelfth Century', *Settimane di studio del Centro italiano di studi sull'alto medioevo*, 33 (Spoleto, 1987), pp. 771–834.

invention of a new ritual act, was nothing short of revolutionary.[13]

Several writers recorded the immediate reaction to the pope's words, and it is clear that Urban's message about the spirituality of the crusade had a remarkable impact on those who heard it. Baldric of Bourgueil described how, after the pope had concluded his sermon, all those who wished to join the expedition:

> immediately sewed the sign of the holy cross onto their clothes. This was, in fact, what the pope had ordered . . . because he had proclaimed the Lord to have said to his followers: *If anyone does not carry his cross and come after me, he cannot be my disciple.*[14]

Ekkehard of Aura wrote that the crusade badge was a 'sign of mortification',[15] and reported that Pope Urban had offered remission of all sins to the crusaders 'if they gave up everything which they possessed . . . and carried the cross after Christ'.[16] Guibert of Nogent believed that those who were preparing to depart for the East 'seemed to have a desire to emulate God',[17] and were therefore taking the cross as a '*stigma* of the Lord's Passion'.[18] And for Fulcher of Chartres, the crusaders 'marked themselves with a sign of the ideal [of *imitatio*] so that they might attain the reality of the ideal'.[19]

In addition to such general statements as these there is also important evidence that illustrates how individual crusaders responded to the idea that they were taking the cross in imitation of Christ. It has already been pointed out in the previous chapter that Tancred Marchisus was believed to have joined the expedition out of a desire to 'follow in the footsteps of the Gospel',[20] and it is clear that the crusade's other leaders shared his sentiment: in their letter to Pope Urban of September 1098, they wrote that 'by your sermons you made us leave everything, both our lands and whatever was in them, and taught us to take up crosses to follow Christ'.[21] Furthermore, charter evidence shows that this idea was not restricted to the upper ranks of first crusaders.[22] The record of the agreement between Wolfker of Kuffern and the Benedictine community of Göttweig stated that 'a certain nobleman called Wolfker, wishing to satisfy that precept of the Gospel, *he who wishes to come after me*, has decided to go to Jerusalem';[23] the endowment of Henry II of Regensburg to the same community proclaimed that the count was 'taking up the cross in accordance with the precept of the Gospel, so that he might go to see

[13] Cf. C. Erdmann, *The Origin of the Idea of Crusade*, trans. M.W. Baldwin and W. Goffart (Princeton, NJ, 1977), pp. 345–8.
[14] Baldric of Bourgueil, 'Historia', p. 16.
[15] Ekkehard of Aura, 'Hierosolymita', *RHC Oc.* 5, p. 19.
[16] *Ibid.*, p. 15.
[17] Guibert of Nogent, 'Dei gesta per Francos', ed. R.B.C. Huygens, *CC:CM* 127 A (Turnhout, 1996), p. 120. For Guibert's use of the idea of *emulatio Dei*, see also *ibid.*, pp. 197, 326.
[18] *Ibid.*, p. 117.
[19] Fulcher of Chartres, *Historia Hierosolymitana (1095–1127)*, ed. H. Hagenmeyer (Heidelberg, 1913), p. 142. See also Guibert of Nogent, 'Dei gesta', p. 321: 'sicut exterius, ita interius baiulavere crucem'.
[20] Ralph of Caen, 'Gesta Tancredi', p. 606.
[21] *Die Kreuzzugsbriefe aus den Jahren 1088–1100*, ed. H. Hagenmeyer (Innsbruck, 1901), no. 16, p. 164.
[22] See Riley-Smith, *First Crusaders*, pp. 62–3.
[23] *Die Traditionsbücher des Benediktinerstiftes Göttweig*, ed. A.F. Fuchs (Vienna, 1931), no. 55, p. 194.

the Lord's Sepulchre'.[24] Similarly, in 1101, Peter of Limoges described how the bishop of Périgueux had set out on crusade, 'carrying Christ's cross to Jerusalem'.[25]

Besides the sources that refer directly to the Gospel texts that Pope Urban was believed to have preached at Clermont, there is also a range of supplementary evidence that indicates the spiritual significance that contemporaries associated with the crusader's cross. The author of the *Gesta Francorum*, for example, wrote that Robert of Flanders 'faithfully bore the sign of the cross every day', a phrase that was both descriptive in its reference to the crusade badge and figurative in its inference to the text of Luke 9:23.[26] Guibert of Nogent expressed a similar idea when he wrote of the suffering that the crusaders had endured whilst on the march to Jerusalem and described how at points they had been 'straining to follow Christ, carrying double crosses, rejoicing that they were able to go beyond the Lord's commands, who had instructed that they take up only one cross'.[27] Elsewhere, he depicted the crusaders as sacrificing themselves for Christ: 'they went out of the camp to him, clearly beyond the desires of the flesh, now carrying his reproach, the mortification of the cross'.[28] Ekkehard of Aura depicted the crusaders as 'carrying the cross after Christ, very much in forced service with Simon',[29] a striking image when one considers that Simon of Cyrene was the first individual to have literally taken Christ's cross and followed him.[30] And, although writing some thirty years later, Fulcher of Chartres believed that the settlers in the Latin East had enjoyed such prosperity because 'God does not wish those to suffer want who vowed to follow him with their crosses, even until the end'.[31] For many writers the very positioning of the crusade badge itself was loaded with symbolic importance. Although many crusaders had undoubtedly sewn the sign of the cross 'onto the front of their clothes',[32] when news of the crusade first reached Bohemond of Taranto he was believed to have been told that the crusaders 'carried the cross of Christ on the right of, or in-between, their shoulders'.[33] This positioning was, of course, evocative of Christ's march to Calvary. When the scribe Galfred recorded that the would-be crusader Emerias of Altejas had 'lifted the cross onto her right shoulder in order to go to Jerusalem',[34] he was obviously referring to Emerias's

---

[24] *Ibid.*, no. 56, p. 197.

[25] 'Un acte de l'évêque Pierre de Limoges (1101)', ed. J. Becquet, *Bulletin de la Société Archéologique et Historique du Limousin*, 112 (1985), p. 18.

[26] *Gesta Francorum*, p. 31. Cf. Peter Tudebode, *Historia*, p. 66.

[27] Guibert of Nogent, 'Dei gesta', p. 178.

[28] *Ibid.*, p. 322. Cf. *Libellus de diversis ordinibus et professionibus qui sunt in aecclesia*, ed. and trans. G. Constable and B.S. Smith, revised edition (Oxford, 2003), pp. 58–9; see above, p. 25.

[29] Ekkehard of Aura, 'Hierosolymita', p. 39.

[30] Matthew 27:32. See E.J. Tinsley, *The Imitation of God in Christ: An Essay on the Biblical Basis of Christian Spirituality* (London, 1960), p. 106.

[31] Fulcher of Chartres, *Historia*, p. 749. See also *ibid.*, p. 154.

[32] Gilo of Paris, *Historia*, p. 24. See also Ekkehard of Aura, 'Hierosolymita', p. 16; Guibert of Nogent, 'Dei gesta', p. 117; 'Narratio Floriacensis de captis Antiochia et Hierosolyma et obsesso Dyrrachio', *RHC Oc.* 5, p. 356.

[33] *Gesta Francorum*, p. 7. Cf. Peter Tudebode, *Historia*, p. 40, and Robert of Rheims, 'Historia', p. 741. See also Fulcher of Chartres, *Historia*, pp. 140–1; OV 5, pp. 14, 206–8; Caffaro, 'De liberatione civitatum orientis', ed. L.T. Belgrano, *Annali genovesi*, 1 (Genoa, 1890), pp. 100, 101, 106.

[34] *Histoire générale de Languedoc*, 3rd edition, ed. J. Vaissète, C. Devic and A. Molinier, 16 vols. (Toulouse, 1872–1904), vol. 5, no. 401, p. 757.

adoption of the crusade badge – but the idea that she had 'lifted' the cross (*levaverat*) was undeniably meant in a figurative sense.[35]

Perhaps the most unexpected consequence of the emphasis on Matthew 16:24 and its variants within the preaching for the First Crusade was the miraculous appearance of *stigmata* upon the bodies of a number of first crusaders.[36] The phenomenon of stigmatism was closely linked with the *imitatio Christi* tradition, especially from the thirteenth century onwards,[37] but unlike later stigmatics, whose bodies were most commonly marked with the five wounds that Christ had suffered during his Passion, the crusaders' *stigmata* manifested themselves in the form of the sign of the cross. The direct connection between this marking and the preaching of the crusade was drawn by Bernold of St Blasien when he recorded how, in 1096, '[Pope Urban] made all those who devoted themselves to this journey mark themselves with the sign of the cross on their clothes; but the sign also appeared on the flesh itself of some of them'.[38] Other writers corroborated this remarkable claim; in his description of the 'various portents' that roused the Germans to join the crusade, Ekkehard of Aura wrote that:

> Some [of the crusaders] were . . . displaying the sign of the cross which had been divinely impressed either on their foreheads or their clothes or in any other place of their body, and they believed themselves by this same *stigma* to have been directed to the army of the Lord.[39]

But these extraordinary revelations were by no means limited to the period of initial recruitment for the expedition. Orderic Vitalis recounted how after the death in Bulgaria of Walter of Poissy – one of the leaders of the crusade's 'first wave' – his comrades noticed that 'the sign of the holy cross appeared on his body'.[40] Elsewhere, Fulcher of Chartres described the shipwreck and drowning of a boatload of crusaders who were bound for the Holy Land in 1097, and noted that after the bodies of the dead were recovered, the survivors 'discovered crosses evidently marked on the flesh above the shoulders'.[41] And Raymond of Aguilers claimed to have witnessed a comparable miracle in 1099 when he inspected the bodies of a number of crusaders who had been killed during a skirmish with the Muslims – he declared that 'all of the dead had crosses on their right shoulders'.[42]

---

[35] See also *Recueil des chartes de l'abbaye de Cluny*, ed. A. Bernard and A. Bruel, 6 vols. (1876–1903), vol. 5, no. 3737, p. 89.

[36] See W.J. Purkis, 'Stigmata on the First Crusade', *Signs, Wonders, Miracles: Representations of Divine Power in the Life of the Church*, ed. K. Cooper and J. Gregory, SCH, 41 (Woodbridge, 2005), pp. 99–108. For a discussion of similar events in Scandinavian sources, see H. Antonsson, '*Insigne Crucis*: A European Motif in a Nordic Setting', *The North Sea World in the Middle Ages: Studies in the Cultural History of North-Western Europe* (Dublin, 2001), pp. 15–32.

[37] See G. Constable, 'The Ideal of the Imitation of Christ', *Three Studies in Medieval Religious and Social Thought* (Cambridge, 1995), pp. 194–217.

[38] Bernold of St Blasien, 'Chronicon', *MGH SS* 5, p. 464.

[39] Ekkehard of Aura, 'Hierosolymita', p. 19.

[40] OV 5, p. 30. Although Orderic's narrative of the crusade was based largely on the *Historia* of Baldric of Bourgueil, Chibnall notes that 'the information in this paragraph occurs only in Orderic'; *ibid.*, p. 30, n. 2.

[41] Fulcher of Chartres, *Historia*, pp. 168–9.

[42] Raymond of Aguilers, *Liber*, ed. J.H. and L.L. Hill (Paris, 1969), p. 102.

Not all of the individuals who laid claim to the miracle of the crusade stigmata were above suspicion. Describing the preparations that the crusaders were making prior to their departure for the East, Baldric of Bourgueil wrote of how:

> Many of the common people were displaying the cross, which had itself grown divinely; but this same [miracle] was taken for granted by certain kinds of young women. This of course was seized upon as entirely fake. Some, in truth, had applied that likeness of a cross with a hot iron.[43]

Another writer confirmed that there were certain crusaders who 'imprinted . . . the sign of the cross to their own flesh with a white-hot iron',[44] whilst Guibert of Nogent described the variety of ways in which some individuals mutilated their bodies so as to denote that they had been touched by the miraculous. One man was supposed to have cut his face and drawn the sign of the cross with the resulting blood; another had blinded himself in the hope that his neighbours would believe that he was some kind of oracle; and yet another had painted the mark of the cross onto his body using fruit dye.[45] By far the most prominent of these fraudsters was Baldwin, an abbot who was chaplain to Godfrey of Bouillon and was later promoted to the archbishopric of Caesarea. According to Guibert, Baldwin had attempted to fake a miraculous *stigma* out of a desire to secure funding to undertake the crusade:

> He carved into the middle of his forehead – I do not know how – that sign of the cross which was customarily made out of some kind of material and attached to clothing. It did not look to have been painted on, but resembled the kind of wound inflicted by a weapon in battle. Having done this, so that his mendacious claim was strengthened, he made it known that an angel had impressed that mark upon him in a vision.[46]

Although this falsification initially paid dividends, Baldwin was eventually exposed as a fraud when his self-inflicted wound became infected.[47] Nevertheless, in his final assessment of the affair, Guibert was sympathetic, not least because of the abbot's conduct during the siege of Antioch. Indeed, Guibert displayed a clear empathy with the motives that had inspired Baldwin's curious behaviour: 'He had of course intended zealous imitation of God (*emulatio Dei*), but he had not carried this out wisely.'[48]

It is this latter phrase in particular that suggests that the phenomenon of the crusade stigmata ought to be studied within a broader context of medieval ideas about how internal spirituality could manifest itself externally. Such ideas are, of course, most famously associated with St Francis of Assisi (d. 1226), who is often inaccurately regarded as 'the first stigmatic' because he was one of the earliest, and certainly the

---

[43] Baldric of Bourgueil, 'Historia', p. 17.
[44] 'Historia de translatione sanctorum magni Nicolai . . . ejusdem avunculi alterius Nicolai, Theodorique . . . de civitate Mirea in monasterium S. Nicolai de Littore Venetiarum', *RHC Oc.* 5, p. 255
[45] Guibert of Nogent, 'Dei gesta', p. 330.
[46] *Ibid.*, p. 197.
[47] See R.D. Smith, *Comparative Miracles* (St Louis, MO, 1965), pp. 23–4, who noted that '[a] verified characteristic of [*bona fide*] stigmata is that the wounds do not become infected'.
[48] Guibert of Nogent, 'Dei gesta', p. 197.

most famous, examples of an individual who shared the five wounds of Christ.[49] It was whilst in retreat on Mount La Verna in 1224 that Francis, immersed in a meditation on the Passion, was said to have received the angelic vision through which *stigmata* were marked upon his hands, feet and side. Later writers believed that the explanation for this marking had been supplied to Francis by Christ himself:

> During this seraphic vision Christ appeared to Saint Francis . . . And these were His words: 'Do you know,' said Christ, 'what I have done to you? I have given you the Stigmata, which are the marks of My Passion, so that you may be My Standard-Bearer . . . In this way you shall be conformed to Me in My death as you have been during your life.'[50]

It is notoriously difficult to separate fact from legend when considering the life of St Francis,[51] but it is clear that the miracle of the stigmata was not a later hagiographical invention. One contemporary, James of Vitry (d. 1240), confirmed that the marking was the result of Christo-mimetic piety when he wrote that Francis had 'followed Him Who was crucified so explicitly that at his death the signs of the wounds of Christ were apparent on his hands, feet, and side'.[52]

The parallels between the descriptions of the stigmatism of St Francis and those of the stigmatism of certain first crusaders are striking. Most obvious is the similarly Christo-centric mental state of the subjects. According to the *Little Flowers*, Francis's retreat on Mount La Verna was spent 'lamenting aloud the Passion of Christ, as though he were watching it with his bodily eyes'.[53] Correspondingly, the evidence considered above clearly shows that ideas of the imitation of Christ were prominent within the preaching of the crusade. Furthermore, the relationship between the devotional activities that were being undertaken and the nature of the subsequent physical marking is also clear in both cases. After his death, Francis was believed to have appeared in a vision to one of his followers and explained why it was that he had been stigmatised in the manner that he had:

> As I was praying [on Mount La Verna], a young man crucified . . . swiftly descended through the sky from heaven. At His marvellous appearance I knelt humbly, and began to contemplate with devotion the boundless love of Jesus Crucified, and the infinite sorrow of His Passion. And His appearance caused so deep a compassion within me that it seemed as though I felt His own Passion in my own body.[54]

---

[49] For a recent study, see N. Yarom, *Body, Blood and Sexuality: A Psychoanalytic Study of St Francis' Stigmata and their Historical Context* (New York, 1992). The biblical origins of 'stigmata' are discussed in C.P. Jones, 'Stigma: Tattooing and Branding in Graeco-Roman Antiquity', *Journal of Roman Studies*, 77 (1987), pp. 150–1.

[50] *The Little Flowers of Saint Francis: With Five Considerations on the Sacred Stigmata*, trans. L. Sherley-Price (London, 1959), p. 166.

[51] See C.H. Lawrence, *Medieval Monasticism: Forms of Religious Life in Western Europe in the Middle Ages*, 3rd edition (Harlow, 2001), pp. 244–5.

[52] James of Vitry, *Sermones ad fratres minores*, ed. H. Felder, *Spicilegium Franciscanum*, 5 (Rome, 1903), p. 35. Cited in Constable, 'Imitation of Christ', p. 219.

[53] *Little Flowers*, p. 150.

[54] *Ibid.*, pp. 182–3.

The crusaders were of course more focused on the idea of bearing Christ's cross than on sharing in the wounds of his Passion, and in this context it is not surprising that the miraculous appearance of *stigmata* on the flesh, both before and during the expedition, always replicated the form and often the evocative positioning of the crusade badge – *super spatulas*[55] or *in dextris humeris*.[56] Such a marking was therefore believed to highlight the most devoted members of the crusading armies: Fulcher of Chartres described the mark as a 'token of faith' (*pignus fidei*) that had been bestowed by God upon his most faithful servants,[57] and Guibert of Nogent referred to the wounds as *sacra stigmata*, divinely imprinted as evidence of the bearer's holiness.[58] Reactions to the attempts to fabricate the miraculous signs are also revealing. Guibert of Nogent's forgiving attitude towards Abbot Baldwin has already been quoted, but it is also worth noting that Guibert referred more generally to the work of the fraudsters, writing that those who conducted acts of self-mutilation did so in order to show that 'the divine was alive in them'.[59] This yearning to demonstrate one's internal spirituality by manufacturing external wounds was not limited to the First Crusade,[60] but it does provide a tangible indication that the fraudsters felt the need to be seen to be imitating Christ.

In drawing comparisons between the experience of St Francis and that of the stigmatics of the First Crusade one could also cite similarities in circumstantial details such as the role of angels and visions in the imposition of the stigmata – almost all of the observers referred to divine revelation in their descriptions of the crusaders' marks,[61] and Abbot Baldwin obviously felt that it was necessary to authenticate his story by claiming that an angel had blessed him with the sign of the cross[62] – but, in a sense, such addenda are superfluous. It is clear enough that the 'miraculous' appearance of the sign of the cross upon the bodies of a number of first crusaders was a direct result of the emphasis on the imitation of Christ in the preaching of the expedition. Equally, it is also clear that the appearances of these *stigmata* bear comparison with the better known stigmatisation of St Francis, who was regarded by some contemporaries as an *alter Christus*, such was the depth of his Christo-mimetic piety.[63] The fact that the crusade stigmata appeared as crosses rather than as wounds in the hands, feet and side should not be seen as problematic, however, for this distinction almost certainly reflects the differences between the devotional milieus of the late eleventh and early thirteenth centuries. Reverence for Christ's wounds was not unknown at the time of the First Crusade – Raymond of Aguilers recounted a vision in which St Andrew instructed the

---

[55] Fulcher of Chartres, *Historia*, p. 169.

[56] Raymond of Aguilers, *Liber*, p. 102.

[57] Fulcher of Chartres, *Historia*, p. 170.

[58] Guibert of Nogent, 'Dei gesta', p. 329.

[59] *Ibid.*, p. 330.

[60] See Constable, 'Imitation of Christ', p. 201, where it is observed in reference to those individuals who later inflicted the wounds of Christ upon themselves that 'self-imposition . . . expresses even more clearly than supernatural intervention the stigmatic's devotion to Christ and desire to imitate His body'.

[61] Raymond of Aguilers, *Liber*, p. 102, testified that 'God was the creator of that cross'. See also Baldric of Bourgueil, 'Historia', p. 17; Ekkehard of Aura, 'Hierosolymita', p. 19; Fulcher of Chartres, *Historia*, pp. 169–70; Guibert of Nogent, 'Dei gesta', p. 329.

[62] Guibert of Nogent, 'Dei gesta', p. 197.

[63] See Constable, 'Imitation of Christ', p. 217.

crusaders to offer five alms 'because of the five wounds of the Lord'[64] – but it had certainly not reached the level of intensity of St Francis's day, where devotion to Christ had shifted towards an increasingly literal mimesis of his human life and sufferings.[65] Moreover, there are at least two other cases of stigmatism that provide a connection between the Christo-mimetic spirituality of the era of the First Crusade with that of the era of St Francis. For the eleventh century, there is Peter Damian's *vita* of Dominic *Loricatus* (d. 1060), where it is recorded that 'Dominic carried the *stigmata* of Jesus on his body, and the banner of the cross was not only depicted on his forehead, but also impressed everywhere on his limbs'.[66] For the thirteenth, there is an entry in Caesarius of Heisterbach's *Dialogue on Miracles*, which describes how 'a certain [Cistercian] novice . . . bowing his head with much reverence . . . felt a cross impressed upon his forehead, and I think that at that moment he was meditating on the Passion'.[67] Both of these examples show that medieval ideas of stigmatism were not as inextricably linked with the five wounds of Christ's Passion as is widely believed. It is therefore evident that St Francis could not possibly have been 'the first stigmatic', for he was anticipated by the *imitatores Christi* of the First Crusade by over a century.

Whilst the adoption of the sign of the cross was the most obvious indication of the crusaders' intent to follow Christ, it is significant that many other aspects of crusading were also comprehended in terms of Christo-mimesis. One of the most prominent themes within the sources was the sacrifice that the crusaders would have to make when they left their homes and families for the East.[68] According to Robert of Rheims, the pope had tried to encourage potential crusaders by reminding them of the words that Christ had used to reassure his earliest followers:

> If the dear love of children, parents or wives holds you back, remember what the Lord says in the Gospel: *He that loves father or mother more than me is not worthy of me. Everyone who has left house or father or mother or wife or children or lands for my name's sake shall receive an hundred-fold and shall inherit everlasting life.*[69]

Urban was therefore believed to be demanding of the crusaders no less than what the

---

[64] Raymond of Aguilers, *Liber*, p. 77. See also *ibid.*, pp. 113–14, where Raymond describes a vision in which Christ ranks the crusaders into five orders according to his five wounds. See below, pp. 43, 51.

[65] See Constable, 'Imitation of Christ', pp. 199–201, who argues that it was only after the fame of St Francis that the term 'stigmata' became specifically associated with Christ's five wounds. See also H.J. Thurston, *The Physical Phenomena of Mysticism* (London, 1952), pp. 32–129.

[66] Peter Damian, 'Vita Dominici Loricati', *PL* 144, col. 1024. See Constable, 'Imitation of Christ', pp. 202–3: 'it is hard to tell how explicitly Damiani's words should be taken . . . Since he was certainly familiar with the figurative use of the term stigmata, he may have been referring to the signs left on Dominic's body by his scourgings and other ascetic disciplines'.

[67] Caesarius of Heisterbach, *Dialogus miraculorum*, ed. J. Strange, 2 vols. (Ridgewood, NJ, 1966), vol. 2, p. 100.

[68] For the broader context, see G. Constable, *Attitudes toward Self-Inflicted Suffering in the Middle Ages* (Brookline, MA, 1982).

[69] Robert of Rheims, 'Historia', p. 728. Citations from Matthew 10:37 and 19:29. See also Fulcher of Chartres, *Historia*, pp. 162–3.

Gospels recorded had been demanded of the disciples: that they abandon their lives and material possessions to follow Christ, and 'to follow' was 'to imitate'.[70] Given what is now known about the financial sacrifices made by many first crusaders and their families,[71] and also about how many crusaders were clustered in kinship groups,[72] this particular aspect of the pope's message is especially striking.

As with the references to the practice of taking the cross, the idea that the crusaders had renounced their worldly goods and accepted voluntary exile for Christ was a popular motif for those who wrote narratives of the expedition. Orderic Vitalis, for example, believed that after the pope had delivered his Clermont address, 'such a deep longing for a pilgrimage overwhelmed countless of his hearers that they determined to sell their lands and abandon all that they had for Christ's sake'.[73] Similarly, Guibert of Nogent wrote that the crusaders had left behind 'their most distinguished wives and their most beloved sons, and disregarded whatever things were held in affection, having set forth in exile',[74] believing that God had 'put in the hearts of the men such contempt for the wild and greedy things of the here and now'.[75] And Geoffrey of Le Chalard described how:

> counts and bishops and countless swarms of faithful people from all the regions of a shaken world were assuming the sign of the cross of Christ. Disregarding the companionship of beloved and dear ones, evidently of fathers and brothers and mothers, and of most precious wives, they were all hastening to fulfil the precepts of the Lord.[76]

A number of individual examples can also be cited. According to Landulf the Younger, the crusader Girismannus had 'abandoned father and mother, sisters and brothers, and also [his] wife and [his] only newborn daughter' in response to the preaching of the archbishop of Milan in 1100,[77] and the anonymous continuator of Gilo of Paris described how Baldwin of Mons was 'leaving behind wife and children, home and castle'.[78] Elsewhere, it was claimed that Raymond of St Gilles had 'abandoned his native land and his paternal goods' to serve the Lord,[79] and Godfrey of Bouillon was believed to have 'left all his possessions for the peace of Christ, and struck out on his way, following Christ who called him on'.[80]

By abandoning their homes and families and taking the cross,[81] the crusaders were therefore widely understood to be fulfilling two of Christ's scriptural injunctions

---

[70] See Constable, 'Imitation of Christ', pp. 145–6.

[71] See G. Constable, 'The Financing of the Crusades in the Twelfth Century', *Outremer: Studies in the History of the Crusading Kingdom of Jerusalem Presented to Joshua Prawer*, ed. B.Z. Kedar, H.E. Mayer and R.C. Smail (Jerusalem, 1982), pp. 64–88; Riley-Smith, *First Crusaders*, especially pp. 129–35.

[72] See Riley-Smith, *First Crusaders*, pp. 93–105.

[73] OV 5, pp. 16–17; see also *ibid.*, pp. 34, 70.

[74] Guibert of Nogent, 'Dei gesta', p. 132; see also *ibid.*, pp. 87–8, 148, 226, 230, 275, 299.

[75] *Ibid.*, pp. 266–7.

[76] Geoffrey of Le Chalard, 'Dictamen de primordiis ecclesiae Castaliensis', *RHC Oc.* 5, pp. 348–9.

[77] Landulf the Younger, 'Historia Mediolanensis', *MGH SS* 20, p. 22.

[78] Gilo of Paris, *Historia*, pp. 16–17.

[79] Raymond of Aguilers, *Liber*, p. 41; see also *ibid.*, p. 117.

[80] Gilo of Paris, *Historia*, pp. 14–15; see also *ibid.*, pp. 12–13.

[81] See also Albert of Aachen, *Historia*, p. 2; Ekkehard of Aura, 'Hierosolymita', pp. 32–3; Fulcher of Chartres, *Historia*, pp. 115–16; *Kreuzzugsbriefe*, no. 22, pp. 178–9.

concerning Christian discipleship. But the parallels between crusading and the imitation of Christ went further still. Whereas the cloistered monk was understood to have followed the call of the Gospel by rejecting the world and 'taking the cross' for the religious life, the nature of the devotional activity of the crusader was far more literal in its mimesis: as the author of the *Gesta Francorum* succinctly put it, the crusaders had set out for the Levant 'saying with one accord that they would all follow the footsteps of Christ'.[82] The crusaders had therefore not only committed themselves to imitating Christ by bearing his cross: as armed pilgrims in the Holy Land, they were literally walking in his footsteps, and it was for this reason that the crusade became popularly known as the 'Way of Christ'.[83]

Reference has already been made in the previous chapter to the fact that, since the early Church, the term *via Christi* had been understood to refer to the imitation of Christ, and how thereafter it became associated with the religious life.[84] But with the First Crusade, the idea of 'following the Way of Christ', like the idea of bearing his cross, shifted from being an abstract theological ideal to being a tangible devotional exercise. According to the author of the *Gesta Francorum*, Pope Urban had applied this language to the crusade at Clermont, where he was supposed to have said that 'if anyone wishes to make a sacrifice for the salvation of his soul, let him have no hesitation in humbly taking the Way of the Lord (*via Domini*)'.[85] It is likely that Baldric of Bourgueil was expanding on this theme[86] when he portrayed the pope's sermon as addressing the depravity of the Christian knighthood in the following terms: 'you are not following the Way that leads you to life . . . Certainly [yours] is the worst way because it is utterly removed from God . . . [but] the Way is short, and the task is slight that will reward you with a never fading crown'.[87]

Given that Pope Urban was credited with preaching the crusade in the prominently Christo-mimetic terms discussed above, it seems more than likely that it was also he who was responsible for first referring to the crusade as the *via Christi*. This aspect of his message also clearly had a deep resonance: Guibert of Nogent noted that the crusade was commonly known as the *via Dei*[88] — a claim that is supported by both narrative and charter sources[89] — and the phrase also appeared in variant forms, such as *via Domini*[90]

[82] *Gesta Francorum*, p. 2. Cf. Peter Tudebode, *Historia*, p. 32.

[83] See, for example, *Gesta Francorum*, p. 7.

[84] See above, pp. 22–3, 24.

[85] *Gesta Francorum*, p. 1. Cf. Peter Tudebode, *Historia*, p. 32.

[86] For the idea that writers such as Baldric proffered a 'theological refinement' of the ideas contained within the *Gesta Francorum*, see J.S.C. Riley-Smith, *The First Crusade and the Idea of Crusading* (London, 1986), pp. 135–52.

[87] Baldric of Bourgueil, 'Historia', pp. 14–15. The reference here was to the 'Two Ways' of which Christ had spoken in Matthew 7:13–14. For medieval understandings of this text, see G.B. Ladner, '*Homo Viator*: Medieval Ideas on Alienation and Order', *Speculum*, 42 (1967), pp. 240–1.

[88] Guibert of Nogent, 'Dei gesta', p. 118. See also *ibid.*, p. 117, where the crusade is referred to as the *iter Dei*.

[89] See, for example, Baldric of Bourgueil, 'Historia', p. 21; Ralph of Caen, 'Gesta Tancredi', pp. 678, 681; 'Historia de translatione sanctorum magni Nicolai', p. 255; *Cartulaire de l'abbaye cardinale de la Trinité de Vendôme*, ed. C. Metais, 5 vols. (1893–1904), vol. 2, pp. 104, 107; *La Chronique de Morigny (1095–1152)*, ed. L. Mirot, Collection de textes, 41 (Paris, 1909), p. 40; OV 5, p. 36.

[90] See, for example, Ekkehard of Aura, 'Hierosolymita', p. 39; *Gesta Francorum*, p. 1; Gilo of Paris,

or *via Iesu Christi*.[91] Similarly, at least one crusader, Stephen of Neublans, was aware that because he lived 'under the secular habit' as an arms-bearer he had committed many sins during his lifetime, 'since the Way in which we walk is polluted'.[92] It seems possible that it was for this reason that he, like so many of his contemporaries, abandoned his home and family to take the cross and follow the Way of Christ to the Holy Sepulchre.

The record of the arrangements that Stephen of Neublans made before he set out for the East also demonstrates how the idea of the *via Christi* laid the foundations for subsequent connections that were drawn between the experience of crusading and the ideal of *imitatio Christi*. In the charter that he drew up prior to his departure Stephen stated that he had 'decided to go to Jerusalem, where God was seen as man and where he spoke with men, and *to worship in the place where his feet have stood*'.[93] This reference to Psalm 131:7, which was also quoted by Fulcher of Chartres on more than one occasion,[94] suggests that the crusaders were aware of the intimate relationship between their undertaking and the human life of Christ. Sensitivity to this relationship was to increase as the crusaders neared Jerusalem, but it seems likely that it was used as a motif in the preaching of the crusade from the outset. According to Baldric of Bourgueil, when Pope Urban called attention to the suffering of the eastern Christians in his Clermont sermon, he was supposed to have called upon the arms-bearers of Christendom to sacrifice themselves for their brethren just as Christ had sacrificed himself for mankind: 'It ought to be a beautiful ideal for you to die for Christ in that city in which Christ died for you.'[95] Similarly, in his letter to the West of 1098 in which he called for further recruits for the crusade, the Greek patriarch of Jerusalem made the following exhortation: 'Come therefore, we pray, to fight in the army of the Lord in the same place in which the Lord fought, in which Christ suffered for us, leaving you an example that you should follow in his footsteps.'[96] In this way, the crusade's preachers were calling upon the arms-bearers of the West to be prepared to perform the ultimate act of *imitatio Christi*: to sacrifice themselves by dying for their brethren.[97]

There has been much written about the issue of death and martyrdom on the First Crusade.[98] There is not space here to rehearse the arguments of previous scholars, nor

---

Historia, p. 52; OV 5, p. 26; 'Chronica prioratus de Casa Vicecomitis', ed. P. Marchegay and É. Mabille, *Chroniques des églises d'Anjou* (Paris, 1869), p. 341. See also *Kreuzzugsbriefe*, no. 15, p. 160, where the crusade is referred to as the *iter Domini*.

[91] *Kreuzzugsbriefe*, no. 16, p. 164.

[92] *Recueil des chartes de l'abbaye de Cluny*, vol. 5, no. 3737, p. 87.

[93] *Ibid.*, p. 88.

[94] Fulcher of Chartres, *Historia*, pp. 162, 331. See also Ekkehard of Aura, 'Hierosolymita', p. 39.

[95] Baldric of Bourgueil, 'Historia', p. 15. See also *ibid.*, p. 101. Baldric also quoted John 15:13, which was to become an important text for crusade propagandists: see especially J.S.C. Riley-Smith, 'Crusading as an Act of Love', *History*, 65 (1980), pp. 177–92.

[96] *Kreuzzugsbriefe*, no. 9, p. 148.

[97] See Tinsley, *Imitation of God in Christ*, p. 110.

[98] See especially J.S.C. Riley-Smith, 'Death on the First Crusade', *The End of Strife*, ed. D.W. Loades (Edinburgh, 1984), pp. 14–31; H.E.J. Cowdrey, 'Martyrdom and the First Crusade', *Crusade and Settlement: Papers Read at the First Conference of the Society for the Study of the Crusades and the Latin East and Presented to R.C. Smail*, ed. P.W. Edbury (Cardiff, 1985), pp. 46–56; J. Flori, 'Mort et martyre des guerriers vers 1100. L'exemple de la prèmiere croisade', *Cahiers de civilisation médiévale*, 34 (1991), pp. 121–39; C. Morris, 'Martyrs on the Field of Battle before and during the First Crusade', *Martyrs*

to cite the plentiful contemporary evidence for the belief that those crusaders who died in the East – whether as a result of illness, execution or death in battle – would merit a martyr's crown.[99] However, what is necessary is to demonstrate how the development of the idea that dead crusaders were 'warrior martyrs' contributed to the belief that the crusaders were imitators of Christ.[100]

A passage from Raymond of Aguilers's *Liber* provides a vivid illustration of the relationship between martyrdom and *imitatio*. Whilst the crusaders were before 'Arqah in April 1099 a Provençal servant called Peter Bartholomew was said to have witnessed a vision in which Christ appeared stretched out on the cross of his Crucifixion, supported by the saints.[101] Pointing to the five wounds he had suffered during his Passion, Christ described to Peter the way in which he had ranked the first crusaders into 'five orders' according to their commitment to the expedition. His most fulsome praise was reserved for those whom he identified as the 'first order':

> The first order is not afraid of spears, or swords, or any other kind of torment. This order is like me. For when I came to Jerusalem, I did not stop to think about swords and lances, clubs and sticks, and lastly the cross. They die for me as I died for them. And I am in them, and they are in me. Upon their death, they are seated to the right of God, where I sat after my Resurrection and Ascension.[102]

Although this episode may well have been intended to serve a political as well as a spiritual purpose – Raymond hoped reporting Christ's words on the remaining four orders would shame recalcitrant crusaders into action[103] – it is obvious enough from this particular example that those crusaders who died in battle were believed to have been willing to sacrifice themselves in imitation of Christ. And for writers who recorded the passing of crusaders who were 'traditional' martyrs – that is to say that they died passively for refusing to apostatise – it was also clear that their subjects were to be regarded as having followed Christ to the last.[104] This idea was central to Guibert of Nogent's description of the suffering and death of a crusader called Matthew, who was killed by the Muslims after he had been captured in battle. Guibert claimed to have known Matthew since childhood, and he eulogised his subject's extraordinary piety, claiming that he had spent so much time in church that:

---

and *Martyrologies*, ed. D. Wood, *SCH*, 30 (Oxford, 1993), pp. 93–105; S. Shepkaru, 'To Die for God: Martyrs' Heaven in Hebrew and Latin Crusade Narratives', *Speculum*, 77 (2002), pp. 311–41.

[99] For a review of the issues surrounding the martyrdom of first crusaders, see N. Housley, *Contesting the Crusades* (Oxford, 2006), pp. 41–2.

[100] H.E.J. Cowdrey, 'Pope Gregory VII and the Bearing of Arms', *Montjoie: Studies in Crusade History in Honour of Hans Eberhard Mayer*, ed. B.Z. Kedar, J.S.C. Riley-Smith and R. Hiestand (Aldershot, 1997), pp. 33–5, shows that similar ideas had been projected by the papacy in 1074.

[101] For the context, see J. France, 'Two Types of Vision on the First Crusade: Stephen of Valence and Peter Bartholomew', *Crusades*, 5 (2006), pp. 1–20.

[102] Raymond of Aguilers, *Liber*, pp. 113–14.

[103] See C. Morris, 'Policy and Visions: The Case of the Holy Lance at Antioch', *War and Government in the Middle Ages: Essays in Honour of J.O. Prestwich*, ed. J. Gillingham and J.C. Holt (Woodbridge, 1984), p. 43; Riley-Smith, *The First Crusade*, pp. 102–3; France, 'Two Types of Vision', p. 17.

[104] See Riley-Smith, 'Death on the First Crusade', p. 20.

his life did not seem to be that of a soldier but rather that of a bishop. In fact, when I recall his dedication in prayer, his piety in speaking and his kindness in giving alms, I am very thankful for his holy exertions, but I mourn for him all the same. Truly, I witnessed him [undertake] such actions through which he merited nothing less than the death of a martyr.[105]

Guibert then advanced the narrative to the point at which Matthew was taken prisoner, and in the subsequent description of his 'passion' it is obvious that Guibert's intention was to portray Matthew as an *imitator Christi*. Refusing to give in to his captors' demands that he convert to Islam, Matthew requested that his death be postponed 'until the sixth day of the week'. The Muslims agreed to his request, assuming that the delay would weaken his resolve, but when the day of his execution finally arrived it transpired that the reason he had requested the postponement was because he wished to die 'on the day on which my Lord Jesus Christ was crucified'. As a result, Guibert believed that Matthew had died a martyr, and 'was carried over to God, whose death he had long desired to imitate (*cuius similitudini mortis inhiaverat*)'.[106]

The reasoning behind Matthew's urgent desire to die on a Friday is striking, but it is by no means the only example of the belief that the crusaders' experiences directly paralleled the narrative of the life of Christ; indeed, awareness of such parallels was understood to have become especially pronounced once the expedition reached Jerusalem in 1099. As the crusaders besieged the holy city, Cono of Montaigu was believed to have stirred the spirits of his comrades by proclaiming that they should 'take up arms in the name of our Lord Jesus Christ, who suffered on a Friday in this very place';[107] a later passage in Orderic Vitalis's narrative went on to describe how 'at the third hour, the time at which the Jews condemned the Lord before Pilate, the Christians, remembering his Passion, received, as it were, new strength, and being filled with fresh courage began to fight as though they had endured nothing before'.[108] In this respect, the timing of the fall of Jerusalem was especially propitious, for Friday was remembered in the liturgical calendar as 'the day on which Christ redeemed the whole world on the cross'.[109] Peter Tudebode highlighted that it was 'at the approach of the hour in which our Lord Jesus Christ deigned to endure his Passion on the cross for us' that Godfrey of Bouillon and Eustace of Boulogne were breaking through the city's defences,[110] and Guibert of Nogent wrote that 'the city was captured by the Franks on the fifteenth day of July, when it was the sixth day [of the week], almost at the hour in which Christ himself was put up on

---

[105] Guibert of Nogent, 'Dei gesta', p. 199.

[106] *Ibid.*, p. 199. The idea of dying on a Friday in imitation of Christ was a hagiographical *topos* that was not unknown before the First Crusade. The sentiment is also found, for example, in John Canaparius, 'Vita S. Adalberti', *MGH SS* 4, p. 595, which was written in *c.*999. In describing the death of St Adalbert of Prague, who was killed by the pagan Prussians on 23 April 997, John Canaparius points out that it was 'feria VI: scilicet ut qua die dominus Iesus Christus pro homine, eadem die homo ille pro Deo suo pateretur.' I am grateful to Professor Hamilton for providing me with this information.

[107] OV 5, pp. 168–9. This speech is peculiar to Orderic.

[108] OV 5, pp. 168–9. Cf. Baldric of Bourgueil, 'Historia', pp. 101–2.

[109] Fulcher of Chartres, *Historia*, p. 299. See also *Gesta Francorum*, p. 90; Gilo of Paris, *Historia*, p. 244; Raymond of Aguilers, *Liber*, p. 151.

[110] Peter Tudebode, *Historia*, p. 139.

the cross'.[111] It should also be noted that Otto of Freising later believed that it was only because of the Christo-mimetic character of the crusaders' processions that Jerusalem had fallen to them at all: 'They were not able to capture Jerusalem with a siege . . . [so] they decided to imitate the humility of the Master and walk around the city with bare feet.'[112] The critical achievement of the first crusaders – liberating Jerusalem from Islam as Christ had liberated mankind from sin – was therefore believed to provide the ultimate vindication to the idea that they truly were imitators of Christ.

Albert of Aachen provided a convenient summary of the range of ideas that connected crusading with the *imitatio Christi* tradition when he wrote of the crusaders that 'they did not hesitate to die for the love of Christ, whose footsteps they followed with the sign of the holy cross, and for whom they had all left homes and family'.[113] The extension of ideas of the imitation of Christ from the monastic to the secular spheres to which Albert gave witness here was, as has been stressed above, without precedent: there is no extant contemporary evidence that depicts eleventh-century Jerusalem pilgrims as following a *via Christi*, or of taking crosses for the Holy Land in observance of Matthew 16:24 or its variants.[114] The fact that contemporaries such as Ekkehard of Aura, Guibert of Nogent and Ralph of Caen regarded the crusade as such an original devotional undertaking must surely in part be attributed to these radical developments.[115] Indeed, the certainty with which it can be concluded that the fusion of ideas of Christo-mimesis and armed pilgrimage was an innovation of Pope Urban II's has an important bearing upon another long-standing dispute in the historiography of crusade ideology: the authenticity, or otherwise, of the encyclical of Pope Sergius IV (1009–12).[116]

In the light of the evidence presented above it now seems almost certain that this so-called papal letter, which was addressed to both laymen and ecclesiastics and purported to be a call for an armed pilgrimage to the Holy Land that predated Pope Urban's appeal by almost a century, originated in 1095–6, possibly from the Cluniac abbey of Mois-sac.[117] Its purpose was to provide a historical antecedent for the First Crusade, and many of the motifs that it contained were synonymous with those found in Urban's preaching.[118] For this reason alone it is an intriguing source because it reflects the concerns of

---

[111] Guibert of Nogent, 'Dei gesta', p. 293.

[112] Otto of Freising, *Chronica sive historia de duabus civitatibus*, ed. A. Hofmeister, MGH SSRG 45 (Hanover and Leipzig, 1912), p. 314. Cf. *Kreuzzugsbriefe*, no. 18, p. 171.

[113] Albert of Aachen, *Historia*, p. 236.

[114] Erdmann, *Origin of the Idea of Crusade*, p. 345, wrote that the adoption of the sign of the cross was 'unquestionably an innovation'.

[115] Ekkehard of Aura, 'Hierosolymita', p. 39; Guibert of Nogent, 'Dei gesta', pp. 87, 136, 326; Ralph of Caen, 'Gesta Tancredi', pp. 605–6.

[116] See A. Gieysztor, 'The Genesis of the Crusades: The Encyclical of Sergius IV (1009–12)', *Medievalia et Humanistica*, 5 (1948), pp. 3–23, and 6 (1950), pp. 3–34; H.M. Schaller, 'Zur Kreuzzugsenzyklika Papst Sergius IV', *Papsttum, Kirche und Recht im Mittelalter: Festschrift für Horst Fuhrmann zum 65. Geburtstag*, ed. H. Mordek (Tübingen, 1991), pp. 135–53; Bull, *Knightly Piety*, pp. 64–6; C. Morris, *The Sepulchre of Christ and the Medieval West: From the Beginning to 1600* (Oxford, 2005), pp. 136–7. For the text of the letter, see Schaller, 'Kreuzzugsenzyklika', pp. 150–3. See also J. France, 'The Destruction of Jerusalem and the First Crusade', *Journal of Ecclesiastical History*, 47 (1996), pp. 1–17.

[117] See Gieysztor, 'Genesis of the Crusades', 6, pp. 19–31.

[118] See Bull, *Knightly Piety*, p. 65.

First Crusade propagandists, but it is especially interesting because it refers to both the Jerusalem pilgrimage and the undertaking of a campaign to liberate the Holy Sepulchre in terms of the imitation of Christ.[119]

Pseudo-Sergius began his letter by reminding his readers of the torment that Christ had suffered on behalf of mankind, and described the devotion that faithful Christians showed by travelling to the Holy Land:

> Some brethren, led by the love of him [Christ], have gone to that place which he touched with his own feet, lamenting right up as far as Mount Calvary, where he healed us by his own wounds, and venerating at the Mount of Olives, and, above all else, at the Sepulchre in which he lay.[120]

These pilgrims were understood to have left their homes 'to follow the footsteps of Jesus Christ', and were seen to be 'shunning temporal possessions and carrying only their own cross, as if they might become disciples and, as it is ordered, they trod the Way of Jesus (*via Ihesu*) with only the cross'.[121] Pseudo-Sergius then went on to report the destruction of the Holy Sepulchre by Hakim in 1009[122] and to proclaim that he wished to recruit for and lead an expedition to Jerusalem to recover the holy city from Islam. Preparations for such an undertaking were already in motion:

> We find that many people who are from the city situated on the seashore [Genoa or Venice] are now most faithful to us . . . because they have sold their things on their own. For this reason they send away their sons and parents, work on [building] ships, making arms, and preparing themselves through all forms of training, so that they might be able to deliver themselves on those shores across the sea. They are preparing themselves to avenge the Holy Sepulchre, and they desire to fulfil the words of the Gospel where it is written: *And everyone who has left father or mother or brothers or wives or lands, for my name's sake, will receive a hundred-fold and inherit eternal life.*[123]

The ideas of Christo-mimesis present in this passage are not the only similarities between Pseudo-Sergius's 'crusading' plans and those of Pope Urban II. The letter also referred, for example, to the institution of the Peace of God,[124] gave details of the spiritual rewards that were available to those who joined the campaign, and described the participants as seeking to exact vengeance on the Muslims who had defiled the Holy Land.[125] However, the parallels between the language being employed by Pseudo-Sergius to describe Jerusalem pilgrims and early-eleventh-century 'proto-crusaders' and that which was attributed to Pope Urban II are so striking – especially the belief that they were following the *via Ihesu* and bearing Christ's cross to Jerusalem – that one is led

---

[119] Cf. Gieysztor, 'Genesis of the Crusades', 6, pp. 17–19.

[120] Schaller, 'Kreuzzugsenzyklika', p. 150.

[121] *Ibid.*, p. 150.

[122] See Riley-Smith, *First Crusaders*, pp. 25, 28–9.

[123] Schaller, 'Kreuzzugsenzyklika', p. 152.

[124] See Bull, *Knightly Piety*, pp. 65–6.

[125] On the idea of vengeance in the sources for the First Crusade, see Riley-Smith, *The First Crusade*, pp. 48–9, 54–7. For the broader context, see now S. Throop, 'Vengeance and the Crusades', *Crusades*, 5 (2006), pp. 21–38.

to conclude that the letter cannot possibly be authentic. Nevertheless, the fact that the encyclical of Pseudo-Sergius exists at all is a fascinating indication of the way in which propagandists were learning to manipulate the past to legitimise the present and future of crusading activity.[126]

Crusading as an Apostolic Activity

If the ideal of the imitation of Christ was of fundamental importance to the spirituality of the First Crusade, the crusaders' pursuit of *imitatio Christi* was not the only way in which they were seen to be sharing in the pious concerns of the monastic reformers who were their contemporaries. Another ideal that is in evidence across the sources for the First Crusade is that of the *vita apostolica*, the apostolic life of the early Church. It would seem that, for a number of observers, the crusaders were not only understood to be imitating Christ, but also to be living in a manner that was concordant with the values of the *ecclesia primitiva*.[127]

It is well documented that the first Christian community at Jerusalem, as was described within the Acts of the Apostles, was held to be a model for many forms of professed religious life in the eleventh and twelfth centuries.[128] It is equally well known that the spread of the ideal of the *vita apostolica* was central to the eleventh-century papacy's programme of reforming the world.[129] The reformers focused their attention on two specific passages, which were understood to communicate the essence of the *ecclesia primitiva*: 'All the believers were together and had everything in common. Selling their possessions and goods, they gave everything to anyone as he had need';[130] 'All the believers were one in heart and mind. No-one claimed that any of his possessions was his own, but they shared everything they had'.[131] However, evidence for the 'unanimity' of spirit in the early Church is to be found throughout the first four chapters of the Acts of the Apostles, where the 'followers of the Way'[132] were repeatedly described as behaving 'with one mind' (*unanimiter*).[133] Indeed, this sentiment was also prominent in other early Christian texts, such as St Paul's letter to the Philippians, where he instructed his correspondents to 'make my joy complete by being like-minded, having the same love,

---

[126] See also below, pp. 69–71, 150–65.

[127] See E.W. McDonnell, 'The *Vita Apostolica*: Diversity or Dissent', *Church History*, 24 (1955), pp. 15–31; G. Olsen, 'The Idea of the *Ecclesia Primitiva* in the Writings of the Twelfth-Century Canonists', *Traditio*, 25 (1969), pp. 61–86; S.H. Hendrix, 'In Quest of the *Vera Ecclesia*: The Crises of Late Medieval Ecclesiology', *Viator*, 7 (1976), pp. 347–78.

[128] For the context, see especially M.-D. Chenu, 'Monks, Canons, and Laymen in Search of the Apostolic Life', *Nature, Man and Society in the Twelfth Century: Essays on New Theological Perspectives in the Latin West*, ed. and trans. J. Taylor and L.K. Little (Toronto, 1968), pp. 202–38.

[129] See C. Morris, *The Papal Monarchy: The Western Church from 1050 to 1250* (Oxford, 1989), pp. 28–33; J.S.C. Riley-Smith, *The Crusades: A History*, 2nd edition (London, 2005), pp. 5–6. For the context, see K.G. Cushing, *Reform and the Papacy in the Eleventh Century: Spirituality and Social Change* (Manchester, 2005), especially pp. 139–57.

[130] Acts 2:44–5.

[131] Acts 4:32.

[132] See above, p. 22.

[133] Acts 1:14, 2:46, 4:24.

being one in spirit and purpose'.[134] It was these ideas of the *vita communis*[135] that the anonymous author of the *Libellus de diversis ordinibus et professionibus qui sunt in aecclesia* (c.1140) had in mind when he wrote of the Cistercians how:

> harmony of mind has been added to spirit, and having one spirit they live together, feel as one, wishing to differ in nothing one from another, eat similarly, adopting one kind of worship and way of life, so that concord of soul should be expressed by an outer consonance of appearance.[136]

Similarly, the author of the *Libellus* believed that the way of life of the 'canons who establish themselves far from men', such as the Premonstratensians, was also modelled on that of the primitive Church, 'since like the apostles they have to live communally and own no property'.[137] Elsewhere, in his *descriptio diversorum ordinum religiosorum* (c.1143–7), Otto of Freising went so far as to apply the ideal of the apostolic life to all professed religious, regardless of the nature of the vows they had taken:

> All [religious] alike spend their lives on earth in purity of living and conscience, and in chastity like that of the angels in heaven. Having but one heart and mind they dwell as one in monasteries or churches; they sleep at the same time, they rise with one mind (*unanimiter*) for prayer, they take food together in one house, [and] they devote themselves to prayer, to reading, and to work by day and night with inexhaustible vigilance.[138]

It has not gone unnoticed that allusions to the ideals of the *vita apostolica* are scattered across the sources for the First Crusade;[139] indeed, their identification was crucial to Jonathan Riley-Smith's characterisation of the crusade as 'a military monastery on the move'.[140] However, as with the limitations of previous scholarly analysis of the ideal of *imitatio Christi* in early crusading spirituality, the extent to which the crusaders were seen to be following the example of the *ecclesia primitiva* has never been fully brought to light. In fact, it seems possible that the ideal of the apostolic life may even have been present in Pope Urban II's preaching of the crusade from the outset.

The most direct example of the analogy that was drawn between the first crusaders and the brethren of the primitive Church is to be found within the *Historia* of Baldric of Bourgueil. At an early stage in his narrative Baldric described how the crusade *militia* had been formed into an *ecclesia*, and he wrote that:

> In that expedition, the dukes themselves were fighting, and the dukes themselves were keeping watch, so that one could not tell a duke from a knight or a knight from a duke. Moreover, so many things were held in common that scarcely anyone could

---

[134] Philippians 2:2.

[135] For the equation between *vita apostolica* and *vita communis*, see Chenu, 'Monks, Canons, and Laymen', pp. 206–7.

[136] *Libellus de diversis ordinibus*, pp. 44–5.

[137] *Ibid.*, pp. 50–1.

[138] Otto of Freising, *Chronica*, p. 370.

[139] See especially Riley-Smith, 'Death on the First Crusade', pp. 30–1.

[140] Riley-Smith, *The First Crusade*, pp. 150–2.

say that anything was his own; in fact, just as in the primitive Church, nearly *all things were held in common.*[141]

This reference to the crusaders' harmonious way of life was by no means unique. Elsewhere, for example, Baldric put a speech into the mouth of Bohemond of Taranto in which the crusade leader was supposed to have declared to his troops, 'I see you, by the grace of God, all of one mind (*omnes unanimes*), where one man does not dissent in any way from another'.[142] Fulcher of Chartres wrote of the crusaders that:

> Though we were of different tongues, we seemed to be brothers in the love of God and nearly of one mind (*proximi unanimes*). For if anyone lost his possessions, he who found it would keep it carefully for many days until by inquiry he found the loser and returned what was found to him. This was indeed proper for those who were making the pilgrimage in the right spirit.[143]

The egalitarianism of the crusade was also recognised by Guibert of Nogent, who remarked that:

> Surely nobody from any generation has ever heard of any people setting forth from its own locality under God only, without a king or without a prince, so that the great and the small alike might learn to carry the yoke, and so that the servant might not have to care for the lord, nor the lord expect anything but brotherhood (*fraternitas*) from the servant.[144]

It is certain that Guibert was not intending here to imply a connection between the crusaders' *fraternitas* and the ideals of the *vita communis*, for he added that 'we cannot offer examples from the past of this'. Yet it is apparent that in this respect he was out of step with many of his contemporaries, who were in no doubt that the crusaders' way of life was redolent with the values of the primitive Church. Indeed, the crusade army was referred to variously as a *collegium Jerosolimitanorum* and a *congregatio Christianorum*,[145] a *sacra societas fidelium Dei*[146] and a *peregrina ecclesia Francorum*,[147] all terms that were highly suggestive of the communal nature of the first Christian community at Jerusalem.[148]

For many writers it was clear that the air of unanimity that permeated the crusade army had been present from the expedition's earliest stages. Sigebert of Gembloux, for example, described how in 1096 the arms-bearers of the West had committed themselves to the crusade *omnes uno animo*,[149] and Baldric of Bourgueil reported that the Normans

---

[141] Baldric of Bourgueil, 'Historia', p. 28. Cf. OV 5, p. 54.

[142] Baldric of Bourgueil, 'Historia', p. 45. See also *ibid.*, p. 95.

[143] Fulcher of Chartres, *Historia*, p. 203.

[144] Guibert of Nogent, 'Dei gesta', p. 312.

[145] Baldric of Bourgueil, 'Historia', pp. 60, 67. See also Peter Tudebode, *Historia*, pp. 89, 91, who referred to the crusaders as a *collegium Francorum*; OV 5, p. 100.

[146] Robert of Rheims, 'Historia', p. 781.

[147] Raymond of Aguilers, *Liber*, p. 83.

[148] See Riley-Smith, 'Death on the First Crusade', p. 30; Riley-Smith, *The First Crusade*, p. 150.

[149] Sigebert of Gembloux, 'Chronica', *MGH SS* 6, p. 367.

from southern Italy who followed Bohemond of Taranto had done so *unanimiter*.[150] This latter term was also used by Robert of Rheims, who wrote that the crusaders 'all glorified God with one mind',[151] and was echoed by the anonymous continuator of Gilo of Paris's *Historia*, who believed that the crusaders were 'taking up arms with one accord (*concorditer*) for the praise of God'.[152] But the atmosphere amongst the departing crusaders is perhaps summarised best by the words of Ekkehard of Aura, who described how, in 1096, 'so many members of Christ, with different tongues and from different tribes and nations, suddenly came together in one body for the love of Christ'.[153]

The evidence for the spirit in which the crusaders set out for the Holy Land therefore seems to be unambiguous. However, it is striking that some of the most remarkable descriptions of the crusaders' unanimity are to be found in reference to their endeavours in battle: in this respect, it would seem that contemporaries believed that one factor instrumental to the success of the expedition was that the crusaders had fought 'with one mind' (*unanimiter*). Thus Baldric of Bourgueil described how, in the wake of Bohemond of Taranto's address to the crusaders before the Battle of Antioch, 'the Franks, with renewed spirits, attacked the Turks with one mind',[154] and Robert of Rheims recorded that at the Battle of Ascalon, 'Not one of our men was slow, not one of them was discovered to be terrified, but all were inspired by one spirit (*uno spiritu animati*), and they pursued the enemies of the cross of Christ with one mind'.[155] Indeed, the word *unanimiter* was used to describe the military deeds of the crusaders by almost all of the earliest historians of the expedition, from the anonymous author of the *Gesta Francorum*,[156] to Peter Tudebode,[157] Raymond of Aguilers,[158] Guibert of Nogent,[159] Albert of Aachen,[160] and Orderic Vitalis.[161] Peter Tudebode also used a similar expression when he recorded how, during the siege of Antioch, Bohemond of Taranto had instructed the crusaders to 'Go forward with an untroubled mind and with joyful unity (*felici concordia*)'.[162] But in terms of parallel formulae, the most remarkable phrase used to illustrate the crusaders' unanimity is to be found within the *Gesta Francorum*, whose anonymous author reported that the crusaders 'entered battle with one heart and mind (*uno corde et animo*)'.[163] Reference has already been made to the fact that the term *unanimiter* was used in the Acts of the Apostles to describe the way of life of the primitive Church, and an example of how the word was used in the mid-twelfth century by Otto of Freising to

---

[150] Baldric of Bourgueil, 'Historia', p. 21. Cf. OV 5, p. 36.

[151] Robert of Rheims, 'Historia', p. 823.

[152] Gilo of Paris, *Historia*, pp. 12–13.

[153] Ekkehard of Aura, 'Hierosolymita', p. 16.

[154] Baldric of Bourgueil, 'Historia', p. 47. For other examples, see *ibid.*, pp. 42, 50, 67, 77, 101.

[155] Robert of Rheims, 'Historia', p. 876.

[156] *Gesta Francorum*, pp. 19–20, 31, 37, 60, 70.

[157] Peter Tudebode, *Historia*, pp. 48–9, 52, 53, 66, 72, 112.

[158] Raymond of Aguilers, *Liber*, pp. 87, 92, 97.

[159] Guibert of Nogent, 'Dei gesta', p. 294.

[160] Albert of Aachen, *Historia*, pp. 134–6, 268, 322.

[161] OV 5, p. 164.

[162] Peter Tudebode, *Historia*, p. 85.

[163] *Gesta Francorum*, p. 40. Cf. Peter Tudebode, *Historia*, p. 75. See also *Gesta Francorum*, p. 28, where the crusaders fight 'uno corde et mente'. Cf. Peter Tudebode, *Historia*, p. 63.

describe the spirituality of the *vita apostolica* has also been offered.[164] Whether or not it was also being intentionally applied in the same way to the first crusaders is rather more open to interpretation, but the fact that the author of the *Gesta Francorum* was using *unanimiter* interchangeably with *uno corde et animo* – the exact language of Acts 4:32 – suggests that he was drawing a direct connection to the spirit of the *ecclesia primitiva*.

In this context, the comparisons that contemporaries made between the first crusaders and Christ's apostles are given a renewed significance. Ekkehard of Aura, for example, believed that the crusaders were 'truly disciples of Christ',[165] and Raymond of Aguilers noted that a contingent of knights led by Godfrey of Bouillon were 'equal in number to the twelve apostles'.[166] Moreover, in his account of one of Peter Bartholomew's dramatic visions,[167] Raymond reported that Christ had identified the 'second order' of crusaders as being 'similar to the apostles, who followed me, and partook of food with me'; correspondingly, the crusaders who were ranked amongst the 'fifth order' were believed to be like Judas Iscariot or Pontius Pilate, for they were 'not only unwilling to risk danger for me, but also for their brothers', and were thereby failing to follow the dictum of John 15:13.[168] The suggestion that those who abandoned the crusade were like Judas also surfaced in Raymond's account of the miraculous appearance of St Andrew, where they were likened to 'the Lord's traitor, who deserted the apostles and sold his Lord to the Jews'.[169] The inference in both cases was, of course, that the most faithful crusaders were similar to the apostles. This idea is also to be found in Raymond's description of the significance of the date on which the crusaders finally liberated Jerusalem. The fifteenth of July was celebrated in the liturgical calendar as the feast of the *divisio apostolorum*,[170] and the holy city had thus been taken 'on the day the apostles were thrown out of Jerusalem and dispersed throughout all the world. On this same day, the sons of the apostles [i.e. the crusaders] liberated the city and the country for God and for the fathers'.[171]

It could of course be argued that the presence of corresponding descriptions of the relationship between crusading and the apostolic life in the expedition's narrative histories is to be put down merely to the environment in which the texts themselves were written. All of the sources to which reference has been made (including the *Gesta Francorum*) are almost certainly the work of churchmen,[172] and it has been written that the medieval clergy 'thought and spoke and wrote the thoughts and words and phrases of the bible'.[173] Moreover, as has been highlighted above, ideas of the *vita apostolica* were a central part of the intellectual milieu of the late eleventh and early twelfth centuries

---

[164] See above, p. 48.

[165] Ekkehard of Aura, 'Hierosolymita', p. 21.

[166] Raymond of Aguilers, *Liber*, p. 93.

[167] See above, p. 43.

[168] Raymond of Aguilers, *Liber*, pp. 114–15.

[169] *Ibid.*, p. 78.

[170] See Morris, *Papal Monarchy*, p. 29.

[171] Raymond of Aguilers, *Liber*, p. 151. See also Ekkehard of Aura, 'Hierosolymita', p. 23; *Kreuzzugsbriefe*, no. 18, p. 171.

[172] See Morris, 'Gesta Francorum', pp. 55–71.

[173] S.R. Maitland, *The Dark Ages*, 5th edition, ed. F. Stokes (London, 1890), p. 476. Quoted in G. Constable, *The Reformation of the Twelfth Century* (Cambridge, 1996), p. 155.

and it would therefore not be inconceivable that contemporaries applied these ideas to the crusade as part of their attempts to frame their understanding of it.[174] Yet if the presence of the ideals of the apostolic life in the histories of the First Crusade is simply a result of the process of narrativisation, the concurrence of the results is nothing short of extraordinary – especially given that several of the texts are known to have been written independently of one another.[175] It seems more likely, therefore, that the inspiration for the application to crusading of the ideals of the *vita apostolica* was external to the expedition's narrative tradition. In this respect, it is gratifying to find that there is fragmentary evidence to suggest that the initial association between the first crusaders and the brethren of the primitive Church can be attributed to Pope Urban II himself.

As a keen sponsor of the development of the regular canons it is well known that Urban II had a particular concern for the ideals of the *vita apostolica*,[176] and it has even been argued recently that his interest in the renewal and propagation of the spirit of the primitive Church was a key factor in his fixing of Jerusalem as the goal of the First Crusade.[177] But there has been little in this previous scholarship to suggest that Pope Urban's support for the apostolic life directly informed his thinking on the ideology of crusading itself.[178] Nevertheless, according to the author of the *Gesta Francorum*, during his preaching tour of France in 1095–6 Pope Urban was said to have drawn attention to a number of New Testament texts that denoted the suffering that Christ's disciples would have to endure for their faith:

> For the lord pope said, 'Brothers, you must suffer many things for the name of Christ, misery, poverty, nakedness, persecution, need, sickness, hunger, thirst and other such troubles, just as the Lord says to his disciples: "You must suffer many things for my name", and "Do not be ashamed to speak before the faces of men; truly, I will give to you words and eloquence", and afterwards "You will receive a great reward"'.[179]

If the *Gesta* is to be believed it would therefore seem that the crusade was being presented almost as if it were an 'active' apostolic mission,[180] since two of the verses that

---

[174] See Bull, 'Views of Muslims and of Jerusalem', pp. 13–14.

[175] See S.B. Edgington, 'The First Crusade: Reviewing the Evidence', *The First Crusade: Origins and Impact*, ed. J.P. Phillips (Manchester, 1997), pp. 55–77.

[176] Urban II, 'Epistolae et privilegia', *PL* 151, no. 58, cols. 337–9. See also J.C. Dickinson, *The Origins of the Austin Canons and their Introduction into England* (London, 1950); Chenu, 'Monks, Canons, and Laymen', pp. 216–17.

[177] See H.E.J. Cowdrey, 'Pope Urban II and the Idea of Crusade', *Studi medievali*, 36 (1995), pp. 730–3.

[178] The one exception of which I am aware is A. Katzenellenbogen, 'The Central Tympanum at Vézelay, its Encyclopaedic Meaning and its Relation to the First Crusade', *Art Bulletin*, 26 (1944), pp. 141–51.

[179] *Gesta Francorum*, pp. 1–2. Cf. Peter Tudebode, *Historia*, p. 32. Citations from Acts 9:16, 2 Timothy 1:8, Luke 21:15 and Matthew 5:12. See also *Gesta Francorum*, p. 62: 'Istas et multas anxietates ac angustias quas nominare nequeo passi sumus pro Christi nomine'.

[180] R.W. Southern, *Western Society and the Church in the Middle Ages* (Harmondsworth, 1970), p. 252, defined the apostolic life as 'activity within the world, and acceptance of whatever was necessary for this activity of preaching, teaching, converting, healing, and serving'. For the context, see also M.-D. Chenu, 'The Evangelical Awakening', *Nature, Man and Society*, pp. 239–69.

were cited referred to the apostolate of St Paul and to that of his successor, St Timothy. The reliability of this aspect of the *Gesta*'s testimony is, of course, somewhat dubious; there is no reason to believe that its author was ever present at the 'eloquent sermons' he described. But it should be remembered that amongst the participant narratives for the First Crusade[181] the *Gesta*'s representation of Pope Urban's preaching on the importance of taking the cross to follow the *via Domini* appears to have been particularly accurate, and it would therefore seem that the *Gesta*'s author was very much alive to the spiritual motifs that were being used in the crusade message. Indeed, although the idea that crusading was to be regarded as an apostolic activity was not prominent in the other versions of the Clermont sermon, it is striking that in addition to a number of references to the idea that the expedition was an act of Christian charity[182] the response to Urban's sermon was depicted by Robert of Rheims as being reminiscent of the mood within the early Church at Pentecost, when the apostles had been touched by the Holy Spirit:[183]

> When Pope Urban had spoken at length about these things and many more like them . . . all those who were present were moved by the same feeling. They came together as one and shouted: 'God wills it! God wills it!' When the venerable Roman pontiff heard this . . . he gave thanks to God, and, indicating with his hand for silence, he said: 'Dearest brethren, today it has been demonstrated to us what the Lord said in the Gospel: *Where two or three are gathered together in my name, there am I in the midst of them.* You would not have been able to speak with one voice unless the Lord God had been present in your minds. Although the cry came from many of you, the origin of the voice was one.'[184]

Similarly, Baldric of Bourgueil believed that it was the Holy Spirit that had 'animated them [the crusaders] to undertake eagerly such great labours and inspired in them one single concord',[185] and in this context it is all the more striking that the author of the *Gesta Francorum* was not the only writer to describe how those who took the cross in response to the pope's Clermont preaching did so *unanimiter*.[186] Indeed, a later version of the Clermont decrees explicitly stated that Pope Urban had 'established and decreed that . . . whosoever were able to go to deliver Jerusalem and the other churches of Asia

---

[181] On the origins of the *Gesta Francorum*, see J. France, 'The Anonymous *Gesta Francorum* and the *Historia Francorum qui ceperunt Iherusalem* of Raymond of Aguilers and the *Historia de Hierosolymitano itinere* of Peter Tudebode: An Analysis of the Textual Relationship between Primary Sources for the First Crusade', *The Crusades and their Sources: Essays Presented to Bernard Hamilton*, ed. J. France and W. Zajac (Aldershot, 1998), pp. 39–69; J. France, 'The Use of the Anonymous *Gesta Francorum* in the Early-Twelfth-Century Sources for the First Crusade', *From Clermont to Jerusalem: The Crusades and Crusader Societies, 1095–1500*, ed. A.V. Murray (Turnhout, 1998), pp. 29–42; Rubenstein, 'What is the *Gesta Francorum*', pp. 179–204.

[182] Baldric of Bourgueil, 'Historia', pp. 12–15. See also *Kreuzzugsbriefe*, no. 3, p. 137.

[183] See also C. Morris, 'Propaganda for War: The Dissemination of the Crusading Ideal in the Twelfth Century', *The Church and War*, ed. W.J. Sheils, SCH, 20 (Oxford, 1983), pp. 80–1.

[184] Robert of Rheims, 'Historia', p. 729. Citation from Matthew 18:20.

[185] Baldric of Bourgueil, 'Historia', p. 9.

[186] *Gesta Francorum*, p. 2. Cf. Peter Tudebode, *Historia*, p. 32. See also Ekkehard of Aura, 'Hierosolymita', pp. 15, 39.

from the power of the pagans, for the love of God and to obtain remission of all their sins, should set forth bearing arms with one mind (*unanimes*)'.[187]

That Pope Urban may well have been referring to the ideals of the apostolic life in his preaching of the crusade is also hinted at in the language of his surviving correspondence from *c.*1096. In the letter in which he instructed four Catalan counts who had taken the cross for the Holy Land that their crusade vows could be commuted by fighting the Muslims of Iberia, Urban wrote that:

> If the arms-bearers of other provinces have resolved with one mind (*unanimiter*) to go to the aid of the Asian Church and to liberate their brothers from the tyranny of the Saracens, so ought you with one mind (*unanimiter*) and with our encouragement work with greater endurance to help a church near you resist the invasions of the Saracens.[188]

This is, admittedly, the only direct evidence for Urban's use of the evocative term *unanimiter*, but the fact that it was used pleonastically suggests the possibility that he was trying to emphasise the significance of the harmonious or 'apostolic' spirit of the crusade army. Indeed, that this actually was his purpose is supported by the fact that several writers subsequently portrayed Urban's representative on the expedition, the papal legate Adhémar of Le Puy, as having proclaimed the same message.[189] According to Robert of Rheims, before the Battle of Antioch Adhémar had delivered a sermon in which he reminded the crusaders that:

> All who are baptised in Christ are sons of God and brothers to each other. Therefore, let what is joined in one spiritual bond be joined in one love, and let us fight as one, as brothers, for our souls and for our bodies.[190]

In addition, it is striking that it was Adhémar's pastoral guidance that was believed to have been responsible for the maintenance of the spirit of *unanimitas* amongst the crusaders whilst they were on the march. In Guibert of Nogent's version of events, 'after the death of that admirable man, the bishop of Le Puy, who had bonded together the minds of all [the crusaders] in concord and unanimity himself, alternately through pastoral love and discipline, dissension and arrogant behaviour began to take hold and rise up among the princes'.[191] It is certainly intriguing that both Robert and Guibert, who were of course writing independently of each other, believed that Adhémar had been instructing the crusaders about the importance of the ideal of the *vita communis*, but it is impossible to know whether or not they were reflecting a theme within Pope Urban's original preaching for the expedition.

The fragments of evidence assembled here do not by any means prove beyond doubt that the ideals of the *vita apostolica* were used by Pope Urban II in his preaching of the First Crusade. Indeed, it is problematic that most of the evidence on which the preceding analysis has relied comes from narrative sources, and as a result there is the

---

[187] *Decreta Claromontensia*, p. 124.

[188] *Papsturkunden in Spanien: I. Katalonien*, ed. P. Kehr (Berlin, 1926), no. 23, p. 287.

[189] For Adhémar's legation, see *Kreuzzugsbriefe*, no. 2, pp. 136–7.

[190] Robert of Rheims, 'Historia', p. 829.

[191] Guibert of Nogent, 'Dei gesta', p. 262.

risk of instigating an unproductive circular argument about the ultimately irretrievable nature of the pope's actual message. For this reason it is worth pausing briefly to consider a sequence of events that took place four years prior to Urban II's preaching of the crusade, since it is clear that in 1091 the pope had shown an acute concern for the emergence of lay interest in the ideals of the apostolic life.[192] According to the chronicler Bernold of St Blasien:

> In these times [c.1091] there flourished in many places in the kingdom of the Germans the common life, not only among clerics and the most religious monks, but also truly among laymen, who offered themselves and their belongings very devotedly to this common life. Although they did not seem to be dressed in the habit of either clerics or monks, they were by no means believed to have been unequal to those in merit . . . Therefore the envy of the devil incited certain men to rivalry against the most esteemed way of life of these brethren, and made them grind at it with malevolent teeth, even though they could see that [these brethren] were living communally in the model of the primitive Church.[193]

Bernold went on to describe how Pope Urban became embroiled in the conflicts that ensued as a result of this 'grinding of malevolent teeth', and he cited the text of a papal letter in which Urban clearly stated his approval of the idea of a quasi-apostolic lay fraternity:

> We have heard about how some of you are complaining about the custom of your communities, in which you take under your protection and direction laymen who renounce the world and devote themselves and their belongings to the common life. However, we approve of this way of life and of this custom, and having inspected it as if with our own eyes, find it laudable, and all the more worthy of being perpetuated because it has been modelled on the primitive Church (*in primitivae ecclesiae formam impressa est*).[194]

This episode clearly indicates that Urban II was aware of the desires of certain laymen to pursue an apostolic life without committing themselves to full religious profession. In this context, it is not improbable that the ideal of the *vita apostolica* may have subsequently been a constituent part of his preaching for the First Crusade, as he sought to address on a larger scale the sorts of pious impulses he had first encountered in 1091. In doing so, his preaching would certainly have met with the approval of the reformers within the papal entourage who, as has already been noted,[195] were intent on introducing monastic values to the secular world. Indeed, the papal reformers may not have been the only party who endorsed this aspect of the crusade message: as a result of recent research into the financial arrangements that crusaders made prior to their departure for the East, it has been suggested that houses of canons regular may have taken an especially prominent role in supporting the expedition and its participants.[196] As the foremost

---

[192] See Chenu, 'Monks, Canons, and Laymen', pp. 220–1.

[193] Bernold of St Blasien, 'Chronicon', pp. 452–3.

[194] Urban II, 'Epistolae', no. 56, col. 336.

[195] See above, p. 47.

[196] Bull, *Knightly Piety*, pp. 258–62; *Crusade Charters, 1138–1270*, ed. C.K. Slack (Tempe, AZ, 2001),

proponents of new ideas about the 'active' apostolic life it is possible that the canons regular, as well as other contemporaries associated with 'poverty and preaching' such as Peter the Hermit,[197] had seen in crusading a form of lay apostolate of which they were particularly keen to support. Indeed, it is remarkable that the anonymous continuator of Gilo of Paris believed that those crusaders who had set out with Peter the Hermit 'had given no thought to making ready a good supply of provisions, as they hoped such provisions would be readily available everywhere, and that as evangelists and disciples of the Gospel, they would gain their food and clothing in accordance with the Gospel'.[198] Such ideas of mendicancy are of course more normally associated with the way of life of the thirteenth-century friars than they are with the devotions of the crusaders.

Although one cannot prove the case for Pope Urban II's preaching of the First Crusade as an apostolic activity, it seems plausible that he was responsible for the first application of the ideals of the *vita apostolica* to the expedition given that there can be no doubt that he had advocated the crusade as a Christo-mimetic devotion. Indeed, in some respects it is perhaps somewhat artificial to distinguish between the ideas of *vita apostolica* and those of *imitatio Christi*, since both revolved around a central ideal of Christian discipleship; as Tinsley put it, 'the Christian life and activity in Acts, as exemplified in the Christian apostles, is shown to be necessarily an imitation of Christ'.[199] Consequently, the two motifs are often inseparable in the sources. For example, when Otto of Freising later described the preaching and commencement of the crusade, he wrote that:

> All these men, coming from many nations and speaking many different languages, were united in one body. Carrying the cross on their clothes, they were proclaiming themselves in word and in deed to be disciples of the cross of Christ, and trusting in the strength of the cross they set out on their route to the East . . . to fight in the [name of the] Lord against the enemies of the cross.[200]

Furthermore, it would seem that the use of the imitation of Christ and the apostolic life as two foundations of crusading spirituality mirrored developments in professed religious life, at least in terms of the devotional context out of which many of the new religious orders of the era were established. Sir Richard Southern highlighted the important distinctions between the ideals of *imitatio Christi* and *vita apostolica* (particularly as was manifest in the respectively contemplative and active spiritualities of Cistercian monks and Augustinian canons),[201] but he also noted that 'the two strands were never wholly separated. Every new Order and every plan for Christian living contained some elements of both'.[202] He went on to illustrate this point by referring to the

---

pp. ix–x, xix–xxi. But see also Riley-Smith, *First Crusaders*, pp. 126–7.
[197] See Blake and Morris, 'A Hermit Goes to War', pp. 81–4. But see also J.M.B. Porter, 'Preacher of the First Crusade? Robert of Arbrissel after the Council of Clermont', *From Clermont to Jerusalem*, pp. 43–53.
[198] Gilo of Paris, *Historia*, pp. 24–5. See Matthew 10:9–11.
[199] Tinsley, *Imitation of God in Christ*, p. 106.
[200] Otto of Freising, *Chronica*, p. 311.
[201] Southern, *Western Society and the Church*, pp. 250–2.
[202] Ibid., p. 252.

origins of the friars,[203] but it seems that his model for understanding the rudimentary spirituality of new forms of religious life is as applicable to the first crusaders as it is to that of the mendicant orders. For just as the Dominicans were primarily understood to be following an apostolic life in their active ministry,[204] so the crusaders were believed to be assisting their brethren in the East out of fraternal love;[205] and just as the Franciscans were chiefly concerned with the literal imitation of Christ through the adoption of voluntary poverty,[206] so the crusaders were supposed to be following a *via Christi* by taking up their crosses and setting out for Jerusalem.

Conclusion

The ideals of *imitatio Christi* and *vita apostolica* were central to the spirituality of the First Crusade, at least in the eyes of those who composed the first generation of narrative histories of the expedition. However, the fact that most of the evidence for the association of these ideas with crusading comes from ecclesiastics rather than from the crusaders themselves should not be seen as especially problematic for assessing their wider importance to crusader motivation.[207] It is clear that Pope Urban II's message was deliberately framed in such a way as to communicate as effectively as possible the idea that crusading was a Christo-mimetic devotion, for by instituting the sign of the cross as the crusade badge the pope created a powerful visual image of the ideal of *imitatio Christi*.[208] Indeed, it may well be that the reason the ideals of the *vita apostolica* fail to surface in the sources in such a similarly obvious way is owing to the absence of a comparable visual symbol or physical gesture that might have denoted the crusaders' apostolic qualities.[209] There is also no reason to think that the ideals of the imitation of Christ or of the apostolic life were so abstract that they would have been alien to laymen in the first instance.[210] One need only look at the opening testimonies of the *Gesta Francorum* and the *Gesta Tancredi*, the letter from the crusade's leaders in 1098 or the handful of crusader charters to gauge how potent the ideal of *imitatio* was believed to be for those who had not committed themselves to a religious life, while Bernold of St Blasien's contemporary account of the growth of lay fraternities attests to popular awareness of the ideals of the *ecclesia primitiva*.[211] What is more, there is overwhelming evidence to

---

[203] *Ibid.*, pp. 279–84.

[204] See Lawrence, *Medieval Monasticism*, pp. 252–8.

[205] See Riley-Smith, 'Act of Love', pp. 191–2.

[206] Lawrence, *Medieval Monasticism*, pp. 244–52.

[207] Cf. Cushing, *Reform and the Papacy*, p. 2.

[208] For a comparable discussion of 'the presentation of theology in everyday terms', see Riley-Smith, 'Act of Love', especially pp. 180–4, 189–92. See also Morris, 'Propaganda for War', p. 84.

[209] For a stimulating discussion of the way in which the ideal of the *vita apostolica* might have been communicated to the medieval laity, see D. d'Avray 'Popular and Elite Religion: Feastdays and Preaching', *Elite and Popular Religion*, ed. K. Cooper and J. Gregory, SCH, 42 (Woodbridge, 2006), pp. 167–71.

[210] Cf. Bull, *Knightly Piety*, p. 285, where it is argued in relation to developing ecclesiastical ideas of pious violence that 'Many laymen were . . . attuned to the concerns of clerics, but not principally on this sort of abstract level.'

[211] See above, p. 55.

demonstrate the level of interaction and exchange of religious ideas between the laity and their local religious communities.[212] This process can perhaps be shown most succinctly by citing Orderic Vitalis's description of the relationship that a small priory to the south of Meulan enjoyed with her local arms-bearers:

> So the cell of Maule rose by the prudence of devoted monks, and through the abundant gifts of worshippers grew and prospered to the praise of God. For the place was very fertile, with vines and rich fields, watered by the river Mauldre which flowed through it, and strongly defended by a great number of noble knights. These during their lifetime gladly make gifts of their land and other wealth to the church; for the monastic order is honoured by them and in the hour of death it is wholeheartedly sought by them for their souls' good. These knights frequent the cloister with the monks, and often discuss practical as well as speculative matters with them; may it continue a school for the living and a refuge for the dying.[213]

In the light of the evidence presented above, and of the results of recent research into the pious practices of the arms-bearing classes in the period before the First Crusade,[214] there are no grounds for believing that ideas of *imitatio Christi* and *vita apostolica* would have been confined to the world of the monastic cloister in the late eleventh century. On the contrary, it seems almost certain that the reason Pope Urban II implored his audience to escape their sinful existences by 'taking up the cross to follow Christ' was because he was familiar with their devotional needs and knew which spiritual motifs would trigger the most effective level of recruitment for his armed Jerusalem pilgrimage.[215] That the idea of apostolic activity should necessarily be relegated to a position of at least secondary importance in crusading spirituality is testimony to the success of Urban's preaching, not to any failure. It is simply the case that the novelty and potency of his 'preaching of the cross' overshadowed other themes, such as the idea that crusading was an act of Christian charity.[216] It was, in truth, through Pope Urban's 'preaching of the cross' that a connection was established between crusading and the *imitatio Christi* tradition that would prove difficult to break as the movement developed in the twelfth century.

---

[212] See Bull, *Knightly Piety*, especially pp. 115–54. See also Hamilton, *Practice of Penance*, pp. 77–103, where it is argued that there was a dialogue between monastic and secular ideas about penance in the tenth and eleventh centuries.

[213] OV 3, pp. 204–7.

[214] See Bull, *Knightly Piety*, especially pp. 155–203.

[215] For Pope Urban II's relationship with the knightly classes of France, see Riley-Smith, *First Crusaders*, pp. 54, 57–8, 76.

[216] For the absence of the idea of fraternal love in crusader charters, see *ibid.*, pp. 65–6.

CHAPTER THREE

Pilgrimage, Mimesis and the Holy Land, 1099–c.1149

Jerusalem Pilgrimage and the Legacy of the First Crusade, 1099–c.1149

The impact of the liberation of Jerusalem on western Christian mentalities was so profound that one contemporary even compared its significance to Christ's redemption of mankind on the cross.[1] Although Pope Urban did not live to respond to the ultimate achievement of the First Crusade, his successor, Paschal II, was unequivocal in his praise of the *militia Christiana*: he portrayed the crusaders' triumph as the fulfilment of scriptural prophecy and wondered at how 'the eastern Church, after a long period of captivity, is now returned to the glory of its ancient liberty'.[2] Paschal's reaction was indicative of the wider response of Christians across Europe, and the sheer volume of narrative histories that were produced to account for the crusade's success is in itself testimony to the effect that the renewed Christian custody of Jerusalem had on the western psyche.[3] The significance of the Holy Land to the writers of these histories is unquestionable, and much of the language they used in their reports of Urban II's Clermont sermon is a reflection of the triumphalist mood of the early twelfth century. According to Baldric of Bourgueil, the pope had declared that:

> We have deservedly called that land holy, in which there is not one footstep which is not glorified and sanctified by the body or the spirit of the Saviour, or by the glorious presence of the holy Mother of God, or the most beloved company of the apostles, or by the blood spilt by the martyrs.[4]

[1] Robert of Rheims, 'Historia Iherosolimitana', *RHC Oc.* 3, p. 723. See Y. Katzir, 'The Conquests of Jerusalem 1099 and 1187: Historical Memory and Religious Typology', *The Meeting of Two Worlds: Cultural Exchange between East and West during the Period of the Crusades*, ed. V.P. Goss (Kalamazoo, MI, 1986), pp. 103–13; C. Morris, *The Sepulchre of Christ and the Medieval West: From the Beginning to 1600* (Oxford, 2005), pp. 219–53; S. Schein, *Gateway to the Heavenly City: Crusader Jerusalem and the Catholic West (1099–1187)* (Aldershot, 2005), *passim*.
[2] *Die Kreuzzugsbriefe aus den Jahren 1088–1100*, ed. H. Hagenmeyer (Innsbruck, 1901), no. 22, p. 178. See also *ibid.*, nos. 19 and 23, pp. 174–5, 179–81.
[3] See M. Bull, 'Views of Muslims and of Jerusalem in Miracle Stories, c.1000–c.1200: Reflections on the Study of First Crusaders' Motivations', *The Experience of Crusading, Volume One: Western Approaches*, ed. M. Bull and N. Housley (Cambridge, 2003), pp. 13–16; J.P. Phillips, *The Second Crusade: Extending the Frontiers of Christendom* (New Haven and London, 2007), pp. 17–36.
[4] Baldric of Bourgueil, 'Historia Jerosolimitana', *RHC Oc.* 4, p. 14.

Guibert of Nogent depicted the primacy of the Holy Land in comparable terms, writing that:

> If this land is the inheritance of God . . . even before the Lord walked and suffered there, as can be gathered from the sacred and prophetic pages [of Scripture], then what sanctity and reverence did it gain next when the God of majesty became flesh there, was fed, grew up, and moving in his lively way, walked here and there in that land?[5]

It is difficult to know whether such emphasis on the physicality or 'geopiety'[6] of the Holy Land was solely a consequence of the success of the First Crusade.[7] Clearly, the expedition of 1096–1102 was the culmination of a century of increased pilgrim traffic to the East,[8] and the crusaders were by no means the first *Hierosolimitani* to have been aware of the fact that they worshipped '*in the place where his feet have stood*'.[9] Around 1025, for example, a priest known as Jachintus recorded that he had set out for Bethlehem and Jerusalem because he had 'longed to see the most holy places where our Lord Jesus Christ was born, and where he bore his sufferings for the whole world',[10] and in 1053 a pilgrim from Rouergue declared that he had travelled to the East 'to pray and to see the holy places, where Our Lord Jesus Christ deigned to be born, suffer, die, rise again and ascend to heaven'.[11] Indeed, from as early as the fourth century pilgrims had travelled to the Levant in the hope that being present in the lands of the Christian heritage would elucidate their faith.[12] St Jerome vividly described the experiences of a Roman noblewoman who went on pilgrimage in 385,[13] and he recorded that at Jerusalem:

---

[5] Guibert of Nogent, 'Dei gesta per Francos', ed. R.B.C. Huygens, *CC:CM* 127 A (Turnhout, 1996), p. 112.

[6] See A. Jotischky, *The Perfection of Solitude: Hermits and Monks in the Crusader States* (University Park, PA, 1995), pp. 4–5, 153–74.

[7] Cf. N. Housley, 'Jerusalem and the Development of the Crusade Idea, 1099–1128', *The Horns of Hattin: Proceedings of the Second Conference of the Society for the Study of the Crusades and the Latin East*, ed. B.Z. Kedar (Jerusalem, 1992), pp. 27–9; D.F. Callahan, 'Jerusalem in the Monastic Imaginations of the Early Eleventh Century', *Haskins Society Journal*, 6 (1994), pp. 119–27.

[8] See J.S.C. Riley-Smith, *The First Crusaders, 1095–1131* (Cambridge, 1997), pp. 23–39; Morris, *Sepulchre of Christ*, pp. 139–46; Schein, *Gateway to the Heavenly City*, pp. 63–90.

[9] Fulcher of Chartres, *Historia Hierosolymitana (1095–1127)*, ed. H. Hagenmeyer (Heidelberg, 1913), pp. 162, 331; *Recueil des chartes de l'abbaye de Cluny*, ed. A. Bernard and A. Bruel, 6 vols. (Paris, 1876–1903), vol. 5, no. 3737, p. 88. For an early application of this verse to Jerusalem pilgrimage (409), see Paulinus of Nola, *Epistolae*, ed. G. de Hartel, *Corpus scriptorum ecclesiasticorum Latinorum*, 29 (Vienna, 1999), Ep. 49, p. 402.

[10] *Jerusalem Pilgrims before the Crusades*, ed. and trans. J. Wilkinson, 2nd edition (Warminster, 2002), p. 270.

[11] J. Bousquet, 'La fondation de Villeneuve d'Aveyron (1053) et l'expansion de l'abbaye de Moissac en Rouergue', *Annales du Midi*, 75 (1963), p. 538. I am grateful to Professor Riley-Smith for providing me with this reference.

[12] See E.D. Hunt, 'The Itinerary of Egeria: Reliving the Bible in Fourth-Century Palestine', *The Holy Land, Holy Lands, and Christian History*, ed. R.N. Swanson, *SCH*, 36 (Woodbridge, 2000), pp. 34–54; Morris, *Sepulchre of Christ*, pp. 47–58.

[13] *Jerusalem Pilgrims*, pp. 79–91.

She fell down and worshipped before the Cross as if she could see the Lord hanging on it. On entering the Tomb of the Resurrection she kissed the stone which the angel removed from the sepulchre door; then like a thirsty man who has waited long, and at last comes to water, she faithfully kissed the very shelf on which the Lord's body had lain . . . She was [also] shown the pillar of the church which . . . is stained with the Lord's blood. He is said to have been tied to it when he was scourged.[14]

St Jerome was not the only early writer to document the importance of the sites of Christ's Passion to the itineraries of Jerusalem pilgrims. The Piacenza Pilgrim (c.570) described how he had prayed at the basilica of St Sophia, which contained:

the seat where Pilate sat to hear the Lord's case, and . . . the oblong stone which used to be in the centre of the Praetorium. The accused person whose case was being heard was made to mount this stone so that every one could hear and see him. The Lord mounted it when he was heard by Pilate, and his footprints are still on it.[15]

Similarly, in his *Topography of the Holy Land* (c.518), Theodosius wrote that upon the Column of the Flagellation, which was venerated at Mount Sion:

you can see the way he clung to it when he was being scourged as if the marks were in wax. His arms, hands, and fingers clove to it. It shows even today. Also he made on it the impression of his whole face, chin, nose, and eyes as if it had been wax.[16]

Sights such as these could only have served to vivify the Gospel narratives for Jerusalem pilgrims, and it is clear that for some there was an undoubtedly mnemonic aspect to their devotions. In addition to the more well-known practices of collecting palms of Jericho[17] and bathing in the River Jordan,[18] the Piacenza Pilgrim wrote that at Cana he had been shown two of the water-pots that had survived from the wedding feast at which Christ had performed his first miracle,[19] and he described how he 'filled one of them up with wine and lifted it up full onto my shoulders';[20] similarly, at Gethsemane ('the place where the Lord was betrayed'), he recorded the presence of 'three couches on which he reclined and where we also reclined to gain their blessing'.[21]

But for all that the sources from before 1095 demonstrate the reverence that early medieval Christians held for the lands of the biblical narrative — and it should be remembered that the Piacenza Pilgrim was writing some five centuries earlier, when the Holy Sepulchre was held under the guardianship of the Christian Empire,[22] and when ideas of Christo-mimesis were more focused on the Saviour's divinity than on his humanity[23] — there

---

[14] *Ibid.*, pp. 83–4.

[15] *Ibid.*, p. 141.

[16] *Ibid.*, p. 107. For comparable descriptions, see *ibid.*, pp. 119, 140, 179, and cf. pp. 113, 177–8.

[17] See J. Sumption, *Pilgrimage: An Image of Mediaeval Religion* (London, 1975), pp. 173–4.

[18] *Ibid.*, pp. 93, 129–30. For examples of this practice, see *Jerusalem Pilgrims*, pp. 136–7, 190–1, 240–1.

[19] John 2:1–11.

[20] *Jerusalem Pilgrims*, p. 131.

[21] *Ibid.*, p. 138. For the archaeology of these 'couches', see *ibid.*, pp. 305–6.

[22] See Morris, *Sepulchre of Christ*, pp. 41–7.

[23] See G. Constable, 'The Ideal of the Imitation of Christ', *Three Studies in Medieval Religious and Social*

can be no doubt that the First Crusade heralded an important change in contemporary western attitudes towards the Holy Land, which was manifest in the developments of the piety of the Jerusalem pilgrimage. It has already been stressed above that the emphasis on the idea of *imitatio Christi* within the preaching of the First Crusade was understood by contemporaries to be something revolutionary, and it was argued in the preceding chapter that the most striking manifestation of the crusader's Christo-mimesis was the act of taking the cross to follow Christ. There is no extant contemporary evidence to indicate that wearing the sign of the cross was associated with Jerusalem pilgrimage before 1095, but it is significant that it was to become recognised as a feature of the devotions of both crusaders and pilgrims in the twelfth century.[24] For example, the German pilgrim Theoderic, who was travelling in the Holy Land c. 1169–74, described how 'Two miles from the Holy City on the north side stands a small church where the pilgrims have their first view of this city and, moved with great joy, put on their crosses'.[25] These crosses were presumably made of wood,[26] and it would seem that the tradition was for pilgrims to go on to the Calvary chapel, where 'the travellers are accustomed to place their crosses which they have brought there from their own countries, and we saw a great heap of them'.[27] Theoderic's account obviously dates from a slightly later period, but other evidence shows that earlier-twelfth-century writers, who were no doubt under the influence of crusading ideology, began to project their ideas of Christo-mimesis onto pilgrims who had travelled to Jerusalem before 1095.[28] For example, in a charter of 1118, Count Fulk V of Anjou described how his grandfather Fulk Nerra had gone on pilgrimage to the Holy Sepulchre out of a desire '[to follow] the precept of the Lord where he said: *If any man will come after me, let him deny himself and take up his cross and follow me*'.[29] At around the same time,[30] the anonymous biographer of Bishop Altmann of Passau was writing an account of his subject's involvement in the great German pilgrimage of 1064–5, and he described how those who had set out for the East had 'abandoned their homes, families and material possessions, and through the hard road followed Christ, carrying the cross'.[31] Similarly, in his *vita* of the hermit Godric of Finchale, Reginald of Durham described how before the saint had departed for the East in the 1090s, he had:

Thought (Cambridge, 1995), pp. 145–68.

[24] See G. Constable, 'Jerusalem and the Sign of the Cross (with Particular Reference to the Cross of Pilgrimage and Crusading in the Twelfth Century)', *Jerusalem: Its Sanctity and Centrality to Judaism, Christianity, and Islam*, ed. L.I. Levine (New York, 1999), pp. 371–81.

[25] *Jerusalem Pilgrimage 1099–1185*, ed. and trans. J. Wilkinson, J. Hill and W.F. Ryan (London, 1988), p. 310. See also the account of the Russian abbot, Daniel (c. 1106–8), *ibid.*, p. 127.

[26] See *ibid.*, p. 286, where Theoderic reports that 'On Saturdays all the guards of the Calvary [chapel] have the custom of burning them.'

[27] *Ibid.*, p. 286.

[28] See above, pp. 45–7. See also Morris, *Sepulchre of Christ*, pp. 144–6.

[29] F. Comte, *L'abbaye Toussaint d'Angers des origines à 1330: étude historique et cartulaire* (Angers, 1985), no. 102, p. 147.

[30] E. Joranson, 'The Great German Pilgrimage of 1064–1065', *The Crusades and Other Historical Essays Presented to Dana C. Munro by his Former Students*, ed. L.J. Paetow (New York, 1928), p. 8, states that 'this work was composed approximately two generations after the event in question'.

[31] 'Vita Altmanni episcopi Pataviensis', *MGH SS* 12, p. 230. Cf. Riley-Smith, *First Crusaders*, p. 29, n. 21, who believed that this was 'a descriptive phrase prefiguring the crusaders'.

received the sign of the holy cross from a priest and with the Lord did not shun to bear his cross . . . and bearing the sign of the Lord's cross on his shoulders he first went to Jerusalem and then on his way back visited the shrine of St James the Apostle.[32]

Jonathan Riley-Smith took this passage to indicate that Godric had been a first crusader,[33] but given the conventions of the hagiographical genre and the distance from which Reginald was writing (the *vita* must have been composed after Godric's death in 1170),[34] this attribution must surely be far less than a 'certainty'.[35] There is nothing in the *vita* to indicate that Godric ever bore arms or engaged the Muslims in battle,[36] and in the light of Theoderic's contemporaneous testimony about how Jerusalem pilgrims travelled to the East with crosses 'which they have brought there from their own countries', it seems just as possible that Reginald of Durham's description of Godric's departure relates to the devotional norms of the 1170s as it does to those of the 1090s.[37]

The practice of cross-bearing was not the only noticeable development in the pious activities of twelfth-century Jerusalem pilgrims. Reference has already been made to the importance of veneration of the Column of the Flagellation in pilgrimage itineraries from before 1100, but by the time Theoderic was travelling in the East there is evidence to suggest that a new element had entered the pilgrim's devotional routine, for he described how:

[at] the Church of Blessed Mary on Mount Sion . . . there is a venerable Chapel in honour of the Lord Jesus Christ, in which part of a great column stands. The Lord was bound to it by Pilate after he had condemned him to hanging on the cross, and he was ordered to be flogged there. There the pilgrims also have a custom of being flogged according to his example.[38]

Indeed, Theoderic even wrote that he had presented the material in his Guide in the way that he had because 'we think it right to arrange our subjects in the order of Christ's sufferings, who by his grace grants us to suffer with him, that together with him we may reign'.[39] In this way, his approach foreshadowed much of the later medieval devotional literature of the Holy Sepulchre.[40]

There can be little doubt that the new strains of Christo-mimetic piety within the devotional activities of twelfth-century Jerusalem pilgrims were at least in part a result of the emphasis on *imitatio Christi* within early crusading spirituality. However, it also

[32] Reginald of Durham, *Libellus de vita et miraculis S. Godrici, heremitae de Finchale*, Surtees Society, 20 (London, 1847), pp. 33–4. For Godric's second Jerusalem pilgrimage, see *ibid.*, pp. 53–8.
[33] See Riley-Smith, *First Crusaders*, pp. 153, 155 n. 67, 166, 209.
[34] See D. Farmer, *The Oxford Dictionary of Saints*, 4th edition (Oxford, 1997), pp. 214–15.
[35] Riley-Smith, *First Crusaders*, p. 209. See also *ibid.*, p. 239, where the saint's second pilgrimage is associated with Bohemond's crusade of 1107–8.
[36] Although see A. Graboïs, 'Anglo-Norman England and the Holy Land', *Anglo-Norman Studies*, 7 (1984), p. 138, who suggests that Godric of Finchale is synonymous with an English merchant called Godric who was involved in the rescue of King Baldwin I after the Battle of Ramla in 1102.
[37] On Godric's pilgrimages, see also Jotischky, *Perfection of Solitude*, pp. 67–9, 71, 92, 169–70.
[38] *Jerusalem Pilgrimage*, p. 300.
[39] *Ibid.*, p. 296.
[40] See Morris, *Sepulchre of Christ*, pp. 310–23.

seems likely that the developments were a corollary of the achievements of the First Crusade itself, for as Paschal II put it, it was through the crusaders that God had deigned 'to rescue the eastern Church from the hands of the Turks and to open to Christian soldiers the very city of the Lord's suffering and burial'.[41] As a result, the Holy Sepulchre and its environs had become more accessible to the Christians of western Europe than they had been for several generations. Guibert of Nogent was not alone in recording the 'great suffering' of pilgrims who travelled to the East in the years before the First Crusade,[42] but in the wake of the city's liberation Otto of Freising described how 'the faithful were flocking from all parts of the world to pray (*causa orationis*) in the earthly Jerusalem'.[43]

The full range of effects that the Latin custody of the Holy Land had on western piety has been considered in detail elsewhere,[44] but two particular consequences of the establishment of the Frankish settlements for pilgrimage and crusade piety ought to be highlighted. The first of these was a re-engagement with the relics of Christ's Passion. Such relics had of course been a prominent feature of European devotion before 1099,[45] but it is clear that the First Crusade led to a surge in the number of items that were in circulation as many crusaders returned to their homes with a range of objects that were subsequently presented to local churches and other religious communities.[46] Furthermore, the crusaders had made two discoveries that were understood to be of an especial importance: the Holy Lance, which was unearthed during the siege of Antioch in 1098,[47] and a fragment of the True Cross, which the crusaders had located shortly after the liberation of Jerusalem and which was to become something of a talisman to the first Latin kingdom until it was lost during the Battle of Hattin in 1187.[48] The significance of the recovery of these relics is shown not only by the crusade leaders' remark that the Holy Lance had 'not been seen since the time of the apostles',[49] but also by the comments of Raymond of Aguilers, who wrote a vivid account of why the True Cross was of such importance shortly after the relic's *inventio* in 1099:

---

[41] *Kreuzzugsbriefe*, no. 19, p. 175.

[42] Guibert of Nogent, 'Dei gesta', pp. 116–17. See also Riley-Smith, *First Crusaders*, p. 38.

[43] Otto of Freising, *Chronica sive historia de duabus civitatibus*, ed. A. Hofmeister, *MGH SSRG* 45 (Hanover and Leipzig, 1912), p. 316.

[44] See especially B. Hamilton, 'The Impact of Crusader Jerusalem on Western Christendom', *Catholic Historical Review*, 80 (1994), pp. 695–713; Morris, *Sepulchre of Christ*, pp. 219–53; Schein, *Gateway to the Heavenly City, passim*.

[45] See A.H. Bredero, 'Jerusalem in the West', *Christendom and Christianity in the Middle Ages: The Relations between Religion, Church and Society*, trans. R. Bruinsma (Grand Rapids, MI, 1994), pp. 91–5.

[46] See Riley-Smith, *First Crusaders*, pp. 150–2.

[47] See C. Morris, 'Policy and Visions: The Case of the Holy Lance at Antioch', *War and Government in the Middle Ages: Essays in Honour of J.O. Prestwich*, ed. J. Gillingham and J.C. Holt (Woodbridge, 1984), pp. 33–45. Not all of the crusaders accepted the authenticity of the Holy Lance: see J.S.C. Riley-Smith, *The First Crusade and the Idea of Crusading* (London, 1986), pp. 95–8.

[48] See A.V. Murray, '"Mighty against the Enemies of Christ": The Relic of the True Cross in the Armies of the Kingdom of Jerusalem', *The Crusades and their Sources: Essays Presented to Bernard Hamilton*, ed. J. France and W.G. Zajac (Aldershot, 1998), pp. 217–38.

[49] *Kreuzzugsbriefe*, no. 18, pp. 169–70.

All our men rejoiced and we gave praise and thanks to Almighty God, who returned to us not only the city in which he suffered, but also the symbols of his Passion and victory, so that we might embrace him more closely with the arms of faith, the more certain because we beheld the signs of our salvation.[50]

Raymond's comments about the role of object and place in twelfth-century Christian piety provide an apposite link to a second consequence of the establishment of the crusader states: the restoration and renewal of the Christian shrines of the Levant, an undertaking that Bernard Hamilton characterised as 'the rebuilding of Zion'.[51] This process was of course directly related to the idea that the Holy Land itself was a relic,[52] and it was necessary because, as the author of one pilgrim's guide put it in 1109:

Inside the city [of Jerusalem] Christians . . . venerate the scourging of Jesus Christ, his crowning and mocking, and other things he suffered for our sake. But nowadays it is not an easy matter to discover where they took place, particularly because since those days the city itself has so often been overthrown and destroyed.[53]

It is not necessary to reiterate the details of this building programme – suffice to say that it was instituted almost immediately,[54] and that it was approaching its zenith when on 15 July 1149 the redesigned Church of the Holy Sepulchre was consecrated.[55] What is essential, though, is to highlight the motives of the building programme's patrons. Bernard Hamilton wrote that the restoration process was 'a visual expression of the faith of the crusaders . . . and a symbol of their deep devotion to the humanity of Christ',[56] and Jonathan Riley-Smith has recently demonstrated how the devotional experience of the Jerusalem pilgrim was central to the planning and execution of artistic and architectural changes, especially at the Church of the Holy Sepulchre.[57] In this respect it would seem that the 'rebuilding of Zion' was intrinsically related to the spirituality of the First Crusade, for although the crusaders had been successful in liberating 'the very city of the Lord's suffering and burial',[58] it was now the responsibility of those who settled in the East to transform that city into a place that might once again edify the faith of all Christians who came to worship *'where his feet have stood'*.[59] The evidence of the surviving pilgrimage accounts is a measure of the settlers' success. One writer

---

[50] Raymond of Aguilers, *Liber*, ed. J.H. and L.L. Hill (Paris, 1969), p. 154. Cf. *Kreuzzugsbriefe*, no. 22, p. 178.

[51] See B. Hamilton, 'Rebuilding Zion: The Holy Places of Jerusalem in the Twelfth Century', *Renaissance and Renewal in Christian History*, ed. D. Baker, *SCH*, 14 (Oxford, 1977), pp. 105–16.

[52] See Riley-Smith, *The First Crusade*, p. 21, 108, 146.

[53] *Jerusalem Pilgrimage*, p. 174. See also *ibid.*, p. 102.

[54] The Russian abbot who was travelling in the East c.1106–8 wrote of the Church of the Annunciation in Nazareth that '[it] was once laid waste but now the Franks have taken it and rebuilt it thoroughly'. See *ibid.*, p. 164.

[55] See Hamilton, 'Rebuilding Zion', pp. 105–16; Riley-Smith, *First Crusaders*, pp. 23–5; Morris, *Sepulchre of Christ*, pp. 189–200.

[56] Hamilton, 'Rebuilding Zion', p. 116. Cf. Schein, *Gateway to the Heavenly City*, pp. 66, 74–5.

[57] J.S.C. Riley-Smith, *The Crusades: A History*, 2nd edition (London, 2005), pp. 53–61.

[58] *Kreuzzugsbriefe*, no. 19, p. 175.

[59] See Hamilton, 'Impact of Crusader Jerusalem', pp. 699–703, 706–7.

recorded that in a church on the Mount of Olives 'stands a high rock in which lies the stone which the Lord stepped on when he ascended to the heavens, and one can see the imprint of his left foot, fourteen inches long, as if he had stepped barefoot into clay',[60] and another referred to a stone cross that had been erected in Jerusalem, which was 'the same measurements as the cross which was born by the Lord, and which the Jews also made Simon of Cyrene carry'.[61] Similarly, in *c.*1140 an Icelandic abbot recorded that in Jerusalem 'there is the church . . . [of] the Lord's sepulchre and the place where the Lord's cross stood, where one can clearly see Christ's blood on the stone as if it were newly bled',[62] and in *c.*1170 the author of another Guide described the significance of the Sheep Pool as 'the place where those who visit are told that the Wood of the Cross remained for a long time', before adding, perhaps somewhat mischievously, that 'the Templars show you another Pool and say that that is the Sheep Pool'.[63]

This final source not only shows how the Christian custody of the Holy Land had an important effect on the experiences of Jerusalem pilgrims, but also illustrates how religious orders such as the Temple played an important role in providing information for pilgrims. It was of course the brethren of the various religious communities who staffed the new shrine churches of the Latin East and who performed the liturgy that was of such importance to the spiritual life of the crusader kingdom, especially during Holy Week.[64] Indeed, in addition to those religious who were responsible for actively ministering to the pilgrims and settlers of the Frankish Levant, it is clear that the establishment of the Christian territories in the Holy Land led to an influx of monks and hermits from the West,[65] as well as to a revival of Orthodox monasticism.[66] Much to the chagrin of critics such as Bernard of Clairvaux,[67] it would seem that the new opportunity to pursue a religious life in the lands of the Christian heritage held a great allure for these individuals and communities. In this respect, the monastic response to Pope Urban's preaching of the crusade in 1095–6 was but a prelude to the flood of religious who would set out for the East in the wake of the expedition's success.[68]

It would seem, therefore, that the confluence of the idea of crusading as a Christo-mimetic devotion with the renewed access to the Holy Land that the first crusaders' triumphs had afforded had a marked effect on the piety and experiences of Jerusalem

---

[60] *Jerusalem Pilgrimage*, pp. 221–2. See also *ibid.*, p. 231.

[61] *Ibid.*, p. 119.

[62] *Ibid.*, p. 217. See also *ibid.*, pp. 220.

[63] *Ibid.*, p. 240.

[64] See Hamilton, 'Impact of Crusader Jerusalem', pp. 707–10.

[65] See especially Jotischky, *Perfection of Solitude*; see also B. Hamilton, 'The Cistercians in the Crusade States', *One Yet Two: Monastic Tradition, East and West*, ed. M.B. Pennington (Kalamazoo, MI, 1976), pp. 405–22; B.Z. Kedar, 'Gerard of Nazareth, a Neglected Twelfth-Century Writer in the Latin East: A Contribution to the Intellectual History of the Crusader States', *Dumbarton Oaks Papers*, 37 (1983), pp. 55–77; B.Z. Kedar, 'A Second Incarnation in Frankish Jerusalem', *The Experience of Crusading, Volume Two: Defining the Crusader Kingdom*, ed. P.W. Edbury and J.P. Phillips (Cambridge, 2003), pp. 79–92.

[66] See A. Jotischky, 'Greek Orthodox and Latin Monasticism around Mar Saba under Crusader Rule', *The Sabaite Heritage in the Orthodox Church from the Fifth Century to the Present*, ed. J. Patrich (Leuven, 2001), pp. 85–96.

[67] See Jotischky, *Perfection of Solitude*, pp. 1–16; Schein, *Gateway to the Heavenly City*, pp. 124–30.

[68] See also B. Hamilton, 'Ideals of Holiness: Crusaders, Contemplatives, and Mendicants', *International History Review*, 17 (1995), pp. 693–703.

pilgrims in the twelfth century. But in order for those holy places to remain in the custody of western Christians it was necessary for them to be defended from the retaliation of neighbouring Muslim powers.[69] Raymond of Aguilers was one of the first writers to describe the threat that was posed to the nascent Latin settlements by Muslim leaders such as the Fatimid caliph, whom he referred to as the 'Sultan of Babylon':

> He blasphemed God, saying that he would destroy the place of the Lord's birth and the stable in which the Lord had lain, and the place of his Passion and Golgotha, where it is said that the blood of the Lord flowed down whilst he was hanging on the cross, and the place where the Lord was buried, and all the other holy places in the city or nearby that are venerated by the Christian people.[70]

It was because of this unceasing threat to the lands of the Christian heritage that, in spite of the success of the First Crusade, the settlers of the Latin East continued to rely on the military support of the West. It is therefore to the development of the ideas associated with those who travelled to the East as crusaders, as distinct from pilgrims, that the rest of this chapter is devoted.

Crusading to the East, 1102–1144

Although it has recently been suggested that in the first half of the twelfth century widespread enthusiasm for crusading to the East lay 'dormant',[71] it has also been stressed that it would be misleading to see the interval between the First and Second Crusades as a period of complete inactivity because crusades were also projected and launched in 1106–8, 1120–4 and 1128–9.[72] Nevertheless, recruitment for these expeditions was sporadic and often localised,[73] and as a consequence both the documentary and narrative records are much more fragmentary than those of the First Crusade. This is in large part owing to the fact that only the expedition of 1120–4 was directly launched by the papacy,[74] and therefore no 'official' record of the language of the preaching of the crusades of 1106–8 and 1128–9 survives. The number of other less formal military campaigns that were active in the Levant during this period further complicates the situation. In 1108, for example, Bertrand of St Gilles was believed to have been fighting in Lebanon 'for the service of God and the Holy Sepulchre',[75] and in 1110 Sigurd of Norway, who had set out on pilgrimage for the Holy Land in 1107, assisted King Baldwin I with the capture of Sidon; he was subsequently rewarded with a fragment of the True Cross.[76] It seems reasonable to assume that participants in expeditions such as these

---

[69]   See J.S.C. Riley-Smith, 'Peace Never Established: The Case of the Kingdom of Jerusalem', *Transactions of the Royal Historical Society*, 5th ser., 28 (1978), pp. 87–102.

[70]   Raymond of Aguilers, *Liber*, p. 155.

[71]   Riley-Smith, *First Crusaders*, p. 168.

[72]   Riley-Smith, *The Crusades*, pp. 117–20.

[73]   See Riley-Smith, *First Crusaders*, pp. 165–8.

[74]   *Ibid.*, p. 10.

[75]   Caffaro, 'De liberatione civitatum orientis', ed. L.T. Belgrano, *Annali genovesi*, 1 (Genoa, 1890), p. 122. See J.S.C. Riley-Smith, 'Raymond IV of St Gilles, Achard of Arles and the Conquest of Lebanon', *The Crusades and their Sources*, pp. 1–8.

[76]   P. Riant, *Expéditions et pèlerinages des Scandinaves en Terre Sainte au temps des croisades* (Paris, 1865),

were motivated by a quasi-crusading zeal, but the exact nature of their votive obliga-tions and spiritual concerns is unknown.[77] In short, there is simply not enough evidence available to conduct as thorough an assessment of the ideas associated with those who went on crusade in the period 1102–44 as that which can be undertaken for the First Crusade. Yet from the little evidence that does survive, it is clear that the association between military activity in the East, Jerusalem pilgrimage and the defence of the Holy Land remained paramount in the minds of those who promoted or commented upon crusading during this period. It therefore seems plausible that many of those who 'took the cross' in the first half of the twelfth century were motivated by much the same piety as those who had left their homes to follow the *via Christi* in 1096.

The first significant campaign to be launched after the failures of 1101–2[78] was initiated by Bohemond of Taranto, who returned to Europe to gather recruits for a new crusade in 1106.[79] Although several contemporary writers failed to mention that the Holy Sepulchre had played any part in his propaganda for this campaign,[80] it seems likely that when Bohemond began his preaching tour of France he claimed to be recruit-ing for an expedition whose objective was to provide military assistance to the nascent crusader states of the Latin East. Thus Orderic Vitalis described the crusade as 'the third expedition from the West [that] set out for Jerusalem',[81] whose participants not only constituted an *exercitus Christi* but were also *peregrini*,[82] and Suger of St Denis wrote of how Bohemond inspired the people of France to take the *iter Ierosolimitanum*.[83] Simi-larly, one chronicler referred to the undertaking as the *via sancti Sepulchri* — the term which, incidentally, the same chronicler had also used of the First Crusade[84] — and another described how:

> Bohemond, the duke of Antioch and a man of great fame and renown . . . came to the castles and cities of Europe, so that by his instruction [their people] might hasten to go to Jerusalem to liberate those who were being held in captivity, and to give aid to those who were being injured by the attacks of the Turks.[85]

It was almost certainly on this basis that the expedition had received the support of Pope Paschal II; it now seems very unlikely that he had sanctioned the abortive attack on the

---

pp. 173–215.

[77] See J.S.C. Riley-Smith, 'An Army on Pilgrimage' (Forthcoming).

[78] See Riley-Smith, *The First Crusade*, pp. 120–34.

[79] See especially J.G. Rowe, 'Paschal II, Bohemund of Antioch and the Byzantine Empire', *Bulletin of the John Rylands Library*, 49 (1966), pp. 165–202.

[80] See, for example, Albert of Aachen, *Historia Ierosolimitana*, ed. and trans. S.B. Edgington (Oxford, 2007), p. 702; Ekkehard of Aura, 'Hierosolymita', *RHC Oc.* 5, pp. 37–8; Sigebert of Gembloux, 'Chronica', *MGH SS* 6, p. 372; Bartolf of Nangis, 'Gesta Francorum Iherusalem expugnantium', *RHC Oc.* 3, p. 538.

[81] *OV* 3, p. 182.

[82] *OV* 6, pp. 102, 100.

[83] Suger of St Denis, *Vita Ludovici Grossi regis*, ed. and trans. H. Waquet (Paris, 1929), p. 48.

[84] *La Chronique de St Maixent, 751–1140*, ed. and trans. J. Verdon (Paris, 1979), p. 178. For the First Crusade as *via sancti Sepulchri*, see ibid., pp. 154, 168.

[85] 'Chronicon Vindocinense seu de Aquaria', ed. P. Marchegay and É. Mabille, *Chroniques des églises d'Anjou* (Paris, 1869), pp. 171–2.

Byzantine Empire that was to follow.[86] Paschal had conferred the *vexillum sancti Petri* upon Bohemond when they had met early in 1106[87] and had tasked Bruno of Segni with assisting Bohemond in recruiting for the expedition. Bruno was a veteran of Urban II's preaching tour of France of 1095–6,[88] and was therefore well suited for this legation; according to Suger of St Denis, he was responsible for 'summoning and encouraging [support] for the *via sancti Sepulchri*' and ensuring that 'the zeal for the journey to Jerusalem did not grow cool'.[89]

Yet for all the emphasis on Jerusalem and the Holy Land in the speeches and sermons of Bohemond and Bruno, it is also clear that once the preaching tour was under way the prince of Antioch did not conceal the fact that he only intended to proceed to the East once he had successfully conquered the Byzantine Empire and installed a sympathetic puppet on the imperial throne.[90] Consequently, his rhetoric became increasingly anti-Greek as he sought to whip up support for this strategy. One commentator described the stirring address Bohemond gave in Chartres on the day he married the daughter of the king of France:

> Then the duke, who made a fine figure even among the greatest, proceeded to the church, mounted the pulpit before the altar of the blessed Virgin and Mother, and there related to the huge throng that had assembled all his deeds and adventures, urged all who bore arms to attack the Emperor with him, and promised his chosen adjutants wealthy towns and castles. Many were kindled by his words and, taking the Lord's cross, left all their belongings and set out on the road for Jerusalem like men hastening to a feast.[91]

The most obvious *casus belli* was the memory of Alexius Comnenus's abandonment and 'betrayal' of the first crusaders in 1098–9,[92] to which Bohemond must have given personal testimony as he recounted 'the various adventures in which he had played a part'.[93] Indeed, in addition to the eyewitness accounts of those who heard Bohemond speak, an important source for understanding how Bohemond was propagating his anti-Greek message is a letter that was spuriously attributed to the Byzantine emperor, and that supposedly dated from before the First Crusade (*c.* 1091).[94] It purported to be an appeal to the count of Flanders for military assistance from the West, which the Byzantines

---

[86] See Rowe, 'Paschal II, Bohemund of Antioch', pp. 192–6.

[87] Bartolf of Nangis, 'Gesta Francorum', p. 538.

[88] Riley-Smith, *First Crusaders*, p. 78.

[89] Suger of St Denis, *Vita Ludovici*, p. 48.

[90] OV 6, pp. 68–71.

[91] OV 6, pp. 70–1.

[92] See J. Shepard, 'Cross-purposes: Alexius Comnenus and the First Crusade', *The First Crusade: Origins and Impact*, ed. J.P. Phillips (Manchester, 1997), pp. 106–13, 122.

[93] OV 6, pp. 68–71. For a possible attempt to neutralise such propaganda, see J. Shepard, 'The "Muddy Road" of Odo Arpin from Bourges to La Charité-sur-Loire', *Experience of Crusading, Volume Two*, pp. 11–28.

[94] See E. Joranson, 'The Problem of the Spurious Letter of Emperor Alexius to the Count of Flanders', *American Historical Review*, 55 (1949–50), pp. 811–32; M. de Waha, 'La lettre d'Alexis I Comnène à Robert I le Frison', *Byzantion*, 47 (1977), pp. 113–25. For the text of the letter, see *Kreuzzugsbriefe*, no. 1, pp. 129–36.

required because of the 'hostile massacres and indescribable killing and mockery of the [eastern] Christians'[95] that had accompanied the Seljuk advance in the 1070s and 1080s. Although the extant text may well be an adaptation of a genuine missive,[96] the weight of evidence suggests that the surviving version was forged in or around 1106 to promote animosity and vengeful feelings towards the Greeks, who had asked for the help of the West but who had subsequently betrayed those who came to their assistance. But as well as inflaming the passions of his French readership by reminding them of past Byzantine perfidy, the letter's composer also employed a number of more positive motifs, which were almost certainly synonymous with the language of Bohemond's preaching of 1106. That 'Pseudo-Alexius' was able to blend the appeal of the riches of Byzantium with the idea of completing a pilgrimage to the Holy Sepulchre is striking: clearly, the two objectives were not deemed to be incompatible.

Although the Muslim response to the liberation of Jerusalem in 1099 was far from coherent[97] there can be little doubt that when Pseudo-Alexius described the Islamic dominance of Palestine and Asia Minor – 'almost the whole land from Jerusalem to Greece . . . [has] already been invaded by them'[98] – his words were nearly as applicable to the situation in 1106 as they were to the era from which the letter was supposed to originate; one need only consult the contemporary pilgrim accounts of Saewulf (c.1102–3)[99] or Abbot Daniel (c.1106–8)[100] to gain some sense of the dangers faced by the earliest western settlers. Thus whilst Pseudo-Alexius's descriptions of how the Muslims 'desecrate and destroy the holy places in numberless ways'[101] were not wholly accurate for the situation post-1099, it is clear enough that the precarious situation in the East was in itself grounds for a new crusade, and Pseudo-Alexius's letter concluded by exhorting the arms-bearers of the West to 'act while you have time . . . so that you do not lose the kingdom of the Christians and, what is greater, the Sepulchre of the Lord'[102] – a statement that certainly seems to make more sense when applied to the situation of 1106 than to that of 1091.

Given the unquestionably emotive value of the Holy Sepulchre, the use of an idea such as this is not surprising. Far more striking, though, is the way Pseudo-Alexius wove the justification for the attack on Byzantium into his appeal. In addition to the material treasures that awaited the crusaders in Constantinople,[103] he proposed that the crusaders should take the city in order to prevent Byzantium's collection of holy relics from falling into the hands of the infidel, a pre-emptive *furtum sacrum* that would anticipate the diversion of the Fourth Crusade by almost a century:[104]

---

[95] *Kreuzzugsbriefe*, no. 1, p. 131.

[96] See Joranson, 'Spurious Letter', pp. 816–19; Shepard, 'Cross-purposes', pp. 113–14, 116–21.

[97] See C. Hillenbrand, *The Crusades: Islamic Perspectives* (Edinburgh, 1999), pp. 31–88.

[98] *Kreuzzugsbriefe*, no. 1, pp. 132–3.

[99] *Jerusalem Pilgrimage*, p. 100. See also *ibid.*, pp. 101, 112–13.

[100] *Ibid.*, pp. 126, 149–50, 156, 160.

[101] *Kreuzzugsbriefe*, no. 1, p. 132.

[102] *Ibid.*, p. 136.

[103] See also OV 6, pp. 104–5, where Bohemond's shame at the eventual failure of the crusade is attributed to the fact that 'he had promised great kingdoms'.

[104] For the importance of Byzantium's relics to the fourth crusaders, see D.E. Queller and T.F. Madden, *The Fourth Crusade: The Conquest of Constantinople*, 2nd edition (Philadelphia, PA, 1997), pp. 87, 98, 138–9, 194–5, 250 n. 69, 267 n. 38, 285 n. 69. For the broader context, see P.J. Geary, *Furta*

For it is better that you should have Constantinople than the pagans, because in that [city] they have the most precious relics of the Lord, that is to say: the pillar to which he was bound; the whip with which he was scourged; the scarlet-coloured cloak in which he was dressed; the crown of thorns with which he was crowned; the reed which he held in his hands like a sceptre; the clothes of which he was deprived before the cross; the larger part of the wood of the cross on which he was crucified; the nails with which he was fastened upon that cross; [and] the linen cloths which were found in the Sepulchre after his resurrection . . .[105]

The list went on to include relics from other notable figures such as St John the Baptist and St Stephen, but the pre-eminent position of items that related to Christ's Passion is striking, especially given what is known about how potent such relics were for the first crusaders and the settlers of the Latin East.[106] In this respect, it would seem that Colin Morris's recent account of how western Christians perceived Constantinople to be 'a second Jerusalem' is particularly helpful for understanding the ideas that may have inspired recruitment to Bohemond's army.[107]

It remains unclear how far the idea of reaching the Holy Land was a strategic aim of the crusade of 1107–8, and how far the *via sancti Sepulchri* was used by Bohemond as a smokescreen to misdirect pious arms-bearers into recruiting for an expedition that was simply the latest episode in the history of antagonism between the Normans of southern Italy and the Byzantine Empire.[108] It is perhaps stretching cynicism to say that Bohemond would not have wanted to march a new army of crusaders to the Levant – his principality of Antioch was as embattled as the other new crusader states of the Latin East[109] – and in his letter to the pope from the siege at Durazzo in 1108[110] he stressed that he was hoping Paschal would assist the crusaders on their *iter Ierosolimitanum* by joining the army and leading it to the East in person.[111] Although when he wrote the letter Bohemond was clearly a desperate man and was probably seeking papal approval for his attack on the Byzantine Empire for the first time,[112] the devotional intent of many of his rank and file became plain once the army had been disbanded after the signing of the Treaty of Devol. One chronicler recorded that whilst some crusaders turned back to Apulia, 'part of the army set out to worship at Jerusalem',[113] and Orderic Vitalis confirmed that Bohemond had given his permission for them 'to continue on their pilgrimage'.[114] Evidently, the

---

Sacra: Thefts of Relics in the Central Middle Ages, revised edition (Princeton, NJ, 1990).

[105] *Kreuzzugsbriefe*, no. 1, p. 134.

[106] See above, pp. 64–5. See also Riley-Smith, *First Crusaders*, p. 66.

[107] Morris, *Sepulchre of Christ*, p. 59.

[108] See G.A. Loud, *The Age of Robert Guiscard: Southern Italy and the Norman Conquest* (Harlow, 2000), pp. 209–23.

[109] See T. Asbridge, *The Principality of Antioch, 1098–1130* (Woodbridge, 2000).

[110] For the date, see Rowe, 'Paschal II, Bohemund of Antioch', pp. 192–3; Joranson, 'Spurious Letter', p. 824, n. 63.

[111] 'Zur Geschichte des Investiturstreites (englische Analekten II)', ed. W. Holtzmann, *Neues Archiv*, 50 (1935), pp. 280–2.

[112] See Rowe, 'Paschal II, Bohemund of Antioch', p. 195.

[113] 'Narratio Floriacensis de captis Antiochia et Hierosolyma et obsesso Dyrrachio', *RHC Oc.* 5, p. 362. See also 'Historia peregrinorum euntium Jerusolymam', *RHC Oc.* 3, p. 229.

[114] OV 6, pp. 104–5.

idea of reaching Jerusalem and the Holy Sepulchre was of vital importance to many of the crusaders of 1107–8.[115]

Although Bohemond's crusade message was obviously indebted to much of the revolutionary thinking of Pope Urban II, there is not enough direct evidence to prove that those who were preaching in 1106 were exploiting the ideas of *imitatio Christi* and *vita apostolica* that had proved so successful in 1095–6. Nevertheless, given that the senior ecclesiastic accompanying Bohemond through France in 1106 had also been a member of Urban II's entourage ten years earlier, it seems reasonable to assume that the sign of the cross was again being used to symbolise the bearer's intention to follow Christ; indeed, Bruno of Segni himself may well have been chosen precisely because he was experienced in preaching the idea of Christo-mimetic armed pilgrimage. The fact that contemporaries referred to Bohemond as 'a true knight and martyr of Christ'[116] and 'a standard-bearer of the army of Christ'[117] also indicates that motifs associated with the imitation of Christ were in use, as does the language used by Orderic Vitalis, who wrote of Bohemond's crusaders that 'they left all their belongings and took the cross of the Lord'.[118] But perhaps the single most important factor in gauging whether the crusaders of 1107–8 might have been instructed that they were undertaking a comparable spiritual exercise to those who had gone before them in 1096–1102 was that Bohemond's very presence was intended to evoke the memory of the First Crusade. Reference has already been made to the impact that Bohemond's personal appearances were believed to have had on recruitment for the expedition – King Henry I of England feared that the prince of Antioch 'might tempt away his best knights'[119] if he was allowed to cross the Channel – and Orderic Vitalis was not the only contemporary historian to describe how returning first crusaders set an example that others were inspired to follow.[120] This must have been a prominent theme within the crusade message of 1106, and it would have been reinforced by the circulation in France of the first generation of narrative histories of the First Crusade, of which the *Gesta Francorum* was the most popular. Given that the anonymous author's text was replete with ideas of *imitatio Christi* and, although perhaps less obviously, *vita apostolica*, it is difficult to believe that anyone who came into contact with the *Gesta* could have doubted that those who took the cross for the Holy Land, whether in 1096 or 1106, ought to be regarded as followers of Christ.

The reconstruction of Bohemond's crusade message of 1106 is not without its difficulties, but the evidence for his recruitment drive seems plentiful in comparison to what is known about how the crusades of 1120–4 and 1128–9 were preached. The first of these campaigns was triggered by the disaster of the Battle of the Field of Blood (28 June 1119),[121] and it is not therefore surprising that the sources point to the urgency

---

[115] These included Ralph of Caen, who was later to become the chaplain and biographer of Tancred Marchisus; see Riley-Smith, *First Crusaders*, p. 240.

[116] 'Historia peregrinorum', p. 228.

[117] Bartolf of Nangis, 'Gesta Francorum', p. 538.

[118] OV 6, pp. 70–1.

[119] OV 6, pp. 68–9.

[120] OV 5, pp. 322–3. See also Fulcher of Chartres, *Historia*, pp. 115–16; Ekkehard of Aura, 'Hierosolymita', p. 28; Guibert of Nogent, 'Dei gesta', p. 322.

[121] See J.S.C. Riley-Smith, 'The Venetian Crusade of 1122–1124', *I comuni italiani nel regno crociato di Gerusalemme*, ed. G. Airaldi and B.Z. Kedar (Genoa, 1986), pp. 339–50; J.P. Phillips, *Defenders of the*

with which the defence of the Holy Land was propagated in the West. Indeed, it has recently been suggested that Pope Calixtus II was preaching for a new crusade as early as the autumn of 1119,[122] although it was not until the First Lateran Council of 1123 that the expedition was officially documented. The record of the council's decrees stated that:

> We concede to those going to Jerusalem to assist in the defence of the Christian people and to do battle against the tyranny of the infidels remission of their sins, and we place their houses and families and all their goods under the protection of St Peter and the Roman church, just as was established by our Pope Urban.[123]

This statement clearly indicates that contemporaries connected the objectives and privileges of the expedition of 1120–4 with those of the First Crusade, but a more visible similarity between the two campaigns was that, as in the 1090s, those who answered the pope's call to crusade were required to take the sign of the cross as a symbol of their commitment to the expedition. The decree from the Lateran Council went on to warn of the penalties that would be imposed upon those recalcitrant crusaders 'who are known to have placed crosses on their clothing either for the journey to Jerusalem or for that to Spain', and who had yet to fulfil their votive obligations.[124] This directive, which also confirms that preaching for the crusade had been in motion for some time by April 1123, was reiterated in a letter Pope Calixtus addressed to 'all the bishops, kings, counts, princes and other faithful of God [in Iberia]': 'if those who have put the sign of the cross on their clothes . . . have not endeavoured to complete their vows between this Easter and the next, we banish them thereafter from the bosom of the Holy Church until they make amends'.[125] The significance of the inclusion of Iberia in the scope of Pope Calixtus's crusade will be considered in more detail in Chapter Five;[126] it is enough to note here that the sign of the cross was clearly in use in both the eastern and peninsular theatres by the early 1120s.

It is unknown whether Calixtus II used the same ideas of Christo-mimesis that Pope Urban had harnessed in his preaching of the cross in the 1090s; neither of the sources referred to above cited any *exempla* or quoted Gospel texts associated with *imitatio Christi*, although the conciliar decree was certainly not a lengthy or detailed document. Nevertheless, Calixtus's preaching was clearly effective, for Jonathan Riley-Smith has identified crusaders who set out for the Levant from France, Germany and Italy,[127] a number of whom are definitely known to have sworn vows or taken the cross.[128] Indeed, it would seem that the devotional intent of at least one contingent was particularly

---

Holy Land: Relations between the Latin East and the West, 1119–1187 (Oxford, 1996), pp. 14–18.
[122] See Riley-Smith, *First Crusaders*, p. 176.
[123] *Conciliorum oecumenicorum decreta*, ed. J. Alberigo et al. (Freiburg, 1962), pp. 167–8.
[124] *Ibid.*, p. 168.
[125] Calixtus II, *Bullaire*, ed. U. Robert, 2 vols. (Paris, 1891), vol. 2, Ep. 454, pp. 266–7.
[126] See below, pp. 129–30.
[127] See Riley-Smith, 'Venetian Crusade', p. 345; Riley-Smith, *First Crusaders*, pp. 242–4.
[128] See 'Chronicon Altinate', ed. A. Rossi, *Archivio storico italiano*, 8 (1845), p. 153; 'Historia ducum Veneticorum', *MGH SS* 14, p. 73; Fulcher of Chartres, *Historia*, p. 657; 'Documents pour l'histoire de Saint-Hilaire de Poitiers', ed. L. Rédet, *Mémoires de la Société des Antiquaires de l'Ouest* (1847), p. 128.

comparable with that of the first crusaders.[129] Fulcher of Chartres wrote that the Venetians had 'set sail for Syria with a great fleet so that, with the help of God, they might extend Jerusalem and the adjacent region for the advantage and glory of Christendom', but he also noted that before they besieged Tyre in 1124 they had 'celebrated the Nativity of the Saviour in Bethlehem as well as in Jerusalem, as was proper'.[130] It is clear, therefore, that a number of the crusaders of 1120–4 regarded themselves as pilgrims,[131] and it is striking that in spite of the fact that they had set out in response to a disaster in northern Syria they continued to view their efforts in terms of aiding Jerusalem and the Holy Sepulchre.

Much the same can also be said of those who took part in the crusade that targeted Damascus in 1128–9. Even less is known about the language of preaching for this expedition,[132] although given the role of Hugh of Payns it must surely have focused on the need for the West to contribute to the defence of the Holy Land.[133] According to *The Anglo-Saxon Chronicle*, the master of the Temple had:

> summoned people out to Jerusalem; and then there went, with him and after him, as great a number of people as ever did before since the first expedition which was in Pope Urban's day . . . [because] He said that a great battle was set between the Christians and the heathen.[134]

Whether or not Hugh had instructed these crusaders that they were imitating Christ is unknown, but Orderic Vitalis described how a number of those who joined the expedition 'took the Lord's cross and, becoming exiles for Christ's sake, set out for his sepulchre in Jerusalem'.[135] Indeed, *imitatio Christi* was a prominent theme within early Templar spirituality[136] and Hugh's presence may well have inspired potential crusaders in much the same way that Bohemond's personal appearances were reputed to have aroused enthusiasm for his expedition to the East in 1106. Hugh's tour certainly played an important part in boosting the international profile of the Templars.[137]

It is impossible to know for certain whether those arms-bearers who took the cross in the first three decades of the twelfth century did so with the same intent to imitate

---

[129] But see also J.S.C. Riley-Smith, 'Government in Latin Syria and the Commercial Privileges of the Foreign Merchants', *Relations between East and West in the Middle Ages*, ed. D. Baker (Edinburgh, 1973), pp. 109–32; C. Marshall, 'The Crusading Motivation of the Italian City Republics in the Latin East, 1096–1104', *Experience of Crusading, Volume One*, pp. 60–79.

[130] Fulcher of Chartres, *Historia*, pp. 655–6, 693–4.

[131] For a possible reference to the crusaders as *peregrini*, see *ibid.*, p. 657.

[132] See Phillips, *Defenders of the Holy Land*, pp. 36–40.

[133] See also J.P. Phillips, 'Hugh of Payns and the 1129 Damascus Crusade', *The Military Orders: Fighting for the Faith and Caring for the Sick*, ed. M. Barber (Aldershot, 1994), pp. 141–7.

[134] *The Anglo-Saxon Chronicle*, trans. and ed. M.J. Swanton (London, 1996), p. 259. See also Henry of Huntingdon, *Historia Anglorum*, ed. T. Arnold, *Rolls Series*, 74 (London, 1879), pp. 250–1; Robert of Torigni, *Chronica*, ed. R. Howlett, *Rolls Series*, 82 (London, 1889), pp. 113–15; William of Tyre, *Chronicon*, ed. R.B.C. Huygens, CC:CM, 63, 63A (Turnhout, 1986), pp. 618–22.

[135] OV 6, pp. 378–9.

[136] See below, pp. 104–11.

[137] See M. Barber, *The New Knighthood: A History of the Order of the Temple* (Cambridge, 1994), pp. 12–19.

Christ that was attributed to the crusaders of 1096–1102. However, given that contemporaries continually referred to these campaigns in the context of the First Crusade, such an idea seems more than likely. Indeed, in the light of the impact that the custody of the Christian holy places evidently had on western piety, and of the centrality of Jerusalem in the preaching of the expeditions of 1106–8, 1120–4 and 1128–9, it is difficult to believe that those who took the cross during this period could have seen their armed pilgrimages as anything other than Christo-mimetic. Nevertheless, it is not until the major expedition of 1146–9, which has become known as the 'Second' Crusade, that the ideas of *imitatio Christi* that had been so central to the spirituality of the First Crusade can once again be identified beyond question.

Crusading to the East, 1145–1149

The Second Crusade of 1146–9 was proclaimed by Pope Eugenius III in response to the news of the fall of Edessa to Zengi in 1144.[138] As Calixtus II may well have done a quarter-century before him,[139] Eugenius launched his appeal by issuing a general letter, known as *Quantum praedecessores*, on 1 December 1145.[140] The letter began by establishing the precedent for the proposed crusade, which Eugenius saw as a continuation of his predecessors' work for the liberation of the eastern Church, and it made specific reference to the preaching of Pope Urban II and the achievements of the first crusaders, who had 'freed from the filth of the pagans that city in which our Saviour was willing to suffer for us and where he left us with his glorious Sepulchre as a memorial of his Passion'.[141] Eugenius then went on to report how the 'enemies of the cross of Christ' had taken the city of Edessa, and he described the desecration of the city and the murder of its archbishop and clergy. It was the duty of the Christian knighthood, Eugenius claimed, to pay heed to the achievements of their forefathers and rush to the defence of the Holy Land:

> It will be seen as a great sign of nobility and integrity if that which was acquired by the efforts of the fathers is vigorously defended by the good sons. Nevertheless if, God forbid, it should be otherwise, the courage of the fathers will have proved to be diminished in the sons.

---

[138] See G. Constable, 'The Second Crusade as Seen by Contemporaries', *Traditio*, 9 (1953), pp. 213–79; J.G. Rowe, 'The Origins of the Second Crusade: Pope Eugenius III, Bernard of Clairvaux and Louis VII of France', *The Second Crusade and the Cistercians*, ed. M. Gervers (New York, 1992), pp. 79–89; G. Ferzoco, 'The Origin of the Second Crusade', *Second Crusade and the Cistercians*, pp. 91–9; R. Hiestand, 'The Papacy and the Second Crusade', *The Second Crusade: Scope and Consequences*, ed. J.P. Phillips and M. Hoch (Manchester, 2001), pp. 32–53; Phillips, *The Second Crusade, passim*.

[139] See Riley-Smith, 'Venetian Crusade', p. 345.

[140] Note that the text used here is the version of 1 March 1146, which contained minor changes to the version of December 1145. For the earlier version, see Eugenius III, 'Epistolae et privilegia', *PL* 180, no. 48, cols. 1064–6.

[141] Eugenius III, 'Quantum praedecessores', ed. P. Rassow, 'Der Text der Kreuzzugsbulle Eugens III. vom. 1. März 1146', *Neues Archiv*, 45 (1924), p. 302. See also J.M. Powell, 'Myth, Legend, Propaganda, History: The First Crusade, 1140–ca.1300', *Autor de la première croisade: actes du colloque de la Society for the Study of the Crusades and the Latin East 1995*, ed. M. Balard (Paris, 1996), pp. 127–41.

The arms-bearers of the West were therefore called upon to undertake this *opus et labor* for the defence of the eastern Church and for the liberation of their *confratres* in the Levant. As well as outlining the privileges that would be offered to crusaders, such as the remission of sins and the extension of the protection of the Church over their families and possessions, the bull also defined the restrictions on the dress and conduct of the crusaders, emphasising the penitential nature of the expedition.[142]

Much of Eugenius's message was to be restated in his second crusade bull, *Divina dispensatione I* (October 1146),[143] and it seems clear enough that the crusade's strategic objectives in the East centred around the recovery of Edessa;[144] indeed, the city was also directly referred to as the goal of the expedition in a troubadour song from the time, *Chevalier, mult estes guariz*.[145] In this context, it is all the more striking that participants and preachers alike continued to view the undertaking as a form of Jerusalem pilgrimage.[146] For example, one chronicler reported that, in 1146, 'Louis, king of the Franks, fired with zeal by the capture of Mesopotamia by the Turks . . . attached the sign of the cross to himself at Vézelay, and with princes and with a countless number of others, he set out across the sea on pilgrimage',[147] and contemporaries referred to the crusade variously as the *via sancti Sepulcri*,[148] *iter Ierosolimitanum*,[149] *expeditio Hierosolimitana*,[150] and the *iter sacrosanctae peregrinationis*.[151] It was also a *felix peregrinatio*,[152] and its participants a *peregrinus exercitus*.[153] Phrases such as *Iherosolimam profecturus*,[154] *Jerosolymis proficiscens*[155] and *Jerusalem tendens*[156] appeared in charters that were drawn up by second crusaders prior to their departure for the East, and Alelmus of Flichecourt later referred to 1147 as the year in which he had 'set out for Jerusalem with the army of Franks'.[157] Indeed, in addition to his describing the crusade as a *sanctum iter*,[158] in a letter of December 1147, Eugenius himself referred to the expedition as the *iter Ierosolimitanum*.[159]

---

[142] Eugenius III, 'Quantum praedecessores', pp. 302–4.

[143] 'Papsturkunden in Malta', ed. P. Kehr, *Nachrichten von der Gesellschaft der Wissenschaften zu Götingen, Phil.-hist. Kl.* (1899), no. 3, pp. 388–90.

[144] See also Odo of Deuil, *De profectione Ludovici VII in Orientem*, ed. and trans. V.G. Berry (New York, 1948), p. 6; Eugenius III, 'Epistolae', no. 166, cols. 1203–4.

[145] *Les chansons de croisade avec leurs mélodies*, ed. J. Bédier and P. Aubry (Paris, 1909), p. 8.

[146] See also the comments of G.A. Loud, 'Some Reflections on the Failure of the Second Crusade', *Crusades*, 4 (2005), pp. 11–12.

[147] 'Sigeberti continuatio Praemonstratensis', *MGH SS* 6, p. 453.

[148] Odo of Deuil, *De profectione*, p. 2.

[149] *Ibid.*, p. 2.

[150] Otto of Freising, *Chronica*, p. 248.

[151] Suger of St Denis, 'Epistolae', *RHGF* 15, no. 13, p. 488.

[152] *De expugnatione Lyxbonensi*, ed. and trans. C.W. David, with a new foreword and bibliography by J.P. Phillips (New York, 2001), p. 70. See also *ibid.*, pp. 60, 102, 108, 134, 170.

[153] Helmold of Bosau, 'Chronica Slavorum', *MGH SS* 21, p. 58.

[154] *Crusade Charters, 1138–1270*, ed. C.K. Slack (Tempe, AZ, 2001), pp. 18, 26, 44.

[155] *Ibid.*, p. 26.

[156] *Ibid.*, p. 26.

[157] *Ibid.*, p. 34.

[158] Eugenius III, 'Quantum praedecessores', p. 304.

[159] 'Documents relatifs à la croisade de Guillaume Comte de Ponthieu', ed. S. Löwenfold, *Archives de l'Orient latin*, 2 (1884), no. 2, p. 254.

References to the crusade as a form of pilgrimage were far more than convenient turns of phrase. According to Odo of Deuil's account of the expedition,[160] Louis VII was concerned 'not to do . . . anything which ill became a pilgrim',[161] and the evidence for the king's devotional activities on the march is irrefutable.[162] Odo recorded that 'during the entire journey the king never forgot mass or the hours because of floods of rain or the enemy's violence',[163] and that:

> Amid so many hardships his safe preservation was owed to no other remedy than his religion, for he always took communion before he went to attack enemy forces and on his return requested vespers and compline, in such ways always making God the alpha and the omega of his deeds.[164]

Odo also stated that some of the crusaders understood that their purpose was 'to visit the Sepulchre of the Lord and, by the order of the supreme pontiff, to wipe out our sins with the blood or the conversion of the pagans',[165] although the latter part of this statement bears more relation to Bernard of Clairvaux's advocation of the crusade against the Wends than to anything said by Eugenius III.[166]

Odo of Deuil was by no means the only writer to comment upon the importance of the Jerusalem pilgrimage to the ideas of the second crusaders. Otto of Freising, for example, described how one contingent had 'entered the Holy City about Palm Sunday, and celebrated with much devotion of heart the Lord's Passion and Holy Resurrection, going round to those places where those things happened and, so it is said, seeing them eye to eye',[167] and early in 1148 Conrad III himself wrote that it was only after visiting Jerusalem that his army would set out for Edessa.[168] Furthermore, it is clear that the contingent of northern crusaders who contributed to the successful siege of Lisbon were also bound for the Holy Sepulchre;[169] as one chronicler recorded for 1147, 'part of

---

[160] See H. Mayr-Harting, 'Odo of Deuil, the Second Crusade and the Monastery of Saint-Denis', *The Culture of Christendom: Essays in Medieval History in Memory of Denis L.T. Bethell*, ed. M.A. Meyer (London, 1993), pp. 225–41; B. Schuste, 'The Strange Pilgrimage of Odo of Deuil', *Medieval Concepts of the Past: Ritual, Memory, Historiography*, ed. G. Althoff, J. Fried and P.J. Geary (Cambridge, 2002), pp. 253–78; J.P. Phillips, 'Odo of Deuil's *De profectione Ludovici VII in Orientem* as a Source for the Second Crusade', *Experience of Crusading, Volume One*, pp. 80–95.

[161] Odo of Deuil, *De profectione*, pp. 36–8.

[162] Cf. A. Graboïs, 'The Crusade of King Louis VII: A Reconsideration', *Crusade and Settlement: Papers Read at the First Conference of the Society for the Study of the Crusades and the Latin East and Presented to R.C. Smail*, ed. P.W. Edbury (Cardiff, 1985), pp. 94–104, and 'Louis VII Pèlerin', *Revue d'histoire de l'église de France*, 74 (1988), pp. 5–22, who argued that Louis was more concerned with undertaking a penitential pilgrimage than commanding an army. For a restatement of Louis's 'crusading' motives, see Phillips, *Defenders of the Holy Land*, pp. 79–82.

[163] Odo of Deuil, *De profectione*, pp. 128–9.

[164] *Ibid.*, pp. 142–3.

[165] *Ibid.*, p. 70.

[166] See Bernard of Clairvaux, 'Epistolae', *SBO* 8, Ep. 457, pp. 432–3.

[167] Otto of Freising, *Gesta Friderici I imperatoris*, ed. G. Waitz and B. de Simson, *MGH SSRG* 46 (Hanover and Leipzig, 1912), pp. 88–9.

[168] Wibald of Stavelot, 'Epistolae', *RHGF* 15, Ep. 2, p. 534. This was of course for tactical reasons as much as it was an act of piety.

[169] See G. Constable, 'A Note on the Route of the Anglo-Flemish Crusaders of 1147', *Speculum*, 28

the Christian army, making for Jerusalem by boat, with the strength of God drove out the Saracens from the Spanish city of Lisbon (*Olisiponem urbem Hispaniae*), captured it and restored it to the Christians'.[170] Indeed, although the contribution of the northern crusaders to the siege may well have been orchestrated by Bernard of Clairvaux,[171] it is apparent that a number of this contingent's rank and file were anxious about the legitimacy of fighting in Iberia when they had sworn to travel to the East. If the anonymous author of *De expugnatione Lyxbonensi* is to be believed,[172] the bishop of Oporto sought to allay these fears by explaining to the crusaders why their fighting in Iberia was a valid exercise:

> Therefore, be not seduced by the desire to press on with the journey which you have begun; for the praiseworthy thing is not to have been to Jerusalem, but to have lived a good life while on the way; for you cannot arrive there except through the performance of His works. Verily, it is through good work that anyone deserves to come to a glorious end. Therefore, as worthy rivals [strive together] to raise up the fallen and prostrate church of Spain; reclothe her soiled and disfigured form with the garments of joy and gladness.[173]

It is unclear how far the bishop's efforts to communicate to the crusaders the primacy of the heavenly over the earthly Jerusalem were successful – many may have been more persuaded to fight in Iberia because of the promise of booty[174] – and there can be no doubt that several of their number did not feel their efforts at Lisbon had relieved them of their votive obligations, for as one eyewitness put it, after the city had been taken they 'sailed through various dangers, and they arrived, as they had vowed, at the Sepulchre of the Lord'.[175]

Perhaps the most novel explanation of how the idea of pilgrimage had motivated the second crusaders is to be found within the pages of Otto of Freising's *Gesta Friderici*,

(1953), pp. 525–6; G. Constable, 'A Further Note on the Conquest of Lisbon in 1147', *Experience of Crusading, Volume One*, pp. 39–44.

[170] 'Sigeberti continuatio Valcellensis', *MGH SS* 6, pp. 459–60. See also 'Sigeberti continuatio Gemblacensis', *MGH SS* 6, p. 389.

[171] See H. Livermore, 'The "Conquest of Lisbon" and its Author', *Portuguese Studies*, 6 (1990), pp. 1–16; J.P. Phillips, 'St Bernard of Clairvaux, The Low Countries and the Lisbon Letter of the Second Crusade', *Journal of Ecclesiastical History*, 48 (1997), pp. 485–97. But see also A.J. Forey, 'The Siege of Lisbon and the Second Crusade', *Portuguese Studies*, 20 (2004), pp. 1–13, who questions whether the involvement of the northern crusaders was the result of advance planning.

[172] Cf. Livermore, '"Conquest of Lisbon"', p. 16, who argued that *De expugnatione* was composed 'to assure those in East Anglia that the conquest [of Lisbon] was not a departure from the oath to undertake the crusade', and J.P. Phillips, 'Ideas of Crusade and Holy War in *De expugnatione Lyxbonensi* (The Conquest of Lisbon)', *Holy Land, Holy Lands*, pp. 125–6, who suggested that the author may have been responsible for 'some embroidering of the original words . . . to develop the key themes that he wished to stress'. See also E.-D. Hehl, *Kirche und Krieg im 12. Jahrhundert: Studien zu kanonischem Recht und politischer Wirklichkeit* (Stuttgart, 1980), pp. 138–9, 259–61, who shows how the source's author borrowed heavily from canon law.

[173] *De expugnatione*, pp. 78–9.

[174] *Ibid.*, pp. 98, 102, 176.

[175] 'Annales sancti Disibodi', *MGH SS* 17, p. 28. Cf. 'The Lisbon Letter of the Second Crusade', ed. S.B. Edgington, *Historical Research*, 69 (1996), pp. 328–39.

where it was recorded that, in 1146, 'the spirit of the pilgrim God had inspired almost all the western world to take up arms against the people that inhabit the East'.[176] Otto explained how the phrase *spiritus peregrini Dei* had originated from the Sibylline Books, which were in wide circulation at the time and were believed to forecast a 'triumph over the whole Orient',[177] led by an individual whose name began with 'L'; common belief understood this to be none other than King Louis VII. Unsurprisingly, with the benefit of hindsight (the *Gesta* was composed *c.*1156–8), Otto was able to express a healthy cynicism about such a prophecy, believing it to be propagated by charlatans who had taken advantage of the gullibility of the French.[178] But Otto also believed that there was some truth in the idea that the 'spirit of the pilgrim God' had been the inspiration for recruitment to the expedition:

> Not without some rational analogy was that spirit, which sent almost all western men on pilgrimage, called by us 'the spirit of the pilgrim God' . . . for when we say 'the spirit of the pilgrim God', we mean that it was because of God that so many and such great men assumed the habit of the pilgrim.[179]

There can therefore be no doubt that as with those who had taken part in the expeditions of 1106–8, 1120–4 and 1128–9, the crusaders of 1146–9 were almost universally regarded as undertaking a form of armed Jerusalem pilgrimage that was comparable to the First Crusade. As a consequence, it is perhaps to be expected that the ideas of Christo-mimesis that were understood to have been central to the spirituality of the expedition of 1096–1102, and that were very likely to have been a feature of the three intermediate campaigns, were once again in evidence in the 1140s. A letter addressed to Louis VII, for example, possibly written by Wladislas II, the duke of Bohemia, referred to the second crusaders as 'the whole army that wishes to walk in the Way of Christ (*in viam Christi*)',[180] and Odo of Deuil began his account of Louis VII's *profectio* by stating that 'the illustrious king of the Franks and duke of the Aquitanians . . . in order to be worthy of Christ, undertook to follow Him by bearing His cross'.[181] Both these statements indicate that the crusade was still believed to offer the laity a path to spiritual perfection and an opportunity to imitate Christ.

These themes were also taken up explicitly by an unnamed priest who was supposed to have preached to the northern crusaders during the siege of Lisbon.[182] He described how Christ's life was a model to which all Christians could aspire, so that they might correct fault within their lives: 'Wherefore it has happened that corrective rather than destructive punishment has been so allotted to man that to whomsoever

---

[176] Otto of Freising, *Gesta Friderici*, pp. 9–10.

[177] *Ibid.*, p. 10. For the Sibylline Books, see B. McGinn, *Visions of the End: Apocalyptic Traditions in the Middle Ages* (New York, 1979), pp. 117–19. For a discussion of the wider association of Apocalyptic and crusading thought see *ibid.*, pp. 88–9, 149–51; H.-D. Kahl, 'Crusade Eschatology as Seen by St. Bernard in the Years 1146 to 1148', *Second Crusade and the Cistercians*, pp. 35–47.

[178] Otto of Freising, *Gesta Friderici*, p. 11.

[179] *Ibid.*, p. 11. I am grateful to Mr Neil Brinded for his comments on this unusual passage.

[180] E. Pellegrin, 'Membra disiecta Floriacensia', *Bibliothèque de l'École des Chartes*, 117 (1959), p. 22.

[181] Odo of Deuil, *De profectione*, p. 6. See also *Les chansons de croisade*, p. 9.

[182] This priest may in fact have been the author of the text himself; the source's modern editor described this attribution as 'probable'; see *De expugnatione*, p. 146, n. 3.

the Devil has offered himself for the imitation of his pride, the Lord has offered himself for the imitation of his humility.'[183] The priest then went on to exhort the crusaders to continue to follow their Saviour's example: 'And you, most dearly beloved brethren, who have followed Christ as voluntary exiles and have willingly accepted poverty, hear and understand that the prize is promised to those who start but is [only] given to those who persevere.'[184]

As this report of the priest's words indicates, the imitation of Christ necessarily entailed hardship, and one of the most striking expositions on the sacrifices that the second crusaders had had to make to follow Christ was delivered by the bishop of Oporto in 1147. In reference to the crusaders' adoption of voluntary poverty and exile, the bishop was said to have proclaimed that:

> Christ, the mediator between God and men, when he came in person into the world, found very few who were followers of this way and of pure religion; hence, when a certain young man who said that he had fulfilled and kept the law asked him how he could be perfect, he answered, 'Go and sell all,' etc. Weigh carefully what follows: 'He was sad, for he had great possessions.' . . . And what shall we say to all this? How many there are among you here who are richer in possessions than this young man! How many who are higher in the rank of honours! How many who are more fortunate in a prolific stock and a numerous offspring! Yet it is a fact that they have exchanged all their honours and dignities for a blessed pilgrimage in order to obtain from God an eternal reward. The alluring affection of wives, the tender kisses of sucking infants at the breast, the even more delightful pledges of grown-up children, the much desired consolation of relatives and friends – all these they have left behind to follow Christ, retaining only the sweet but torturing memory of their native land.[185]

The analogy that the bishop drew between the second crusaders and the 'rich young man' of Matthew 19:16–30 is striking, especially when one considers how central this passage was to be to the religious conversions of such notable figures as Waldes of Lyons and St Francis of Assisi.[186] Indeed, the bishop went on to describe the crusaders to whom he was preaching as 'the newest mystery of the cross', and, using a Pauline phrase associated with *imitatio Christi* that Guibert of Nogent had also applied to the first crusaders, explained how the contingent of Anglo-Norman, Flemish and Rhineland arms-bearers assembled before him had gone forth 'out of the camp, bearing the reproach of the cross'.[187] In this way, the second crusaders' sacrifices were depicted as being directly analogous to that which Christ had made on Calvary.[188]

The bishop of Oporto was not alone in describing the hardship that the second crusaders had had to endure to follow Christ. In a letter addressed to Louis VII in which he sought to demonstrate his support for the expedition, Peter the Venerable described the 1140s as a time of 'new grace', in which the deeds and miracles of Christian tradition

---

[183] *Ibid.*, pp. 150–1.

[184] *Ibid.*, pp. 152–3.

[185] *Ibid.*, pp. 70–3.

[186] See L.K. Little, *Religious Poverty and the Profit Economy in Medieval Europe* (London, 1978), pp. 120–8, 146–52.

[187] *De expugnatione*, p. 72. Citation from Hebrews 13:13. Cf. Guibert of Nogent, 'Dei gesta', p. 322.

[188] See Morris, *Sepulchre of Christ*, p. 3.

were being renewed, and in which the second crusaders had made an extraordinary display of piety:

> For what honours, what riches, what pleasures, what home or parents can hold them back? And yet, leaving everything, they have chosen to follow their Christ, to toil for him, to fight for him, to die for him and to live for him.[189]

Peter's closing words were of course evocative of a theme that had been especially prominent in the narrative histories of the First Crusade, and he was not the only writer to depict the second crusaders' willingness to die in battle as a form of martyrdom. For example, one account of the siege of Lisbon described how after the city had been taken successfully by the northern crusaders, 'the bodies of our martyrs were buried outside the camp'.[190] Similarly, Odo of Deuil was in no doubt that those who had died on crusade in the East had achieved a martyr's crown. In a particularly vivid passage, he described how those crusaders who had sacrificed themselves for their fellow men were following Christ's example:

> For lords to die so that their servants might live would have been an incident calling for lamentation, had not the Lord of all given an example thereof. The flowers of France withered before they could bear fruit in Damascus. In saying this I am overcome by tears, and I groan from the bottom of my heart. Concerning this tragedy, however, the sober mind can comfort itself with the solace that this and earlier examples of their valour will live on in the world and that their death, whereby their errors were swept away through fervent faith, has won [for them] the martyr's crown.[191]

In many respects, therefore, the ideals of *imitatio Christi* that were circulating at the time of the Second Crusade were no different to those that had first been applied to the *milites Christi* of the First Crusade. However, analysis of one final contemporary source suggests that there may have been a subtle distinction between the Christo-mimetic spirituality associated with the two expeditions. In a sermon that has been dated to between April and June 1147, Peter the Venerable preached an address, *De laude Dominici Sepulchri*, which can only have been intended to inspire recruitment for the Second Crusade.[192] Echoing the mood of *Quantum praedecessores*, the sermon evoked the memory of the liberation of Jerusalem in 1099 and praised the first crusaders for their willingness to offer their souls and sacrifice their bodies for Christ: 'you did not at all repay anything worthy of equalling the very great gifts given to you by him . . . but you indicated that you wished to'.[193] Turning to address Christ himself, Peter attempted

---

[189] *The Letters of Peter the Venerable*, ed. G. Constable, 2 vols. (Cambridge, MA, 1967), vol. 1, Ep. 130, p. 328.
[190] 'Annales sancti Disibodi', p. 28.
[191] Odo of Deuil, *De profectione*, pp. 118–19. For another description of the dead crusaders as martyrs, see *ibid.*, p. 130.
[192] Peter the Venerable, 'Petri Venerabilis Sermones tres', ed. G. Constable, *Revue bénédictine*, 64 (1954), pp. 232–54. See also V.G. Berry, 'Peter the Venerable and the Crusades', *Petrus Venerabilis 1156–1956: Studies and Texts Commemorating the Eighth Centenary of his Death*, ed. G. Constable and J. Kritzeck, *Studia Anselmiana*, 40 (Rome, 1956), pp. 141–62.
[193] Peter the Venerable, 'Sermones tres', p. 247.

to stir his audience by employing ideas of Christo-mimesis that were also reported to have been used by Pope Urban II fifty years earlier:

> You have been made the Way (*via*) for those who, in this pilgrimage, are proceeding to their homeland, through the humility of the flesh which you took up; you appear to them through the majesty of divine power as truth (*ueritas*) and life eternal (*vita sempiterna*).[194]

However, at the heart of Peter's sermon was a hymn of praise for the Holy Land in which he set out the importance of protecting the landmarks of the Christian heritage. His attention focused on the Holy Sepulchre, and he signalled its significance as the place that had been sanctified by the Resurrection.[195] But the Sepulchre was also used as a metaphor for the acceptance of Christ, and Peter implored those crusaders to whom he was preaching to adopt the following maxim:

> I will imitate this sepulchre of his, in that just as his body was held in the middle of the earth, I will hold in my heart, which is in the middle of my breast, his eternal memory.[196]

This equation between *imitatio Sepulchri* and *imitatio Christi* appears to have been something of a progression from the ideas that had been circulating in *c.*1096, and almost certainly reflects the impact that the renewed western custody of the Holy Sepulchre had had on the Christians of Europe in the first half of the twelfth century.[197] If the language of Peter's sermon is anything to judge by, one must conclude that the idea of fighting for Christ '*in the place where his feet have stood*' must have been every bit as emotive for the second crusaders as it had been for their predecessors, and possibly even more so.

Ideas of Christo-mimesis appear to have been fundamental to the spirituality of crusading to the East during the period 1102–49. Less can be said about the way in which the association between crusading and the *vita apostolica* developed in the first half of the twelfth century. The fact is that the primary sources for the period 1102–44 are silent on the ideas of *vita communis* and apostolic activity that appeared in some of the narrative histories of the First Crusade. Nevertheless, by the time of the Second Crusade, for which the source material is more substantial, there is some fragmentary evidence for a continuation of these themes.

Some of the most prominent references to ideas that are perhaps best described as 'quasi-apostolic' are to be found within *De expugnatione Lyxbonensi*. From the outset, the author of this text went to great lengths to demonstrate the importance of unity to the successes of the second crusaders who fought at Lisbon. In his description of the gathering of forces at Dartmouth, for example, he wrote that:

> Among these people of so many different tongues the firmest guarantees of peace and friendship were taken; and, furthermore, they sanctioned very strict laws, as,

---

[194] *Ibid.*, p. 254. Cf. John 14:6; Baldric of Bourgueil, 'Historia', pp. 14–15.
[195] Peter the Venerable, 'Sermones tres', p. 234.
[196] *Ibid.*, p. 243.
[197] Cf. Morris, *Sepulchre of Christ*, pp. 249–50.

for example, a life for a life and a tooth for a tooth. They forbade all display of costly garments.[198]

This harmonious spirit was also later observed by the bishop of Oporto, who was said to have praised the crusaders because they were joined in a 'unanimous fellowship (*unanimis societas)'*.[199] It was to the dangers of straying from this spirit of unanimity that Hervey of Glanvill was said to have pointed when he exhorted a group of dissenters to remain and fight with the rest of the crusaders in Lisbon before proceeding to the East.[200] Moreover, the final victory over the Muslims of Lisbon was understood to have been a direct result of the fact that the crusaders had fought *unanimiter*:[201]

> Indeed, for when we were now almost at the entrance of the gates, concord would have been broken had not our God interposed the right hand of his propitiation. But from the beginning of our association he always exercised the clemency of his goodness towards us, so that when from many and uncontrollable causes of discord even our leaders in desperation lost control of their tempers, then at last the breath of the Holy Spirit, as it were, repelling the chill of a misty cloud by a certain gleam of the noonday sun, re-established the grateful bond of a returning concord.[202]

It is difficult to know whether these references were intended to evoke the spirituality of the *ecclesia primitiva*. Parallels can certainly be drawn with the language of the histories of the First Crusade, but it is noticeable that the author of *De expugnatione* did not draw any direct analogy between the crusaders who fought at Lisbon and the brethren of the primitive Church. Indeed, when the bishop of Oporto implored the crusaders to assist with the siege of Lisbon on the basis that it was the duty of all Christians to help their brethren, it is striking that it was not to any apostolic model that he was said to have resorted: 'Weigh not lightly your duty to your fellow men; for as St Ambrose says, "He who does not ward off an injury from his comrades and brothers, if he can, is as much at fault as he who does the injury".'[203]

More secure evidence for the influence of the ideals of the *vita apostolica* on the second crusaders is to be found within Odo of Deuil's *De profectione*, although it would appear that it was only after the Templars had taken effective control of King Louis's army in January 1148 that ideas of unanimity began to permeate the actions of the crusaders who were fighting in the East.[204] Odo described how the master of the Temple, Everard of Barres, was 'to the army an example of goodness', and how:

> the king liked the example which they [the Templars] set and was glad to imitate it, and he wanted the army to be influenced in that direction, for he knew that,

---

[198] *De expugnatione*, pp. 56–7.
[199] *Ibid.*, p. 70. See also J.A. Brundage, 'St. Bernard and the Jurists', *Second Crusade and the Cistercians*, pp. 29–30.
[200] *De expugnatione*, pp. 104–6.
[201] See also 'Annales sancti Disibodi', p. 28, where the northern crusaders are described as fighting *unanimiter*.
[202] *De expugnatione*, pp. 166–7.
[203] *Ibid.*, pp. 78–9.
[204] See Barber, *New Knighthood*, p. 67; Phillips, 'Odo of Deuil's *De profectione*', p. 90.

even if extreme hunger should weaken them, unity of spirit (*unitas animi*) would also strengthen them in their weakness.[205]

It seems reasonable to assume that the *exemplum* to which Odo referred was nothing less than the fact that the Templars lived a communal life which was itself modelled on the *vita apostolica*. Certainly Bernard of Clairvaux saw in the Templars the same apostolic spirituality that was claimed by other new forms of religious life in this period. He described the Templars as living in 'brotherly love, devoted obedience, [and] voluntary poverty',[206] and in one passage of his *De laude novae militiae*, he made a direct comparison between the way of life of the Templars and that of the brethren of the primitive Church:

> They live the common life (*in communi*), a clearly delightful and sober way of life, without wives and without children. And so that their evangelical perfection should not be wanting, they live in one house . . . without anything of their own, careful to preserve the unity of the [Holy] Spirit in the bond of peace. You might say that the whole multitude has one heart and soul (*cor unum et animam unam*).[207]

Furthermore, it is striking that the Templars were known to contemporaries not only as *milites* but also *commilitones* – a term that evoked a unity of spirit and purpose[208] – and the *Primitive Rule* of the Temple went to great lengths to stress the importance of observing the *vita communis*, so much so that if a 'sickly sheep' was identified amongst the 'society of faithful brothers', it was stated that he should be removed at once.[209] On the basis of the record of Odo of Deuil it would seem that such principles were not simply abstractions. It is clear that the Templars' influence on King Louis's army in 1148 was immediate, and that their tactical decision to form the crusaders into fraternities yielded surprisingly successful results; as Odo put it, 'when permission had been granted by the commander, all attacked the Turks with one mind (*unanimiter*), and they killed those whom they could overtake, thus avenging the death of their comrades and their own losses'.[210] Indeed, the formation of confraternities during both the First and Second Crusades indicates how far the ideals of the *vita apostolica* had a practical application for crusade armies on the march.[211]

---

[205] Odo of Deuil, *De profectione*, pp. 124–5.

[206] Bernard of Clairvaux, 'Liber ad milites Templi de laude novae militiae', *SBO* 3, p. 222.

[207] *SBO* 3, p. 220.

[208] See, for example, *Die ursprüngliche Templerregel*, ed. G. Schnürer (Freiburg, 1903), pp. 130, 131, 132, 136, 150; *SBO* 3, p. 213; *Cartulaire général de l'ordre du Temple 1119?-1150*, ed. Marquis d'Albon (Paris, 1913), nos. 16, 21, 63, 64, 85 and 244, pp. 10, 15, 46, 48, 64, 165.

[209] *Die ursprüngliche Templerregel*, p. 151. See also *ibid.*, pp. 140, 148–9.

[210] Odo of Deuil, *De profectione*, pp. 126–7. For a discussion of the military impact of the formation of these confraternities, see J.P. Phillips and M. Hoch, 'Introduction', *Second Crusade*, p. 10.

[211] See J. Richard, 'La confrèrie de la croisade: à propos d'un épisode de la prèmiere croisade', *Études de civilisation médiévale, IXe–XIIe siècles: mélanges offerts à Edmond-René Labande par ses amis, ses collègues, ses élèves* (Poitiers, 1974), pp. 617–22.

Conclusion

It would seem that although Odo of Deuil and the anonymous author of *De expugnatione Lyxbonensi* were both aware of the importance of ideas of concord and unanimity to the successes or failures of the second crusaders, any direct connections between crusading and the ideals of the *vita apostolica* had faded by the mid-twelfth century. In some respects this is not surprising. The idea of crusading as an apostolic activity had always been secondary to that of *imitatio Christi* in First Crusade spirituality, and the effective transmission of the idea of the crusader's 'apostolate' must undoubtedly have suffered after the literalisation of the idea of 'taking the cross to follow Christ' had proved so successful. Indeed, the almost immediate dominance of *imitatio Christi* over *vita apostolica* in crusading spirituality mirrors the contemporaneous developments in the ideologies of many of the new religious orders of the eleventh and twelfth centuries. At the end of the previous chapter, reference was made to Sir Richard Southern's belief that ideas of Christo-mimesis and apostolic activity were an inseparable feature of all the new religious foundations of the period, but it is important to note that he qualified that statement by stressing that 'every new plan tended to go in one direction or the other: to concentrate *either* on evangelical imitation *or* apostolic usefulness'.[212]

In the wake of the recovery of Jerusalem in 1099, and of the subsequent establishment of a permanent western Christian presence in the Holy Land, the emphasis on 'evangelical imitation' in the spirituality of crusaders and pilgrims who set out for the Levant became of paramount importance. Indeed, the evidence cited in this chapter has led some historians to believe that the relationship between crusade and *imitatio Christi* was endemic in the twelfth century.[213] It is therefore striking that when one turns to analyse the detail of the preaching of the Second Crusade by Pope Eugenius III and Abbot Bernard of Clairvaux, the idea of armed pilgrimage as a Christo-mimetic devotion is completely absent. In fact, the Cistercians appear to have been attempting to institute a theology of the cross that was quite different to that of Pope Urban II.

---

[212] R. W. Southern, *Western Society and the Church in the Middle Ages* (Harmondsworth, 1970), p. 252.
[213] See, for example, J.S.C. Riley-Smith, 'Crusading as an Act of Love', *History*, 65 (1980), pp. 178–9.

CHAPTER FOUR

The Cistercian Influence on Crusading Spirituality,

c. 1128–1187

The Cistercian Preaching of the Second Crusade

It has often been suggested that *Quantum praedecessores*, the letter by which Pope Eugenius III signalled the official proclamation of the Second Crusade, was of great significance to the institutional development of the crusading movement. Indeed, Giles Constable went so far as to say that *Quantum praedecessores* marked:

> a fundamental step in the development of the crusades and of crusading thought . . . Built on the growth and events of half a century, this bull set the pattern for the juridical development of the crusade and as such laid the basis of the crusade as an institution in European history.[1]

However, even though *Quantum praedecessores* was regarded within the papal curia as being of use for almost a generation,[2] it is now clear that Eugenius's contribution to the 'juridical development' of crusading needs to be reassessed. He may well not have been the first pope to issue a general letter for a crusade to the East,[3] and it is obvious that he did not wish to be thought of as an innovator. One of his letter's central themes was that he was following the example of 'our predecessors the Roman pontiffs [who] have worked for the liberation of the eastern Church', and the privileges that he offered to second crusaders were propagated as being the same as those that 'our aforesaid predecessor Pope Urban instituted'.[4] In this respect, he was the latest in a line of pontiffs who were determined to link their appeals for military assistance for the Latin East to the memory of the First Crusade,[5] and Penny Cole has concluded that Eugenius

---

[1] G. Constable, 'The Second Crusade as Seen by Contemporaries', *Traditio*, 9 (1953), p. 253.

[2] See below, pp. 111–17.

[3] See J.S.C. Riley-Smith, 'The Venetian Crusade of 1122–1124', *I comuni italiani nel regno crociato di Gerusalemme*, ed. G. Airaldi and B.Z. Kedar (Genoa, 1986), pp. 339–50; J.S.C. Riley-Smith, *The Crusades: A History*, 2nd edition (London, 2005), pp. 119–20.

[4] Eugenius III, 'Quantum praedecessores', ed. P. Rassow, 'Der Text der Kreuzzugsbulle Eugens III. vom. 1. März 1146', *Neues Archiv*, 45 (1924), pp. 302, 304.

[5] See, for example, *Die Kreuzzugsbriefe aus den Jahren 1088–1100*, ed. H. Hagenmeyer (Innsbruck, 1901), no. 19, p. 175; *Conciliorum oecumenicorum decreta*, ed. J. Alberigo *et al.* (Freiburg, 1962), pp. 167–8.

believed *Quantum praedecessores* to be 'merely a written formulation and application of all that Urban had intended when he launched the first great expedition'.[6] Yet in spite of the fact that Eugenius claimed to be closely adhering to the ideas and practices that had been instituted by Pope Urban II,[7] there can be no doubt that one of the motifs that had been fundamental to the preaching of the First Crusade was overlooked in *Quantum praedecessores*: that crusaders should be regarded as imitators of Christ.

Given the prominence of *imitatio Christi* in early crusading spirituality it is astonishing that this theme is missing from the text of *Quantum praedecessores*. There was only one reference in Eugenius's letter to the practice of the crusader taking the cross,[8] but no connection was drawn between this act and the scriptural verses that Pope Urban was reported to have cited in his Clermont sermon, or the spirituality with which they were associated. The precision with which *Quantum praedecessores* was composed is unquestionable,[9] and it therefore seems highly improbable that the absence of the rhetoric of *imitatio Christi* was an oversight. Indeed, if this had been the case, it is striking that it was not corrected in the revised text of the bull that was promulgated in March 1146, or included in either version of *Divina dispensatione*, which were issued in October 1146 and April 1147 respectively.[10] Furthermore, these letters, which were obviously fundamental to the ideological foundations of the Second Crusade, did not exist in a vacuum; on the contrary, they were a vital tool in encouraging recruitment for the expedition across Europe. One contemporary who was closely involved with the participation of the Germans in the crusade described how *Quantum praedecessores* was distributed and read aloud at large-scale public events,[11] and it might therefore be assumed that the ideal of *imitatio Christi* would be elaborated upon by those charged with the dissemination of Eugenius's crusade message. However, the surviving evidence suggests that such an assumption would be completely unfounded.

Much of the responsibility for the wider preaching of the Second Crusade fell to Bernard of Clairvaux,[12] who had himself had a hand in the final draft of *Quantum praedecessores* in March 1146.[13] The role of crusade preacher was not one that he had sought for himself, and he was conscious of the conflict between his role in the politics of the

---

[6] P.J. Cole, *The Preaching of the Crusades to the Holy Land, 1095–1270* (Cambridge, MA, 1991), p. 41.

[7] See also Eugenius III, 'Epistolae et privilegia', *PL* 180, no. 166, cols. 1203–4.

[8] Eugenius III, 'Quantum praedecessores', p. 304. 'Auctoritate etiam apostolica prohibemus, ut de omnibus, que illi, qui crucem acceperint, quiete possederint, nulla deinceps questio moveatur, donec de ipsorum reditu vel obitu certissime cognoscatur.'

[9] See J.P. Phillips, *The Crusades, 1095–1197* (Harlow, 2002), pp. 63–5; J.P. Phillips, *The Second Crusade: Extending the Frontiers of Christendom* (New Haven and London, 2007), pp. 37–60.

[10] For the texts, see 'Papsturkunden in Malta', ed. P. Kehr, *Nachrichten von der Gesellschaft der Wissenschaften zu Göttingen, Phil.-hist. Kl.* (1899), no. 3, pp. 388–90; Eugenius III, 'Epistolae', no. 166, cols. 1203–4.

[11] Otto of Freising, *Gesta Friderici I imperatoris*, ed. G. Waitz and B. de Simson, *MGH SSRG* 46 (Hanover and Leipzig, 1912), p. 60.

[12] See Constable, 'Second Crusade, pp. 244–7, 276–8; E. Willems, 'Cîteaux et la seconde croisade', *Revue d'histoire ecclésiastique*, 49 (1954), pp. 116–51; M. Meschini, *San Bernardo e la seconda crociata* (Milan, 1998); Phillips, *The Second Crusade*, pp. 60–98.

[13] See J.G. Rowe, 'The Origins of the Second Crusade: Pope Eugenius III, Bernard of Clairvaux and Louis VII of France', *The Second Crusade and the Cistercians*, ed. M. Gervers (New York, 1992), pp. 84, 87.

world and his commitment to the cloister; as he wrote to the archbishop of Mainz in condemnation of the unlicensed preaching of the German monk called Radulf, 'the duty of a monk is not to teach but to pray'.[14] Nevertheless, the importance of Bernard's preaching for stimulating recruitment to the expedition is undisputed. By his own admission, the impact of his sermons was profound – '*I have declared and I have spoken*', he reported to Pope Eugenius, '. . . towns and castles are emptied, and now one may scarcely find one man among seven women, so many women are there widowed while their husbands are still living'.[15] The fervour that Bernard's preaching tour inspired was confirmed by Odo of Deuil, who described how 'the abbot . . . who bore a hardy spirit in his frail and almost lifeless body, hastened about, preaching everywhere, and soon the number of those bearing the cross had been increased immeasurably'.[16] The enthusiasm that surrounded Bernard's preaching was on a par with the events that had accompanied Pope Urban II's appeal fifty years beforehand,[17] and it would seem that the appeal of the abbot's message was universal. Otto of Freising described how Bernard had been instrumental not only in persuading Louis VII and the French to join the crusade, but also in encouraging the participation of Conrad III and the Germans: 'The abbot . . . persuaded the king with Frederick, the son of his brother, and other princes and distinguished men to take up the cross, performing many miracles in public and also in private.'[18] In some respects, by recruiting two of Europe's most powerful monarchs, Bernard had even surpassed the achievements of Pope Urban himself.

The wording of Bernard's sermons can never be fully reconstructed, but his Second Crusade message was repeated in a series of letters that were addressed to those to whom he could not preach in person.[19] As Jean Leclercq demonstrated,[20] these letters were certainly tailored to suit individual recipients and to address any pertinent local conditions,[21] but they were all constructed around a series of central ideas and stock phrases. Consequently, it is reasonable to assume that these letters, which have been described as 'among the most powerful crusade propaganda of all time',[22] and the common motifs they contain, provide an accurate reflection of the language that Bernard himself had used when preaching the crusade across Europe in 1146–7.

[14] Bernard of Clairvaux, 'Epistolae', *SBO* 8, Ep. 365, p. 321. For Radulf's preaching, see also Otto of Freising, *Gesta Friderici*, pp. 58–9. See also Cole, *Preaching of the Crusades*, pp. 43–5.

[15] *SBO* 8, Ep. 247, p. 141. Citation from Psalm 39:6.

[16] Odo of Deuil, *De profectione Ludovici VII in Orientem*, ed. and trans. V.G. Berry (New York, 1948), pp. 10–11.

[17] See J.S.C. Riley-Smith, *The First Crusade and the Idea of Crusading* (London, 1986), pp. 31–57.

[18] Otto of Freising, *Gesta Friderici*, pp. 58–9. Cf. 'Sigeberti continuatio Praemonstratensis', *MGH SS* 6, p. 453. See also J.P. Phillips, 'Papacy, Empire and the Second Crusade', *The Second Crusade: Scope and Consequences*, ed. J.P. Phillips and M. Hoch (Manchester, 2001), pp. 15–31.

[19] See *SBO* 8, Ep. 363, p. 312; Ep. 458, p. 434.

[20] J. Leclercq, 'L'encyclique de saint Bernard en faveur de la croisade', *Revue bénédictine*, 81 (1971), pp. 282–308, and 82 (1972), p. 312; J. Leclercq, 'Pour l'histoire de l'encyclique de saint Bernard sur la croisade', *Études de civilisation médiévale, IXe–XIIe siècles: mélanges offerts à Edmond-René Labande par ses amis, ses collègues, ses élèves* (Poitiers, 1974), pp. 479–90.

[21] See, for example, Bernard of Clairvaux, 'Letter to the English People', *The Letters of St Bernard of Clairvaux*, trans. B. Scott James (Sutton, 1998), pp. 462–3, where Bernard warns against the maltreatment of Jews.

[22] Riley-Smith, *The Crusades*, p. 122.

Across the letters,[23] Bernard repeated Pope Eugenius's call for a crusade to the East, and he highlighted how the recent Muslim resurgence in the Holy Land signalled a threat for Jerusalem and the Holy Sepulchre:

> The enemy of the cross has begun to show his sacrilegious head there, and to devastate with the sword that blessed land, that land of promise. Alas, if there should be none to resist him, he will soon invade the very city of the living God, destroy the workshop of our redemption, and defile the holy places which have been adorned by the blood of the immaculate lamb.[24]

Bernard's preaching for the crusade was therefore more focused on the defence of the Holy Sepulchre than it was on any specific strategic objectives, such as the recovery of Edessa. However, perhaps the most notable difference between Bernard's letters and those of Pope Eugenius was that the imagery of the cross figured far more prominently in the former than it had done in the latter. In his letter to 'the people of eastern France and Bavaria', Bernard entreated his audience to:

> Take up (*suscipere*) the sign of the cross and you will obtain indulgence in equal part for all the sins which you have confessed with a contrite heart. If the cloth itself is bought, it is of little value; if it is worn with devotion on the shoulder, it is without doubt worth the kingdom of God. They do well, therefore, those who have taken up this heavenly sign; and they also do well . . . [those] who hurry to take hold of (*apprehendere*) what will be, for them, their salvation.[25]

The sign of the cross was therefore at the heart of Bernard's crusade message, and one need only consult Odo of Deuil's description of events at Vézelay in March 1146 to gauge how powerful a recruiting device the symbol continued to be:

> when heaven's instrument poured forth the dew of the divine word, as he was wont, with loud outcry people on every side began to demand crosses. And when he had sowed, rather than distributed, the parcel of crosses which had been prepared beforehand, he was forced to tear his own garments into crosses and to sow them abroad.[26]

Nevertheless, it is striking that at no point in Odo's account, or in any of the other narratives of Bernard's preaching tour, is the abbot reported to have referred to the Gospel passages that would have portrayed the crusaders as fulfilling Christ's scriptural injunction to 'take up their crosses'. The fact that this motif was also missing from each and every one of his surviving crusade letters is equally remarkable, and suggests that at no stage did Bernard make any positive efforts to identify the crusade badge as a mark of the bearer's Christo-mimetic piety.[27]

---

[23] See especially *SBO* 8, Ep. 363, pp. 311–17; Ep. 458, pp. 434–7. See also Bernard of Clairvaux, 'Letter to the English People', pp. 460–3.

[24] *SBO* 8, Ep. 363, p. 312; Ep. 458, p. 435.

[25] *SBO* 8, Ep. 363, p. 315. See also Ep. 458, p. 436.

[26] Odo of Deuil, *De profectione*, pp. 8–9.

[27] Cf. Cole, *Preaching of the Crusades*, pp. 59–60, who argued that, for Bernard, crusading was associated with 'suffering and self-sacrifice in imitation of Christ', and Y. Katzir, 'The Second Crusade and the Redefinition of *Ecclesia*, *Christianitas* and Papal Coercive Power', *Second Crusade and the Cistercians*, p. 9,

It could of course be argued that because ideas of the imitation of Christ were so embedded within popular understandings of crusading spirituality neither Bernard nor Eugenius felt that a Gospel citation or an explicit reference to the ideal of *imitatio* was necessary. However, given the proven effectiveness of the idea that by taking the cross the crusader was 'following in the footsteps of Christ', this seems unlikely – especially as both men were clearly aware of the need to provide *exempla* from which their audiences could draw inspiration. Reference has already been made to how Eugenius called on second crusaders to recollect and live up to the achievements of their forefathers,[28] and the theme also figured prominently in Bernard's crusade letters, where it was argued that further territorial losses in the Holy Land would be a source of 'confusion and endless shame for our generation':

> What are you doing, brave men? What are you doing, servants of the cross? Will you really give holy things to dogs and pearls to pigs? What a great number of sinners have confessed their sins with tears and obtained forgiveness after the swords of the fathers cleared the filth of the pagans![29]

Given what is now known about the importance of family tradition to participation in twelfth-century crusading activity,[30] it is no surprise to find that this theme was taken up by a number of contemporaries. Odo of Deuil, who was obviously familiar with the detail of *Quantum praedecessores*,[31] referred repeatedly to the example that had been set by the first crusaders,[32] and towards the end of his account of Louis VII's campaign he reported that the king had attempted to rally his troops by saying:

> 'Let us follow the route of our fathers, whose incomparable valour endowed them with renown on earth and glory in heaven . . .' To these remarks they [the army] answered: 'We do not want to and cannot depreciate our fathers' renown, but events went more easily for them than they have thus far for us.'[33]

Similarly, Conrad III wrote that the Byzantines had treated the second crusaders with more respect than 'was ever shown to our ancestors',[34] and during the siege of Lisbon Hervey of Glanvill was reported to have brought a number of disobedient crusaders into line by warning them that they were in danger of becoming 'the objects of universal infamy and disgrace':

who believed that the crusaders 'undertook the obligation to imitate Christ' in response to Bernard's preaching.

[28] Eugenius III, 'Quantum praedecessores', pp. 302, 303.

[29] *SBO* 8, Ep. 363, p. 313. See also Ep. 458, pp. 435–6.

[30] See, for example, E. Siberry, 'The Crusading Counts of Nevers', *Nottingham Medieval Studies*, 34 (1990), pp. 64–70; J.S.C. Riley-Smith, 'Family Traditions and Participation in the Second Crusade', *Second Crusade and the Cistercians*, pp. 101–8; J.S.C. Riley-Smith, *The First Crusaders, 1095–1131* (Cambridge, 1997), *passim*.

[31] See Odo of Deuil, *De profectione*, p. 94, where he refers to the prohibition that Eugenius had placed on the crusaders taking dogs and falcons and on the nature of their clothing. Cf. Eugenius III, 'Quantum praedecessores', p. 304; *SBO* 8, Ep. 458, p. 436.

[32] See Odo of Deuil, *De profectione*, pp. 58, 78.

[33] *Ibid.*, pp. 130–2.

[34] Wibald of Stavelot, 'Epistolae', *RHGF* 15, Ep. 2, p. 534.

Nay more, recalling the virtues of our ancestors, we ought to strive to increase the honour and glory of our race rather than cover tarnished glory with the rags of malice. For the glorious deeds of the ancients kept in memory by posterity are the marks of both affection and honour. If you show yourselves [to be] worthy emulators of the ancients, honour and glory will be yours, but if unworthy, then disgraceful reproaches.[35]

It is obvious that the emphasis on the 'deeds of the fathers' within the letters of Bernard and Eugenius had struck a resounding chord with the arms-bearers of western Europe,[36] and their success shows that the two men must have been closely attuned to their audience's mindset.[37] In this context, it is therefore all the more striking that they had not referred directly to the *imitatio Christi* tradition. Indeed, the only biblical *exemplum* that Eugenius had employed in *Quantum praedecessores* was that of Mattathias of the Maccabees – but even then he chose to present his subject not as an example of a warrior who had fought with divine approval,[38] but as an individual who 'did not hesitate at all to relinquish all he had in the world to preserve the laws of his fathers'.[39] Given that their references to the *strenuitas patrum* were so numerous and so forthright, it does not seem logical to conclude that Bernard and Eugenius would have hoped or assumed that their references to the crusade badge would have led their audience to infer a connection to the ideal of *imitatio Christi*. Fortunately, however, the evidence is such that it is not necessary to rely on an argument *ex silentio*, for when the texts of Bernard's letters are analysed closely, the efforts of the Cistercians to redefine crusading ideology become increasingly obvious.

An initial indication of how Bernard was attempting to distance crusading from the *imitatio Christi* tradition can be observed in reference to his choice of language. The Latin verb Bernard used most frequently to describe the adoption of the crusade badge was *suscipere*,[40] but this was not a term that appeared in the Vulgate to express the idea of taking the cross to follow Christ; in Matthew 10:38 it is rendered as *accipere*, Matthew 16:24, Mark 8:34 and Luke 9:23 as *tollere*, and Luke 14:27 as *baiulare*. The frequency with which *suscipere* was used in Bernard's letters – and the fact that the other verbs were conspicuous by their absence – suggests that Bernard was consciously trying to create a new vocabulary for crusading. This was not wholly without success, for in a

---

[35] *De expugnatione Lyxbonensi*, ed. and trans. C. W. David, with a new foreword and bibliography by J.P. Phillips (New York, 2001), pp. 104–7. J.P. Phillips, 'Ideas of Crusade and Holy War in *De expugnatione Lyxbonensi (The Conquest of Lisbon)*', *The Holy Land, Holy Lands, and Christian History*, ed. R.N. Swanson, *SCH*, 36 (Woodbridge, 2000), p. 134, believed that this speech was 'clearly influenced by *Quantum praedecessores*'.

[36] Cf. Constable, 'Second Crusade', p. 253, n. 205.

[37] See, for example, S. Barton, *The Aristocracy in Twelfth-Century León and Castile* (Cambridge, 1997), pp. 3, 42–6, where it is argued that the aristocratic classes of León and Castile were increasingly becoming aware of a sense of lineage and family heritage in the twelfth century.

[38] For the early use of Maccabean imagery in crusade literature, see Riley-Smith, *The First Crusade*, pp. 91–2. See also *Papsturkunden für Templer und Johanniter*, ed. R. Hiestand, 2 vols. (Göttingen, 1972–84), vol. 1, no. 8, p. 215.

[39] Eugenius III, 'Quantum praedecessores', p. 303.

[40] See, for example, *SBO* 8, Ep. 363, p. 315; Ep. 457, p. 433; Ep. 458, p. 436. See also Nicholas of Clairvaux, 'Epistolae in persona S. Bernardi', *PL* 182, Ep. 467, col. 672.

letter from an unidentified 'W.' to King Louis VII, one individual, who styled himself as *dux et miles et servus crucis*, described his desire to 'take the cross (*suscipere*) from the hands of the most holy abbot of Clairvaux'.[41] Nevertheless, given that many of the preachers who used Bernard's letters would have been relying on vernacular translations rather than on the original Latin texts,[42] it could be argued that such linguistic subtleties were inconsequential. However, the most striking innovation in Bernard's 'preaching of the cross' was not in the verbs that he used to describe the act, but in his portrayal of the significance of the crusade badge itself. Indeed, on close examination it is evident that Bernard's understanding of crusading spirituality was quite different to that attributed to Pope Urban II.[43]

It has already been described above how, at the Council of Clermont, Urban was understood to have instituted the crusade badge as a *signum mortificationis*[44] and a *stigma passionis dominicae*.[45] In this way, the sign of the cross was presented as a symbol of the crusader's *imitatio Christi*, and Urban was understood to have stressed that it was through the crusader's Christo-mimetic efforts and acts of self-sacrifice that he would earn a satisfactory penance.[46] The emphasis in Bernard's preaching was quite different. He portrayed the cross as a *signum vitae*, which was symbolic of the crusade indulgence, the unique gift that God was offering to those who responded to the perilous situation he had contrived to bring about in the East:

> [God] puts himself into a position of necessity, or feigns to do so, so that he can give back rewards to those fighting for him: forgiveness of sins (*indulgentia delictorum*) and eternal glory. Therefore I call blessed this generation that can take hold of a time of such indulgence, to be alive in such a jubilee year that is pleasing to the Lord. The blessing is spread throughout the whole world, and everyone is flocking to this sign of life.[47]

In Bernard's soteriology the crusader was not therefore participating in a self-sanctifying act, but was being shown the mercy of God.[48] That Bernard was not alone in advocating this new theology of the cross is shown by the appearance of similar phrasing in the letters of two of his closest associates. Pope Eugenius, who as Bernardo Pignatelli

---

[41] 'Un document sur Saint Bernard et la seconde croisade', ed. J. Leclercq, *Revue Mabillon*, 43 (1953), p. 2. Leclercq suggested that the most likely candidate for authorship was Welf VI, duke of Bavaria, and that the letter should probably be dated to March or April 1147.

[42] See *SBO* 8, Ep. 458, pp. 436–7. See also *De expugnatione*, p. 70, which records the presence of translators amongst the northern crusaders who fought at Lisbon.

[43] Cf. Constable, 'Second Crusade', pp. 249–52; É. Delaruelle, 'L'idée de croisade chez Saint Bernard', *Mélanges Saint Bernard* (Dijon, 1953), pp. 53–67.

[44] Ekkehard of Aura, 'Hierosolymita', *RHC Oc.* 5, p. 19.

[45] Guibert of Nogent, 'Dei gesta per Francos', ed. R.B.C. Huygens, *CC:CM* 127 A (Turnhout, 1996), p. 117.

[46] See Riley-Smith, *The First Crusade*, pp. 27–9; M. Bull, *Knightly Piety and the Lay Response to the First Crusade: The Limousin and Gascony, c.970–c.1130* (Oxford, 1993), pp. 166–71.

[47] *SBO* 8, Ep. 363, p. 314; cf. Ep. 458, p. 435. For the Bernardine indulgence, see J.S.C. Riley-Smith, *What were the Crusades?*, 3rd edition (Basingstoke, 2002), pp. 62–4.

[48] Riley-Smith, *The Crusades*, p. 124, believed that 'with Eugenius and Bernard the emphasis shifted from the penitent's self-imposed punishment to God's merciful kindness'.

had been a former pupil of the abbot of Clairvaux,[49] described the crusade badge as the *signum vivificae crucis*,[50] and Nicholas of Clairvaux, who was one of Bernard's secretaries,[51] referred to the cross as a *signum salutis*.[52] It is apparent, therefore, that short of abandoning the sign of the cross as the crusade badge altogether the Cistercians were making every possible effort to dissociate crusading from the ideal of the imitation of Christ, and were using the opportunity to institute a completely new understanding of the crusader's spiritual privileges.

Although a number of contemporary writers picked up on Bernard's use of *suscipere* to describe the act of taking the cross,[53] the evidence presented in Chapter Three has already shown that the efforts of the Cistercians to redefine the significance of the crusade badge were not successful, for the idea that the second crusaders were imitators of Christ appears to have been widespread outside Bernard's inner circle. With the benefit of hindsight, this is not surprising. Given that Bernard and Eugenius had made repeated efforts to draw a connection between the First and Second Crusades, they perhaps ought to have expected that their preaching would inadvertently trigger the memory of the Christo-mimetic spirituality of the First Crusade. Indeed, the Cistercians were certainly not the only ones alive to the idea of reviving the achievements of the past, and it is striking how far the circumstances surrounding the launch of the Second Crusade coincided with commemoration of the triumphs of 1096–9.[54] It has been suggested, for example, that the 'crusading window' of St Denis,[55] which included depictions of the first crusaders' siege and capture of Jerusalem, ought to be dated to the mid-1140s;[56] it would certainly have provided a suitable backdrop to the ceremony Louis VII took part in before his departure for the East.[57] It has also been shown that Louis's chaplain, Odo of Deuil, may well have consulted narrative histories of the First Crusade such as the *Gesta Francorum* and the *Liber* of Raymond of Aguilers as part of his preparations for the expedition.[58] Furthermore, Jay Rubenstein has recently argued that Louis VII's crusading piety was cultivated by his reading of a manuscript that he had been presented in 1137 by an individual called William Grassegals, who claimed to have been a first crusader.[59] The manuscript included the First Crusade narratives of Fulcher

---

[49] See J.N.D. Kelly, *The Oxford Dictionary of Popes* (Oxford, 1986), pp. 172–3.

[50] Eugenius III, 'Epistolae', no. 166, col. 1203.

[51] See J. Leclercq, 'Saint Bernard et ses secrétaires', *Revue bénédictine*, 61 (1950), p. 220.

[52] Nicholas of Clairvaux, 'Epistolae', no. 467, col. 672. Cf. *SBO* 8, Ep. 457, p. 433.

[53] See, for example, 'Cartulaire de l'abbaye de Saint-Sulpice-la-Forêt', ed. P. Anger, *Bulletin et mémoires de la Société Archéologique d'Ille-et-Vilaine*, 35 (1906), no. 51, p. 350; Odo of Deuil, *De profectione*, p. 8; Leclercq, 'Un document', p. 2. See also *Papsturkunden für Templer und Johanniter*, vol. 1, no. 53, p. 253; Alexander III, 'Epistolae et privilegia', *PL* 200, nos. 626 and 1504, cols. 601, 1295.

[54] On the 'post-history' of the First Crusade, see now Phillips, *The Second Crusade*, pp. 17–36.

[55] See E.A.R. Brown and M.W. Cothren, 'The Twelfth-Century Crusading Window of the Abbey of Saint-Denis', *Journal of the Warburg and Courtauld Institutes*, 49 (1986), pp. 1–40.

[56] For the date, see J.P. Phillips, *Defenders of the Holy Land: Relations between the Latin East and the West, 1119–1187* (Oxford, 1996), p. 107.

[57] See Odo of Deuil, *De profectione*, pp. 14–19.

[58] See J.P. Phillips, 'Odo of Deuil's *De profectione Ludovici VII in Orientem* as a Source for the Second Crusade', *The Experience of Crusading, Volume One: Western Approaches*, ed. M. Bull and N. Housley (Cambridge, 2003), pp. 83–4.

[59] J. Rubenstein, 'Putting History to Use: Three Crusade Chronicles in Context', *Viator*, 35 (2004),

of Chartres and Raymond of Aguilers, and opened with a dedicatory letter in which the donor referred to the 'miracle' of the liberation of Jerusalem and encouraged Louis to be mindful of the deeds of his predecessors:

> I, W. Grassegals by name, from the country of Vélay, knight by rank, devoted to the edifice of the church of Blessed Mary of Le Puy, and rejoicing in the Lord to have been present at the grace of the aforesaid victory [in the East], propose to give to you, Lord Louis, most glorious king of the Franks as well as most victorious Duke of Aquitaine, this book, outstanding in its presentation and description of such admirable material. In this way you might look in this book with the eye of reason as if in a mirror at the images of your ancestors – Hugh the Great, Robert Count of Flanders, and others – and you might follow their footsteps on the path of virtue.[60]

Rubenstein's thesis is tempting, and if he is correct it would imply that ideas of *imitatio Christi* would have been at the heart of Louis VII's thinking on crusading spirituality for some time before the preaching of Eugenius III and Bernard of Clairvaux in 1145–7. Indeed, as Rubenstein himself points out, the manuscript illumination of Christ suffering on the cross (fol. 27r) would certainly have provided Louis with a stirring image 'of what it meant to travel east as a pilgrim-warrior and campaign there against the enemies of the faith'.[61] In short, the atmosphere of commemoration that was manifest in the 1140s,[62] and to which Eugenius and Bernard had unquestionably contributed, must surely have played a part in the Cistercians' failure to communicate their message successfully.

It may be that Bernard had hoped that his preaching of the cross as a *signum vitae* in an *annus iubileus* would prove more powerful than the more literalistic interpretation that had been offered at Clermont by Urban II. If this was the case, Bernard would have grossly underestimated the spiritual charge of Christo-mimetic warfare in the Holy Land for the arms-bearers of the West. It is probably closer to the truth to judge that his subtle use of Scripture and advanced theology of the cross was simply beyond the intellectual reach of most of his contemporaries,[63] and in some respects the fact that the sign of the cross continued to be so loaded with the symbolism of *imitatio Christi* fifty years after the proclamation of the First Crusade is testimony more to Pope Urban's ingenuity than to Bernard's failings. Nevertheless, the fact that the Cistercians were demonstrably attempting to redefine the significance of the crusade badge still begs the question why they were preaching the spirituality of crusading in different terms to those that had been used so effectively in 1095–6.

One possible explanation for the omission of ideas of Christo-mimesis in the Cistercian preaching of the Second Crusade may be the strategic vision that Eugenius and Bernard evidently had for the conflict.[64] In *Divina dispensatione II* (April 1147), Eugenius described how campaigns were being initiated against the enemies of the cross of

---

pp. 131–68. For the date, see *ibid.*, pp. 150–2.

[60] *Ibid.*, p. 134. For the Latin, see Fulcher of Chartres, *Historia Hierosolymitana (1095–1127)*, ed. H. Hagenmeyer (Heidelberg, 1913), p. 827.

[61] Rubenstein, 'Three Crusade Chronicles', pp. 159–60, 168.

[62] See also M. Bull, 'The Capetian Monarchy and the Early Crusade Movement: Hugh of Vermandois and Louis VII', *Nottingham Medieval Studies*, 40 (1996), pp. 25–46.

[63] Cf. Cole, *Preaching of the Crusades*, p. 61.

[64] See Constable, 'Second Crusade', pp. 255–6.

Christ on a number of fronts, and he indicated that those crusaders who fought *contra Saracenos* in Iberia or *contra Sclavos* in the Baltic would receive the same spiritual privileges as those who set out for the Holy Land;[65] Bernard reiterated this position when he wrote to assure the crusaders in the North that they would be rewarded with 'the same forgiveness of sins as those who set out towards Jerusalem'.[66] The multi-directional scope of the crusade was also widely noted by contemporaries. Most famously, the chronicler Helmold of Bosau confirmed that 'To its initiators it seemed that one part of the army should be sent to the eastern regions, another to Spain, and a third against the Slavs who live next to us,'[67] and he later wrote of the conquest of Lisbon that 'this alone was successful of the entire work which the pilgrim army (*peregrinus exercitus*) achieved'.[68]

The extension of crusading against the pagans of the Baltic was a new development in the movement's history in 1147,[69] but it is clear that attempts to persuade the arms-bearers of Iberia of the legitimacy of crusading against the Muslims of al-Andalus had been fraught with difficulty since the early twelfth century. As will be suggested in Chapter Five, this was in large part owing to the unique attraction of the idea that the crusade was a Christo-mimetic Jerusalem pilgrimage-in-arms, with which penitential warfare that took place away from the Holy Land could not possibly compare. Given the renewed devotional significance that the Holy Land had taken on in the first half of the twelfth century, it therefore seems possible that the Cistercian attempts to isolate crusading warfare from ideas of *imitatio Christi* may have been the result of an acute awareness of the desire of western arms-bearers to follow Christ by fighting 'in the place where his feet have stood', and of a desire to detach crusading from its Jerusalem-centric roots so that it might be propagated more effectively in other theatres of war.

Whilst this idea is not wholly without merit, two factors militate against it being a fully satisfactory explanation. First of all, the inclusion of the campaigns that were being fought in Iberia and the Baltic in the scope of the crusade cannot be proved to have been part of the strategists' thinking from the outset. It seems certain that crusade privileges were only extended to the Baltic in response to a direct local appeal, for Otto of Freising wrote that 'the Saxons, refusing to set out for the East because they had as neighbours certain tribes who were devoted to the obscenity of idolatry, took the cross in the same way so that they might proceed against these tribes in war'.[70] Similarly, it is clear that any help that Bernard of Clairvaux may have enlisted for Afonso Henriques's siege of Lisbon was in reply to a request from the Portuguese king. As Bernard wrote, 'we have received the letters and greetings of your Highness . . . What we have done in this matter will be revealed by the outcome, as you will see for yourself'.[71] A comparable series of events

---

[65] Eugenius III, 'Epistolae', no. 166, col. 1203.

[66] *SBO* 8, Ep. 457, p. 433.

[67] Helmold of Bosau, 'Chronica Slavorum', *MGH SS* 21, p. 57. See Constable, 'Second Crusade', p. 223.

[68] Helmold of Bosau, 'Chronica Slavorum', p. 58.

[69] See Constable, 'Second Crusade', p. 257; Riley-Smith, *The Crusades*, pp. 123–4; I.M. Fonnesberg-Schmidt, *The Popes and the Baltic Crusades, 1147–1254* (Leiden, 2007), pp. 27–43.

[70] Otto of Freising, *Gesta Friderici*, p. 61.

[71] *SBO* 8, Ep. 308, p. 228. See H. Livermore, 'The "Conquest of Lisbon" and its Author', *Portuguese Studies*, 6 (1990), pp. 1–16; J.P. Phillips, 'St Bernard of Clairvaux, The Low Countries and the Lisbon

must also have taken place in reference to the campaigns that were being waged on the peninsula's east coast by Alfonso VII of León-Castile, for in 1148 Pope Eugenius wrote that he had 'willingly allowed . . . [the king] to make an expedition against the tyranny of the infidels'.[72] The propagation of the Second Crusade across such a wide geographical area was therefore a reaction to developing circumstances in the mid-1140s rather than an ambitious project formulated in the papal curia, and it is therefore implausible that Eugenius and Bernard would have felt the need to begin to separate crusading from its geographical origins in the East as early as March 1146. Indeed, that this cannot possibly have been a consideration is evident from the tone of their letters themselves, from which it is obvious that every effort was being made to channel the geopiety associated with Jerusalem and the Holy Sepulchre into recruitment for the crusade.

Even the most cursory examination of the letters of Eugenius and Bernard reveals that the Cistercians were sensitive to the unique importance of the Holy Land as a relic of the life of Christ. Reference has already been made to the fact that in *Quantum praedecessores* Eugenius had described Jerusalem as 'that city in which it was our Saviour's will to suffer for us and where he left us with his glorious Sepulchre as a memorial of his Passion',[73] but the most striking examples of how the Cistercians were harnessing the idea of defending the Holy Land can be found in the letters of Bernard:

> The earth is troubled and shaken because the Lord of heaven has begun to lose his land, the land in which he was seen, and in which he lived among men for more than thirty years. His land, which he honoured with his birth, glorified with his miracles, sanctified with his blood and enriched with his tomb. His land, in which the voice of the turtledove was heard, when the son of the Virgin praised the life of chastity. His land, in which the flowers of his resurrection first blossomed.[74]

The emphasis on the geopiety of the Holy Land was also evident in the letters of Nicholas of Clairvaux, who made use of several of the stock phrases that were also a feature of his master's letters. In a letter addressed to the count and nobles of Brittany in April or May 1146, Nicholas wrote that:

> The earth is troubled and shaken because the king of heaven has lost his land, the land *where his feet have stood*. The enemies of his cross . . . are working to destroy the places of our redemption, and they are straining to profane the places sanctified by Christ's blood; chief amongst those places of the Christian religion is the Sepulchre in which the Lord of all was buried, and where his funeral shroud was bound together. All of these things they are striving to pull down.[75]

Letter of the Second Crusade', *Journal of Ecclesiastical History*, 48 (1997), pp. 485–97. But see also A.J. Forey, 'The Siege of Lisbon and the Second Crusade', *Portuguese Studies*, 20 (2004), pp. 1–13.

[72] Eugenius III, 'Epistolae', no. 296, col. 1346. See J.F. O'Callaghan, *Reconquest and Crusade in Medieval Spain* (Philadelphia, PA, 2003), pp. 44–6.

[73] Eugenius III, 'Quantum praedecessores', p. 302.

[74] *SBO* 8, Ep. 458, p. 435. See also Ep. 363, p. 312. On this passage, see Riley-Smith, *The Crusades*, p. 122.

[75] Nicholas of Clairvaux, 'Epistolae', no. 467, col. 671. See also the language of his letter to the Byzantine Emperor, *ibid.*, no. 468, cols. 672–3.

These examples show that for Bernard and his associates the crusade was not just an opportunity to gain spiritual privileges by fighting for God, irrespective of the theatre of conflict, but that it was also understood to be imperative that the arms-bearers of the West defend the landmarks of Christian tradition. Indeed, the emphasis placed in the Cistercian preaching on the importance of the earthly Jerusalem has frequently been underestimated,[76] for it is clear that they were deeply concerned to protect the holy places in the Levant. In this respect, Bernard's crusade letters of 1146–7 expressed the same affection and concern for the Holy Land that he had earlier expressed in his *De laude novae militiae*.[77] In that treatise, for example, he had highlighted the especial significance of the Holy Sepulchre for the devotional experiences of western Christians:

> I think that it is not just the sweetness of ordinary devotion that is poured out when one is contemplating on the physical resting place of the Lord, even if it is only with physical eyes . . . How sweet it is for pilgrims after the great fatigue of their long journey, and the many dangers on land and sea, to find peace at last in that place where they know very well that their own Lord found peace! I think that at that moment, because of their delight, they do not feel the hardship of the road or calculate the inconvenience of the costs, but grasp the reward for their effort and the prize of the journey, according to the words of Scripture: *They rejoice exceedingly when they have found the tomb*.[78]

Similarly, Bernard acknowledged elsewhere that the patriarch of Jerusalem was especially favoured by God because 'You alone . . . have been chosen by the Lord to be his own bishop . . . you enter his tabernacle every single day, and you *adore him in the place where his feet have stood*'.[79] In this context, Bernard must therefore be seen to have been demanding of second crusaders that they offer a temporary contribution to the defence of the Holy Land, a cause to which the Templars had dedicated their lives: 'These delights of the world, this treasury of heaven, this inheritance of all faithful people is yours, most beloved believers of the faith. It is entrusted to your wisdom and strength.'[80]

Although the idea of reaching the heavenly Jerusalem was not entirely absent in Bernard's preaching for the Second Crusade – he wrote that the *via Ierosolimitana* was not to be closed to those who fought in the Baltic, for example[81] – it is striking that it was the earthly Jerusalem that was paramount in his thinking when recruiting for the expedition to the East. In this respect, there is no trace of his trying to convince second crusaders who vowed to fight for Christ in the East that 'the praiseworthy thing is not

---

[76] Cf. A. Jotischky, *The Perfection of Solitude: Hermits and Monks in the Crusader States* (University Park, PA, 1995), p. 12, who argued that 'Bernard's emphasis is not on the defense of the holy places . . . but on the necessary spiritual benefits of the crusade for the participants'. See also Constable, 'Second Crusade', p. 247; Katzir, 'Second Crusade', p. 9; S. Schein, *Gateway to the Heavenly City: Crusader Jerusalem and the Catholic West (1099–1187)* (Aldershot, 2005), pp. 121–2.

[77] For Bernard's concern for the Latin East, see also his letters to Queen Melisende, *SBO* 8, Ep. 206, p. 65; Ep. 289, pp. 205–6; Ep. 254, pp. 297–8; Ep. 255, p. 299.

[78] Bernard of Clairvaux, 'Liber ad milites Templi de laude novae militiae', *SBO* 3, p. 236. Citation from Job 3:22.

[79] *SBO* 8, Ep. 393, p. 365.

[80] *SBO* 3, p. 239.

[81] *SBO* 8, Ep. 457, p. 433.

to have been to Jerusalem, but to have lived a good life while on the way'.[82] Bernard's preaching for the Second Crusade did not attempt to modify the increased devotional attachment to the physicality of the Holy Land; rather, he was directly tapping into the fervent geopiety that had developed in the West since the liberation of Jerusalem in 1099. Consequently, it does not follow that the reason he was moving to isolate crusading from ideas of Christo-mimesis was because he was trying to play down the geographical significance of the earthly Jerusalem in his preaching; indeed, if anything, it renders the absence of the ideal of *imitatio* all the more striking.

In order to understand why Bernard and his associates were consciously trying to institute a new theology of the cross it is expedient to examine contemporary Cistercian perspectives on the ideal of *imitatio Christi* itself. To conduct a full study of such perspectives here would of course be impractical, and the analysis that follows is restricted to sources that are relevant to the relationship between crusading, pilgrimage and monasticism. In this way, it will be shown that the main reason the Cistercians placed such a premium on the earthly Jerusalem was because they believed it might lead Christians to contemplate and strive for the heavenly city.[83] To do that, however, required a lifetime's votive commitment, and it will be argued that the Cistercians believed that it was only those who abandoned the world for full religious profession who could truly be considered to be *imitatores Christi*.

Bernard of Clairvaux, imitatio Christi *and the Templars*

It has already been observed that Bernard of Clairvaux's presentation of the crusade badge as a *signum vitae* denoted a shift away from the literal interpretation of Matthew 16:24 that Urban II was said to have offered at the Council of Clermont in 1095. Indeed, it is noteworthy that in another context Bernard wrote that 'a literal reading [of Scripture] should not lead us to presuppose the spiritual meaning'.[84] On closer examination it would seem that Bernard's desire to move away from the association between crusading and the ideal of *imitatio Christi* of Matthew 16:24 was almost certainly related to his interpretation of another biblical passage, 2 Corinthians 5:16: 'Wherefore henceforth, we know no man after the flesh (*secundum carnem*). And if we have known Christ after the flesh, now we know him so no longer.' As Colin Morris has shown,[85] for Bernard, this verse did not just refer to the understanding of the saviour's human sufferings that was cultivated by physical contact with the relics and sites of the Passion: it was also a call for all Christians to advance to a deeper knowledge of Christ's divinity. In this way, Bernard believed that devotion to Christ's humanity, which was endemic in crusading

---

[82] *De expugnatione*, pp. 78–9.

[83] Cf. P. Raedts, 'St Bernard of Clairvaux and Jerusalem', *Prophecy and Eschatology*, ed. M. Wilks, SCH Subsidia, 10 (Oxford, 1994), pp. 169–82.

[84] *SBO* 3, p. 219.

[85] C. Morris, 'Christ after the Flesh: 2 Corinthians 5.16 in the Fathers and in the Middle Ages', *The Ampleforth Journal*, 80 (1975), pp. 44–51. I am grateful to Professor Morris for providing me with this reference. See also M.L. Dutton, 'Intimacy and Imitation: The Humanity of Christ in Cistercian Spirituality', *Erudition at God's Service*, ed. J.R. Sommerfeldt, *Studies in Cistercian Medieval History*, 11 (Kalamazoo, MI, 1987), pp. 33–69.

and pilgrimage spirituality in the first half of the twelfth century,[86] was but a precursor to spiritual advancement and maturity:

> I think this is the principal reason that the invisible God willed to be seen in the flesh and to converse with men as a man. He wanted to recapture the affections of carnal men who were unable to love in any other way, by first drawing them to the salutary love of his own humanity, and then gradually raising them to a spiritual love.[87]

A crusade or pilgrimage to the East therefore provided Christians with an opportunity to engage with Christ on an elementary level by being present in '*the place where his feet have stood*', but it was only the first step towards the imitation of Christ. As Bernard put it, superficial devotion to Christ 'is most lovely . . . [but] if anyone shall break open the nut, he shall find within what is still more pleasant and far more delightful'.[88]

Examples of how these principles were enacted can be seen in two of Bernard's other letters that make reference to the Second Crusade. The first of these was addressed to the sister of Henry de Stopho, a second crusader who had chosen to join the Cistercian order rather than fulfil his crusade vow.[89] Bernard began his letter by acknowledging that the crusade was a virtuous activity for those who sought to aid their salvation, but he went on to recall the story of Mary and Martha (Luke 10:38–42) to demonstrate to Henry's sister how her brother's profession into the Cistercian order meant that he had chosen 'with Mary the best part'.[90] Thus instead of seeking the earthly Jerusalem with the second crusaders, Henry was understood to have 'turned his face towards that true Jerusalem' by adopting the contemplative life. In this respect, the passage echoed the tone of a letter to which reference was made in Chapter One, in which Bernard informed the bishop of Lincoln that one of his parishioners had completed his Jerusalem pilgrimage without ever setting foot in the Holy Land by remaining with Bernard at Clairvaux.[91] However, in the letter that relates to Henry de Stopho, Bernard made it clear that, by joining the Cistercian order, it was through the imitation of Christ that his subject had chosen to seek out the heavenly Jerusalem:

> He has not put aside the intention with which he took the sign [of the cross], he has done something far better: he has become poor for the poor Christ, and he has set out to return, under the habit of religion, to the house of the poor Christ.[92]

---

[86] See also C. Morris, *The Papal Monarchy: The Western Church from 1050 to 1250* (Oxford, 1989), pp. 376–8.

[87] Bernard of Clairvaux, 'Sermones super Cantica Canticorum', *SBO* 1, p. 118. Cited in Dutton, 'Intimacy and Imitation', p. 39.

[88] Bernard of Clairvaux, 'Sermones', *SBO* 4, p. 320. Cited in Morris, 'Christ after the Flesh', p. 50.

[89] *SBO* 8, Ep. 459, p. 437.

[90] See G. Constable, 'The Interpretation of Mary and Martha', *Three Studies in Medieval Religious and Social Thought* (Cambridge, 1995), pp. 1–141.

[91] *SBO* 7, Ep. 64, pp. 157–8. See above, pp. 14–15.

[92] *SBO* 8, Ep. 459, p. 437. See G. Constable, '*Nudus nudum Christum sequi* and Parallel Formulas in the Twelfth Century: A Supplementary Dossier', *Continuity and Discontinuity in Church History: Essays Presented to George Hunston Williams on the Occasion of his 65th Birthday*, ed. F. Forrester Church and T. George, *Studies in the History of Christian Thought*, 19 (Leiden, 1979), pp. 83–91.

A still more striking example of Bernard's very precise understanding of the ideal of *imitatio Christi* can be seen in a letter he addressed in the mid-1140s to his fellow Cistercian abbots. He began by expressing his deep affection for his Cistercian brothers, and stated that he shared not only in their joys but also in their hardships. The latest of these hardships, it would seem, was that 'certain brethren . . . have scorned our holy way of life and are striving to embroil themselves in the turmoil of the world'. This was a reference to the desire of certain Cistercian monks and lay brethren to abandon the Order to join the armies of the Second Crusade – behaviour which Bernard knew to be contrary to the nature of the vows they had sworn:

> Why do you seek the glory of the world when you have chosen to lie forgotten in the house of God? Why are you wandering through the countryside when you are professed to lead a life of solitude? Why do you sew the cross on your clothes, when you always carry it (*baiulare*) in your heart, if you keep the religious life?[93]

Bernard's belief that 'the object of monks is to seek out not the earthly but the heavenly Jerusalem, and this not by proceeding with their feet but by progressing with their feelings' has already been quoted,[94] but in the final question that he put to his Cistercian brethren one can sense his frustration at their failure to understand the subtleties of his crusade preaching and the nature of their own devotional commitments. This letter makes it clear that, for Bernard, the imitation of Christ was (quite literally) at the heart of the monastic life, and that the crusade badge was intended to be symbolic of a quite different spirituality. For a member of the Cistercian order to abandon the heavenly for the earthly Jerusalem was therefore a patently retrograde step,[95] and revealed a palpable misunderstanding of the ideal of *imitatio Christi* itself. It is therefore no surprise that Bernard demanded that all those monks or lay brothers who joined the crusade should be excommunicated.

The evidence considered above suggests that Bernard believed the only true way to follow Christ and to go beyond 'fleshly' knowledge was to renounce the secular world for full religious profession.[96] In this respect, the crusade – whilst undeniably helpful and meritorious – was too elementary, because it was a temporary form of lay devotion that emphasised the primacy of the earthly over the heavenly Jerusalem. Nevertheless, Bernard's letters should not lead one to conclude that he believed the imitation of Christ to be restricted to the contemplative life, for by the mid-twelfth century the idea of 'full religious profession' was no longer solely equated with the traditional Benedictine model of coenobitic monasticism that Bernard and the Cistercians exemplified. Indeed, when one considers the language that Bernard used to promote the Order of the Temple, which was perhaps the most innovative of the new religious orders that

---

[93] *SBO* 8, Ep. 544, pp. 511–12.

[94] *SBO* 8, Ep. 399, pp. 379–80.

[95] See also Bernard's letters concerning the pilgrimage of the Cistercian abbot of Morimond, Arnold, in 1124. *SBO* 7, Ep. 4, 5, 6 and 7, pp. 24–46.

[96] Cf. *Libellus de diversis ordinibus et professionibus qui sunt in aecclesia*, ed. and trans. G. Constable and B.S. Smith, revised edition (Oxford, 2003), pp. 38–41, whose author wrote of the Cistercians that 'They so live in their houses that, remaining in the flesh, since they forsake and transcend the fleshly, they are justly said to be above the flesh. Let anyone who sees them wonder at such a change in human infirmity, for though they are on the earth they are said to be not of it.'

were founded in the eleventh and twelfth centuries, it becomes clear that he believed that the way of life of the Templar presented the Christian arms-bearer with a unique opportunity to follow Christ by making a lifetime's votive commitment to the perform-ance of acts of sacred violence. In this way, Bernard understood the spirituality of the Templar to be quite distinct from that of the crusader.

The Order of the Temple was established in Jerusalem in 1120 by a group of knights, led by Hugh of Payns, who sought to provide protection for pilgrims travelling in the Holy Land.[97] As the contemporary accounts of Jerusalem pilgrims attest,[98] they were undertaking a most necessary role; indeed, the foundation of the Templars was but one of a series of measures being implemented by western Christians to provide a new infrastructure for the growing numbers of pilgrims who were travelling to the Levant, especially in the wake of the liberation of Jerusalem in 1099.[99] The most significant other contemporary foundation was the Order of the Hospital of St John of Jerusa-lem,[100] whose independence was confirmed in the papal decree *Pie postulatio voluntatis* in 1113, wherein it was stated that the role of the Hospitaller was to see to 'the support of pilgrims and to the needs of the poor'.[101] Nevertheless, although the Hospital would later take on a broader responsibility for the welfare of the Jerusalem pilgrim after its militarisation (probably in the mid-1120s),[102] it was the Temple that was the first military order to combine martial action with spiritual contemplation, and thus it was the Templar who could first claim to be 'a religious man who goes forward as an armed knight . . . [to] kill the enemy without blame'.[103]

Contemporaries were certainly aware of the novelty of the Templars' way of life. In the Order's *Primitive Rule*, which was drawn up in Latin at the Council of Troyes in 1129,[104] the Templars were described as a 'new kind of religion' (*novum genus religionis*) and a 'knighthood of religion' (*milicia religionis*).[105] Similarly, in his *De laude novae mili-tiae* (1129x31),[106] Bernard of Clairvaux wrote that 'This is a new kind of knighthood, unknown to previous generations, in which twofold warfare (*conflictus geminus*) is fought ceaselessly and in equal measure, against both flesh and blood [on earth] and against evil spirits in the heavens'.[107] The idea that the Templars were engaged in 'twofold warfare' was of the utmost importance, and in c.1129 Guigo of La Grande Chartreuse wrote to Hugh of Payns to offer guidance on how the Templars might balance the active and

---

[97] William of Tyre, *Chronicon*, ed. R.B.C. Huygens, *CC:CM* 63, 63 A (Turnhout, 1986), pp. 553–5.

[98] *Jerusalem Pilgrimage 1099–1185* ed. and trans. J. Wilkinson, J. Hill and W.F. Ryan (London, 1988), pp. 100, 101, 112–13, 126, 149–50, 156, 160.

[99] See M. Barber, 'The Charitable and Medical Activities of the Hospitallers and Templars', *A History of Pastoral Care*, ed. G.R. Evans (London, 2000), pp. 148–68.

[100] See especially J.S.C. Riley-Smith, *The Knights of St John in Jerusalem and Cyprus, c.1050–1310* (London, 1967).

[101] *Papsturkunden für Templer und Johanniter*, vol. 2, no. 1, p. 195.

[102] See Riley-Smith, *First Crusaders*, p. 163.

[103] *Die ursprüngliche Templerregel*, ed. G. Schnürer (Freiburg, 1903), p. 147.

[104] See M. Barber, *The New Knighthood: A History of the Order of the Temple* (Cambridge, 1994), pp. 14–18.

[105] *Die ursprüngliche Templerregel*, p. 147.

[106] For the date, see D. Carlson, 'The Practical Theology of St Bernard and the Date of the *De laude novae militiae*', *Erudition at God's Service*, pp. 133–47.

[107] *SBO* 3, p. 214.

contemplative aspects of their devotions:

> It is, of course, a mistake if we wage war on external enemies and do not transcend internal ones first . . . We must therefore conquer ourselves, O most beloved brethren, so that we may go forth to fight external enemies securely. Let us rid our minds of vices before we purge our lands from pagans.[108]

Such language was of course reminiscent of ideas that were present in some of the narrative histories of the First Crusade,[109] and it is well documented that the devotional warfare of the Templars was associated with the ideological foundations of the crusading movement.[110] The substantial difference, however, was that where the First Crusade had seen the fusion of meritorious warfare and penitential pilgrimage, the devotions of the Templars associated holy war with professed religion; where the first crusaders had fought for God and the Holy Sepulchre for a limited period, the Templars had committed themselves to fight *infatigabiliter*.[111] In this way, the Templars formalised the concept that the first crusaders had followed a quasi-monastic way of life.[112] Indeed, where writers such as Guibert of Nogent and Robert of Rheims had described the first crusaders as being more like monks than knights,[113] in regarding the Templars Bernard of Clairvaux believed that the religious and secular ways of life had merged beyond distinction:

> Thus in a wonderful and unique way they are distinguished [from other arms-bearers] by being meeker than lambs but fiercer than lions. I am in doubt as to whether it would be preferable to call them monks or knights, unless perhaps it would be proper to refer to them as both. For it is to be understood that they lack neither the gentleness of the monk nor the strength of the soldier.[114]

Bernard's great intellectual rival, Peter the Venerable, made a similar observation some twenty years later when he asked of the Temple's third master, Everard of Barres:

> Who will not rejoice, who will not exult that you have not just gone forth to a single conflict, but to a double one, just as the apostle says, in which you fight *against spiritual wickedness* with the virtues of the heart, and against physical enemies with the strength of your bodies. In one of these you have assumed all of the qualities of holy monks and hermits; in the other you have exceeded the intention of all professed religious . . . You are monks by your virtues and knights by your deeds, filling one role spiritually and exercising the other physically.[115]

---

[108] *Lettres des premiers Chartreux*, 2 vols. (Paris, 1962–80), vol. 1, Ep. 2, p. 154.

[109] See Riley-Smith, *The First Crusade*, pp. 119, 147.

[110] See A.J. Forey, 'The Emergence of the Military Order in the Twelfth Century', *Journal of Ecclesiastical History*, 36 (1985), pp. 175–95. See also J.S.C. Riley-Smith, *What were the Crusades?*, 3rd edition (Harlow, 2002), pp. 82–3.

[111] *SBO* 3, p. 214.

[112] See J.A. Brundage, 'Crusades, Clerics and Violence: Reflections on a Canonical Theme', *Experience of Crusading, Volume One*, pp. 147–56.

[113] See Riley-Smith, *The First Crusade*, pp. 150–2, 154–5.

[114] *SBO* 3, p. 221.

[115] *The Letters of Peter the Venerable*, ed. G. Constable, 2 vols. (Cambridge, MA, 1967), vol. 1, Ep. 172, p. 408. Citation from Ephesians 6:12.

The Templars' way of life was not without its critics, however, and the concern that surrounded the novelty of the Temple as a religious foundation is evident from the letter Hugh *Peccator* sent to the *milites Templi* in 1129.[116] Although the issue of this letter's authorship has not been settled beyond doubt,[117] it seems most likely that its words of encouragement came from the Order's founder, Hugh of Payns, whilst he was seeking recognition for the Templars at the Council of Troyes. The letter provides an intimate insight into the contemporaneous upheavals in the religious landscape of the early twelfth century, and is an important example of how apologists for the new religious orders sought to justify their existence and explain their role in the *ecclesia Dei*. In response to questions of whether the Temple was a legitimate alternative to the more traditional forms of religious life, Hugh *Peccator* was clear:

> See, brothers, if all the members of the body have one function, the body itself is not able to continue at all. Listen to the apostle: *If the foot should say: 'I am not an eye, I am not of the body', is it not therefore of the body?* Those who are the most humble are often of the most use. The foot touches the earth but it carries the whole body. Do not deceive yourselves: each one shall receive his reward according to his work. The roofs of the houses receive the rain and the hail and the wind; but if there were no roofs, what would become of the painted walls?[118]

This acknowledgement of unity in diversity was at the heart of the religious milieu of the period, and Hugh's choice of quotation from 1 Corinthians 12:15 echoed the sense of other commonly cited passages, such as the 'many rooms but one house of God' of John 14:2.[119] As he then went on to state, the Templars' uniqueness was required because no other religious were exclusively committed 'to bearing arms against the enemies of the faith and peace for the defence of Christians'.[120] In this respect, the Templars were understood by apologists to offer an *exemplum* to those *militia saeculari* who were living a life 'in which Christ was not the cause',[121] and the juxtaposition of ideas of *militia* and *malitia* was a central theme in Bernard of Clairvaux's *De laude novae militiae*,[122] where he

---

[116] See A.J. Forey, *The Military Orders from the Twelfth to the Early Fourteenth Centuries* (Basingstoke, 1992), pp. 16–17; B. Smalley, 'Ecclesiastical Attitudes to Novelty, c. 1100–c. 1250', *Church, Society and Politics*, ed. D. Baker, *SCH*, 12 (Oxford, 1975), pp. 113–31.

[117] See C. Sclafert, 'Lettre inédite de Hughes de Saint-Victor aux chevaliers du Temple', *Revue d'ascetique et de mystique*, 34 (1958), pp. 275–99; D. Selwood, 'Quidam autem dubitauerunt: The Saint, the Sinner, the Temple and a Possible Chronology', *Autor de la première croisade: actes du colloque de la Society for the Study of the Crusades and the Latin East 1995*, ed. M. Balard (Paris, 1996), pp. 221–30; S. Cerrini, 'La fondateur de l'ordre du Temple à ses frères: Hugues de Payns et le *Sermo Christi militibus*', *Dei gesta per Francos: Crusade Studies in Honour of Jean Richard*, ed. M. Balard, B.Z. Kedar and J.S.C. Riley-Smith (Aldershot, 2001), pp. 99–110.

[118] 'Un document sur les débuts des Templiers', ed. J. Leclercq, *Revue d'histoire ecclésiastique*, 52 (1957), p. 87. Citation from 1 Corinthians 12:15.

[119] See G. Constable, 'The Diversity of Religious Life and Acceptance of Social Pluralism in the Twelfth Century', *History, Society and the Churches: Essays in Honour of Owen Chadwick*, ed. D. Beales and G. Best (Cambridge, 1985), pp. 38–40.

[120] 'Un document', p. 87.

[121] *Die ursprüngliche Templerregel*, p. 130.

[122] See A. Graboïs, '*Militia* and *Malitia*: The Bernardine Vision of Chivalry', *Second Crusade and the Cistercians*, pp. 49–56.

expounded the inherent virtue of the devotional activities of the Templars:

> And now, as an example (*ad imitationem*), or at least for the humiliation of our knights [of the West] who are clearly not fighting for God but for the Devil, we will describe briefly the customs and life of these knights of Christ. Let us consider how they might behave at home and also in battle, how they might act in public, and in what way the knights of God might be different from those of the world.[123]

In the light of contemporaneous devotional trends it is perhaps not surprising that the ideal of *imitatio Christi* was presented as central to the spirituality of the Templars.[124] Examples of how ideas of Christo-mimesis were applied to various forms of professed religious life in the late eleventh and twelfth centuries have already been provided above,[125] and in some respects the brethren of the Temple were seen to be no different to those who abandoned the world to join new orders such as the Cistercians or Carthusians.[126] However, given the revolutionary nature of their way of life, it is equally unsurprising to find that the Templars' Christo-mimesis was presented as being somewhat more literal than that of the contemplative monk, and in this respect Templar apologists seemed to borrow as much from early crusading spirituality as they did from the ideas of the monastic reformers; indeed, given that the language by which those ideas were expressed was often identical, it is sometimes impossible to know which influence was the more formative. An overlap can be found, for example, in Otto of Freising's description of the origins of the Order:

> Some individuals despised themselves for Christ's sake, and considering that it was not without cause that they wore the belt of military service, set out for Jerusalem, and there they began to undertake a new kind of knighthood by fighting against the enemies of the cross of Christ. By perpetually carrying the mortification of the cross on their bodies they seemed by their life and profession not to be knights but monks.[127]

Like both the cloistered monk and the first crusader, the Templar was therefore understood to have abandoned the world and taken up the cross to follow Christ. In the first of a series of papal privileges granted to the Templars, *Omne datum optimum* (now redated to 1138),[128] Pope Innocent II echoed Baldric of Bourgueil's report of Pope Urban's preaching of the *via Christi* at Clermont by describing how the Templars' renunciation of the world was a dismissal of the 'broad way which leads to death', and he

---

[123] *SBO* 3, p. 219. The idea of teaching by model was of profound importance in the twelfth century; see C. W. Bynum, *Docere verbo et exemplo: An Aspect of Twelfth-Century Spirituality* (Missoula, MT, 1979).

[124] For the spirituality of the military orders, see also T. Licence, 'The Templars and the Hospitallers, Christ and the Saints', *Crusades*, 4 (2005), pp. 39–57.

[125] See above, pp. 22–7.

[126] For a broader discussion of this theme, see now T. Licence, 'The Military Orders as Monastic Orders', *Crusades*, 5 (2006), pp. 39–53.

[127] Otto of Freising, *Chronica sive historia de duabus civitatibus*, ed. A. Hofmeister, *MGH SSRG* 45 (Hanover and Leipzig, 1912), p. 320.

[128] Riley-Smith, *The Crusades*, p. 79.

stated that they had instead chosen to follow the 'hard road which leads to life'.[129] The Templars' adoption of the *arduum iter* was symbolised by the fact that they had 'taken up the Lord's cross', a *signum vivifice crucis* that they always carried on their chests.[130] This idea was also taken up in *Milites Templi* (1144) by Innocent's successor, Pope Celestine II, where a direct reference was made to the Gospel passage that Urban II was reported to have quoted in his preaching of the First Crusade:

> The knights of the Temple of Jerusalem, new Maccabees during a time of grace, relin-quishing worldly desires and abandoning personal possessions, have followed Christ by taking up his cross. It is through them that God liberates the eastern Church from the filth of the pagans, and defeats the enemies of the Christians.[131]

The fact that Matthew 16:24 was applied in this way to the Templars only months before the composition of *Quantum praedecessores* is striking, and renders Eugenius III's omission of the verse from his crusade letters all the more significant; clearly, the papal curia of the mid-1140s had not forgotten how the idea of 'taking Christ's cross' might be applied to those who committed themselves to acts of devotional warfare.

That connections between the Templars and ideas of *imitatio Christi* were also drawn more widely is evident from the language of certain charters that recorded a number of early donations to the Order. By becoming poor for the poor Christ, the Templars were seen to represent a manifestation of the religious poverty that was espoused by so many of the new religious orders,[132] and it was for this reason that they were referred to vari-ously as *pauperes commilitones Christi*[133] and *pauperes milites Templi*.[134] Indeed, on his entry to the Order in 1130, Ramon Berenguer III stated explicitly how he wished to join the Temple because 'the merciful God, who was rich in all things, became poor for me . . . and so I have been made poor for him, so that he might deem me to be worthy of enter-ing into the riches of his glory'.[135] In 1145 another individual declared that he was join-ing the Temple because he was 'wishing to comply [with the Gospel] . . . where it says: *Anyone who does not renounce everything he possesses cannot be my disciple*'.[136] More striking still are the entries in the cartulary of the Templar commandery at Richerenches.[137] In June 1138, a charter drawn up by 'Brother Rostan' to document Hugh of Bourbouton's entry into the Order recorded that:

> In the name of God: I, Hugh of Bourbouton, hearing and needing to fulfil such great precepts of the Lord which are set forth in the Gospel where it says *If any man will come after me, let him deny himself, and take up his cross, and follow me*, hastily attending to

---

[129] *Papsturkunden für Templer und Johanniter*, vol. 1, no. 3, p. 205. Citation from Matthew 7:13–14. Cf. Baldric of Bourgueil, 'Historia Jerosolimitana', *RHC Oc.* 4, p. 15.

[130] *Papsturkunden für Templer und Johanniter*, vol. 1, no. 3, pp. 207, 205.

[131] *Ibid.*, no. 8, p. 215. See also *ibid.*, no. 15, p. 222.

[132] *Die ursprüngliche Templerregel*, p. 151; *SBO* 3, p. 222.

[133] *Cartulaire général de l'ordre du Temple 1119?–1150*, ed. Marquis d'Albon (Paris, 1913), nos. 188 and 244, pp. 129, 165. See also *Die ursprüngliche Templerregel*, pp. 130, 131, 132, 135, 136, 150.

[134] *Cartulaire général de l'ordre du Temple*, nos. 20 and 129, pp. 13, 90.

[135] *Ibid.*, no. 33, p. 25. See also nos. 68 and 207, pp. 51, 144.

[136] *Ibid.*, no. 371, p. 237.

[137] I am grateful to Dr Jochen Schenk for providing me with these references.

the defence of my soul, have seen the way of safety. Truly denying myself, my wife, my son and daughter, my land and my possessions, I present and offer myself to the Lord God, and to Blessed Mary his mother, and to the Poor Knights of the Temple of Christ of Jerusalem . . .[138]

Some time later Brother Rostan drew up a similarly worded document for another donor, Bertrand *de Balmis*. By this point, however, the scribe obviously deemed that anyone consulting the cartulary would be so familiar with the association of Matthew 16:24 and recruitment to the Temple that he only supplied the text in an abbreviated form:

> In the name of God: I, Bertrand *de Balmis*, hearing and needing to hold to such great precepts of the Lord, and also to the teaching of the Lord Jesus in the Gospel [where he said] to his disciples *Si quis vult post me venire a. s. e. t. c. s. e. s. m.*, am following such sayings of his and am denying myself and taking up the cross on my chest and following the Lord. [Thus] for my sins and for those of my family, I present and offer myself to the Lord Jesus Christ, and to his mother Mary, and to the Knights of the Temple of Jerusalem . . .[139]

Indeed, the evidence from the Richerenches cartulary suggests that Rostan established a precedent that later scribes followed: in 1157, for example, a charter was drawn up for William *Gaucelmus* that replicated precisely the earlier abbreviation of Matthew 16:24.[140]

It was not only in their willingness to take up the cross for a life of religious poverty that the Templars were understood to be following Christ, however. For Hugh *Peccator*, the combination of action and contemplation that the Templars espoused in their daily lives was itself modelled on Christ's example: 'Christ himself, who you ought to follow, worked on earth fighting wicked and evil men before ascending to heaven to sit untroubled at the right hand of the father.'[141] Similarly, Bernard of Clairvaux depicted Christ's expulsion of the money-changers from the Temple in Jerusalem as a blueprint for the Templars' defence of the Holy Land: 'This devoted army, moved by the example of their king, rightly believe that it is more shameful and more intolerable by far for the holy places to be polluted by the infidels than to be infested with merchants'.[142] In this respect, the emphasis on the Christo-mimetic character of the Templars' military activities echoed the appeal that the Greek patriarch of Jerusalem had issued in 1098 for the arms-bearers of the West to 'fight in the army of the Lord in the same place in which the Lord fought'.[143] It would seem, in fact, that the most prominent motif of *imitatio Christi* to appear in early Templar *apologia* related to the inherent dangers that were associated with fighting for the Lord; as Orderic Vitalis put it, the Templars were 'admirable knights who devote their lives to the bodily and spiritual service of God and, rejecting all the things of this world, face martyrdom daily'.[144]

---

[138] *Cartulaire de la commanderie de Richerenches de l'ordre du Temple (1136–1214)*, ed. Marquis de Ripert-Monclar (Avignon and Paris, 1907), no. 3, p. 5. See also Riley-Smith, *First Crusaders*, pp. 164–5.

[139] *Cartulaire de la commanderie de Richerenches*, no. 33, p. 36.

[140] *Ibid.*, no. 146, p. 134.

[141] 'Un document', p. 88.

[142] *SBO* 3, p. 222.

[143] *Kreuzzugsbriefe*, no. 9, p. 148.

[144] OV 6, pp. 310–11.

It was described in Chapter Two how the first crusaders' willingness to sacrifice themselves for Christ was understood to be the consummate act of *imitatio Christi*.[145] In this context, it is to be expected that the idea of martyrdom would also be central to the ideology of the Temple, the brethren of which had devoted the remainder of their lives to defending the faith; as the *Primitive Rule* stated, 'it is certain that you especially are entrusted with the duty of laying down your lives for your brothers'.[146] This citation is indicative of how John 15:13 came to be regarded as a foundation text for Templar observance. That the idea of self-sacrifice was to be regarded as a paradigm of Christo-mimesis is clearly illustrated by a later passage in the *Rule*, which described how the Templar was required to swear that 'I will take the cup of salvation, that is by my death, I will imitate (*imitabor*) the death of my Lord, because just as Christ laid down his life for me, thus I am ready to lay down my life for my brothers'.[147] If Simonetta Cerrini is correct in concluding that the Latin version of the *Rule* constituted a redraft of a presentation that Hugh of Payns made to the Council of Troyes in the vernacular,[148] it is all the more striking that the ecclesiastics of the council believed that the notion of *imitatio* was more suited to Templar spirituality than *ultio*, for in the later Old French version of the *Rule*, which Cerrini believes was based on Hugh's original presentation, this statement was redacted as follows: '*Calicem salutaris accipiam*. Ce est a dire: Je penrai le calice de salu. Ce est: Je vengerai la mort de Jhesu Crist por ma mort. Car ensi come Jhesu Crist mist son cors por moi, et je sui apareilliés en tel maniere metre m'arme por mes freres.'[149]

It is no exaggeration to say that John 15:13 was the most frequently cited scriptural text in early sources that describe the Christo-mimetic piety of the Templars.[150] In *Omne datum optimum*, for example, Innocent II described how:

> Just like true Israelites and warriors most prepared for holy war, aflame with the torch of true charity, with your actions you carry out the word of the Gospel, in which it is said: 'Greater love no-one has than this, that a man lay down his life for his friends.' And in accordance with the words of the shepherd on high, you do not fear at all to lay down your lives for your brothers and to defend them from the incursions of the pagans.[151]

Similarly, in 1138x42, Innocent wrote that the Templars had 'followed Christ, and are continually prepared to lay down their lives for their brothers',[152] and in 1144 Celestine

---

[145] See above, pp. 42–5.

[146] *Die ursprüngliche Templerregel*, p. 146. The Old French translation emphasised the precedent by adding the phrase 'ensi comme fist Jhesu Crist'. See *La règle du Temple*, ed. H. de Curzon (Paris, 1886), p. 58.

[147] *Die ursprüngliche Templerregel*, p. 136. Citation from Psalm 116:13.

[148] S. Cerrini, 'A New Edition of the Latin and French Rule of the Temple', *The Military Orders: Welfare and Warfare*, ed. H. Nicholson (Aldershot, 1998), p. 212.

[149] *La règle du Temple*, pp. 63–4.

[150] In addition to the sources quoted in the text, see also, for example, 'Un document', p. 87; *SBO* 8, Ep. 175; *Cartulaire général de l'ordre du Temple*, no. 59, pp. 42–3; *Papsturkunden für Templer und Johanniter*, no. 17, p. 223; *Letters of Peter the Venerable*, vol. 1, Ep. 172, p. 408; 'Epistola A. Dapiferi militiae Templi', *RHGF* 15, pp. 540–1.

[151] *Papsturkunden für Templer und Johanniter*, vol. 1, no. 3, pp. 205–6.

[152] 'Bullaire du Temple', *Cartulaire général de l'ordre du Temple*, no. 3, p. 374.

II described how 'They do not fear to lay down their lives for their brothers, and they defend pilgrims setting out for the holy places . . . from the attacks of the pagans'.[153] A comparable observation was made by Bishop Ulger of Angers in c. 1128x49 when he described how the Templars:

> have chosen to fight against the enemies of God, who are pursued from the holy city of Jerusalem and other parts of the East; they do not hesitate to give their lives and to pour out their blood until they erase the wicked gentiles from the most sacred of places, which the Lord chose for his nativity, his life and his Passion.[154]

The application of ideas of Christo-mimesis to the Templars must be attributed in large part to the efforts of Bernard of Clairvaux.[155] It is well known that Bernard played an important role in the redrafting of the Templars' *Primitive Rule*, and therefore no coincidence that he revisited many of the themes within that *Rule* in his *De laude novae militiae*. The notion that the Templar lived for a *mors sacra*, for example, was especially prominent. 'How blessed are the martyrs who die in battle', Bernard wrote; 'Rejoice, mighty athlete, if you live and conquer in the Lord; but leap up and glory even more if you die and are brought together with the Lord.'[156] However, the most important reference to this idea was reserved for another passage, where Bernard asked the rhetorical question of the Templar, 'Why should he fear living or dying when for him *to live is Christ and to die is gain?*'[157] This citation from Philippians 1:21 is of the utmost importance, and an awareness of how it was used by Bernard is critical for understanding his reading of Templar spirituality. Indeed, for all their Christo-mimetic sacrifices on the field of battle, it was also the fact that they were contemplatives, for whom 'to live is Christ (*vivere Christus est*)', that was central to Bernard's presentation of the Templars as *imitatores Christi*.

It was suggested above that Bernard believed that devotion to the sites of the Holy Land was valuable as a way for Christians to engage with their Saviour on a basic level, but that in order for Christians to follow Christ it was necessary for them to advance beyond this elementary stage of 'fleshly' knowledge. There can be no clearer example of how Bernard sought to cultivate such spiritual development than in the second half of his *De laude novae militiae*, where his efforts were obviously focused on the devotional lives of the Templars. The significance of the second half of *De laude* has often been overlooked,[158] but when seen within the context of Bernard's understanding of 2 Corinthians 5:16, its importance becomes clear. Indeed, it is totally misleading to refer to *De laude* as being separated into two 'halves', for the passages that deal overtly with the way of life of the Templars make up only the first five of the treatise's thirteen chapters – eleven pages out of twenty-six in the edition of Leclercq and Rochais[159]– with the remaining eight chapters being meditative texts on the most significant sites of the Holy Land: Bethlehem,

---

[153] *Papsturkunden für Templer und Johanniter*, vol. 1, no. 8, p. 215.

[154] *Cartulaire général de l'ordre du Temple*, no. 21, p. 15.

[155] See M.L. Bulst-Thiele, 'The Influence of St. Bernard of Clairvaux on the Formation of the Order of the Knights Templar', *Second Crusade and the Cistercians*, pp. 57–65.

[156] *SBO* 3, p. 215.

[157] *SBO* 3, p. 214. Citation from Phillipians 1:21.

[158] Cf. Barber, *New Knighthood*, p. 46.

[159] *SBO* 3, pp. 214–24 and 224–39 respectively.

Nazareth, the Mount of Olives and the Valley of Jehoshaphat, the River Jordan, Calvary, the Holy Sepulchre, Bethphage, and Bethany. However, as David Carlson has highlighted, it is striking that these chapters were ordered 'not geographically . . . [but] in approximate order of the major events of Christ's life'.[160] It would seem, therefore, that Bernard intended to eulogise on the spiritual significance of each site so that he might encourage the Templars to go beyond the physical and thus enable them to declare that 'although we have known Christ after the flesh, now we know him so no longer'.

Bernard's purpose is perhaps illustrated best by focusing on his discussions of Bethlehem and the Holy Sepulchre. Naturally, the town of Christ's birth was the first of the eight sites to be considered, and Bernard opened his analysis by describing its importance as the place where the Word was made flesh: 'Bethlehem, the house of bread, was the place in which he, the living bread, descended from heaven, was born of the Virgin, and first appeared [to mankind].'[161] Bernard then used the image of the animals approaching Christ in the manger as a metaphor for the simple Christian's attempts to come to know his Saviour:

> In the same place, the stable is pointed out to the pious draught animals, and in that stable is the hay from the virgin meadow; there the cow may become acquainted with his owner and the ass with the stable of his Lord . . . Because long ago man did not understand the splendour in which he was made, he has been compared with senseless beasts and he is made similar to them. The Word of God and the Bread of Angels was made the food of animals so that man might chew over this fodder and regain his lost dignity.[162]

The implication of this metaphor was then fully drawn out when Bernard turned to cite the text of 2 Corinthians 5:16:

> From being cattle, he is changed back into a man again, so that he might be able to say with St Paul: 'And if we have known Christ after the flesh (*secundum carnem*), now we know him so no longer' . . . For he who finds life in the words of Christ no longer searches for the flesh.[163]

In this way, Bethlehem was understood to signify not only the value of engaging with Christ on a 'fleshly' level, but also the importance of advancing beyond that elementary stage to spiritual maturity:

> For only a child needs a cup of milk, and only an animal needs to feed on hay . . . Nevertheless it is one and the same fodder from the heavenly pastures that is chewed over sweetly by cattle and eaten by man. It gives strength to the adult and provides nourishment for the young.[164]

---

[160] Carlson, 'Practical Theology', pp. 138–9.
[161] *SBO* 3, p. 224.
[162] *SBO* 3, pp. 224–5.
[163] *SBO* 3, p. 225.
[164] *SBO* 3, p. 225.

Bernard followed a similar line of thought in his meditation on the Holy Sepulchre,[165] where he delineated a connection between the sense of 2 Corinthians 5:16 and the ideal of *imitatio Christi*. He began by describing how the Sepulchre was relevant not only as a relic of Christ's death and resurrection, but also as a catalyst for a deeper devotion to the example of Christ's life and death: 'The life of Christ has given me a rule (*regula*) for living, and his death has redeemed me from death. One has prepared life, while the other has destroyed death. The life is hard but the death is precious; in fact, both are very necessary.'[166] He went on to develop the theme by arguing that 'since it was equally necessary for us to live piously and to die fearlessly, he taught us to live by his life and to die by his death',[167] before calling upon the ideal of the *via Christi*, which had been fundamental to ideas of Christo-mimesis since the days of the early Church:

> It was deemed to be altogether necessary that he delay his death and condescend to live as man among men for some time, so that by his frequent and truthful speeches he might awaken us to invisible things, by his marvellous works he might add to our faith, and by his rectitude he might guide our behaviour . . . He presented himself to us as Life in the Gospel, saying *I am the Life*.[168]

To imitate Christ was to follow his example of sobriety, justness and piety, to speak the truth and to share in the indignities he had suffered,[169] and Bernard therefore exhorted his audience 'to imitate his examples, to venerate his miracles, to believe his teachings, and to be grateful for his sufferings':

> Although he was rich, he became poor for us. From greatness he became small, and from being raised on high he became humble. From being strong he became weak, because he endured hunger and thirst and was tired by his travels. He also suffered many other things not out of necessity, but by his own free will. This was, for him, a kind of foolishness. But, for us, does it not represent the path of discretion (*via prudentiae*), the form of righteousness (*forma iustitiae*), and the model of sanctity (*exemplum sanctitatis*)?[170]

These passages demonstrate that Bernard believed the Templars to be *imitatores Christi* not only because they were willing to follow Christ's example by taking up the cross and offering themselves as a sacrifice for their brethren, but also because as professed religious who were contemplative in the Holy Land they were understood to be advancing beyond an elementary reverence of '*the places where his feet have stood*' to a deeper understanding of the spiritual significance of those places. As he wrote at the beginning of *De laude*, 'the temporal glory of the earthly city does not distract us from the goodness of the heavenly city, but adds to it, at least so long as we are not in doubt that the one is the figure of the other, and that it is the heavenly city which is our mother'.[171] The

---

[165] Cf. Schein, *Gateway to the Heavenly City*, p. 73.

[166] *SBO* 3, pp. 229–30.

[167] *SBO* 3, p. 230.

[168] *SBO* 3, pp. 234–5.

[169] *SBO* 3, p. 234.

[170] *SBO* 3, pp. 234–5.

[171] *SBO* 3, p. 219.

contrast between Bernard's attitudes towards the spirituality of the Templar and that of the crusader could therefore hardly be more obvious, for it was only the Templar for whom the phrase *'to live is Christ'* had any real meaning. Indeed, the difference is highlighted all the more clearly when one notices that as well as appearing in his treatise on the Templars, Philippians 1:21 was also used by Bernard in his crusade preaching of 1146. However, in his letters for the Second Crusade, Bernard adapted the phrase to the following: 'Now, O mighty soldiers, O men of war, you can fight without danger, where to conquer is glory *and to die is gain.'*[172] The exclusive application to the Templars of the phrase *vivere Christus est* suggests that whilst Bernard undoubtedly viewed the crusade as a way for the pious layman to secure spiritual rewards, he believed the Temple to be the only suitable vocation for those who wished to carry out acts of sacred violence and at the same time fulfil a desire to follow Christ. In short, it was the important distinction that Bernard drew between the spirituality of the Templar and that of the crusader that appears to have been at the heart of his revolutionary interpretation of the crusader's cross. It would seem that, for Bernard, it was the Templars who were the real inheritors of the Christo-mimetic spirituality of the First Crusade.

The Cistercian Influence on the Preaching of Crusades, 1150—1187

In spite of the Second Crusade's many dramatic failures,[173] the ecclesiastical authorities of the West did not lose interest in promoting the defence of the Holy Land in the forty years between the farcical retreat from Damascus in 1148 and the fall of Jerusalem to Saladin in 1187. Indeed, the immediate reaction of senior churchmen to the events of 1147–9 was that efforts to aid the beleaguered Latin East should be redoubled, especially after the death of Raymond of Antioch in June 1149.[174] Accordingly, in the spring of 1150, Abbot Suger of St Denis led the initiative for launching a new crusade to the East, which he hoped would be led once again by Louis VII.[175] Although his plans for the expedition were never realised, the language of the correspondence exchanged between Suger, Bernard of Clairvaux, Peter the Venerable and Pope Eugenius gives some indication of how the crusade might have been promoted had it come to fruition. All four men displayed their awareness of the threats facing the settlers of the Latin East, and indicated their belief in the fundamental importance of defending the Holy Land.[176] In a letter sent to

---

[172] *SBO* 8, Ep. 363 and 458, pp. 315, 436. For a confused reference to this idea in one of the narrative sources for the Second Crusade, see *De expugnatione*, p. 156.

[173] See, for example, Constable, 'Second Crusade', pp. 266–76; G. Constable, 'A Report on a Lost Sermon by St Bernard on the Failure of the Second Crusade', *Studies in Medieval Cistercian History Presented to Jeremiah O'Sullivan* (Spencer, MA, 1971), pp. 49–54; E. Siberry, *Criticism of Crusading, 1095–1274* (Oxford, 1985), pp. 77–80; Cole, *Preaching of the Crusades*, pp. 52–9; G.A. Loud, 'Some Reflections on the Failure of the Second Crusade', *Crusades*, 4 (2005), pp. 1–14.

[174] See Phillips, *Defenders of the Holy Land*, pp. 102–3.

[175] See B.M. Bolton, 'The Cistercians and the Aftermath of the Second Crusade', *Second Crusade and the Cistercians*, pp. 131–40; Phillips, *Defenders of the Holy Land*, pp. 100–18; G. Constable, 'The Crusading Project of 1150', *Montjoie: Studies in Crusade History in Honour of Hans Eberhard Mayer*, ed. B.Z. Kedar, J.S.C. Riley-Smith and R. Hiestand (Aldershot, 1997), pp. 67–75; T. Reuter, 'The "Non-Crusade" of 1149–50', *Second Crusade*, pp. 150–63.

[176] In addition to the letters quoted in the text, see also Suger of St Denis, 'Epistolae', *Oeuvres complètes*

Bernard of Clairvaux, for example, Peter the Venerable apologised for his absence from the council of war that Abbot Suger had organised at Chartres for 8 May,[177] but stressed that the crusade project nevertheless had his wholehearted support:

> Who would it not move if by some disaster that Holy Land, which was taken from the yoke of the pagans by the great efforts of our fathers (*tantis patrum laboribus*) and by the shedding of so much Christian blood not so long ago, was to be subdued by the wicked and the blasphemous once again? Who would it not move if such a salutary journey for penitent sinners, which it is proper to believe, has now saved innumerable thousands of pilgrims from hell and restored them to heaven for fifty years, should be closed because the Saracens stand in the way?[178]

Of the four men, it was Bernard who was the most vocal in his support for the expedition – perhaps understandable given his pivotal role in the preaching of the Second Crusade and the criticism he had received for its failure[179] – and it appears that the council at Chartres had made moves to elect him as both the spiritual and military leader of the new crusade.[180] However, this was not a role that he felt suited for, and in a letter to Pope Eugenius in which he portrayed the losses in the East as a 'second Passion of the Lord' he looked to the head of the Church to lead a new crusade to the Holy Land, declaring that 'it is the time to take out both swords in defence of the eastern Church':

> If you love Christ with that triple love . . . with all your heart, with all your soul, and with all your strength, as is proper, then you will not hold back or neglect your duty while his bride [the Holy Land] is in such great danger; but rather you will support her with whatever strength, zeal, authority and power you can muster. A unique danger demands a unique effort. The foundations [of the Church] are shaking violently, and the building will be ruined imminently if efforts are not made at once to support it.[181]

Bernard's extraordinary enthusiasm for the crusade project is also evident from the letter that he wrote to Peter the Venerable after the council at Chartres:

> A great and important enterprise of the Lord has become known all over the world. Clearly, it is great because the king of heaven is losing his land, the land of his inheritance, the land *where his feet have stood* . . . The places which came into contact with the prayers of the prophets and the miracles of the Saviour and which were

---

de Suger, ed. A. Lecoy de la Marche (Paris, 1867), Ep. 18 and 24, pp. 268–9, 280–2; *SBO* 8, Ep. 380, p. 344; Eugenius III, 'Epistolae', nos. 382 and 390, cols. 1414–15, 1419; *Letters of Peter the Venerable*, vol. 1, Ep. 165 and 166, pp. 398–400.

[177] See V.G. Berry, 'Peter the Venerable and the Crusades', *Petrus Venerabilis 1156–1956: Studies and Texts Commemorating the Eighth Centenary of his Death*, ed. G. Constable and J. Kritzeck, *Studia Anselmiana*, 40 (Rome, 1956), pp. 159–62.

[178] *Letters of Peter the Venerable*, vol. 1, Ep. 164, p. 397. See also G.R. Knight, *The Correspondence between Peter the Venerable and Bernard of Clairvaux: A Semantic and Structural Analysis* (Aldershot, 2002), pp. 201–25.

[179] Bernard of Clairvaux, 'De consideratione ad Eugenium papam', *SBO* 3, pp. 410–13, contains Bernard's response to his critics.

[180] *SBO* 8, Ep. 256, pp. 163–5; 'Sigeberti continuatio Praemonstratensis', *MGH SS* 6, p. 455. See also Bolton, 'Cistercians and the Aftermath', p. 138.

[181] *SBO* 8, Ep. 256, pp. 163–4.

consecrated by the life and blood of Christ are threatened. What will this mean except that the foundations of our salvation, the riches of the Christian people, will be taken away?[182]

It is noteworthy that the phrasing that Bernard was using of the projected expedition in this private correspondence was consonant with the language of his earlier crusade letters, and it therefore seems reasonable to assume that had the crusade advanced beyond the planning stages its preachers would have recycled some of the motifs that had proved so effective in 1146–7. As it was, Pope Eugenius's support for the expedition was less than inspirational – he described the project as an 'immense work of piety', but stopped short of issuing a general letter for the new venture[183] – and any momentum that the strategists had had ground to a halt by midsummer 1150.[184] Nevertheless, it is striking that the profound awareness of the importance of maintaining the Christian custody of the holy places and of defending the Holy Land from its enemies did not fade with the deaths of Suger of St Denis in 1151, Bernard of Clairvaux and Pope Eugenius in 1153, and Peter the Venerable in 1156. In fact, it is evident that their ideas were to remain central to the preaching of crusades to the East in the period 1150–87.

In the years between the Second and Third Crusades numerous appeals were issued that called for western military assistance for the settlers of the Latin East. In general, the surviving evidence can be divided into three groups: first, appeals that were sent directly from the Christians in the Holy Land to their brethren in the West, such as the numerous letters directed at Louis VII in the early 1160s,[185] and the letter sent to the West by the patriarch of Jerusalem, Amalric of Nesle, in 1166;[186] second, direct appeals from the papacy to the arms-bearers of the West, which were frequently issued in response to news from the Levant, such as *Quantum praedecessores III* (1165),[187] *In quantis pressuris* (1166),[188] *Inter omnia* (1169),[189] *Cor nostrum* (1181),[190] and *Cor nostrum II* (1184);[191] and third, letters sent by the papacy to other churchmen authorising their preaching of crusades, such as those which Adrian IV addressed in November 1157 to Samson,

[182] *SBO* 8, Ep. 521, p. 483.

[183] Eugenius III, 'Epistolae', no. 382, cols. 1414–15.

[184] See Bolton, 'Cistercians and the Aftermath', pp. 138–9; Constable, 'Crusading Project', pp. 74–5; Reuter, 'The "Non-Crusade"', pp. 157–8.

[185] Louis VII, 'Epistolae', *RHGF* 16, nos. 91, 121–6, 194–7 and 243–5, pp. 27–8, 36–40, 59–63, 79–81. See Phillips, *Defenders of the Holy Land*, pp. 140–9.

[186] 'Documents', ed. C. Riant, *Archives de l'Orient latin*, 2 vols. (Paris, 1881–4), vol. 1, Ep. 2, pp. 386–7. See Phillips, *Defenders of the Holy Land*, pp. 151–3.

[187] Alexander III, 'Epistolae', no. 360, cols. 384–6. See J.G. Rowe, 'Alexander III and the Jerusalem Crusade: An Overview of Problems and Failures', *Crusaders and Muslims in Twelfth-Century Syria*, ed. M. Shatzmiller (Leiden and New York, 1993), pp. 112–32.

[188] *Papsturkunden für Templer und Johanniter*, vol. 1, no. 53, pp. 251–3. See Phillips, *Defenders of the Holy Land*, pp. 150–1.

[189] Alexander III, 'Epistolae', no. 626, cols. 599–601. See Phillips, *Defenders of the Holy Land*, pp. 186–208.

[190] Alexander III, 'Epistolae', no. 1504, cols. 1294–6. See Phillips, *Defenders of the Holy Land*, pp. 246–51.

[191] *Papsturkunden in Sizilien*, ed. P. Kehr (Göttingen, 1899), no. 26, pp. 329–30. See Phillips, *Defenders of the Holy Land*, pp. 251–66.

archbishop of Rheims,[192] an unidentified clerical audience,[193] and Peter of Rovira, the master of the Temple in Spain,[194] and those which Alexander III sent in 1169 and 1173 to Henry, archbishop of Rheims.[195] The circumstances surrounding each of these appeals have been the subject of research elsewhere,[196] and it is therefore unnecessary to reconstruct the narrative of events in the Latin East in the third quarter of the twelfth century. Instead, the present analysis will focus on the thematic similarities of the appeals that were issued in the period between the collapse of the crusade project of 1150 and the fall of Jerusalem in 1187, in order to demonstrate the influence of ideas that had been propagated by Pope Eugenius III and Abbot Bernard of Clairvaux in 1146–7. In this respect, it is striking that although Jerusalem and the Holy Sepulchre continued to be of central importance to crusade propaganda, it was the Christian warriors who had sacrificed their blood for the Holy Land since 1095 rather than Christ's sacrifice on the cross that was understood to be the most important *exemplum* of crusading piety. Not once during this period did crusade preachers turn to the ideas of Christo-mimesis that had proved so effective in 1095–6.

As one might expect, there were many references to the plight of the Latin East and the threats that a resurgent Islam posed to the Holy Sepulchre in the crusade appeals of 1150–87, and it would be redundant to cite the detail of each and every call 'for the liberation and defence of the holy places';[197] a selection of examples will suffice. In June 1166, for example, in one of the few original passages in *In quantis pressuris*, Pope Alexander III called for crusaders to fight *contra Sarracenos* in 'that land, which our Lord and Redeemer Jesus Christ sanctified with his bodily presence'.[198] Similarly, in December 1173, Alexander wrote to Henry of Rheims requesting that the archbishop preach for a new crusade because of the 'extreme danger' that was threatening '*the place in which the feet of the Lord have stood*'.[199] And in *Ingemiscimus et dolemus* (1173x4), the pope continued to lament the situation in 'that Holy Land, which God the redeemer of all thought worthy of his bodily presence and in which, for our redemption, he wished to take up the flesh and suffer the gallows of the cross'.[200] However, perhaps the most dramatic appeal to have survived from this period was that which the patriarch of Jerusalem, Amalric of Nesle, addressed to 'the archbishops, bishops, abbots, prior, provosts, princes, dukes, courtiers, marquises, counts, and all the sons of the holy mother Church' in 1166.[201] He described the threat posed to the eastern Church by the 'enemies of the Holy Cross', and pleaded for the arms-bearers of the West to assist immediately in the defence of Jerusalem and the Holy Land:

---

[192] Adrian IV, 'Epistolae et privilegia', *PL* 188, no. 157, cols. 1537–8.

[193] *Papsturkunden in Spanien: I. Katalonien*, ed. P. Kehr (Berlin, 1926), no. 77, pp. 359–60. The surviving text of this letter is incomplete.

[194] *Ibid.*, no. 78, pp. 360–2.

[195] Alexander III, 'Epistolae', nos. 627, 1047 and 1102, cols. 601–2, 927–8, 962–3.

[196] Phillips, *Defenders of the Holy Land*.

[197] Adrian IV, 'Epistolae', no. 157, col. 1538. See also *Papsturkunden in Spanien*, nos. 77 and 78, pp. 359–60, 362.

[198] *Papsturkunden für Templer und Johanniter*, vol. 1, no. 53, p. 253.

[199] Alexander III, 'Epistolae', no. 1047, col. 927. See also *ibid.*, no. 1505, col. 1296.

[200] *Papsturkunden für Kirchen im Heiligen Lande*, ed. R. Hiestand (Göttingen, 1985), no. 109, p. 276.

[201] 'Documents', *Archives de l'Orient latin*, Ep. 2, pp. 386–7.

Come therefore, most beloved brothers, to liberate your mother, before evil slaves come who threaten to destroy her! Come to the holy places, consecrated by the bodily presence of our Saviour! If you wish to be partners in the same redemption which was produced in that place through the most precious blood of Jesus Christ, hurry to set it free![202]

Although Amalric's letter contained a vivid reference to the Passion of Christ – 'the Lamb of God, who bore the sin of the world, was deceived, beaten and died for us, and he redeemed us on the cross'[203] – it is striking that no connection was made between this image and the idea that the crusaders who responded to the appeal would be taking the cross in imitation of Christ. In truth, Amalric was one of the few propagandists from this period who failed to supply any biblical or historical *exempla* for crusading whatsoever, but even if he had drawn an analogy between Christ's Passion and the crusader's cross he would have been out of step with his contemporaries. The simple fact of the matter is that between 1150 and 1187 the idea of the *strenuitas patrum* to which Pope Eugenius III had first alluded in December 1145 had replaced *imitatio Christi* as the most prominent motif used by those who sought to recruit for crusades to the East.

The idea of the *strenuitas patrum* is to be found across the sources. In 1161, for example, Bohemond of Antioch wrote to Louis VII expressing the 'great sadness' in the Holy Land, reminding the king 'How shameful it will be to all people and to you if this land, land in which so much of your ancestors' blood was shed . . . a land which has acquired such fame, may be allowed to be violated and destroyed by wicked people!'[204] Similarly, in 1163, Geoffrey Fulcher, a preceptor of the Temple, wrote to Louis as a representative of those settlers in the Holy Land who approached the king 'as supplicants with knees bent to your heart of charity, humbled at your feet; out of kindness we ask and await your help'. Geoffrey reminded Louis of the importance of the Holy Land as 'the place of our redemption',[205] and in a subsequent letter wrote that:

Before the rest of Christendom is taken, you must help us . . . therefore let those who are God's make ready, and those who value the name of Christianity, let them come to set free our kingdom and our land of freedom, so that the brave blood of our fathers shall not be proven disgraceful and irredeemable in the hands of the sons.[206]

The motif of the *strenuitas patrum* was also used repeatedly by the papacy. For example, having reissued Eugenius III's *Quantum praedecessores* in 1165 with only the most minor of adjustments, Pope Alexander's second crusade encyclical, *In quantis pressuris*, appealed once again to his audience's sense of family duty: 'Thus just as your ancestors and predecessors, not without shedding a great deal of their blood . . . liberated that land from the filth of the pagans, so you too must be bound by that example, to reach out bravely to its liberation and defence.'[207] Elsewhere in the letter the pope quoted a key passage from *Quantum praedecessores* verbatim:

[202]   *Ibid.*, p. 387.
[203]   *Ibid.*, p. 386.
[204]   Louis VII, 'Epistolae', no. 91, p. 28.
[205]   *Ibid.*, no. 195, p. 61.
[206]   *Ibid.*, no. 197, p. 63.
[207]   *Papsturkunden für Templer und Johanniter*, vol. 1, no. 53, p. 252.

It will be seen as a great sign of nobility and integrity if that which was acquired by the efforts of the fathers is vigorously defended by the good sons. Nevertheless if, God forbid, it should be otherwise, the courage of the fathers will have proved to be diminished in the sons.[208]

Three years later, Alexander continued to tap into the same idea when he issued *Inter Omnia*:

When long ago [Jerusalem] came under the power of the Saracens because of the sins of the Christian people, men of virtue rose up, and having wiped out and driven off the heathen, they restored the Holy Land to the faith of Christ once again. And after raising the banner of faith there, they returned the Sepulchre of the Lord . . . [to the custody] of the Christian people.[209]

Furthermore, in 1173, Alexander wrote that it was 'not without a great flowing of blood by the power of kings, princes and the other faithful of Christ' that the Holy Land had been delivered 'out of the hands of impious men'.[210] In 1181, he called to mind the memory of previous crusades once again by writing in *Cor nostrum* of 'that land for which our forefathers poured out their blood'.[211] And in a letter that dates from the same time, *Cum orientalis terra*, he instructed the clergy that when preaching for the projected campaign they should remind their audience of the sacrifice of their *patres et genitores*: '[tell them that] they should go quickly to that land, for whose liberation ancestors and fathers shed their blood, and [that] they should fight against the enemies of the cross of Christ with might and strength'.[212]

In terms of their use of the *strenuitas patrum* as an *exemplum* for crusading, Alexander and his contemporaries were unquestionably influenced by the Cistercian preaching of the Second Crusade. But, as *exempla*, the *strenuitas patrum* and the *imitatio Christi* were not necessarily mutually exclusive, and it is therefore striking that whilst the efforts of Eugenius III and Bernard of Clairvaux to distance crusading from ideals of Christo-mimesis had failed in the short term, some of their revolutionary ideas about the 'preaching of the cross' continued to hold currency in the period before the Third Crusade. Indeed, although Bernard's advanced theology of the crusade indulgence was only used by the papal curia for a limited period,[213] his stripping of the crusade badge of its Christo-mimetic qualities was followed universally by those who appealed for crusades to the East before 1187. In *Inter omnia*, for example, no connections were drawn between the sacrifice that Christ had made on the cross and the symbol that the crusader would bear on his chest, even though Pope Alexander had highlighted that Christ 'gave himself up for us, as a fragrant offering and sacrifice to God'.[214] Indeed, the scriptural citations that Alexander quoted in this letter were taken from two of the

---

[208] *Ibid.*, p. 252. Cf. Eugenius III, 'Quantum praedecessores', p. 303.
[209] Alexander III, 'Epistolae', no. 626, col. 600.
[210] *Ibid.*, no. 1047, col. 927.
[211] *Ibid.*, no. 1504, col. 1294.
[212] *Ibid.*, no. 1505, cols. 1296–7.
[213] See Riley-Smith, *What were the Crusades?*, pp. 59–64; Riley-Smith, *The Crusades*, pp. 133–4.
[214] Alexander III, 'Epistolae', no. 626, cols. 599–600.

Pauline Epistles rather than from Matthew 10:38 or 16:24,[215] and instead of following Christ, the crusader was therefore being entreated to go to his aid (*ad subventionem*) and to fight in defence of his patrimony, in return for the sacrifice that he had made on the cross and in imitation of the *viri virtutis* of past generations.

The ideology associated with crusading to the East in the period 1150–87 had there-fore certainly advanced beyond the ideas of *imitatio Christi* that had been conceived in 1095 by Pope Urban II, but it is clear that the crusade's origins in the Jerusalem pilgrimage tradition were secure enough. The importance of the emphasis on the Holy Land in the sources considered above is unquestionable, and it is striking that pro-spective expeditions continued to be referred to variously as *sanctum iter*,[216] *iter sancti Sepulcri*,[217] *iter Dominici Sepulcri*,[218] *labor Hierosolymitana*,[219] and *labor peregrinationis*.[220] Furthermore, in *Cor nostrum*, Alexander III highlighted the explicit importance of the Holy Sepulchre for all those crusaders who set out for the East: 'To all who are willing to visit the Sepulchre of the Lord for its present need, whether they die on the journey, or they arrive at that place, we enjoin the hardship of this journey as penance . . . and for remission of all sins.'[221] In this respect, the idea that participants in a crusade to the East were undertaking an armed pilgrimage remained unchanged in the first century of the movement's history.

Conclusion

Although the penitential disciplines that Pope Eugenius III and Abbot Bernard of Clair-vaux had sought to impose upon the second crusaders were undoubtedly influenced by Cistercian austerity,[222] it now seems that neither individual sought to inculcate crusad-ers with the ideas of Christo-mimesis that were central to the spirituality of their Order and that had also been fundamental to Pope Urban II's preaching of the First Crusade in 1095–6. For Bernard, the temporary nature of the crusaders' votive obligations was insufficient for them to be regarded as true followers of Christ, and although he understood an expedition to the East to be worthwhile because it allowed pilgrims and crusaders to engage with their Saviour on a 'fleshly' level, the pursuit of *imitatio Christi* was believed to be restricted to those who had committed themselves to a lifetime of religious profession. It was for this reason that Bernard sought to encourage the brethren of the Order of the Temple in the East to devote attention to the spiritual meaning of their surroundings, and to remind them that the Holy Land was significant not only because it had witnessed Christ's humanity, but also because it could stimulate

---

[215] *Ibid.*, cols. 599–600. Citations from 2 Corinthians 5:15 and Ephesians 5:2.

[216] *Ibid.*, nos. 360 and 626, cols. 386, 601; *Papsturkunden für Templer und Johanniter*, vol. 1, no. 53, p. 253.

[217] 'Documents', *Archives de l'Orient latin*, Ep. 2, p. 387.

[218] *Ibid.*, p. 387; *Papsturkunden für Templer und Johanniter*, vol. 1, no. 53, p. 253; Alexander III, 'Epistolae', no. 1504, col. 1296.

[219] Alexander III, 'Epistolae', no. 1505, col. 1296.

[220] *Ibid.*, no. 1504, col. 1295.

[221] *Ibid.*, col. 1296.

[222] See Riley-Smith, *The First Crusade*, p. 155; J.A. Brundage, 'St Bernard and the Jurists', *Second Crusade and the Cistercians*, pp. 29–31.

devotion of his divinity. The earthly Jerusalem was therefore presented as a valuable first stage in the journey towards the heavenly city, a contemplative undertaking that was, of course, necessarily related to the imitation of Christ, but that could not be fulfilled by witnessing the temporal city alone. In this framework, the idea that the adoption of the crusader's cross could signify that the bearer had fulfilled Christ's scriptural injunctions to follow him was understood to be too elementary, and Bernard and his associates therefore reinvented the crusade badge as a *signum vitae* that was symbolic of their advanced understanding of the crusade indulgence. However, to supplement this new approach it was also necessary for the Cistercians to supply fresh *exempla* to inspire potential crusaders, and instead of teaching the arms-bearers of the West that they were following Christ, Bernard and Eugenius stressed to their audience that it was necessary for them to undertake the crusade as a duty to their bloodline and as a way of upholding the traditions and achievements of their ancestors. Nevertheless, although there is a good deal of evidence to suggest that the idea of the *strenuitas patrum* struck a resounding chord in the West in the mid-1140s, the eventual outcome of retaining the sign of the cross as the symbol of the crusade was that Bernard and Eugenius were unable to separate the mainstream of crusading activity from the *imitatio Christi* tradition as it is clear they had intended. For all their efforts, they were swimming hopelessly against the tide of contemporary devotion, and in this respect their attempts to distinguish the spirituality of the crusader from that of the Templar should be counted amongst the many failures associated with the Second Crusade.

In this light, it is perhaps all the more striking that the Cistercian preaching of the Second Crusade had such an important legacy in the third quarter of the twelfth century.[223] During this period, the idea that the crusader's cross could serve as a symbol of Christo-mimesis appears to have been completely forgotten by those responsible for preaching crusades to the East; instead, the *exemplum* of the *strenuitas patrum* that had been so central to the thinking of Eugenius and Bernard was adopted wholesale, and it is significant that the wording of Eugenius's *Quantum praedecessores* proved to be invaluable to the composition of subsequent crusade encyclicals, especially during the pontificate of Alexander III. Indeed, recent scholars have suggested that Alexander's recycling of passages from *Quantum praedecessores* may have been a sign of weakness or of his indifference to the situation in the Holy Land,[224] but when one considers the realities of the nexus of family ties that bound the West to the settlers of the Latin East it may in fact have seemed prudent for the papal curia to reissue a bull that had previously proved so successful in recruiting crusaders. Rather than a sign of apathy, Alexander's repeated use of the motifs within *Quantum praedecessores* should perhaps be seen as an attempt to connect with the crusading traditions that were clearly developing amongst the arms-bearers of the West to whom his appeals were addressed. More research is needed on the ideological response of the Christian faithful to calls to crusade in 1157, 1165,

---

[223] For another treatment of Bernard's influence, see Schein, *Gateway to the Heavenly City*, pp. 122–3, 176, 178.

[224] See, for example, Rowe, 'Alexander III and the Jerusalem Crusade', p. 120, who believed that the 1165 reissue of *Quantum praedecessores* was 'faded and worn', and Phillips, *Defenders of the Holy Land*, pp. 150–1, who wrote that it was an 'uninspired bull'. C. Tyerman, *The Invention of the Crusades* (Basingstoke, 1998), p. 14, described the preparation of crusade encyclicals during this period as 'a pattern of unadventurous plagiarism'.

1166, 1169, 1173, 1181 and 1184, but it is clear that for the popes, at least, the history and example of the early crusades and the continued threats facing Jerusalem and the Holy Sepulchre were believed to be the most potent motifs that could be harnessed for recruiting for armed pilgrimages to the East before 1187.

CHAPTER FIVE

The Introduction of Crusading to Iberia, 1095–c.1134

The Impact of Crusading Ideology in Iberia, 1095–c.1120

In the preceding four chapters it has been argued that the idea of Christo-mimetic Jerusalem pilgrimage was central to contemporary understandings of crusading to the East in the twelfth century. However, it is now accepted by most historians that crusading activity was by no means limited to the Levant, and was in fact extended to include a number of other theatres of war both within and without western Europe.[1] In order to establish how important pilgrimage was to the broader development of the crusade ideal, the following two chapters will now consider how crusading evolved when introduced to one of those other theatres.

There can be little doubt that in terms of both chronology and local conditions, the Iberian peninsula presents itself as a suitable candidate for a case study of this kind. The preaching of a crusade in Iberia can be identified within thirty years of the proclamation of the First Crusade, and the peninsula was therefore established as a crusading frontier some time before crusades were launched in the Baltic or against schismatics, heretics or western secular powers.[2] Indeed, the fact that Iberia presented opportunities for warfare against an Islamic foe also meant that, until recently, the peninsula was often regarded as playing a pivotal role in the genesis of crusade ideology.[3] Scholars such as Carl Erdmann characterised the eleventh-century conflicts between Christians and Muslims in Iberia as proto-crusades,[4] and Derek Lomax argued that 'although the first crusaders were Frenchmen fighting in Spain, there was no reason why their status should

---

[1] See, for example, J.S.C. Riley-Smith, *What were the Crusades?*, 3rd edition (Basingstoke, 2002).

[2] *Ibid.*, pp. 12–22. See also N. Housley, 'Crusades against Christians: Their Origins and Early Development, c.1000–1216', *Crusade and Settlement: Papers Read at the First Conference of the Society for the Study of the Crusades and the Latin East and Presented to R.C. Smail*, ed. P.W. Edbury (Cardiff, 1985), pp. 17–36; I.M. Fonnesberg-Schmidt, *The Popes and the Baltic Crusades, 1147–1254* (Leiden, 2007).

[3] But see also M. Bull, 'Views of Muslims and of Jerusalem in Miracle Stories, c.1000–c.1200: Reflections on the Study of First Crusaders' Motivations', *The Experience of Crusading, Volume One: Western Approaches*, ed. M. Bull and N. Housley (Cambridge, 2003), p. 37.

[4] C. Erdmann, *The Origin of the Idea of Crusade*, trans. M.W. Baldwin and W. Goffart (Princeton, NJ, 1977), pp. 136–40, 155–6, 288–9.

not later be extended to those fighting for Jerusalem'.[5] This position must now be regarded as untenable for a number of reasons. First of all, it is clear that although there is some indication that arms-bearers from France were involved in sporadic peninsular campaigns against Muslim powers in the eleventh century, there is very little evidence that their exploits were regarded as being religious in cause or penitential in character.[6] Even though the exact circumstances in which Pope Alexander II offered remission of sins to those who set out for Spain in *c.*1063 may remain unresolved,[7] as Marcus Bull has pointed out, 'the most striking feature of the supposed Barbastro indulgence, even if the maximal interpretation is placed upon it, is its isolation'.[8] More broadly, Angus MacKay and Richard Fletcher argued convincingly that eleventh-century warfare between Iberian Christians and Muslims was often driven by political and material exigencies rather than by any ideological imperative,[9] a fact that was exemplified by the career of the historical Cid, who fought as a mercenary warrior for both Christian and Muslim paymasters.[10] The most inescapable problem with the validity of the idea of the 'proto-crusade' in eleventh-century Iberia is, however, a conceptual one. As has already been described above, contemporaries regarded Pope Urban II's proclamation of the crusade in 1095 as extremely innovative because it fused radical concepts of meritorious warfare and Christo-mimesis with more traditional ideas of penitential pilgrimage. There is no trace whatsoever of any comparable fusion of acts of pious violence and pilgrimage in Iberia before 1095,[11] and it is striking that contemporaries were more inclined to draw analogies between crusading and entry into monastic life than they were to make references to precedents created by peninsular warfare against Islam. More practically, one of the surviving records of decrees from the Council of Clermont explicitly stated that the first crusaders should not set out 'to gain honour or money', from which it might be inferred that the crusade was regarded as being different in character from other military exploits against Islam with which western arms-bearers might be famil-iar.[12] In short, it would seem that when Pope Urban proclaimed the First Crusade in 1095 most Iberian arms-bearers would probably have had only a limited contact with

---

[5] D.W. Lomax, *The Reconquest of Spain* (London, 1978), p. 59. See also J.F. O'Callaghan, *Reconquest and Crusade in Medieval Spain* (Philadelphia, PA, 2003), pp. 24–7.

[6] M. Bull, *Knightly Piety and the Lay Response to the First Crusade: The Limousin and Gascony, c.970–c.1130* (Oxford, 1993), pp. 70–114.

[7] *Ibid.*, pp. 72–81. See also A. Ferreiro, 'The Siege of Barbastro, 1064–5: A Reassessment', *Journal of Medieval History*, 9 (1983), pp. 129–44.

[8] Bull, *Knightly Piety*, p. 111.

[9] A. MacKay, *Spain in the Middle Ages: From Frontier to Empire, 1000–1500* (London, 1977), pp. 15–26; R.A. Fletcher, 'Reconquest and Crusade in Spain, *c.*1050–1150', *Transactions of the Royal Historical Society*, 5th ser., 37 (1987), pp. 31–47. See also C.J. Bishko, 'The Spanish and Portuguese Reconquest, 1095–1492', *A History of the Crusades*, vol. 3, ed. H.W. Hazard (Madison, WI, 1975), p. 399.

[10] See R.A. Fletcher, *The Quest for El Cid* (London, 1989). See also S. Barton, 'Traitors to the Faith? Christian Mercenaries in al-Andalus and the Maghreb, *c.*1100–1300', *Medieval Spain: Culture, Conflict and Coexistence. Studies in Honour of Angus MacKay*, ed. R. Collins and A. Goodman (New York, 2002), pp. 23–45; S. Barton, 'Spain in the Eleventh Century', *The New Cambridge Medieval History*, vol. 4.2, ed. D. Luscombe and J.S.C. Riley-Smith (Cambridge, 2004), pp. 154–90.

[11] Cf. Bull, *Knightly Piety*, pp. 111–12.

[12] *Decreta Claromontensia*, ed. R. Somerville, *The Councils of Urban II. I.* (Amsterdam, 1972), p. 74. See J.S.C. Riley-Smith, *The First Crusaders, 1095–1131* (Cambridge, 1997), p. 106.

the notion of penitential warfare, and absolutely no experience of 'proto-crusading'. In this context, it is perhaps not surprising that the novelty of the First Crusade proved to be as attractive to some of the arms-bearers of Iberia as it was to those who hailed from north of the Pyrenees.[13]

Although the exact number of first crusaders who came from Iberia is unknown, there can be no doubt that their numbers were sufficient enough to raise serious concerns in the papal curia about the consequences of the absence of the arms-bearing classes from the peninsula. Pope Urban might well have anticipated that his proclamation of the crusade would attract recruits from Iberia; he must certainly have believed Jerusalem pilgrimage to be as potent for Spaniards as it was for other western Christians, for in his attempt to stimulate ideas of reconquest[14] in 1089 he had portrayed peninsular penitential warfare as being of an equivalent value to a journey to the East.[15] In a letter whose addressees included Count Berenguer Ramon II of Barcelona, Pope Urban had framed his offer of spiritual rewards to all those who undertook the restoration of Tarragona, a Catalan frontier town and a papal fief, in the following terms:

> We exhort those who wish to go on pilgrimage, either to Jerusalem or to some other place, in the spirit of penance and devotion, to direct the costs and all the effort of that journey to the restoration of the church of Tarragona, so that, with God's help, an episcopal seat might be established there in safety, and so that the same city might be filled with Christian people to stand as a wall and an outer defence against the opposition of the Saracens. With God's mercy, we offer you the same indulgence that you would earn if you were to complete such a long pilgrimage.[16]

It is unclear whether or not Pope Urban was writing in response to news of a planned Catalan pilgrimage, although the inclusion of the phrase *vel partes alias* suggests that any report he had received about the destination of a proposed undertaking was not specific. It seems more likely therefore that Jerusalem pilgrimage was simply being used in 1089 to provide a measure of the spiritual value of the liberation and restoration of Tarragona[17] – a striking idea that must certainly mark an important developmental step in Urban's formulation of the crusade ideal.[18]

---

[13] See, for example, A. Ubieto Arteta, 'La participación navarro-aragonesa en la primera cruzada', *Príncipe de Viana*, 8 (1947), pp. 357–84; J. Goñi Gaztambide, *Historia de la bula de la cruzada en España* (Vitoria, 1958), pp. 59–62; S. Barton, *The Aristocracy in Twelfth-Century León and Castile* (Cambridge, 1997), pp. 155–6; S. Barton, 'From Tyrants to Soldiers of Christ: The Nobility of Twelfth-Century León-Castile and the Struggle against Islam', *Nottingham Medieval Studies*, 44 (2000), pp. 35–6. Cf. Bull, *Knightly Piety*, p. 98, who believed that 'the Spanish response to the First Crusade does not seem to have been considerable'.

[14] On this loaded term, see especially Fletcher, 'Reconquest and Crusade', *passim*; O'Callaghan, *Reconquest and Crusade*, pp. 1–22.

[15] Cf. Goñi Gaztambide, *Historia*, pp. 55–9.

[16] Urban II, 'Epistolae et privilegia', *PL* 151, no. 20, cols. 302–3. See also Pope Urban's 'Postquam a nobis' (July 1089), in F. Fita, 'Sobre un texto del arzobispo don Rodrigo', *BRAH*, 4 (1884), p. 370.

[17] But see also *Papsturkunden in Spanien: I. Katalonien*, ed. P. Kehr (Berlin, 1926), no. 22, pp. 286–7, and Urban II, 'Epistolae', no. 52, cols. 331–3, where the equation with Jerusalem pilgrimage is not repeated.

[18] Cf. H.E. Mayer, *The Crusades*, trans. J. Gillingham, 2nd edition (Oxford, 1988), pp. 27–9.

Pope Urban's letter is not the only surviving evidence that points to eleventh-century Iberian devotion to the Holy Land. In 1075, for example, King Alfonso VI of León-Castile discovered that he had in his possession at Oviedo 'an incredible treasure', a chest that had been spirited away from Toledo before the city had been conquered by the Muslims, which contained relics of:

> the wood of the Cross; the Lord's blood; the Lord's bread, that is from his Last Supper; the Lord's Sepulchre; the Holy Land where the Lord stood; the robe of St Mary and the milk of the said virgin and mother of God; [and] the Lord's garment which was divided by lot and his gravecloth . . .[19]

Scholars have demonstrated the importance of relics of Christ's Passion for stimulating contemporary devotion to Jerusalem and the Holy Land,[20] and in this context it is therefore understandable why Pope Urban's crusade message of 1095–6, which may well have been transmitted to Iberia by some of the Spanish ecclesiastics who were present at the Council of Clermont,[21] proved popular with certain arms-bearers from across the peninsula.[22] Nevertheless, in spite of his extensive preaching in France for the liberation of the Holy Sepulchre, Urban was nothing but concerned about the participation in the First Crusade of warriors from the Christian regions of Iberia because, as he put it in a letter addressed to the Catalan counts of Besalú, Empurias, Roussillon and Cerdaña in c. 1096, 'it is no virtue to rescue Christians from the Saracens in one place only to expose them to the tyranny and oppression of the Saracens in another'.[23] Urban's well-founded fear was that the draining of manpower from the peninsula would destabilise an already fragile military situation, and he therefore told the four Catalan counts, each of whom had taken the cross, that instead of fighting in the Levant they could have their crusade vows commuted by taking up arms in defence of their native soil:

> We are persistently entreating your lordships on behalf of the city or rather the church of Tarragona, and we order you to persevere with the restoration of that place with all possible means for the remission of sins . . . Of course, if anyone should die on this expedition for God and for the love of his brothers, he should not doubt that he will certainly receive forgiveness of his sins and find a share of eternal life through the most compassionate mercy of our God. Thus if any of you has resolved to go to Asia, it is here instead that he should endeavour to fulfil the desire of his devotion [i.e. his crusade vow].[24]

[19] C. Morris, 'Memorials of the Holy Places and Blessings from the East: Devotion to Jerusalem before the Crusades', *The Holy Land, Holy Lands, and Christian History*, ed. R.N. Swanson, *SCH*, 36 (Woodbridge, 2000), pp. 95–6.

[20] See H.E.J. Cowdrey 'Pope Urban II and the Idea of Crusade', *Studi medievali*, 36 (1995), pp. 733–42; C. Morris, *The Sepulchre of Christ and the Medieval West: From the Beginning to 1600* (Oxford, 2005), pp. 146–53.

[21] See R. Somerville, 'The Council of Clermont (1095) and Latin Christian Society', *Archivum Historiae Pontificae*, 12 (1974), pp. 64–5, 71–2, 73.

[22] First crusaders from 'Galicia' and 'Hispania' are referred to in Ekkehard of Aura, 'Hierosolymita', *RHC Oc.* 5, p. 16; Sigebert of Gembloux, 'Chronica', *MGH SS* 6, p. 367; 'Notitiae duae Lemovicenses de praedicatione crucis in Aquitania', *RHC Oc.* 5, pp. 350–1.

[23] *Papsturkunden in Spanien*, no. 23, p. 288.

[24] *Ibid.*, p. 287–8.

Pope Urban's letter to the Catalan counts is not the only evidence to have survived which illustrates the problems that the preaching of the First Crusade caused in Iberia. On 14 October 1100, Urban's successor, Pope Paschal II, wrote a letter to Alfonso VI in which he reiterated his predecessor's policy of trying to redirect the crusading piety of Iberian arms-bearers, who in this case had probably been stirred to join a third wave of first crusaders by the liberation of Jerusalem in the previous year; Paschal assured Alfonso that the individuals in question could earn *venia peccatorum* by fighting in his 'kingdoms and counties' instead.[25] The excitement that the success of the First Crusade caused in Iberia had also affected the clergy, for on the same day the pope wrote to Spanish ecclesiastics to inform them that 'just as the knights' they were forbidden from deserting their homes to make for Jerusalem because of the *feritas Moabitarum*.[26] Six months later, on 25 March 1101, Paschal wrote to the clergy and laity of León-Castile once again, imploring them to focus their efforts in Spain rather than in the Holy Land. He told them it was not the time to desert their homelands, 'which are attacked daily by the raids of the Moors and the Moabites', and ordered those who had set out for the East to return to their homes at once.[27] However, his letter also showed that he was aware of the allure of the earthly Jerusalem, and of the ignominy that might accompany the crusaders' returning home with their vows unfulfilled.[28] To compensate, he tried to reinforce the idea that knights could gain spiritual rewards by fighting Islam in Iberia, but the desperation in his tone suggests that he was aware of the relative appeal of crusading to the East and of penitential warfare within the peninsula:

> Therefore we order you all with renewed command that you attack the Moabites and the Moors in your parts [of Christendom], persisting with all strength. In that place, by the generosity of God, you may complete your penance; in that place you can grasp the remission and grace of the holy apostles Peter and Paul and of their apostolic church.[29]

The surviving letters of Pope Urban and Pope Paschal indicate that the positive response of Iberian arms-bearers to the preaching of the First Crusade was regarded as extremely problematic,[30] but it is certain that they cannot have been the only missives despatched to explain how peninsular crusaders could have their vows commuted by fighting for the security of their homelands. Indeed, the case of King Pedro I of Aragón shows that the papacy's efforts to redirect the energies of Iberian crusaders were not as uniform a failure as the repetitive nature of the evidence cited above would appear to suggest. Pedro had taken the cross for the third wave of the First Crusade in 1100,[31] but instead of setting out for the East he chose to fulfil his vow by campaigning near

---

[25] Paschal II, 'Epistolae et privilegia', *PL* 163, no. 26, col. 45.

[26] *Ibid.*, no. 25, col. 45.

[27] *Ibid.*, no. 44, cols. 64–5.

[28] This humiliation was not restricted to crusaders from Iberia: Stephen of Blois, for example, had deserted the First Crusade at Antioch in 1098 and was shamed into joining the third wave of crusaders in 1101 by 'the private nagging of his formidable wife'. See J.S.C. Riley-Smith, *The First Crusade and the Idea of Crusading* (London, 1986), p. 120.

[29] Paschal II, 'Epistolae', no. 44, col. 65.

[30] See Bull, *Knightly Piety*, p. 97.

[31] Goñi Gaztambide, *Historia*, p. 67, n. 11.

Zaragoza, where he was said to have borne the *vexillum Christi*.[32] One contemporary described Pedro as the *rex crucifer*,[33] and the king's designation of a newly established settlement as 'Juslibol' (the name is believed to be a vulgarisation of *Deus lo vult*)[34] suggests that Pedro found it easy to channel his initial enthusiasm for the crusade to the East into more local military projects. In so doing, he was undoubtedly reflecting the will of the papacy, but it would seem that his co-operation with papal requests was the exception rather than the rule because at least two of the addressees of Urban's letter of *c.*1096, Geoffrey III of Rousillon and William Jordan of Cerdaña, ignored the pope's request to look to the defence of Tarragona and set out for Jerusalem irrespective of his instructions.[35]

It seems likely that at the heart of the problem of preventing Iberian arms-bearers from deserting the peninsula for the Holy Land was the fact that the crusade was not only regarded as an opportunity to gain spiritual rewards by fighting for God: it was also understood to be a form of pilgrimage. When one considers the highly charged nature of Pope Urban's preaching of the crusade as a Christo-mimetic devotional activity, and the reaction of contemporaries to the use of the sign of the cross as the crusade badge, the comparative appeal of fighting peninsular Islam is thrown into sharp relief. In spite of his best efforts, Pope Urban's utterances about the relative merits of travelling to Jerusalem to liberate the Holy Sepulchre and restoring the church of Tarragona must have sounded distinctly hollow,[36] and the fact that at this early stage of the crusading movement's development the sign of the cross was inextricably linked with the idea of imitating Christ by fighting '*in the place where his feet have stood*' goes a long way to explaining the reluctance of individuals such as the counts of Rousillon and Cerdaña to abandon their original plans of travelling to the East. As far as one can tell, although Pope Urban had commented in 1098 that 'in our days by means of Christian strength, [God] has conquered the Turks in Asia and the Moors in Europe',[37] he had no mind to include Iberia within the scope of the First Crusade,[38] and there is no evidence from *c.*1095–1102 to suggest that there was any general preaching for penitential warfare in the peninsula as there is for, say, the third wave of the First Crusade in 1101.[39] In this respect, if the evidence for Pedro of Aragón's bearing of the cross at Zaragoza is reliable, it would appear that he was acting independently of papal proclamations,[40] and his understanding of the significance of the crusade badge would certainly have been at odds with that of most of his contemporaries. In fact, the only comparable example

---

[32] F. Fita, 'El Concilio Nacional de Palencia en el año 1100 y el de Gerona en 1101', *BRAH*, 24 (1894), p. 232. See Ubieto Arteta, 'La participación navarro-aragonesa en la primera cruzada', p. 370.

[33] Goñi Gaztambide, *Historia*, p. 67, n. 13.

[34] See O'Callaghan, *Reconquest and Crusade*, p. 33.

[35] See Riley-Smith, *First Crusaders*, pp. 71, 207, 225.

[36] *Papsturkunden in Spanien*, no. 23, p. 287.

[37] Urban II, 'Epistolae', no. 237, col. 504. Bull, *Knightly Piety*, p. 97, suggested that this equation was being made to dissuade Aragonese arms-bearers from joining the First Crusade.

[38] Cf. Goñi Gaztambide, *Historia*, pp. 61–2. N. Housley, 'Jerusalem and the Development of the Crusade Idea, 1099–1128', *The Horns of Hattin: Proceedings of the Second Conference of the Society for the Study of the Crusades and the Latin East*, ed. B.Z. Kedar (Jerusalem, 1992), p. 32, argued that it is 'crystal clear that Urban II's conception of the crusade was a broad one'.

[39] See Riley-Smith, *First Crusaders*, pp. 75–7.

[40] Cf. Goñi Gaztambide, *Historia*, p. 67.

of a broader understanding of a first crusader's votive obligation that survives is that which Orderic Vitalis attributed to Helias of La Flèche, the count of Maine. Helias had taken the cross in 1096, but fearing that the king of England would take advantage of his absence in the East to gain further lands in northern France, Helias was said to have declared that:

> My [original] desire was to fight against the infidel in the name of the Lord, but now it appears I have a battle nearer home against the enemies of Christ. Every man who opposes truth and justice proves himself an enemy of God . . . I will not abandon the cross of our Saviour which I have taken up as a pilgrim, but will have it engraved on my shield and helmet and all my arms . . . Fortified by this symbol I will move against the enemies of peace and right, and defend Christian lands in battle. And so my horse and my arms will be clearly marked with a holy sign [i.e. the cross] and all foes who attack me will be fighting against a knight of Christ.[41]

The apparent ease with which Helias felt able to redirect his crusading piety is striking, but it is plain nonetheless that he was understood to have been conscious that his actions against 'the enemies of Christ' in France did not relieve him of his votive obligation, for he added that he would have to 'wait for a better time when I might fulfil my vow', presumably by completing a journey to the Holy Sepulchre.[42] Returning to Iberia, one is forced to conclude that the papacy's offer to crusaders from the peninsula of local penitential warfare as a means of vow commutation has more in common with the experience of Emerias of Altejas than it does with the later projection of Spain as a second front of crusading activity. Emerias was a woman from Toulouse who had taken the cross in 1098, but who was encouraged by her bishop to commute her crusade vow by founding a hospice for the poor.[43] In both Emerias's case and that of the Iberian first crusaders, the alternative penitential activities proposed by the respective ecclesiastical authorities simply seem to have been regarded as being more suitable than those that the individuals in question had originally vowed to undertake: penitential warfare for pious knights and charitable foundations for wealthy noblewomen. At the time of the First Crusade, the papacy must therefore be seen to be reacting to the pious aspirations of the Spanish rather than seizing the opportunity to extend crusading warfare to the peninsula, and one is left with the impression that the Church was faced with an uphill struggle if it was to convince the arms-bearers of Iberia that it was as rewarding to fight against the Muslims of al-Andalus as it was to engage with Islam in the Holy Land.[44]

Papal efforts to foster ideas of penitential warfare in Iberia, which had been initiated by Pope Urban II,[45] were somewhat erratic in the first two decades of the twelfth century. Indeed, although Pope Paschal had instructed the clergy of Braga in Portugal in a letter of 1108×11[46] that they 'ought to encourage the minds of the faithful [to fight] against

---

[41] OV 5, pp. 228–31.

[42] See also Riley-Smith, *The First Crusade*, pp. 40–1.

[43] *Histoire générale de Languedoc*, 3rd edition, ed. J. Vaissète, C. Devic and A. Molinier, 16 vols. (Toulouse, 1872–1904), vol. 5, p. 757. See Riley-Smith, *First Crusaders*, p. 108.

[44] See also Barton, 'From Tyrants to Soldiers of Christ', pp. 28–48.

[45] Cf. O'Callaghan, *Reconquest and Crusade*, pp. 24–32.

[46] Goñi Gaztambide, *Historia*, pp. 67–8, believed this letter to be a response to the Uclés disaster of

the attacks of the Moabites so that, abstaining from sin, they might obtain the grace of God',[47] such nebulous proclamations appear to have been shots in the dark, and it was not until *c.* 1116 that the papacy was involved in the coherent projection of campaigning against Islam on the Iberian mainland.[48]

According to the *vita* of Oleguer of Tarragona, which cannot have been written until at least two decades after the events it was describing, shortly after he had returned from his triumphant expedition to the Balearics of 1114–15 Count Ramon Berenguer III of Barcelona had set out for Rome to seek an audience with Pope Paschal II. During his time in the apostolic city, and as a result of his dialogues with the pope, he was said to have been supplied with 'letters of remission and obedience to stir up kingdoms of faith against a people of faithlessness, the Saracens of Spain',[49] which suggests that Paschal had authorised the preaching of a penitential war in Catalonia. The pope's sponsorship of Ramon Berenguer's specific proposal – an assault on the coastal town of Tortosa – is also supported by epistolary evidence. In a letter of 23 May 1116 Paschal praised the count for his faithfulness and for his recent victories over the Muslims of the Balearics, where he had exerted himself 'against the enemies of the Christian people', and he reported his awareness of the fact that his correspondent was now understood to be working 'for the conquest of the Moors and Moabites in Tortosa and [other] parts of Spain'.[50] Although the letter stopped short of portraying the campaign as a penitential activity, it did confirm that the pope had offered the protection of the apostolic see to Ramon Berenguer, and the subsequent preaching activity of a papal legate, Cardinal Boso of St Anastasia, indicates that Paschal intended to support the count's efforts to recruit for the expedition.[51] Nevertheless, there is no evidence to show that the efforts of Ramon Berenguer or Cardinal Boso came to anything, and it has been suggested that the Tortosa project failed largely because it was eclipsed by contemporary events in Aragón.[52]

The conquest of Zaragoza in 1118 by King Alfonso I of Aragón,[53] known to history as 'the Battler',[54] provides the first unambiguous evidence of the papacy actively directing penitential warfare on the Iberian mainland.[55] According to the chronicler of St Maixent, a group of senior ecclesiastics, who may have included the newly elected Pope Gelasius II amongst their number, 'confirmed the way of Spain' at a church council that was convened in Toulouse in 1118,[56] possibly as a result of the preaching tour of

---

1108, but Fita, 'Concilio Nacional de Palencia', p. 219, dated it to March 1111. For the narrative of events at Uclés, see Lomax, *Reconquest of Spain*, pp. 72–3.

[47] Fita, 'Concilio Nacional de Palencia', p. 219.

[48] The 'crusade' to the Balearics of 1113–15 will be dealt with in Chapter Six.

[49] 'Vita sancti Olegarii', *España Sagrada*, 29 (Madrid, 1775), p. 475.

[50] F. Fita, 'Renallo Gramático y la conquista de Mallorca por el conde de Barcelona don Ramón Berenguer III: Apéndice de documentos', *BRAH*, 40 (1902), no. 11, p. 73.

[51] See Bull, *Knightly Piety*, pp. 108–9.

[52] B.F. Reilly, *The Contest of Christian and Muslim Spain, 1031–1157* (Cambridge, MA, and Oxford, 1992), p. 179.

[53] See J.M. Lacarra, 'La conquista de Zaragoza por Alfonso I (18 diciembre 1118)', *Al-Andalus*, 12 (1974), pp. 65–96.

[54] *Crónica de San Juan de la Peña*, ed. A. Ubieto Arteta, *Textos medievales*, 4 (Valencia, 1961), p. 68.

[55] Cf. J.S.C. Riley-Smith, *The Crusades: A History*, 2nd edition (London, 2005), p. 116.

[56] *La Chronique de Saint-Maixent, 751–1140*, ed. and trans. J. Verdon (Paris, 1979), p. 186. See also J. Verdon, 'Une source de la reconquête chrétienne en Espagne: la Chronique de Saint-Maixent', *Mélanges*

Cardinal Boso in 1117–18.[57] The meaning of this rather vague phrase is elucidated by a letter that Pope Gelasius himself addressed on 10 December 1118 to 'the army of Christians besieging Zaragoza and to all supporters of the Catholic faith'.[58] Clearly, the council of Toulouse had discussed the assignment of spiritual privileges to those who fought in a military campaign in the Ebro valley under King Alfonso. Gelasius's letter was evidently part of an ongoing correspondence with the army and was intended not only to reassure those who were engaged in the siege but also to attract more recruits for the expedition. As such, it defined the spiritual reward that participants might receive in the broadest of terms:

> Those who are labouring, or who will labour, in the service of the Lord, and those who have said in advance that they will donate, or those who will donate in future, anything to the church of the city [of Zaragoza], which was destroyed by the Saracens and Moabites, so that it can be rebuilt, or to the clergy serving God there, so that they may be supplied as necessary, will obtain remission and forgiveness of their penances according to the extent of their labours and the cost of their benefactions to the church, at the judgement of the bishops in whose parishes they live.[59]

There can be no doubt that this letter is evidence that those who fought alongside Alfonso at Zaragoza could have expected to receive remission of sins, but it is striking that the exact nature of that remission was to be determined by local clergy rather than mandated by the papacy. Moreover, the fact that Pope Gelasius was emphasising the value of military contributions alongside more peaceful and restorative ones highlights how penitential warfare was coming to be regarded as a customary channel of pious activity. Yet for all that the Zaragoza campaign and its antecedents in 1108x11 and 1116 indicate that the papacy was authorising penitential warfare in Iberia, there is nothing to suggest that these undertakings were regarded as crusades.[60] At no point in the period *c.*1102–*c.*1120 was pious violence in the peninsula compared to an expedition to Jerusalem, and there is no evidence that participants swore vows or were entreated to take the sign of the cross in imitation of Christ.[61] If these campaigns *were* crusades, the complete absence of evidence of these potent elements is astonishing, especially given Pope Paschal II's direct experiences with many first crusaders and Pope Gelasius II's pedigree within the papal chancery.[62] Indeed, such is the certainty with which the language, symbolism and privileges of crusading can suddenly be identified in Iberia in the early 1120s, unless further evidence comes to light it must be concluded that these earlier campaigns belong to a separate tradition of penitential war.[63]

offerts à René Crozet, ed. P. Gallais and Y.-J. Riou, 2 vols. (Poitiers, 1966), vol. 1, pp. 273–82.

[57] See Bull, *Knightly Piety*, p. 109.

[58] Gelasius II, 'Epistolae et privilegia', *PL* 163, no. 25, col. 508.

[59] *Ibid.*, col. 508.

[60] Cf. Riley-Smith, *The Crusades*, p. 116.

[61] Cf. Goñi Gaztambide, *Historia*, p. 62.

[62] See J.N.D. Kelly, *The Oxford Dictionary of Popes* (Oxford, 1986), p. 163.

[63] See Riley-Smith, *First Crusaders*, pp. 51–2; Housley, 'Crusades against Christians', pp. 17–36; C. Tyerman, *The Invention of the Crusades* (Basingstoke, 1998), p. 15. In this respect, I follow the schema of R.A. Fletcher, *St James's Catapult: The Life and Times of Diego Gelmírez of Santiago de Compostela* (Oxford, 1984), pp. 297–8; Fletcher, 'Reconquest and Crusade', pp. 42–3; and Bull, *Knightly Piety*, p. 113. But

The Extension of Crusading to Iberia and the iter per Hispaniam

It has already been described in Chapter Three how, at the First Lateran Council in April 1123, Pope Calixtus II confirmed his earlier proclamation of a crusade to the East, an expedition that was launched in response to the news of the defeat at the Battle of the Field of Blood in 1119.[64] It is significant that when on that occasion Pope Calixtus spoke of the need for those who had not yet set out on crusade to fulfil their vows, he referred to 'those . . . who are known to have placed crosses on their clothing either for the journey to Jerusalem or for that to Spain'.[65] This decree makes it absolutely clear that at some point before April 1123 the sign of the cross was being used to symbolise an individual's votive obligation to go on crusade in Iberia, and, moreover, that it was being promulgated that crusaders in Spain would be rewarded with the same spiritual privileges as those who participated in the expedition to the East. This position was clarified by Pope Calixtus in the letter he wrote to 'all the bishops, kings, counts, princes and other faithful of God [in Iberia]', almost certainly from the Lateran Council of 1123 itself.[66] Calixtus began by describing the threat faced by the Spanish church 'through the oppression of the pagans', before moving to his *exhortatio*:

> We appeal to your affection, as if God, on whose behalf we are acting, were exhorting you through us. And so, dearest sons, we are encouraging you with all the prayers that we can offer so that you might never cease from working hard for the defence of your brothers and for the liberation of the churches. Thus with apostolic authority and the power granted to us by God, we willingly offer to all those fighting firmly on this expedition the same remission of sins that we offered to the defenders of the eastern Church. But if those who have put the sign of the cross on their clothes for this purpose have not endeavoured to complete their vows between this Easter and the next, we banish them thereafter from the bosom of the Holy Church until they make amends.[67]

The letter went on to confirm that Oleguer of Tarragona was to act as the expedition's papal legate;[68] other evidence indicates that legatine authority was also granted to the archbishop of Compostela, Diego Gelmírez.[69] Thus at some point in the early years of his pontificate, and certainly before April 1123, Pope Calixtus II had proclaimed a crusade to the East and at around the same time had authorised crusading within the Iberian peninsula for the first time.[70] After three decades of efforts to stem the flow

---

see also Housley, 'Jerusalem and the Development of the Crusade Idea', pp. 32–6.

[64] See above, pp. 72–4.

[65] *Conciliorum oecumenicorum decreta*, ed. J. Alberigo *et al.* (Freiburg, 1962), p. 168.

[66] For the date, see J.S.C. Riley-Smith, 'The Venetian Crusade of 1122–1124', *I comuni italiani nel regno crociato di Gerusalemme*, ed. G. Airaldi and B.Z. Kedar (Genoa, 1986), p. 345.

[67] Calixtus II, *Bullaire*, ed. U. Robert, 2 vols. (Paris, 1891), vol. 2, Ep. 454, pp. 266–7.

[68] It is certainly intriguing that the preaching of the crusade was not later recorded in Oleguer's *vita*. See Riley-Smith, 'Venetian Crusade', p. 348.

[69] Diego had been appointed papal legate for the provinces of Mérida and Braga in 1120. For his crusade legation, see Riley-Smith, 'Venetian Crusade', p. 347.

[70] For the response to Calixtus's preaching in Iberia, see Goñi Gaztambide, *Historia*, pp. 78–9; Riley-Smith, 'Venetian Crusade', p. 348; O'Callaghan, *Reconquest and Crusade*, pp. 38–9.

of manpower from Iberia and to promote the merits of penitential warfare within the peninsula, the papacy had suddenly shifted policy by extending crusading to another theatre of war and, as a result, ostensibly detaching the crusade ideal from its Jerusalem-centric roots.[71] It is impossible to know for certain what factors inspired Calixtus to abandon the approach of his predecessors, but a hypothetical reconstruction of events is possible using a variety of contemporary source material. Indeed, it would seem that far from attempting to isolate crusading from its association with the Jerusalem pilgrimage tradition, the idea of fighting to and for the Holy Sepulchre was being introduced into Iberia as a means of propagating peninsular warfare against Islam.

An important clue as to the role the Holy Land may have played in the extension of crusading to Iberia is provided by the text of a letter sent to Diego Gelmírez by the patriarch of Jerusalem and the prior of the Holy Sepulchre in *c.*1120. As has been noted elsewhere,[72] this letter, which was preserved by the compilers of the *Historia Compostellana*,[73] was one of several appeals that were sent to the West in the wake of the defeat at the Battle of the Field of Blood.[74] It described the perilous situation in the Latin East, and appealed passionately for the archbishop of Compostela to assist in the settlers' plight:

> Every day we are attacked, every day we are slaughtered and taken captive . . . [but] we are prepared to die for the name of Jesus before we abandon the holy city of Jerusalem, the Cross of the Lord and the most sacred Sepulchre of Christ . . . O most distinguished archbishop, we implore you with bended knees and with floods of tears to come to help us![75]

The letter went on to emphasise that the arms-bearers of Iberia should not hesitate 'to die in Jerusalem for the name of Christ, where the son of God did not hesitate to be crucified and die for us', and entreated the archbishop of Compostela to send an *exercitus Christi* to assist in the defence of the Holy Sepulchre:

> If indeed you had not heard our call, or not seen our messengers or letters, perhaps you might have some excuse. But is this the case? You must come, you must come! And whosoever comes to our aid will receive remission of all sins, for with the help of God we are loosening the bonds [of sin] and placing them upon the shoulders of the Lamb, who takes away the sins of the world.[76]

Although it has been stressed elsewhere that there is no evidence of any direct response to the patriarch's letter,[77] there is the strong possibility that its receipt in

---

[71] For the significance of the pontificate of Calixtus II to the early development of crusading in Spain, see also N. Housley, *Contesting the Crusades* (Oxford, 2006), pp. 100–5.

[72] See J.P. Phillips, *Defenders of the Holy Land: Relations between the Latin East and the West, 1119–1187* (Oxford, 1996), pp. 14–18.

[73] On this text, see especially B.F. Reilly, 'The *Historia Compostelana*: The Genesis and Composition of a Twelfth-Century Spanish *Gesta*', *Speculum*, 44 (1969), pp. 78–85; Fletcher, *St James's Catapult*, p. 301.

[74] *Historia Compostellana*, ed. E. Falque Rey, CC:CM 70 (Turnhout, 1988), pp. 270–2. See also Phillips, *Defenders of the Holy Land*, pp. 15–17.

[75] *Historia Compostellana*, p. 271.

[76] *Ibid.*, p. 272.

[77] Phillips, *Defenders of the Holy Land*, pp. 16–17.

Compostela may well be connected to the subsequent extension of crusading to the Iberian peninsula. It is well known that Diego Gelmírez enjoyed a close relationship with Pope Calixtus II[78] – it was under Calixtus that Compostela was elevated to metropolitan status in 1120, for example[79] – and Calixtus's personal connections also meant that he had a special concern for events in both the Holy Land and in Iberia. As Guy of Burgundy, he was not only cousin to King Baldwin II of Jerusalem,[80] but also brother to Raymond (d. 1107), the first husband of Queen Urraca of León-Castile (r. 1109–26), and uncle to Urraca's son, who was to become King Alfonso VII (r. 1126–57).[81] It is therefore not impossible to believe that Diego had made the pope aware of the appeal he had received from the patriarch of Jerusalem, and that at the same time that he was preaching for a crusade to the East Calixtus was reminded of the problems that earlier crusade appeals had caused in Spain.[82] In simultaneously proclaiming a crusade in Spain as the equal of a campaign to the East, Calixtus might therefore be seen to be anticipating potential difficulties with arms-bearers from Iberia responding positively to his call to take the cross for the Holy Land.[83] However, this argument poses something of a conceptual problem because, as has been stressed above, in c. 1120 the idea of crusading was intrinsically linked with the Jerusalem pilgrimage tradition and literal ideas of Christo-mimesis that could only be fulfilled by travelling to '*the place where his feet have stood*'. It is therefore of the greatest significance that the proclamation of the crusade in Spain in the early 1120s coincides with the first appearances of a motif that was to become fundamental to peninsular crusading: the *iter per Hispaniam*.[84]

Simply put, the idea of the strategists appears to have been that crusaders fighting in Spain would open another route to the Holy Sepulchre by liberating Iberia and North Africa from the rule of Islam. In this way, the efforts and goals of crusaders fighting in Iberia were presented as being synonymous with those of crusaders who set out for the Holy Land via Hungary and Asia Minor. It is surely no coincidence that one of the most striking expressions of this idea was delivered by Diego Gelmírez himself at a council held in Compostela in January 1124.[85] According to the *Historia Compostellana*, the council had been called in an attempt to resolve the discord between Queen Urraca and her son Alfonso, but proceedings had concluded with Archbishop Diego proclaiming an expedition 'against the Moors', participation in which was to be rewarded with *plenaria absolutio*:

---

[78] See Fletcher, *St James's Catapult*, pp. 192–222.

[79] Calixtus II, *Bullaire*, vol. 1, nos. 146–8, pp. 216–19.

[80] See Riley-Smith, *First Crusaders*, p. 177.

[81] For the crusading traditions of the comital house of Burgundy, see *ibid.*, pp. 94–5, 102, 247.

[82] *Historia Compostellana*, pp. 24–6, 77–8, preserved the letters that Pope Paschal II had written to try to dissuade Iberian first crusaders in 1100 and 1101.

[83] Barton, *Aristocracy*, p. 155, notes that 'By 1120 … large numbers of Galicians were taking up the cross to campaign in the Near East.'

[84] See Housley, 'Jerusalem and the Development of the Crusade Idea', pp. 35–6.

[85] There is some confusion over the dating of this council; several historians have followed Goñi Gaztambide's incorrect date of January 1125. But *Historia Compostellana*, p. 378, records that 'concilium in tertio anno sui archiepiscopatus XV K. Februarii Compostelle celebrauit', and Calixtus II, *Bullaire*, vol. 1, nos. 146–8, pp. 216–19, show that it was in February 1120 that Compostela was elevated to a metropolitan see. The council must therefore have been held in January 1124.

> And finally in that council, with a loud voice, he proclaimed, praised and commended
> an expedition against the Moors, for the suppression and undoing of pagans, and for
> the glorification and edification of Christians. To all those who accepted to go on that
> expedition as a penance, he granted absolution of all sins by the authority of Almighty
> God, Son and Holy Spirit, and of the blessed apostles, Peter, Paul and James and all
> of the saints.[86]

The *Historia*'s compilers went on to state that the reward for participation in the *expeditio* was to be offered to 'the kings and counts and other princes, the knights and also the footsoldiers', before concluding with a description of how the general preaching of the campaign was to be set in motion.[87]

The *excitatoria* that the council produced 'for the archbishops, bishops, abbots and the rest of the clergy to proclaim, praise and expound to all the people' was preserved in the *Historia*. It was attributed to Archbishop Diego, who styled himself as archbishop of Compostela and papal legate, and who began by addressing both spiritual and secular leaders by quoting from St Paul's Epistle to the Romans: '*The hour has come for you to rise from your slumber*'.[88] Diego went on to describe how although Christ had called for help the people of Christendom had refused to go to his aid, and he therefore entreated the arms-bearers of Iberia to seize the opportunity to join the 'camp of Christ' from where they might gain remission of sins as *athletas Christi* in an *exercitus Domini*. He also delineated the temporal privileges that participants could expect to receive, such as the protection of their property, and stated that in all his proposals he was following the decree of Pope Calixtus II (*iuxta domini Pape edictum*). However, the most dramatic aspect of his appeal was the way he cited the example of the first crusaders to inspire his audience, and linked the projected crusade in Spain with the *iter Iherosolimitanum*:

> Just as the knights of Christ, the faithful sons of the Holy Church, opened the way to
> Jerusalem with much labour and spilling of blood, so we should become knights of
> Christ and, after defeating his wicked enemies the Saracens, open the way to the same
> Sepulchre of the Lord through Spain, which is shorter and much less laborious.[89]

This was, of course, an extraordinary proposal and Diego's suggestion that the *iter per Hispaniam* was 'shorter and much less laborious' was almost certainly rhetorical.[90] But in the wake of the symbolic recovery of the former Visigothic capital of Toledo in 1085,[91] the recent victory against the Almoravids at Zaragoza in 1118 and, above all, the 'miraculous' success of the First Crusade in 1099,[92] this remarkable project cannot have been dismissed as pure fantasy.[93] That it was actually taken quite seriously is shown

---

[86] *Historia Compostellana*, p. 378.

[87] *Ibid.*, p. 378.

[88] *Ibid.*, p. 379. Citation from Romans 13:11.

[89] *Ibid.*, pp. 379–80.

[90] For an alternative treatment of the *iter per Hispaniam*, see P. J. O'Banion, 'What has Iberia to do with Jerusalem? Crusade and the Spanish Route to the Holy Land in the Twelfth Century' (Forthcoming).

[91] See O'Callaghan, *Reconquest and Crusade*, p. 30.

[92] See Riley-Smith, *The First Crusade*, pp. 132–4.

[93] Cf. M. Bull, 'The Capetian Monarchy and the Early Crusade Movement: Hugh of Vermandois and Louis VII', *Nottingham Medieval Studies*, 40 (1996), p. 28, who argued that 'Pressure on Fatimid Egypt

by the speed with which the idea appears to have spread across the peninsula in the mid-1120s.

The principal secular supporter for the *iter per Hispaniam* in the early twelfth century was Alfonso I of Aragón.[94] Alfonso's enthusiastic response to the idea of opening another road to the Holy Sepulchre through Iberia is perhaps not surprising. His brother Pedro had already established a tradition of crusading piety in the royal house of Aragón by taking the cross in 1100,[95] and Alfonso himself had of course been victorious in the penitential war that Pope Gelasius II had directed against the Muslims of Zaragoza in 1118. It is in fact in relation to this victory at Zaragoza that Alfonso's embracing of crusade ideology can first be identified, for this campaign was but the latest episode in the history of Aragonese territorial expansion into the Ebro valley,[96] and in the early 1120s, in order to secure the various gains that had been made in the previous two decades, Alfonso began to establish a number of military confraternities in the region, perhaps inspired by the foundation of the Templars in the East in 1120.[97] The statutes that survive for these confraternities demonstrate that from at least as early as 1122 Alfonso saw the Aragonese expansion into the Ebro as being part of a larger context of crusading activity.

The first of these confraternities was established at Belchite at some point between February and May 1122,[98] although the only record for its privileges is contained within a document produced by the Council of Burgos in 1136.[99] Whilst it is therefore difficult to isolate which elements of the confraternity's privileges were retained from an earlier document and which were introduced later, there is no reason to believe that the statement of the confraternity's aims does not date from the time of its establishment in 1122.[100] In its foundation charter, the *milicia confraternitas Cesaraugustane* was described by Alfonso of Aragón as being established 'for the preservation, defence and expansion of the Christian people, and for the suppression and destruction of the arrogance and aggression of the faithless pagans'.[101] It was a *milicia Christi* and an *exercitus Dei*, over which Alfonso himself was the *princeps confrater et defensor*. Along with grants of generous privileges, Alfonso ordained that the brothers should 'never make peace with the pagans, but let them strive for all their days to harass and assault them'.[102] The charter

from the west would certainly have been of benefit to the Latin position in Palestine.'

[94] See J.M. Lacarra, *Alfonso el Batallador* (Zaragoza, 1978). For the lack of a response to Diego Gelmírez's preaching in León-Castile, see Barton, 'From Tyrants to Soldiers of Christ', pp. 38–9.

[95] Cf. Bull, 'The Capetian Monarchy', pp. 27–9.

[96] See C. Stalls, *Possessing the Land: Aragon's Expansion into Islam's Ebro Frontier under Alfonso the Battler, 1104–1134* (Leiden, New York and Cologne, 1995), pp. 4–58.

[97] See E. Lourie, 'The Confraternity of Belchite, the Ribat, and the Temple', *Viator*, 13 (1982), pp. 159–76; A.J. Forey, 'The Military Orders and the Spanish Reconquest in the Twelfth and Thirteenth Centuries', *Traditio*, 40 (1984), pp. 197–8; A.J. Forey, 'The Emergence of the Military Order in the Twelfth Century', *Journal of Ecclesiastical History*, 36 (1985), pp. 180, 189.

[98] For the date, see A. Ubieto Arteta, 'La creación de la cofradía militar de Belchite', *Estudios de edad media de la corona de Aragón*, 5 (1952), pp. 427–34.

[99] See P. Rassow, 'La cofradía de Belchite', *Anuario de historia del derecho español*, 3 (1926), pp. 200–26.

[100] See Bull, *Knightly Piety*, pp. 102–3.

[101] Rassow, 'Cofradía de Belchite', p. 220.

[102] *Ibid.*, p. 221.

went on to record the conditions of service at Belchite and the varying nature of the spiritual rewards offered to those who contributed to the confraternity's efforts. This section's opening clause established a clear analogy between a lifetime's commitment to defending Christians in Spain and other avenues of religious observance, and bears obvious comparison with the contemporary establishment of the Order of the Temple:

> Any Christian, whether cleric or layman, who may wish to become a brother of this confraternity … at the castle which is called Belchite, or at any other castle which is suitable for this enterprise (*expeditio*), should undertake to fight for the defence of Christians and in the service of Christ for the rest of his life. He will, after having made confession, be absolved of all his sins as if he were entering upon the life of a monk or a hermit.[103]

The specific influence of crusading ideology upon the foundation at Belchite is most clearly illustrated in the charter's closing phrases, wherein the broader framework for the confraternity's operations was delineated. First, the charter cited scriptural passages that were crucial to the association between crusading and the ideal of the imitation of Christ in the early twelfth century:

> Therefore, most beloved brothers, you must make haste with an eager soul to the joy of so much remission, remembering the precepts of the Lord: *He who follows me will not walk in darkness*; and *he who throws away his life because of me, he will keep it in eternal life*; and *he who does not take up his cross and follow me is not worthy of me*.[104]

The charter then concluded by describing the idea of the *iter per Hispaniam* and connecting the success of the First Crusade with more recent victories in the Balearics and in the Ebro:

> Indeed, by the same remission, the Sepulchre of the Lord was delivered out of captivity, and also Majorca, Zaragoza, and other places; similarly, with God's favour, the *iter Jherusalemitanum* will be opened from this direction, and the church of God, which hitherto has been held under the captivity of slavery, will be made free.[105]

Within a matter of years of the establishment of the confraternity at Belchite, Alfonso had founded a similar organisation at Monreal del Campo. This second foundation cannot be precisely dated, but it seems most likely to have been some point in 1128.[106] The confraternity of Monreal del Campo was another *militia Christi* whose *raison d'être* was the liberation of the *iter per Hispaniam*. According to the surviving source that documents its establishment – a letter subscribed by Archbishop William of Auch to encourage recruitment and benefaction from Gascony – Alfonso had founded the confraternity so that, under his leadership, it would 'bring battle to and overcome all the Saracens on this side of the sea, and open a road to Jerusalem across the straits [of Gibraltar]'.[107] The

---

[103] *Ibid.*, p. 224.
[104] *Ibid.*, p. 225. Citations from John 8:12; Matthew 10:39; John 12:25; Matthew 10:38.
[105] *Ibid.*, p. 225.
[106] For the date, see Stalls, *Possessing the Land*, p. 260, n. 122.
[107] For the document, see *Documents para el estudio de la reconquista y repoblación del valle del Ebro*, ed.

letter also highlighted the value of the spiritual reward offered by membership of the confraternity, suggesting that 'just as the *Iherosolimitani*', the *confratres* of Monreal del Campo would be completely absolved of sin.[108]

Aside from the information provided in the statutes quoted above, very little is known about the ideals or achievements of the confraternities Alfonso of Aragón founded in the 1120s; it is worth noting that neither organisation was mentioned in his famous will of 1131.[109] However, one supplementary reference (albeit nebulous) to the activities of the *milicia Christi* of Belchite is provided by Orderic Vitalis in his account of Alfonso's raids deep into al-Andalus in 1125–6. Indeed, these raids themselves are probably indicative of the extent to which the king was committed to the practical fulfilment of the *iter per Hispaniam*,[110] and it is striking that as a preliminary to that expedition Orderic recorded that alongside a French contingent fighting the Muslims of the Ebro were the *fratres de Palmis*.[111] Marjorie Chibnall identified these *fratres* as the brothers of Belchite, and she argued that the term was 'probably derived from the spathe, or sword-shaped bract of palm trees', and associated it with the fact that later in the twelfth century the brethren of some Spanish military orders were known as the *fratres de spata*.[112] However, it is more likely that the designation of the *fratres de Palmis* had a deeper resonance with the brothers' projected desire to liberate an alternative road to the Holy Sepulchre. The association of the palm tree with Jerusalem pilgrimage was long-standing, and it does not therefore seem implausible that the permanent *confratres* of Belchite might have used an image of the palm as a badge that was symbolic of their ultimate goal: to reach the Holy Land and collect real palm branches, as was customary for those who had completed an *iter Iherosolimitanum*. In this way, they would have been distinguished from those crusaders whom they fought alongside, whose adoption of the sign of the cross was of course understood to denote a temporary votive obligation. If this analysis of the derivation of the term *fratres de Palmis* is accurate, it gives further indication of the importance of pilgrimage ideology to the development of crusading in Iberia.

It would seem, therefore, that from at least the early 1120s Alfonso of Aragón saw himself and his men as crusaders who were participating in an armed pilgrimage to the Holy Land that differed from the First Crusade only in terms of the route that was being taken. In this respect, it is telling that when Orderic Vitalis described Alfonso's final campaign at Fraga, he wrote of the 'unconquerable determination of the magnificent prince and the armies of the Christians, who wore the cross of Christ (*Christi cruce signatos*) and were strengthened with invincible courage',[113] and that, like the army of

J.M. Lacarra, 2 vols., *Textos medievales*, 62–3 (Zaragoza, 1982–5), vol. 1, no. 173, pp. 182–4; also *Colección diplomática de Alfonso I de Aragón y Pamplona (1104–1134)*, ed. J.A. Lema Pueyo (San Sebastian, 1990), no. 141, pp. 206–8.

[108] *Colección diplomática de Alfonso*, no. 141, p. 208.

[109] A.J. Forey, 'The Will of Alfonso I of Aragón and Navarre', *Durham University Journal*, 73 (1980), p. 64, suggested that the absence of the confraternities from the will indicates that neither institution ever became well-established. For the text of the will, see *Colección diplomática de Alfonso*, nos. 241 and 284, pp. 356–65, 446–8.

[110] On the subsequent campaign, see OV 6, pp. 404–6. See also O'Callaghan, *Reconquest and Crusade*, pp. 37–8.

[111] OV 6, pp. 400–1.

[112] OV 6, p. 400, n. 2.

[113] OV 6, pp. 410–11.

the kingdom of Jerusalem,[114] Alfonso was also reputed to have always carried a fragment of the True Cross into battle.[115] Furthermore, it should also be noted that amongst those who fought alongside Alfonso in the Ebro were a number of former first crusaders, including Gaston IV of Béarn, Rotrou of Perche and Centulle of Bigorre.[116] These men were understood to have been central to Alfonso's military efforts – the confraternity of Monreal del Campo was believed to have been established 'with the advice and help of Count Gaston', for example[117] – but Marcus Bull has noted that 'returning French first crusaders transferred their enthusiasm into the Spanish theatre only very gradually',[118] and emphasised that in spite of the network of family ties that connected Gascony with Aragón[119] it was not until 1117 that Gaston of Béarn can be clearly identified as engaging enthusiastically in peninsular reconquest. Perhaps it had taken an idea as potent as opening a road to the Holy Sepulchre through Iberia to stir his enthusiasm, and that of men like him, for campaigning in Spain;[120] his interest in pilgrimage had certainly not waned since his return from the East in 1101.[121] If this is the case, it certainly raises the question whether the *via de Hispania* that was confirmed at the Council of Toulouse in 1118 was synonymous with the *iter per Hispaniam* that Diego Gelmírez spoke of at Compostela in 1124.[122]

Alfonso's fixation with the idea of opening the *iter per Hispaniam* also goes a long way to explaining the content of his remarkable will, which was initially drawn up in 1131 and confirmed shortly before his death in 1134. The motivation behind the creation of this document – the execution of which would have seen the kingdom of Aragón divided between the Hospitallers, Templars and canons of the Holy Sepulchre – has been a cause of some controversy, but in the light of what has been said above it is perhaps to be expected that the present writer is in agreement with the conclusions of Alan Forey rather than those of Elena Lourie.[123] When Alfonso's career is considered as

---

[114] See A. V. Murray, '"Mighty against the Enemies of Christ": The Relic of the True Cross in the Armies of the Kingdom of Jerusalem', *The Crusades and their Sources: Essays Presented to Bernard Hamilton*, ed. J. France and W. G. Zajac (Aldershot, 1998), pp. 217–38.

[115] 'Chronica Adefonsi imperatoris', ed. A. Maya Sánchez, *Chronica Hispana saeculi XII, CC:CM 71* (Turnhout, 1990), p. 43.

[116] See J. M. Lacarra, 'Los franceses en la reconquista y repoblación del valle del Ebro en tiempos de Alfonso el Batallador', *Cuadernos de historia*, 2 (1968), pp. 65–80; L. H. Nelson, 'Rotrou of Perche and the Aragonese Reconquest', *Traditio*, 26 (1970), pp. 113–33; Bull, *Knightly Piety*, pp. 99–107; Riley-Smith, *First Crusaders*, pp. 165–6.

[117] *Colección diplomática de Alfonso*, no. 141, p. 207.

[118] Bull, *Knightly Piety*, p. 99.

[119] *Ibid.*, p. 107.

[120] For the involvement of other Gascons in the Aragonese reconquest of the 1120s, see *ibid.*, pp. 106–7.

[121] *Ibid.*, pp. 99–100.

[122] *La Chronique de Saint-Maixent*, pp. 154, 168, 178, used the word *via* of the crusades of 1096–1102 and 1106–8, which at least suggests the possibility that the campaign of 1118 was regarded as a form of pilgrimage.

[123] See E. Lourie, 'The Will of Alfonso I, "El Batallador", King of Aragon and Navarre: A Reassessment', *Speculum*, 50 (1975), pp. 635–51; Forey, 'The Will of Alfonso I of Aragón', pp. 59–65; E. Lourie, 'The Will of Alfonso I of Aragon and Navarre: A Reply to Dr. Forey', *Durham University Journal*, 77 (1984), pp. 165–72.

a whole, the bequest to these three religious institutions, whilst impractical, does not seem as bizarre as Lourie would have us believe;[124] indeed, the wording of the letter of 1128 describing the foundation of the confraternity of Monreal del Campo suggests that the Templars already had a presence in Aragón.[125] But what connected the brethren of the Temple, Hospital and the Holy Sepulchre was not so much their potential for assisting in the promotion of the reconquest (the canons of the Holy Sepulchre clearly never held a military role, and the Hospital may not yet have been militarised) as their intrinsic association with the Holy Land.[126] It is easy to demonstrate how potent the Holy Land was for Alfonso during his lifetime, and how important crusading ideology was to the royal house of Aragón in the early twelfth century; thus it does not seem improbable that Alfonso's bequest was motivated by a deep-rooted piety. Indeed, if Alfonso's plans for the *iter per Hispaniam* had come to fruition, the presence of the Temple and Hospital in Aragón would have been particularly apposite given the practical role that the Orders played in providing an infrastructure for pilgrimage, either through defending pilgrims and securing pilgrim routes, or by caring for the sick poor. Although undoubtedly over-ambitious, Alfonso's will may therefore have been much more far-sighted than has previously been suggested.

Conclusion

In the light of the evidence presented above there can be little doubt that ideas of Jerusalem pilgrimage were fundamental to the introduction of crusading to Iberia, and it therefore seems reasonable to infer that the use from *c.*1120 of the sign of the cross as the badge of a crusader fighting in Spain was intended to highlight the association with the ideas of Christo-mimesis that had been central to the spirituality of the First Crusade. The power of that spirituality was thus being harnessed by propagandists such as Diego Gelmírez in a revolutionary way, with the actions of crusaders in Iberia being portrayed as united with those who chose to follow the road to the Holy Land taken by the first crusaders. Their routes may have been different, the propagandists taught, but their goal was identical, and thus it may have been hoped that peninsular crusading would come to hold the same status as an expedition that set out to the East via the Bosphorus. In this respect, the preaching of the *iter per Hispaniam* was instrumental to the extension of crusading to Iberia because it acknowledged the primacy of the Holy Sepulchre in the mental constructions of crusading in the early twelfth century.

It remains unclear whether the proclamation of a crusade in Iberia by Pope Calixtus II at some point before April 1123 was an attempt to stem a potential flow of manpower to the East. If, as Richard Fletcher argued, 'Spaniards of the eleventh and early twelfth

---

[124] Lourie, 'The Will … A Reassessment', *passim*, argued that the bequests were part of a conspiracy to neutralise papal or Castilian intervention and thus secure an Aragonese succession.

[125] *Colección diplomática de Alfonso*, no. 141, p. 207. The *confratres* of Monreal del Campo benefited from exemptions from taxation 'quemadmodum militia confraternitatis Ierosolimitana'. See A.J. Forey, *The Templars in the Corona de Aragón* (London, 1973), pp. 6–9.

[126] See Forey, 'The Will of Alfonso I of Aragón', pp. 64–5. For the militarisation of the Hospital, see Riley-Smith, *First Crusaders*, pp. 163–4. See also A.J. Forey, 'The Military Orders and the Spanish Reconquest', pp. 197–234.

centuries were not interested in a programme of reconquest',[127] then the introduction of crusading to the peninsula in the 1120s might simply be seen as an independent and proactive attempt to stimulate ideas of *reconquista* – ideas that were only gradually being rediscovered in the period before the First Crusade and which the reform papacy was particularly keen to revive. The pattern of events of *c.* 1089–*c.* 1116 would suggest, however, that the change in policy implemented by Calixtus II was as much a response to circumstances as it was an inspired project that anticipated the eventual scope of the Second Crusade by more than twenty years.[128]

---

[127] Fletcher, 'Reconquest and Crusade', p. 34.
[128] It is striking that the evidence that survives from the early 1120s consists of efforts to force recalcitrant Iberian crusaders to complete their unfulfilled vows, rather than material that relates to the proactive preaching of crusading in Spain.

CHAPTER SIX

The Development of Crusading Spirituality in Iberia,

c. 1130–c. 1150

Diego Gelmírez, the Cult of St James and the Liber sancti Jacobi

In the previous chapter it was suggested that the first archbishop of Compostela, Diego Gelmírez, was acutely aware of the problems that the advent of crusading to the East had caused in the Iberian peninsula and that as a result he was one of a number of individuals who were instrumental in propagating the idea of the *iter per Hispaniam* in Iberia in the early 1120s. Diego is an intriguing character, whose political and ecclesiastical dealings led his modern biographer to describe him as 'Saint James's Catapult', and it is perhaps not surprising that he played such a prominent role in the early development of crusading in Iberia, especially given his close connections with Pope Calixtus II.[1] Indeed, it should be noted that as well as preaching the crusade in Spain at Compostela in 1124, Diego was also a witness to the foundation charter of the confraternity of Belchite, which suggests that there may well have been a more co-ordinated strategy for promoting crusading in Iberia than has previously been thought.[2] However, in spite of the fact that the *excitatoria* from the council at Compostela of 1124 recorded how spiritual rewards offered to crusaders in Iberia were granted not only on the authority of SS. Peter and Paul but also on that of St James the Great,[3] there has been a division of opinion in the secondary literature about whether or not Diego Gelmírez saw in the crusading movement an opportunity to enhance the standing of the cult of St James itself. José Goñi Gaztambide argued that although Diego had been able to use the

---

[1] R.A. Fletcher, *Saint James's Catapult: The Life and Times of Diego Gelmírez of Santiago de Compostela* (Oxford, 1984).

[2] See J. Goñi Gaztambide, *Historia de la bula de la cruzada en España* (Vitoria, 1958), p. 80; R.A. Fletcher, 'Reconquest and Crusade in Spain, c. 1050–1150', *Transactions of the Royal Historical Society*, 5th ser., 37 (1987), p. 46.

[3] *Historia Compostellana*, ed. E. Falque Rey, CC:CM 70 (Turnhout, 1988), pp. 378–80. Cf. Paschal II, 'Epistolae et privilegia', *PL* 163, no. 44, col. 65: 'Vobis ergo omnibus iterata praeceptione praecipimus ut in vestris partibus persistentes Moabitas et Mauros totis viribus impugnetis: ibi largiente Deo vestras poenitentias peragatis: ibi sanctorum apostolorum Petri et Pauli et apostolicae eorum Ecclesiae remissionem et gratiam percipiatis.' See also J.S.C. Riley-Smith, 'The First Crusade and St. Peter', *Outremer: Studies in the History of the Crusading Kingdom of Jerusalem Presented to Joshua Prawer*, ed. B.Z. Kedar, H.E. Mayer and R.C. Smail (Jerusalem, 1982), pp. 41–63.

prestige of the apostle's cult to elevate Compostela to metropolitan status, the appeal of the Holy Sepulchre was simply too great for him to have effectively harnessed devotion to St James as propaganda for campaigns against peninsular Islam.[4] Conversely, Richard Fletcher believed that 'by temperament and early experience Diego was a man of the world. He had the wit to see that his world was changing and the intuition to grasp how change might be made to suit his apostle's – his own – purposes',[5] and he noted that during the second quarter of the twelfth century 'the notion of St. James as a patron saint of warfare against Islam emerges clearly for the first time'.[6] Although Fletcher stressed that there are few traces of ideas of crusade or reconquest in the *Historia Compostellana*, the same cannot be said of another contemporary source, the *Liber sancti Jacobi*. The first three sections of this chapter will therefore explore how propagandists for Compostela sought to use the *Liber sancti Jacobi* to cultivate an association between St James, the pilgrimage to Compostela and the development of crusading ideology in Iberia. In so doing, it will be demonstrated that the idea of the *iter per Hispaniam* was not the only pilgrimage motif used to propagate crusading in Iberia in the early twelfth century.

The *Liber sancti Jacobi* is a complicated source.[7] It has been described as 'a compendium of individual items that collectively compose an encyclopaedia for the pilgrimage and cult of Saint James'[8] and as 'the pre-eminent literary source for the medieval veneration of St James of Compostela'.[9] It consists of five books, each of which was probably written independently before the subsequent compilation in the mid-twelfth century. The so-called *Codex Calixtinus* (the original manuscript of the *Liber*) has been dated to between 1139 and 1173,[10] and it has been argued recently that a date c.1138–45 ought

---

[4] Goñi Gaztambide, *Historia*, p. 80. See also N. Housley, 'Jerusalem and the Development of the Crusade Idea, 1099–1128', *The Horns of Hattin: Proceedings of the Second Conference of the Society for the Study of the Crusades and the Latin East*, ed. B.Z. Kedar (Jerusalem, 1992), p. 36.

[5] Fletcher, *St James's Catapult*, p. 114.

[6] *Ibid.*, p. 298.

[7] Whilst there is as yet no critical edition of the *Liber sancti Jacobi* as a whole, the source is now readily accessible through a recent transcription of the *Codex Calixtinus*, the twelfth-century manuscript held in the Compostela Cathedral library [LSJ: CC]. This latest work replaces an earlier transcription published as *Liber sancti Jacobi: Codex Calixtinus*, i. *Texto*, ed. W.M. Whitehill (Santiago de Compostela, 1944). A facsimile of the manuscript itself was published as *Liber sancti Jacobi: Codex Calixtinus de la catedral de Santiago de Compostela* (Madrid, 1993). For a recent edition of the *Liber's* fifth book, see *The Pilgrim's Guide to Santiago de Compostela: A Critical Edition*, ed. A. Stones, J. Krochalis, P. Gerson and A. Shaver-Crandell, 2 vols. (London, 1998).

[8] T.F. Coffey, L.K. Davidson and M. Dunn, *The Miracles of Saint James: Translations from the Liber sancti Jacobi* (New York, 1996), p. xiii.

[9] J. van Herwaarden, 'Saint James in Spain up to the 12th century', *Wallfahrt kennt keine Grenzen*, ed. L. Kriss-Rettenbeck and G. Möhler (Munich and Zurich, 1984), pp. 235–47.

[10] The *terminus ante quem* is certain, as it was in 1173 that Arnaldus de Monte made a copy of the *Liber* for his monastery at Ripoll. The *terminus post quem* is generally accepted as 1139 because of internal dating evidence (a letter attributed to Pope Innocent II attesting to the veracity of the *Liber's* contents). For the *Codex Calixtinus*, see especially M.C. Díaz y Díaz, *El Códice Calixtino de la catedral de Santiago: estudio codicológico y de contenido* (Santiago de Compostela, 1988). For the date, see *ibid.*, pp. 77–81.

to be preferred for the earliest stages of work on the text.[11] The five books of the *Liber* detailed the liturgy relating to the worship of St James, a collection of miracles attributed to him (which can be dated to *c.*1135x39),[12] a history of his martyrdom and the *translatio* of his relics to Galicia, a book detailing the legendary exploits of Charlemagne in Spain (which can be dated to *c.*1130x45),[13] and a guide for prospective pilgrims that offered practical and spiritual advice for the safety and enrichment of their journey.

Although parts of the *Liber* are verifiably ascribed to certain well-known individuals (such as three of the *miracula* of Book II to St Anselm), the overarching attribution of the work to Pope Calixtus II – hence *Codex Calixtinus* – is unquestionably spurious, as some of the passages he was supposed to have written must be dated to after his death in 1124.[14] It therefore seems most likely that the compiler (or compilers) of the *Liber* assumed the pseudonym 'Calixtus' to lend cachet to certain passages of their work[15] – a phenomenon that was not uncommon in the central Middle Ages. Indeed, Giles Constable has described the eleventh and twelfth centuries as the 'golden age' of medieval forgery, and he has demonstrated how numerous authors issued their works under false names in the hope of lending authenticity and authority to their writings.[16] If this was indeed the compiler of the *Liber*'s intent, the choice of Calixtus II was a logical one, especially given his family connections with the Iberian peninsula and his obvious historical associations with and favour for Santiago de Compostela. The exact identity of the compiler himself is still open to question, although the *Liber*'s contents have led many to conclude that he was a Frenchman; the shadowy figure of a Poitevin named Aymery Picaud is often suggested to be a likely candidate.[17]

The authorship of the *Liber sancti Jacobi* is an issue that will almost certainly remain unresolved but, as Constable highlighted,[18] a more interesting question about forgeries is not who wrote them but why they were made in the first place. The fundamental purpose of the *Liber sancti Jacobi* is hinted at by the spurious attribution of the work to Pope Calixtus II and is a subject about which historians are almost universally agreed: the

---

[11] *Pilgrim's Guide*, vol. 1, p. 15.

[12] For the date, see *Pilgrim's Guide*, vol. 1, pp. 59–60. The youngest miracle of Book II can be dated to 1135. A number of *miracula* were later appended to the *Codex Calixtinus*'s fifth and final book; the earliest of these can be dated to 1139.

[13] For the date, see *ibid.*, vol. 1, p. 60.

[14] But cf. R.W. Southern, 'The English Origins of the "Miracles of the Virgin"', *Mediaeval and Renaissance Studies*, 4 (1958), pp. 206–7, who believed there was 'nothing . . . intrinsically improbable' about Pope Calixtus being responsible for the production of the *Codex*, and *Pilgrim's Guide*, vol. 1, p. 17, whose modern editors believed that his direct involvement was 'not out of the question'.

[15] See van Herwaarden, 'Saint James in Spain', p. 242.

[16] G. Constable, 'Forgery and Plagiarism in the Middle Ages', *Archiv für Diplomatik*, 29 (1983), pp. 1–41. See also C.N.L. Brooke, 'Approaches to Medieval Forgery', *Medieval Church and Society* (London, 1971), pp. 100–20; A. Grafton, *Forgers and Critics: Creativity and Duplicity in Western Scholarship* (Princeton, NJ, 1990).

[17] See, for example, van Herwaarden, 'Saint James in Spain', p. 244; A. Moisan, 'Aimeri Picaud de Parthenay et le "Liber sancti Jacobi"', *Bibliothèque de l'École des Chartes*, 143 (1985), pp. 5–52. On the 'authorship' of the *Liber*, see also *Pilgrim's Guide*, vol. 1, pp. 15–27; Díaz y Díaz, *El Códice Calixtino*, pp. 81–7.

[18] Constable, 'Forgery and Plagiarism', p. 2.

propagation and aggrandisement of the cult of St James of Compostela.[19] It is evident that the *Liber sancti Jacobi* was conceived, at least in part,[20] as a means not only of promoting pilgrimage to Santiago de Compostela, but also of developing the idea that the Iberian peninsula should be regarded as another frontier of crusading warfare. Whilst there are many unresolved issues surrounding the *Liber*'s commissioning, compilation and authorship, it seems that the most likely answers to the questions raised become apparent when the work is viewed in the context of the contemporary intellectual climate at Compostela, particularly under the leadership of Diego Gelmírez. It would seem, therefore, that the *Liber sancti Jacobi*, as it survives in the *Codex Calixtinus*, was a work undertaken most probably in Compostela by a group of scholars – possibly including French canons of the cathedral chapter[21] – who were tasked with producing a definitive statement on the history, traditions and liturgy of the cult of St James to complement the official *registrum* of the *Historia Compostellana*. Indeed, as one of the sermons in the *Liber*'s first volume stated, the work was devised 'so that no one may dare to write anything about him [St James] except the authentic things that this codex which is called *Iacobus* contains'.[22]

This argument for the rationale behind the *Liber*'s creation is supported by the wording of its introductory letter, which was spuriously attributed to Pope Calixtus[23] and which set out the purposes of the compilation and instructions on how its contents were to be used. The letter suggests that the *Liber*'s compilers wished their work to be placed within the chronology *c.*1130x40, as it was addressed to 'the basilica of Cluny . . . William, patriarch of Jerusalem, Diego, archbishop of Compostela and to all orthodox people'.[24] (Diego Gelmírez was archbishop between 1120 and 1140, and William I held the patriarchate between 1130 and 1145.)[25] Pseudo-Calixtus explained that he was sending a copy of the *Liber* to each of his correspondents, 'since in all of the parts of the world more eminent supporters in dignity or honour than you cannot be found';[26] his desire for his work to be associated with Cluny, Jerusalem and Compostela must surely be taken as an attempt to lend further credibility to its contents. Pseudo-Calixtus then went on to describe the piecemeal process by which the *Liber* was compiled, and stated that the work had been undertaken 'so that the disciples of St James might find bound together in one volume the material (*legenda*) necessary for reading on his feast days'.[27] He then offered further evidence for the veracity of the *Liber*'s contents, in what seems to have been a plea for acceptance from an anxious scholar:

---

[19] See van Herwaarden, 'Saint James in Spain', p. 244; LSJ: CC, p. XX. But see also C. Hohler, 'A Note on *Jacobus*', *Journal of the Warburg and Courtauld Institutes*, 35 (1972), pp. 31–80, and the comments by J.L. Nelson in her review of *The Pilgrim's Guide* in *Bulletin of the Confraternity of Saint James*, 65 (March 1999), p. 26.

[20] For the additional possibilities, see Coffey *et al.*, *Miracles of Saint James*, p. xxxv.

[21] See Díaz y Díaz, *El Códice Calixtino*, p. 311, n. 1; *Pilgrim's Guide*, vol. 1, pp. 25–6; LSJ: CC, p. XX.

[22] LSJ: CC, p. 87.

[23] See Calixtus II, *Bullaire*, ed. U. Robert, 2 vols. (Paris, 1891), vol. 1, p. LXXXI.

[24] LSJ: CC, p. 7.

[25] For William's dates, see B. Hamilton, *The Latin Church in the Crusader States: The Secular Church* (London, 1980), p. 373.

[26] LSJ: CC, p. 7.

[27] LSJ: CC, p. 7.

Let no one think that anything written here has come from my own mind, but rather from authoritative books; both Testaments, of course, and also from the holy doctors Jerome, Ambrose, Augustine, Gregory, Bede, Maximus, Leo, and many other Catholic writers. Thus it should be understood that that which is contained in the first book has been openly extracted [from the works of others]. The other things that are written down in the subsequent books in a historical manner I either saw with my own eyes, or I found written, or I learned from truthful reporting, and wrote it down.[28]

There followed a more explicit description of how the *Liber*'s contents should be used:

Whatever is written in the first two books [the liturgy and *miracula*] . . . may be sung and read in churches at matins and masses, according to ordinance, for it is authentic and described with great authority. And whatever is written in the following books . . . may be read in refectories at meals, for it too is of great authority. But what is contained in the first two books is quite sufficient for reading at matins. And if all the sermons and miracles of Blessed James that are contained in this codex cannot be read in church on his feast days because of their length, they may of course be read afterwards throughout each week in the refectory, and certainly at least on the day on which his feast took place.[29]

From this brief overview of the text's provenance, content and stated purpose, it seems clear enough that the *Liber sancti Jacobi* ought to be regarded within the broader context of contemporaneous efforts by religious institutions to forge specific identities for themselves.[30] A full analysis of how this process manifested itself at Compostela is beyond the scope of this chapter; for the present purpose, attention will be focused on demonstrating how certain sections of the *Liber* – specifically the *miracula* of Book II and the *Historia Turpini* of Book IV – were redacted for the purpose of linking St James with crusading ideology and establishing a mythical-historical context for crusading in Iberia.

St James of Compostela as a Patron of Crusading Warfare

The use of *miracula* by religious institutions has been well documented in recent scholarship, where it has been stressed that the compilation of miracle stories was by no means universal to all cult centres but was in fact a response to particular circumstances at a given time.[31] On this basis, examination of the environment in which *miracula* were assembled is revealing, and Marcus Bull's case study of the eleventh-century compilation of the miracles of St Faith at Conques provides one example of how *miracula* could be collected during a period of remarkable growth in a cult's resources and prestige, and how the miracles themselves could be used as part of a strategy of expansion.[32] In

---

[28] LSJ: CC, p. 7.
[29] LSJ: CC, p. 8.
[30] See below, pp. 150–3.
[31] See M. Bull, *The Miracles of Our Lady of Rocamadour: Analysis and Translation* (Woodbridge, 1999), pp. 10, 43–55.
[32] *Ibid.*, pp. 50–1.

this respect, the assembly of the *miracula sancti Jacobi* can be seen as comparable to the process at Conques, as the compilers of both collections appear to have had similar intentions: to promote more widely the saint in question and to forge an institutional identity for a growing cultic centre. But the fact that *miracula* were produced for St James at all is striking given that, as Benedicta Ward has shown, the miraculous was of a lesser importance to those pilgrims who set out for Compostela, which was known first and foremost as one of the three great penitential shrines of Christendom.[33] What is therefore particularly interesting about this compilation is the manner in which St James is depicted in the *miracula*, and consequently what image of the cult Pseudo-Calixtus chose to project.

The miracles attributed to St James have a number of remarkable qualities. First, in spite of the relative longevity of the shrine at Compostela, only twenty-two miracles were recorded in Book II of the *Liber sancti Jacobi*; this has been described as a 'paltry number when compared to the more than two hundred that Gregory of Tours collected about Martin of Tours . . . [and the] more than 250 miracles attributed to St. Thomas Becket between 1171 and 1177 at his tomb or around Canterbury'.[34] Furthermore, it should be noted that on the whole the miracles chosen for inclusion in the *Liber* were relatively contemporary to the work's creation. Of the twenty-two recorded, the earliest dated from the ninth century, two were placed in the earlier eleventh century, five during the period 1064x1099, and thirteen during the first third of the twelfth century (1100x35).[35] Eighteen of the stories were attributed to the pen of Pope Calixtus,[36] as was the statement that opened the collection that offered an explanation of how the twenty-two miracles had been selected:

> Let no one think that I have written down all the miracles and stories that I have heard about him, but only those that I am satisfied are true and are based on the truest assertions of the most truthful people. For if I had written down all the miracles that I have heard about him in many places and in the stories of many people, hand and parchment would have worn out before the stories did.[37]

This kind of editorial strategy does not appear to have been unique; the prologue to the miracles of Our Lady of Rocamadour (produced 1172–3) contained a similar disclaimer:

> there has been such a vast number of miracles before our own day that it has been impossible to hold them in our memory or write them down . . . So we propose to limit our narration to what we have seen with our own eyes or what we have learned from reliable people with sure accounts to give.[38]

---

[33] B. Ward, *Miracles and the Medieval Mind: Theory, Record and Event, 1000–1215* (Aldershot, 1987), pp. 110–26.

[34] Coffey *et al.*, *Miracles of Saint James*, p. xlvi. The following translations are adapted from the texts published in this book.

[35] Only one miracle (no. XX) is without any dating evidence.

[36] Cf. Southern, '"Miracles of the Virgin"', p. 207, who thought it possible that Calixtus could have compiled the miracles whilst Archbishop of Vienne (1088–1119).

[37] LSJ: CC, p. 159.

[38] Bull, *Miracles of Our Lady*, p. 97. For Bull's analysis of this phenomenon, see *ibid.*, p. 39.

It would appear, therefore, that this collection of St James's miracles was carefully con-structed. From this, it follows that the *miracula* that were included were ones whose content suited the image that the cult's advocates wished to present.

Pseudo-Calixtus claimed that the purpose of his collection was to move the hearts of listeners 'toward the sweetness and love of the heavenly kingdom',[39] and he repeated his instruction that the miracles should be 'read diligently in churches and refectories on the feast days of this apostle and on other days if it be pleasing'.[40] The collection's central theme was the wide range of miracles worked by St James who, as God's inter-cessor for mankind, 'pours out a display of his powers over those who do not cease to make their appeals to him'.[41] Pilgrims to Compostela were inevitably highly favoured in the stories and, with only one exception, the miracles' recipients were those who had undertaken a pilgrimage to St James or those who had made a vow to do so. However, it is interesting to note that the miracles were not focused on his shrine or its relics them-selves,[42] and the stories often taught important lessons, such as the penitential value of the Compostelan pilgrimage,[43] the importance of fulfilling vows,[44] and the necessity of offering charity to pilgrims.[45]

Whilst these stories therefore supported the broad agenda of the *Liber sancti Jacobi* – the efficacy of the penitential pilgrimage to Compostela – it is worth highlighting the social background from which a large number of those who benefited from the miracles came. In particular, the *miracula* portrayed the saint as being closely associ-ated with the arms-bearing classes. Nine of the twenty-two miracles were witnessed by *milites*, the assistance of *heroes* was described twice, one narrative referred to a *vir inclitus*, and *comites* were aided in two of the stories.[46] Only five other professions were mentioned (a sailor, a bishop, a serf, a merchant and a tanner), and it has been sug-gested elsewhere that this 'chivalric orientation' of the cult of St James led to the saint eventually becoming 'a figure of identification all over Europe for the new rising group of the lesser nobility'.[47] However, Marcus Bull observed a similar trend in the miracles of Our Lady of Rocamadour, and he argued that 'the frequency of arms-bearers in the stories must to a large extent be a simple function of their greater wealth and mobility, and their relative freedom from the sorts of domestic, agricultural or occupational ties that would have inhibited members of other groups'.[48] Whilst there is no doubt some truth in this, analysis of the context in which some of the *milites* were aided by St James would suggest that there was a further significance to the relationship. Indeed, in some

[39] LSJ: CC, p. 159.
[40] LSJ: CC, p. 159. See Ward, *Miracles and the Medieval Mind*, p. 111.
[41] LSJ: CC, p. 161.
[42] On the peripatetic nature of the saint's miraculous powers, see Coffey *et al.*, *Miracles of Saint James*, p. xlvi.
[43] LSJ: CC, pp. 161–2.
[44] LSJ: CC, pp. 163–4.
[45] LSJ: CC, pp. 164–5, 165–6.
[46] *Milites* were assisted in miracles I, IX, XII, XIII, XV, XVI and XX; the *heroes* appeared in miracles IV and VI; the *vir inclitus* is the subject of miracle XXI; and the two counts were referred to in miracles I and XVIII.
[47] K. Herbers, 'The Miracles of St. James', *The Codex Calixtinus and the Shrine of St. James*, ed. J. Williams and A. Stones, *Jakobus-Studien*, 3 (Tübingen, 1992), p. 20.
[48] Bull, *Miracles of Our Lady*, p. 75.

cases, it was precisely because of their profession and, in particular, their commitment to fighting Muslims, that these arms-bearers had benefited from the saint's protection and patronage.

It is clear from the content of the first miracle that issues of Christian-Muslim relations in the Iberian peninsula would be a feature of the entire collection. The chapter's heading established that the story would describe how St James freed twenty men 'from the captivity of the Moabites', and the text of the miracle itself began with a description of the political situation in Iberia in the early twelfth century: 'During the time of King Alfonso the rage of the Saracens burned fiercely in parts of Spain.'[49] This reference was almost certainly to Alfonso VI of León-Castile, who had of course been responsible for many of the Christian advances in the later eleventh century – his most famous victory being the reconquest of Toledo in 1085 – and, indirectly, for the beginning of the Almoravid involvement in the peninsula's history.[50] The action of the miracle itself arose out of this new Islamic aggression. Pseudo-Calixtus described how 'A certain count called Ermengol, seeing that the Christian religion was oppressed by the onset of the Moabites, set out to war supported by the strength of his army and attacked [the Muslims] as if he believed that he and his men were invincible'.[51] However, the count was overcome by his enemies and, along with twenty of his companions, was imprisoned by the Muslims in the city of Zaragoza; here, they prayed to St James to liberate them. The resolution of the narrative was predictable enough: St James appeared, the soldiers' chains were broken, and they were guided to safety. One of the soldiers eventually made the pilgrimage to Compostela, and it was in this way that his testimony came to be recorded by Pseudo-Calixtus.

St James was therefore established in this first narrative as one who came 'out of mercy in aid of those in the snares of their oppressors' and offered his support to those suffering 'from unspeakable captivity'.[52] The themes of freedom from captivity, or of divine assistance to Christians who were under some kind of Muslim oppression, were also repeated in several other narratives.[53] For example, the final miracle of the collection recorded how 'a certain citizen of Barcelona' had made the pilgrimage to Compostela in 1100, where 'he had asked from the apostle only that he might free him from captivity by his enemies, if by accident he should fall into such a situation'.[54] On a subsequent journey to Sicily, this individual was then 'captured at sea by Saracens . . . and bought and sold thirteen times at trade fairs and markets. But in fact those who bought him were not able to hold him because [on each occasion] his bonds and

---

[49] LSJ: CC, pp. 159, 161.

[50] See J.F. O'Callaghan, *Reconquest and Crusade in Medieval Spain* (Philadelphia, PA, 2003), p. 30.

[51] LSJ: CC, p. 161.

[52] LSJ: CC, p. 161.

[53] See O.R. Constable, 'Muslim Spain and Mediterranean Slavery: The Medieval Slave Trade as an Aspect of Muslim-Christian Relations', *Christendom and Its Discontents: Exclusion, Persecution, and Rebellion, 1000–1500*, ed. S.L. Waugh and P.D. Diehl (Cambridge, 1996), pp. 264–84. See also M. Bull, 'Views of Muslims and of Jerusalem in Miracle Stories, c.1000–c.1200: Reflections on the Study of First Crusaders' Motivations', *The Experience of Crusading, Volume One: Western Approaches*, ed. M. Bull and N. Housley (Cambridge, 2003), pp. 34–7.

[54] LSJ: CC, p. 177.

chains were ground down by St James.'[55] After a journey that had taken the man from the Mediterranean to such distant places as India and Africa, he was finally returned to Spain, where St James explained why he had had such a run of bad luck: 'You have fallen into these dangers because when you were in my cathedral you asked me only for the deliverance of your body and not for the salvation of your soul.' Imparting the mercy of the Lord upon him, St James then freed the man for a final time:

> And so the man, released from his bonds, began to return openly to the land of the Christians through the cities and castles of the Saracens, carrying a piece of the chain in his hands as proof of this great miracle . . . And when he encountered a pagan who tried to capture him, the man showed him the part of the chain and his adversary immediately fled from him.[56]

Although not quite as dramatic, the seventh miracle (dated to 1101) also occurred as a result of an incident of piracy in the Mediterranean. Pseudo-Calixtus described how:

> a certain sailor called Frisonus was guiding a ship that was sailing over the sea, filled with pilgrims who were wishing to go to the Sepulchre of the Lord in the region of Jerusalem so that they could pray there. [At some point on the way] a Saracen called Avitus Maimon, who wanted to march all the pilgrims away with him into the land of the Moabites as captives, approached Frisonus's ship for the purpose of fighting.[57]

During the mêlée that ensued, Frisonus himself – 'bearing his iron breastplate and his helmet and his shield' – fell into the sea, and he prayed to St James to rescue him and his boatload of pilgrims. The saint's intervention was immediate. Frisonus was miraculously returned to his ship, and:

> by the strength of God and the assistance of St James, the ship of the Saracens was immediately seized and put to the test by a powerful storm. [Subsequently] the ship of the Christians, with St James leading by divine approval, reached the desired place; and Frisonus, having visited the Sepulchre of the Lord, in the same year went to St James in Galicia.[58]

St James's ability to protect those who were persecuted by Muslims was therefore unambiguous. However, other examples went further, and the ninth miracle provided a more explicit illustration of the saint offering direct support to Christians fighting against Muslims, in this instance in the Holy Land. Pseudo-Calixtus described how, in 1103:

> a certain glorious and most noble arms-bearer of Frankish stock (*genere Francorum*), who was near Tiberias in the region of Jerusalem, vowed that if the Apostle James would give him the power to conquer and destroy the Turks in battle, he would go to the saint's shrine. With the help of God, the apostle bestowed such power on him that he overcame completely all of the Saracens who did battle with him.[59]

[55] LSJ: CC, p. 177.
[56] LSJ: CC, p. 177.
[57] LSJ: CC, p. 166.
[58] LSJ: CC, p. 166.
[59] LSJ: CC, p. 167.

The broader framework of the nineteenth miracle was the advancement of the reconquest, and in particular the saint's direct involvement in its progress.[60] The narrative began at Compostela, where an anchorite attached to the cathedral overheard the prayers of a group of peasants. In reaction to their addressing the saint as a *bonus miles*, Pseudo-Calixtus described how:

> That most holy man of God became indignant at these words, and because the peasants had called him [St James] a knight he said to them in censure, 'You most stupid peasants, you foolish people. You should not address St James as a knight but as a fisherman, remembering that time when, at the Lord's calling, he left the life of a fisherman, followed the Lord and became a fisher of men.'[61]

Although Pseudo-Calixtus had shown a desire to propagate St James's militaristic characteristics elsewhere in the *miracula* — he had, for example, depicted the saint as 'sitting on a horse as if he was a knight',[62] and described him as both a *miles Dei*[63] and a *miles invictissimi imperatoris*[64] — it was in this narrative that St James's transformation into a warrior was complete:

> On the night following the day in which that most holy man had related this about Blessed James, the saint appeared, fitted out in the whitest clothes, also bearing military arms . . . made out as if he were a knight, and holding two keys in his hand. After calling three times, James spoke in this way: 'O Stephen, servant of God, you who ordered that I should not be called a knight but a fisherman, I am appearing to you in this way so that you no longer doubt that I am able to fight for God as his champion, that I go before the Christians in the fight against the Saracens, and that I arise as the victor for them.'[65]

In order to demonstrate his powers of intercession and his concern for the Christians of Iberia, the saint described how the keys he was holding would open the gates of the city of Coimbra: 'At the third hour tomorrow I will return to the power of the Christians the city which has been pressed under siege by King Fernando for seven years.' It soon transpired that Coimbra had indeed fallen to the army of Fernando of Castile — thus placing the miracle in July 1064 — and the narrative closed with the hermit accepting the 'rebranding' of St James as the *bonus miles*: 'And so when what had been uttered beforehand became known to be true, Stephen, the servant of God, asserted that for those calling out to him in battle St James was stronger than all others, and he preached that anyone fighting for truth should call upon him.'[66]

Whilst a number of themes can be identified in the miracles compiled by Pseudo-

---

[60] This miracle was not original to the *Liber sancti Jacobi*, and appeared in an earlier form in the *Historia Silense* (c.1109x18). See M.C. Díaz y Díaz, *Visiones del mas alla en Galicia durante la alta edad media* (Santiago de Compostela, 1985), pp. 121–43.

[61] LSJ: CC, p. 175.

[62] LSJ: CC, p. 164.

[63] LSJ: CC, p. 164.

[64] LSJ: CC, p. 174.

[65] LSJ: CC, p. 175.

[66] LSJ: CC, p. 175.

Calixtus, the attempt to develop the militaristic nature of the cult of St James is striking. The saint was variously presented as knight, liberator of Christian captives, and divine assistant to those fighting the Muslims of Spain and further afield. This theme does of course bear comparison with the appearance of soldier saints in the histories of the First Crusade,[67] such as at the Battle of Dorylaeum in 1097,[68] and more famously during the Battle of Antioch in June 1098.[69] Of the latter, the anonymous author of the *Gesta Francorum* recorded that:

> Then also appeared from the mountains a countless host of men on white horses, whose banners were all white. When our men saw this, they did not understand what was happening or who these men might be, until they realised that this was the succour sent by Christ, and that the leaders were St George, St Mercurius and St Demetrius.[70]

The portrayal of saints as *milites Christi* was not, therefore, without precedent in hagiographical tradition. It was, however, something of an innovation in the history of the cult of St James of Compostela, and the relating of the saint's dramatic appearance to the indignant anchorite of the nineteenth miracle may well have been intended to counter the objections of those who might protest at this radical development. To reinforce the point that the compilers of the *Liber sancti Jacobi* appear to have had specific ideas in mind about how they wished to promote the cult of St James, it is a useful exercise to compare briefly these *miracula* with another contemporary collection. The comparison is all the more pertinent because the miracles in question relate to another relic from the same individual: the hand of St James, which was in the custody of Reading Abbey.[71]

The twenty-eight miracles of the hand of St James are recorded in a manuscript that dates from around 1200, and it is likely that they were compiled in the last decade of the twelfth century.[72] The collection presents a marked contrast to the *miracula* ascribed to the saint by Pseudo-Calixtus and demonstrates the differing priorities of the cults of St James of Reading and of Compostela. Whereas St James of Compostela was presented as a miracle worker of international reach and seemingly limitless powers, the miracles of St James of Reading 'could be those at any healing shrine of the period'.[73] Twenty-five out of the twenty-seven miracles show evidence of the saint's abilities as a healer (contrasting with the three from the *Liber sancti Jacobi*), almost all the miracles are recorded

---

[67] See Riley-Smith, 'First Crusade and St. Peter', pp. 52–6; J.S.C. Riley-Smith, *The First Crusade and the Idea of Crusading* (London, 1986), p. 105.

[68] See Raymond of Aguilers, *Liber*, ed. J.H. and L.L. Hill (Paris, 1969), p. 45.

[69] See also B. Hamilton, '"God Wills It": Signs of Divine Approval in the Crusade Movement', *Signs, Wonders, Miracles: Representations of Divine Power in the Life of the Church*, ed. K. Cooper and J. Gregory, SCH, 41 (Woodbridge, 2005), pp. 88–98.

[70] *Gesta Francorum et aliorum Hierosolimitanorum*, ed. and trans. R. Hill (Oxford, 1962), p. 69. Cf. Peter Tudebode, *Historia de Hierosolymitano itinere*, ed. J.H. and L.L. Hill (Paris, 1977), pp. 111–12.

[71] See B. Kemp, 'The Miracles of the Hand of St James', *Berkshire Archaeological Journal*, 65 (1970), pp. 1–19; B. Kemp, 'The Hand of St James at Reading Abbey', *Reading Medieval Studies*, 16 (1990), pp. 77–96.

[72] See Kemp, 'Miracles of the Hand', p. 1.

[73] Ward, *Miracles and the Medieval Mind*, p. 116.

as taking place at the shrine in Reading itself, or at least in the immediate vicinity, and the recipients were drawn from all strata of society.[74] Nevertheless, the compilers of the Reading *miracula* showed an awareness of and a degree of association with the shrine in north-west Spain. The final story (dated to 1127) told of a knight who had shown particular devotion to St James during his lifetime: 'Being bound in special devotion to this apostle, he had twice visited the apostle's home in Galicia, accompanied on the second journey by . . . [his son] as comrade and fellow traveller.'[75] The narrative then went on to describe the father's anguish at his son's near-fatal illness, but also referred to the fact that he was 'confident of the apostle's grace towards him, on account of his devotion to the apostle'. St James was then reported to have healed the knight's son, and both individuals subsequently made a pilgrimage to Reading in thanksgiving.

In contrast with the Reading collection, it can therefore be shown that Pseudo-Calixtus consciously ascribed to St James a considerably broad array of miraculous powers, which the saint was capable of exercising over a wide-ranging area. Whilst St James was primarily represented as an advocate and protector of pilgrims – the role that was fundamental to his portrayal across the whole of the *Liber* – one of the most significant trends within the *miracula* was St James's patronage of arms-bearers. However, the assistance given to these individuals was not solely restricted to their time as pilgrims; if this had been the case, it could be argued that such a trend might simply have been the result of demographics.[76] In some cases, St James's patronage manifested itself whilst the arms-bearers were performing their traditional social function: fighting.[77] And in some of those scenarios, the enemy was Muslim, with conflicts taking place both in Iberia and in the Holy Land. The association of St James with the promotion of ideas of peninsular reconquest, and more broadly with crusading warfare in general, whilst not overwhelmingly explicit, was therefore certainly nascent in the *miracula sancti Jacobi*.[78] It was, however, an association that was illustrated most vividly in the folios of the fourth book of the *Liber sancti Jacobi*, the *Historia Turpini*.

The Historia Turpini *as a Foundation Legend for Crusading in Iberia*

The fourth book of the *Liber sancti Jacobi* consists of a text that was to reach a near-legendary status in the medieval period: the *Historia Turpini*, often known as *Pseudo-Turpin*.[79] This so-called *Historia* purported to be an eyewitness account by Archbishop

[74] Kemp, 'Miracles of the Hand', p. 4: 'Not all the miracles were worked specifically by the Hand, but apart from no. XXV, all were related directly or indirectly to the Hand or to Reading where it was kept . . . The largest number of cures resulted from the drinking by the invalid of "water of St. James", which . . . was water in which the reliquary containing the Hand had been dipped.'

[75] *Ibid.*, p. 18.

[76] Cf. Bull, *Miracles of Our Lady*, pp. 74–6.

[77] Aside from the cases considered above, St James's assistance of soldiers in what might be called 'combat situations' can be shown in miracles XV and XX. See also miracle XI, whose recipient may well have been an arms-bearer.

[78] See Bull, 'Views of Muslims and of Jerusalem', pp. 25–38, who argued that miracle stories such as these 'can throw valuable light on some of the most important contemporary perceptions that activated crusading enthusiasm'.

[79] See G. Spiegel, *Romancing the Past: The Rise of Vernacular Prose in the Middle Ages* (Berkeley, CA, 1993), pp. 55–98.

Turpin of Rheims of the deeds of Charlemagne in Spain, but the attribution of the work's authorship is unquestionably spurious. Although the *Codex Calixtinus* contains the earliest surviving manuscript of the *Historia Turpini*, as with much of the material selected for inclusion in the *Liber*, Pseudo-Turpin's work may well have existed in an earlier form.[80] Reference has already been made to the inclination of twelfth-century writers to ascribe their work to others[81] – hence the attribution of the *Codex Calixtinus* itself – and the *Historia Turpini* is another example of this trend. The author's actual identity is uncertain. His prominent use of Scripture has been highlighted elsewhere,[82] and one scholar has concluded that he was, in fact, a monk of Cluny.[83] This attribution certainly seems plausible as Cluny's sponsorship of the Compostelan pilgrimage is well known, and Pseudo-Turpin's work would certainly have been appropriate material for reading in the refectory as it was replete with moralistic *exempla*.[84] Others have argued that Pseudo-Turpin may have originated from St Denis, and that the *Historia* was part of a programme designed to legitimise the abbey's claims to primacy and to enhance the authority of the Capetian kings.[85] However, regardless of its original author's provenance and intent,[86] the redaction that survives as part of the *Liber sancti Jacobi* provides further evidence of Pseudo-Calixtus's desire to promote the cult of St James and, more specifically, to associate the saint with the development of crusading ideology in Iberia.

Before embarking on a study of Pseudo-Turpin's work, it is worth considering briefly the historicity of Charlemagne's campaigns in Spain. It seems clear enough that Charlemagne enjoyed only limited military successes in the peninsula, and his sole expedition to the Ebro valley in 778 has recently been described as 'disastrous'.[87] The *Historia Turpini* was therefore based on the loosest of historical detail. Indeed, Christopher Hohler expressed great astonishment that such a gross misrepresentation of the past did not lead contemporaries to question the nature of the *Liber sancti Jacobi* itself. He characterised Pseudo-Turpin's work as 'the twelfth-century equivalent of *1066 And All That*',[88] and believed that the *Liber* was originally the manual of a nomadic grammar master that was used to teach boys Latin. As Hohler saw it, 'The critical moment in the fortunes of *Jacobus* was when Turpin's reminiscences escaped from the schoolroom and

[80] *An Anonymous Old French Translation of the* Pseudo-Turpin Chronicle, ed. R.N. Walpole, (Cambridge, MA, 1979), pp. 21–2.

[81] See above, pp. 141–2.

[82] *The Pseudo-Turpin, edited from Bibl. Nat. Ms. 17656*, ed. H.M. Smyser (Cambridge, MA, 1937), p. 4.

[83] *Ibid.*, pp. 4–5.

[84] See, for example, the *exempla* that consider the misappropriation of the alms of the dead (LSJ: CC, p. 204), the need to confront vices (pp. 208, 210, 217), and the importance of honouring the poor (p. 209).

[85] See Pseudo-Turpin, ed. Walpole, p. 21; I. Short, 'A Study in Carolingian Legend and its Persistence in Latin Historiography (XII–XVI Centuries)', *Mittellateinisches Jahrbuch*, 7 (1972), pp. 129–30; G. Spiegel, 'The Cult of St. Denis and Capetian Kingship', *Journal of Medieval History*, 1 (1975), pp. 43–69; E.A.R. Brown, 'Saint-Denis and the Turpin Legend', *The Codex Calixtinus and the Shrine of St. James*, ed. J. Williams and A. Stones, *Jakobus-Studien*, 3 (Tübingen, 1992), pp. 51–88.

[86] See also *The Anglo-Norman* Pseudo-Turpin Chronicle *of William de Briane*, ed. I. Short (Oxford, 1973), pp. 1–2, where it is suggested that the *Historia Turpini* was originally intended for consumption in the courts of the laity.

[87] *Medieval Iberia: An Encyclopaedia*, ed. E.M. Gerli (New York and London, 2003), pp. 225–6.

[88] Hohler, '*Jacobus*', p. 37.

began to be regarded as literature and even as history'.[89] That moment was the 'discovery' of the *Liber* at Compostela by a monk from Ripoll in 1173, and Hohler argued that from then on the *Liber* has been fundamentally misunderstood.

The difficulty with accepting Hohler's conclusions on the function of the *Historia Turpini*, and consequently on the *Liber sancti Jacobi* as a whole, is that he did not really take into account the nature of twelfth-century perspectives of the past and, in particular, the use of myth and legend by twelfth-century writers.[90] Amy Remensnyder's recent study of monastic foundation legends has shown the importance of 'imaginative memory' to the writers of such texts, and she has demonstrated that these legends, which often depicted kings such as Clovis, Pippin the Short and, above all, Charlemagne, as the founders of the religious houses in question, 'belong in the realm of what was believed to be true, rather than what was seen to be fiction'.[91] She argued that foundation legends were created in response to a variety of needs:

> In moments of stress, when the community's independence or very existence is in jeopardy, the construction of a common past assures the group of its (threatened) identity . . . Equally, the past may become a means of conceptualizing and understanding present phenomena . . . Finally, the past may become legitimating, glorifying – even sanctifying – for the present . . . it can serve as the basis for the fashioning of new identities [and] new traditions.[92]

Similar work has been conducted by scholars who have studied the role of 'imaginative memory' in the creation of legends for the new religious orders, such as the Hospitallers,[93] Cistercians,[94] and Carmelites,[95] and by those who have considered how the writers of twelfth-century cultural or family histories 'potently evoked the past to validate the present'.[96] Marcus Bull has summarised the work of historians in this field as follows:

> to regard the foundation stories as simply 'bad' history would be to miss the central point that they were creative exercises whose authors sought to project the ideals

---

[89] *Ibid.*, p. 63.

[90] For the broader context, see G. Constable, 'Past and Present in the Eleventh and Twelfth Centuries: Perceptions of Time and Change', *L'Europa dei secoli XI e XII fra novità e tradizione: sviluppi di una cultura* (Milan, 1989), pp. 135–70.

[91] A.G. Remensnyder, *Remembering Kings Past: Monastic Foundation Legends in Medieval Southern France* (Ithaca and London, 1995), p. 2.

[92] *Ibid.*, pp. 3–4.

[93] *Les légendes de l'Hôpital de Saint-Jean de Jérusalem*, ed. A. Calvet (Paris, 2000).

[94] C.H. Berman, *The Cistercian Evolution: The Invention of a Religious Order in Twelfth-Century Europe* (Philadelphia, PA, 1999); E. Freeman, *Narratives of a New Order: Cistercian Historical Writing in England, 1150–1220* (Turnhout, 2002).

[95] A. Jotischky, *The Carmelites and Antiquity: Mendicants and their Pasts in the Middle Ages* (Oxford, 2002).

[96] J. Dunbabin, 'Discovering a Past for the French Aristocracy', *The Perception of the Past in Twelfth-Century Europe*, ed. P. Magdalino (London, 1992), p. 2. See also R.H.C. Davis, *The Normans and their Myth* (London, 1976); N.L. Paul 'Crusade and Family Memory before 1225', unpublished Ph.D. thesis (Cambridge, 2005).

and concerns of the institutions in which they were writing back into an earlier age, in order to confer legitimacy and status on their present-day circumstances. In other words, the past was not a neutral quantity preserved for its own sake; it was, rather, a tool which could be used selectively and carefully in the fashioning of institutional identities.[97]

When considered in this light, Hohler's belief that the *Historia Turpini* should be reduced to the level of Sellar and Yeatman is untenable. Rather, Pseudo-Turpin's work as it survives in the *Liber sancti Jacobi* should be regarded as integral to the development of an institutional identity for the cult of St James of Compostela, and should also be considered to be illustrative of how propagandists were seeking to create a mythical-historical context for crusading in Spain. Although it is not until the book's final chapters – a description of the threat posed by Islam in Iberia in the early twelfth century and a forged papal crusade encyclical – that the redactors' purposes become completely transparent, it seems obvious enough that the text of the *Historia* itself was being used to establish an ideological framework for crusading in Iberia by marking out traditions and relationships between ideas of pilgrimage and holy war in the peninsula. In this respect, the *Historia Turpini* can be seen to have been advancing one of the themes that was manifest in the *miracula sancti Jacobi*: that St James was a patron of warfare against the Muslims of Spain.[98]

The prologue of the *Historia Turpini* consists of a letter addressed to Leoprand, the dean of Aachen, the text of which makes it clear that Pseudo-Turpin sought to establish his reliability as an eyewitness to Charlemagne's fourteen years of campaigning in Spain. Styling himself as a 'diligent companion of the great Emperor Charlemagne', Pseudo-Turpin set out that his *Historia* would record how 'our most famous Charlemagne liberated Spain and Galicia from the control of the Saracens'.[99] This was a necessary work, it was claimed, because Leoprand had been unable to find in the royal chronicles of St Denis a detailed account of the king's exploits in Spain, and Pseudo-Turpin's direct involvement in events meant that he was more than qualified to recount the details of 'the expedition to and reconquest (*conversio*) of Spain and Galicia'.[100]

The connection between St James, the pilgrimage to Compostela and Charlemagne's military activity in Spain was established from the very beginning of the *Historia*. Following from the *Liber sancti Jacobi*'s third book,[101] Pseudo-Turpin gave brief mention in his first chapter to the 'prehistory' of the cult of St James in Spain, recording St James's apostolic mission to the country, his preaching in Galicia, his return to Jerusalem and subsequent execution by King Herod,[102] and the eventual *translatio* of the saint's body to the north-west of the peninsula.[103] That the cult of St James was eventually forgotten,

---

[97] Bull, *Miracles of Our Lady*, p. 24.

[98] Bull, *Miracles of Our Lady*, p. 25, advocated the complementary study of miracles and foundation legends. See also Constable, 'Forgery and Plagiarism', pp. 20–1.

[99] LSJ: CC, p. 199.

[100] LSJ: CC, p. 199, n. 1.

[101] LSJ: CC, pp. 185–91. This volume was crucial to the *Liber*'s programme of establishing Compostela's institutional identity as it described the *translatio* of St James's relics to Galicia.

[102] Acts 12:2.

[103] Cf. J. van Herwaarden, 'The Origins of the Cult of St. James of Compostela', *Journal of Medieval History*, 6 (1980), pp. 1–35.

and that Spain had resorted to paganism, was also lamented.[104] Turning his attention to Charlemagne, Pseudo-Turpin went on to describe how:

> After many laborious campaigns in many parts of the world . . . Charlemagne suc-
> ceeded in capturing innumerable cities from one coast [of Europe] to the other, seiz-
> ing them from the hands of the Saracens by the strength of his own invincible arm
> and with the help of God, and bringing them under Christian rule. Exhausted by
> such draining toil and effort, he resolved to no longer enter battle so that he might
> get some rest.[105]

At this time, however, the emperor witnessed a remarkable stellar portent:

> He gazed at a road of stars that was in the sky, which began near the North Sea,
> stretched between Germany and Italy, Gaul and Aquitaine, crossed straight through
> Gascony, the Basque country, Navarre and Spain as far as Galicia. It was here that
> the body of St James lay, although this was unknown at the time. For several nights
> Charlemagne examined these stars and began to think over what their significance
> might be.[106]

Pseudo-Turpin claimed that the meaning of this *caminus stellarum* was eventually revealed to Charlemagne in a remarkable dream in which St James appeared before the emperor; the episode was illustrated in the *Codex Calixtinus* by a miniature in the folio that pre-ceded the *Historia Turpini*.[107] The motifs contained within this vision are striking, and it is therefore worth quoting Pseudo-Turpin's report of the saint's speech in full:

> I am James the apostle, Christ's disciple, son of Zebedee, brother of John the Evan-
> gelist, whom our Lord in his ineffable goodness deemed worthy to be chosen on the
> Sea of Galilee to preach to his people. I was killed by the sword of King Herod, and
> my body now lies buried unrecognised in Galicia, which is at the present time still
> suffering under Saracen oppression. I am astonished that you, who have conquered
> so many cities and lands, have not liberated my land from the Saracens. Therefore I
> give you notice that because God has made you more powerful than any of the other
> kings of the world, he has chosen you from amongst all others to prepare my way
> and deliver my country from the hands of the Moabites, so that you might earn for
> yourself a crown of everlasting reward. The meaning of the road of stars that you saw
> in the sky is that you will set out from here for Galicia with a great army to conquer
> the faithless pagan people, liberate my way, set free my land, and visit my church and
> my tomb. And after you all people from one end of the earth to the other will go
> there to obtain forgiveness of their sins from the Lord, and will tell of God's wonders
> and miracles and sing his praise. And there will be pilgrims there from your lifetime

---

[104] LSJ: CC, p. 201.

[105] LSJ: CC, p. 201.

[106] LSJ: CC, p. 201.

[107] *Codex Calixtinus*, f. 162r; reproduced in LSJ: CC, p. 191. Depictions of the 'Dream of Charlemagne' became prevalent across the medieval and early modern period; see, for example, Domenico Laffi, *A Journey to the West: The Diary of a Seventeenth-Century Pilgrim from Bologna to Santiago de Compostela*, trans. J. Hall (Leiden, 1997), p. 118.

until the end of the world. Now go, therefore, with all the speed that you possibly can. I will be your helper in all things, and I will ensure that because of your labours you will be crowned in heaven by the Lord, and that your name will be praised for eternity.[108]

This passage was fundamental to the *Historia Turpini*'s contribution to the creation of an institutional identity for Santiago de Compostela and to Pseudo-Turpin's efforts to create a kind of 'foundation legend' for twelfth-century crusading in Iberia. The account of St James's speech contained a number of remarkable ideas, many of which had direct parallels to the language Pope Urban II was reported to have used at Clermont when proclaiming the First Crusade. Most obviously, just as the first crusaders had been charged with the recovery of Christ's patrimony in the Holy Land,[109] Charlemagne was understood to have been tasked with the liberation of St James's *terra* from the oppression of the Moabites – a term that undoubtedly gave the speech a contemporary resonance.[110] However, perhaps the more striking aspect of the speech was that just as Pope Urban was said to have fused ideas of penitential warfare with those of Jerusalem pilgrimage, St James was reported to have entreated Charlemagne not only to free Iberia, but also to liberate the *iter* to Compostela and thus make St James's shrine accessible to all Christian pilgrims. In so doing, Charlemagne was destined to become the first 'quasi-crusader' in Spain and to inaugurate a new age of pilgrimage to Compostela, for which he would receive both secular and spiritual rewards: his name would be 'praised for eternity', and he would be 'crowned in heaven by the Lord'.

Pseudo-Turpin reported that St James had appeared to Charlemagne on three separate occasions before the emperor eventually 'gathered together a great army and marched off to fight the infidels in Spain'.[111] The narrative of this first campaign was relatively brief, taking up only five of the *Historia*'s twenty-six chapters. The only complete description Pseudo-Turpin offered of its progress was of how, at the siege of Pamplona, the walls of the city had 'fallen of their own accord' after three months and as a result of the miraculous intervention of St James.[112] In the aftermath of this siege, Charlemagne's mercy to those Muslims who converted to Christianity, and retribution on those who did not, was reported by Pseudo-Turpin as inducing 'the other Saracens . . . [to come] from far and wide to submit to Charlemagne, send him tribute and surrender their cities to him, and soon the whole land was under his control'.[113] The third chapter of the *Historia* then recorded the full extent of Charlemagne's Iberian conquests and the fact that 'some of these cities were captured without a battle, others with extensive fighting and the greatest skill'.[114] Indeed, Pseudo-Turpin named all the cities in turn in order to

---

[108] LSJ: CC, p. 201.

[109] See Riley-Smith, *The First Crusade*, pp. 21, 48–9, 108, 114, 146, 152, 154.

[110] O'Callaghan, *Reconquest and Crusade*, p. 16, described how 'the word Moabites was used most often to refer to the Almoravids, a Muslim sect who invaded Spain in the late eleventh century'. R. Dozy, *Recherches sur l'histoire et la litterature de l'Espagne pendant le Moyen Âge*, 3rd edition, 2 vols. (Paris, 1881), vol. 2, pp. 375–6, believed that Pseudo-Turpin was deliberately using the word 'Moabite' to draw attention to the Almoravid threat.

[111] LSJ: CC, p. 201.

[112] LSJ: CC, pp. 201–2.

[113] LSJ: CC, p. 202.

[114] LSJ: CC, p. 202.

demonstrate how 'the whole of Spain, that is to say al-Andalus, Portugal, the lands of the *Serrani* and *Pardi*, Castile, the Moorish territories, Navarre, Álava, Vizcaya, Vasconia and Pallars, all yielded to Charlemagne's rule'.[115] He also made the astonishing claim that Charlemagne had reached beyond the Iberian mainland, not only taking the Balearic Islands to the east but also crossing into North Africa, where his conquests ranged as far as modern Tunisia. Perhaps naturally, though, the emperor's time in Spain was said to have concluded with the completion of a pilgrimage to Compostela and El Padrón, the Galician coastal town that had grown up around the site where the boat bearing the relics of St James had supposedly reached shore in the first century. It was here that Charlemagne 'gave thanks to God and St James for having brought him that far, and planted his lance in the sea, declaring that he could not go any further'.[116]

The substantial part of Pseudo-Turpin's work was, however, devoted to events that followed Charlemagne's first victorious period of campaigning in the Iberian peninsula. In this respect, it seems more than likely that the *Historia*'s narrative development was influenced by events in the Iberian peninsula in the late eleventh and early twelfth centuries. Pseudo-Turpin described how, after Charlemagne returned to France, leaving Iberia in peace, the peninsula was overrun by 'a certain pagan king from Africa called Aigolandus, [who] conquered the whole of Spain with his armies, drove the Christians out from the towns and the cities, and killed those whom Charlemagne had left to defend the land'.[117] This invasion by aggressive Muslim peoples from North Africa closely paralleled the threat presented to the Christians of Iberia by the arrival of the Almoravids in 1086,[118] and Charlemagne's exemplary reaction to the news – he was described as immediately setting out for the peninsula – was almost certainly intended to illustrate that he was the paradigm of a Christian warrior.[119] The narrative of Charlemagne's second Iberian campaign spanned chapters VI–X of the *Historia*; his third campaign was considered in chapters XI–XIX. However, rather than addressing Pseudo-Turpin's account of events chronologically, it is expedient to draw attention to some of the themes with which these chapters were most obviously concerned to demonstrate further how it was hoped that the *Historia* would contribute to the cultivation of crusade ideology in Iberia.

First of all, it is clear that from at least the third campaign onwards conflict between Christians and Muslims in Iberia was considered to be a form of holy war. In his eleventh chapter Pseudo-Turpin reported that Charlemagne had returned to France to recruit more men for his armies, and he described how the emperor 'enlisted both friends and enemies, fellow countrymen and foreigners . . . and I, Turpin, on the Lord's authority, blessed and absolved from all their sins those whom the Emperor took with him to Spain to conquer the infidels'.[120] Pseudo-Turpin went on to testify that he had 'exhorted the faithful people by the worthy precepts of Christ to fight bravely, and gave them absolution from their sins'.[121] Although the *Historia* did not go so far as to depict campaigning in the

---

[115] LSJ: CC, p. 202.
[116] LSJ: CC, p. 202.
[117] LSJ: CC, p. 203.
[118] See O'Callaghan, *Reconquest and Crusade*, pp. 30–1.
[119] LSJ: CC, p. 203.
[120] LSJ: CC, p. 206.
[121] LSJ: CC, p. 207.

peninsula as a meritorious act in itself – in fact Pseudo-Turpin's proclamations seem to bear more relation to the absolution granted in advance to those who fought at Civitate in 1053 than they do to more developed understandings of penitential violence[122] – it nevertheless laid some of the theoretical groundwork for ideas that were to be drawn upon in the forged papal crusade encyclical that appeared in the book's final chapter.

A related theme that recurred within the narratives of the encounters between the armies of Charlemagne and Aigolandus was the certainty that, like those who had died at Civitate, those Christians who fell in battle in Iberia would become martyrs,[123] from which Pseudo-Turpin concluded that 'those who fight for Christ gain their salvation'.[124] This idea was referred to most vividly in the deathbed speech ascribed to Roland, one of Charlemagne's most trusted warriors. Following the successful conclusion of the third and final campaign in the peninsula, Pseudo-Turpin had turned his attention to describing the *restauratio* of Iberia and the eventual withdrawal of Charlemagne's victorious armies, which led inexorably towards a consideration of the legendary rout at Roncesvalles,[125] where:

> Not one of the twenty thousand Christian soldiers escaped with his life. Some were driven through with lances, some beheaded by swords, some cut down by axes, some pierced by arrows and javelins, some beaten to death with staves, some flayed alive with knives, some burned on fires, others hanged from trees.[126]

Roland was amongst the many 'martyrs of Christ' who fell at Roncesvalles,[127] and in his final words he was reported to have hoped that all those who had died for Christ in Iberia would be treated mercifully and be rewarded with a martyr's crown:

> Then, stretching his hands towards the Lord, he offered up this prayer for those who had died in the previous battle: 'May your heart be moved to be merciful, O Lord, to those of your faithful servants who died in battle today. They came from distant parts of the world to this foreign land to wage war on the faithless people, to exalt your holy name, to avenge your precious blood and to proclaim your faith. But now they lie killed by the hands of the Saracens. And I ask you, O Lord, to wipe away their sins mercifully, deliver their souls and rescue them from the torments of hell. Send your holy archangels to them to rescue their souls from the land of darkness and guide them into the heavenly kingdom, where together with your blessed martyrs they may be found worthy to reign for eternity with you, who lives and reigns with God the Father and the Holy Spirit for ever and ever. Amen.'[128]

The sacrifices made by those who had died at Roncesvalles were also said to have been remembered by Charlemagne himself;[129] indeed, it is striking that the arrangements

---

[122] See J.S.C. Riley-Smith, *The First Crusaders, 1095–1131* (Cambridge, 1997), pp. 47–9.
[123] See, for example, LSJ: CC, pp. 204–5, 206, 217.
[124] LSJ: CC, p. 205.
[125] See also *Pilgrim's Guide*, vol. 2, pp. 26, 28, 62–4.
[126] LSJ: CC, p. 216.
[127] LSJ: CC, p. 218.
[128] LSJ: CC, p. 219.
[129] See also *Pilgrim's Guide*, vol. 2, pp. 62–4.

that the emperor made to commemorate the dead were also understood to incorporate those who would follow their example by dying for Christ in the peninsula in any future conflict. Pseudo-Turpin reported that Charlemagne had ordained that on the anniversary of the deaths of Roland and his companions, the canons of the church of St Romain in Blaye where Roland's remains had been interred would say thirty masses and psalters 'for all those who accepted, or for those who will accept, martyrdom in Spain for the love of God'.[130] Furthermore, after he had returned to Paris, Charlemagne was understood to have prayed to St Denis to ensure that these masses and psalters would be efficacious:

> Then, standing next to his body, he [Charlemagne] prayed to Blessed Denis, for the salvation of . . . those Christians who accepted the martyr's crown for the love of God in wars against the Saracens in Spain. The next night, Blessed Denis appeared to the sleeping king and woke him saying: 'For those who, inspired by your instruction and your example of probity, died or who will die in wars against the Saracens in Spain, I have secured forgiveness of all their transgressions.'[131]

Whilst the concept of warrior martyrs was not exclusively linked to crusading the two ideas were very closely related,[132] and some of the contexts in which Pseudo-Turpin described the ideas of martyrdom in his *Historia* suggest that a direct connection between those who died in Iberia and those who died on the First Crusade ought to be inferred. First of all, in his report of Roland's deathbed speech, Pseudo-Turpin portrayed those who fought for Christ in Iberia as having adopted a kind of voluntary exile:

> O Lord Jesus Christ, for whose faith I left my homeland and came to these foreign regions to exalt Christianity, with whose aid I have been victorious in many battles against the faithless Saracens, and have endured numerous blows, disasters, many wounds, reproaches, derision, fatigue, heat and cold, hunger and thirst, and anxieties, to you in this hour I now entrust my soul.[133]

In this respect, Pseudo-Turpin appears to have been following in the footsteps of writers such as Guibert of Nogent, who depicted the hardships endured by the first crusaders in terms of self-inflicted suffering, as has been described above.[134]

Secondly, a theme that was common to the *Historia Turpini* and a number of the crusade histories of the early twelfth century was the idea that, like the first crusaders, Charlemagne and his warriors were understood to be taking part in a vendetta

---

[130] LSJ: CC, pp. 222–3. See also *ibid.*, p. 225, for Charlemagne's commemoration of the Battle of Roncesvalles.

[131] LSJ: CC, p. 223.

[132] C. Morris, 'Martyrs on the Field of Battle before and during the First Crusade', *Martyrs and Martyrologies*, ed. D. Wood, *SCH*, 30 (Oxford, 1993), p. 103, argued that it was 'the First Crusade which inserted the idea [of warrior martyrs] into the common stock of Western thought'. See also H.E.J. Cowdrey, 'Pope Gregory VII and Martyrdom', *Dei gesta per Francos: Crusade Studies in Honour of Jean Richard*, ed. M. Balard, B.Z. Kedar and J.S.C. Riley-Smith (Aldershot, 2001), pp. 3–11.

[133] LSJ: CC, p. 219.

[134] See above, pp. 39–41, 74, 79–81.

against both Muslims and Jews.[135] According to Pseudo-Turpin, as he lay dying Roland had addressed his sword with the following words, which evoked some of the popular ideas of vengeance that were prevalent in early crusading ideology:

> Through you the Saracens are destroyed, the faithless people killed, the Christian religion exalted, the praise, glory and fame of God secured. O how many times have I avenged through you the name of our Lord Jesus Christ, how many times have I slain the enemies of Christ, what number of Saracens have I killed with you, what number of Jews and other faithless people have I destroyed to exalt the Christian faith! Through you the justice of God is fulfilled, the hand and foot of the habitual robber is cut off from the body. How many times have I killed with you the faithless Jew or Saracen, how many times have I, so I think, avenged the blood of Christ![136]

But perhaps the most compelling evidence for a connection between the martyrdom of Charlemagne's warriors and that of the arms-bearers of the First Crusade can be inferred from Pseudo-Turpin's description of one particular episode relating to death in battle. On the evening before an engagement with a prince from Navarre:

> Charlemagne asked the Lord to show him which of his men were going to die in battle. The following day, when Charlemagne's warriors had put on their armour, the sign of the cross of the Lord appeared in red on the shoulders of those who were destined to die; it showed on the back of their breastplates. When Charlemagne saw this, he immediately had them isolated in his chapel so that they could not die in battle . . . [But following that battle] Charlemagne returned to those whom he had shut away for safety and found them lifeless. There were around one hundred and fifty of them in number. Oh most blessed company of Christian warriors! Even though they did not die by the sword of the persecutor, they were not deprived of the martyr's palm.[137]

This passage has such a strong similarity to the reports of the crusade *stigmata* that featured in some of the histories of the First Crusade that one is forced to question its originality. In both cases, the discovery of the sign of the cross 'on the back of the shoulders' was believed to indicate that the bearer was especially chosen by God, and the mark frequently appeared only after the crusader in question had died.[138] It is impossible to know for sure whether Pseudo-Turpin was adapting the miracle of the crusade *stigmata* to suit his own purposes, but given that the Latin of a later section in which he described how Charlemagne's warriors 'were wading in blood right up to their ankles'[139] is remarkably close to the wording used by Fulcher of Chartres in his

---

[135] See Riley-Smith, *The First Crusade*, pp. 48–9, 54–7, 153–4. For the context, see now S. Throop, 'Vengeance and the Crusades', *Crusades*, 5 (2006), pp. 21–38.

[136] LSJ: CC, p. 218. Cf. Hohler, '*Jacobus*', p. 34, n. 14, whose analysis of this passage revealed some further misconceptions about the twelfth century: 'it is not the duty of Christian warriors to "avenge God" but to protect the fatherless etc.; and the contrary statement has no place in a work in Latin and therefore written by an ecclesiastic for clerics'.

[137] LSJ: CC, p. 210.

[138] See above, pp. 35–9.

[139] LSJ: CC, p. 210: 'Tanta sanguinum effusio die illa agitur, quod victores usque ad bases in sanguine

account of the massacre at Jerusalem in 1099,[140] and that Pseudo-Calixtus also later stated that he had consulted a *codex Iherosolimitane ystorie*,[141] it is at least a possibility that the Compostelan redactors of the *Historia Turpini* had access to or were inspired by Fulcher's *Historia Hierosolymitana*.[142]

The 'crusading' ideas within the *Historia Turpini* are certainly not as precise or well-defined as those contained within contemporary texts that originated from the papacy of from other leading churchmen of the twelfth century, such as Bernard of Clairvaux.[143] Nevertheless, it seems more than likely that in his references to Charlemagne and his warriors adopting self-imposed exile, being absolved from sin, liberating the *terra* of St James and the *iter* to Compostela, exacting vengeance upon Muslims and Jews, accepting martyrdom and being marked with quasi-crusade *stigmata*, Pseudo-Turpin was attempting to create a precedent for crusading in Iberia. Thus far the connections between the appearance of such motifs in the *Historia Turpini* and the development of crusade ideology in the peninsula have mostly had to be inferred. However, Book IV of the *Liber sancti Jacobi* contained three appendices, each attributed to Pseudo-Calixtus, from which it is evident that the material contained within the *Historia* was intended specifically to establish a foundation legend for crusading in Spain.

The first of Pseudo-Calixtus's contributions (chapter XXIV) began by describing the *inventio* of Bishop Turpin's body, who was depicted as being another 'martir Christi'. Pseudo-Calixtus reiterated that 'those who accepted martyrdom in Spain for the faith of Christ are crowned with merit in the heavens', and he argued that although Charlemagne and Turpin had not died at Roncesvalles, they too should be considered martyrs, before confirming that, in fulfilment of Charlemagne's wishes, from the time of the Battle of Roncesvalles onward masses had been celebrated on 16 June 'not only for Charlemagne's dead warriors, but also for all those who, from the time of Charlemagne up to the present day, have become martyrs for the faith of Christ in Spain and in the extremities of Jerusalem'.[144] Following this pseudo-papal assertion of the ultimate spiritual reward for those who had died fighting for Christ, the penultimate chapter of the *Liber sancti Jacobi*'s Book IV considered how the political situation in Iberia had developed from the time of Charlemagne down to the twelfth century. Although initially there had been peace, Pseudo-Calixtus described how Almanzor (d. 1002) had sought to restore Galicia and Spain to Muslim rule. The stories of the desecration that Almanzor had inflicted, and particularly that which had been wrought at Compostela, have obvious parallels with the reports of Urban II's Clermont sermon in which the

---

natabant.'

[140] Fulcher of Chartres, *Historia Hierosolymitana (1095–1127)*, ed. H. Hagenmeyer (Heidelberg, 1913), p. 301: 'quod si inibi essetis, pedes vestri sanguine peremptorum usque ad bases tingerentur.' See also B.Z. Kedar, 'The Jerusalem Massacre of July 1099 in the Western Historiography of the Crusades', *Crusades*, 3 (2004), pp. 15–75.

[141] LSJ: CC, p. 229.

[142] But cf. M. Bull, 'The Capetian Monarchy and the Early Crusade Movement: Hugh of Vermandois and Louis VII', *Nottingham Medieval Studies*, 40 (1996), p. 43, who believed that this probably referred to the *Historia Iherosolimitana* of Robert of Rheims.

[143] On the difficulties of strictly defining 'crusading' ideas, see now N. Housley, *Contesting the Crusades* (Oxford, 2006), pp. 20–1.

[144] LSJ: CC, p. 227.

pope described the defilement of Jerusalem and the Holy Sepulchre. However, although Pseudo-Calixtus recorded a number of episodes of the violation of Spanish churches, Almanzor's incursions into Iberia had not led to a permanent Islamic presence in the peninsula and the chapter closed by reiterating the idea that for a long time the Saracens had been unable to successfully take the country (*patria*) of St James.[145]

It was therefore not until the final chapter of the *Liber's* Book IV that the full contemporary significance of the *Historia Turpini* was realised, for here Pseudo-Calixtus set out the text of a letter in which he directly proclaimed a crusade for Iberia, which was referred to as the *iter Yspania*. It should be noted from the outset that Ulysse Robert rightly considered this bull to be a forgery,[146] but in spite of the bogus nature of its origins it is remarkable that the text of the letter has received little scholarly attention. It was not, for example, considered by Goñi Gaztambide in his *Historia de la bula de cruzada in España*, and it has not been mentioned in any of the other major histories of the development of crusading in Iberia. Given the spurious attributions to Pope Calixtus elsewhere in the *Liber sancti Jacobi*, there can be little doubt that the letter was appended to the *Historia Turpini* at Compostela by those who sought to mould Pseudo-Turpin's work into propaganda for the cult of St James. But more could be said. It is known that there is a crusade bull of Pope Calixtus II's, now lost, that the pope referred to indirectly in his surviving letter of 1123,[147] and it is therefore a possibility that the Pseudo-Calixtine bull in the *Liber sancti Jacobi* was modelled on the missing *bona fide* bull. Pseudo-Calixtus's general letter proclaiming a crusade in Iberia is replete with the hallmarks of later crusading encyclicals (*narratio, exhortatio* and *privilegia*), and it must certainly have been formulated by individuals who were familiar with such documents. But even if one leaves aside the admittedly slight proposition that this letter was based on a genuine crusade bull, it can still nonetheless be considered to be amongst the most fascinating of forgeries.

Dated to the Lateran Council of 1123, from where the real Pope Calixtus II had confirmed crusade privileges for those fighting in Spain or the Holy Land and had written another letter proclaiming the crusade in Iberia, Pseudo-Calixtus began his letter by marking out the predicament faced by the Christians of the Iberian peninsula.[148] He described the desecration of churches, the persecution, torment and slavery endured in Spain at the hands of the Muslims, and also called to mind the 'thousands upon thousands' of martyrs who had sacrificed their lives there, before issuing his *exhortatio*: 'Therefore, I appeal to your affection, my little sons . . . to go to Spain to fight the Saracens. Those who will have gone there willingly will be rewarded with great payment.' He then turned his attention to the deeds of Charlemagne, describing the 'countless labours' the emperor had gone through in his battles against the *gens perfidia*. The letter imagined how at an eighth-century council in Rheims, Charlemagne's *consocius*, Archbishop Turpin, had 'with divine authority freed from the chains of all their sins all those who were in Spain to conquer the faithless people, to spread Christianity, liberate

---

[145] LSJ: CC, pp. 227–8.
[146] Calixtus II, *Bullaire*, vol. 1, pp. LXXXI–LXXXII. Robert reproduced the bull as no. 449 in vol. 2, pp. 261–2.
[147] *Ibid.*, vol. 2, no. 454, pp. 266–7.
[148] LSJ: CC, p. 228.

Christian captives, and to accept martyrdom out of divine love'.[149] But in his boldest move, Pseudo-Calixtus then drew a direct line between Archbishop Turpin's supposed absolution of sin for those who fought in Iberia and the later preaching of the First Crusade by Pope Urban II. In so doing, he was completely rewriting the history of the crusading movement:

> All the popes who came afterwards have confirmed this same [indulgence], all the way to our own time with the testifying of blessed Pope Urban, that illustrious man, who at the Council of Clermont in France, in the presence of around one hundred bishops, asserted this same [indulgence], when he proclaimed the journey to Jerusalem, as the book of the *Ystoria Iherosolimitana* tells us. This same [indulgence] we now strengthen and affirm, so that all who will have gone with the sign of the cross of the Lord raised on their shoulders to fight the faithless people either in Spain or in the far reaches of Jerusalem, as we have said above, on behalf of God and the holy apostles, Peter, Paul and James, and all the saints, and with our apostolic blessing, may be absolved from all their sins which they have confessed to their priests and for which they will have been doing penance.[150]

Pseudo-Calixtus further connected the deeds of Charlemagne with his own call to crusade by confirming that all those who died whilst fighting the Muslims of Iberia would be rewarded with the crown of martyrdom. He stressed the urgency of his appeal – 'surely there has never been so great a need to go [to Spain] . . . as there is today' – before setting out the instructions for how the crusade was to be preached. The letter then closed by blessing both preachers and crusaders alike, and advocated that its contents should be widely copied and disseminated.[151]

When considered within the context of this remarkable document, it seems more than likely that the redaction of the *Historia Turpini* contained within the *Liber sancti Jacobi*, although doubtless based on an earlier work, was commissioned and executed, probably at Compostela, as part of the programme of developing an institutional identity for the cult of St James and as a means of providing a historical framework or 'foundation legend' for crusading activity in Spain. Through the examination of such a legend, it is possible to see the minds of crusade propagandists at work, as they sought to create a model for crusading in Iberia that the knighthood of Christendom might aspire towards. The *Historia Turpini* therefore reads like a long *exemplum*, with the closing letter of Pseudo-Calixtus acting as the moralistic direction. The letter's positioning in the *Liber*'s text – just after observations about the relative peace that had endured in Spain since Charlemagne's time – was surely not accidental. It seems certain that the letter's purpose was to invigorate the Christian arms-bearers of the West to respond to the new threat posed by the aggressive Islam of North Africa.

The association of Charlemagne with crusading ideas was not original to Pseudo-Turpin, and the emperor's role as an *exemplum* of Christian knighthood was recorded in several histories of the First Crusade, including Robert of Rheims's report of Urban II's Clermont sermon:

---

[149] LSJ: CC, pp. 228–9.
[150] LSJ: CC, p. 229.
[151] LSJ: CC, p. 229.

> Let the stories (*gesta*) about your predecessors move you and incite your souls to strength: the probity and greatness of King Charlemagne and of Louis his son and of your other kings, who destroyed the kingdoms of the pagans and extended into them the boundaries of Holy Church.[152]

Jonathan Riley-Smith has demonstrated that most of the leaders of the First Crusade were conscious of a connection to the Carolingian dynasty, and that romantic portrayals of Charlemagne as 'the conquering Christian emperor, waging warfare against the pagans in Spain and Saxony' held popular currency in the late eleventh century, as did narratives describing the emperor's legendary pilgrimage to the Holy Land.[153] It is therefore not surprising that in order to encourage recruitment for crusading in Iberia, Charlemagne was overtly depicted by Pseudo-Turpin as a 'proto-crusader'. Indeed, Pseudo-Turpin demonstrated that the precedent set by Charlemagne had been honoured by his immediate successors:

> After Charlemagne's death there were many kings and princes who fought the Saracens in Spain: Clovis, who was the first Christian king of the Franks, Clothaire, Dagobert, Pippin, Charles Martel, Charles the Bald, Louis and Carloman. All these succeeded in conquering some parts of Spain, but abandoned others. Charlemagne, however, subjugated the whole of Spain during his lifetime.[154]

In this way, Pseudo-Turpin was tracing a direct connection between the achievements of Charlemagne and the potential for the Christian arms-bearers of the twelfth century to follow his example. That his efforts were well received is evident from the subsequent interest that was taken in his text. Aside from survival in more than 170 Latin manuscripts, the *Historia Turpini* was translated into many vernaculars, including Old French, Provençal, Galician, Anglo-Norman, Middle High German, Welsh and Old Norse,[155] and it has been argued recently that Pseudo-Turpin's work was especially popular with noble families who were involved in crusading in both Iberia and in the Holy Land.[156]

When the *miracula sancti Jacobi* and *Historia Turpini* are studied in tandem, it seems clear enough that significant efforts were being made in the second quarter of the twelfth century by propagandists working at Santiago de Compostela to associate the cult of St James with the development of crusading in Iberia. The saint was portrayed in the *miracula* as having a particular concern for the arms-bearing classes of Europe, whom he supported not only because they had made (or had vowed to make) a pilgrimage to his shrine, but also because they were involved in fighting Islam both in Iberia and the Holy Land. This depiction of the saint's patronage of 'crusading' warfare was elucidated further in the *Historia Turpini*, where Pseudo-Turpin demonstrated that St James himself

---

[152] Robert of Rheims, 'Historia Iherosolimitana', *RHC Oc.* 3, p. 728.

[153] Riley-Smith, 'First Crusade and St. Peter', pp. 47–9. See also Bull, 'The Capetian Monarchy', p. 43. Charlemagne's pilgrimage was also mentioned by Pseudo-Turpin: see LSJ: CC, p. 216.

[154] LSJ: CC, pp. 202–3. Pseudo-Turpin's knowledge of dynastic history was wayward to say the least.

[155] See Pseudo-Turpin, ed. Walpole, p. 5; Short, 'Study in Carolingian Legend', pp. 127–52. See also H. Richter, '*Militia Dei*: A Central Concept for the Religious Ideas of the Early Crusades and the German *Rolandslied*', *Journeys toward God: Pilgrimage and Crusade*, ed. B.N. Sargent-Baur (Kalamazoo, MI, 1992), pp. 107–26.

[156] See Paul, 'Crusade and Family Memory', pp. 172–7.

had been directly responsible for the involvement of Charlemagne and his warriors in the original reconquest of the Iberian peninsula in the eighth century. Having been called upon to liberate St James's *terra* and to open a road to his tomb, Charlemagne was depicted as having participated in an armed pilgrimage in the peninsula, which set a precedent for others to follow. Indeed, the author of the *Pilgrim's Guide*, which constituted the fifth book of the *Liber sancti Jacobi*, claimed that the 'first station of prayer (*primus locus orationis*)' in Spain for those who travelled to Compostela in the twelfth century was a site that was known as the *crux Karoli*:

> [It] is called the Cross of Charlemagne because it is here that with axes and picks and spades and other implements Charlemagne, going to Spain with his armies, once made a road, and he raised on it the sign of the cross of the Lord. And then, kneeling facing Galicia, he poured out his prayer to God and Saint James. On account of this, the pilgrims, bending the knee towards the land of Saint James, are accustomed to pray, and each one plants his own standard of the cross of the Lord.[157]

By opening the pilgrim road to Compostela and by returning to Spain repeatedly to continue the fight against the Muslims of North Africa, Charlemagne and his men were therefore understood to be commendable models of proto-crusading piety. The fact that the spiritual privileges that Archbishop Turpin of Rheims was supposed to have instituted for their military campaigns was presented by Pseudo-Calixtus as providing a precedent for Pope Urban II's preaching of the First Crusade is a clear illustration of how 'imaginative memory' was being used to establish a foundation legend for crusading in Iberia. There can therefore be little doubt that José Goñi Gaztambide was incorrect in concluding that the cult of St James could not have been used to propagate crusades in Spain.

Nevertheless, the fact that Pseudo-Turpin and Pseudo-Calixtus (if they were indeed separate writers) were making such pains to institute a mythical-historical framework for peninsular warfare against Islam begs the question why a foundation legend for crusading in Iberia was believed to be necessary in the first place; it certainly seems to give the lie to the idea that eleventh-century Spain was a breeding ground for crusade piety. Perhaps it was beginning to be felt in *c.* 1140 that the strategy of opening the *iter per Hispaniam*, which was described in the previous chapter, was too ambitious.[158] It may be that without the direction of a man such as Alfonso I of Aragón enthusiasm for the idea became dormant, especially when there had not been any recent military successes to compare to the victories at Toledo, Jerusalem or Zaragoza. Perhaps it indicates that the *iter per Hispaniam* had proved ineffective in recruiting for campaigns in the peninsula, and that continued references to worshipping at the Holy Sepulchre had only perpetuated the drain of manpower to the East that had proved so problematic at the turn of the century. It is striking that, at some point in the 1130s, the instinctive response of a certain noble from León-Castile who wished to undertake a severe penance was that he should 'go on a pilgrimage to Jerusalem' rather than fight against the Muslims of al-Andalus.[159] Either way, the propagation of the Compostelan foundation myth and

---

[157] *Pilgrim's Guide*, vol. 2, pp. 26–7.
[158] But see below, pp. 177–8.
[159] 'Chronica Adefonsi imperatoris', ed. A. Maya Sánchez, *Chronica Hispana saeculi XII, CC:CM* 71

the presentation of Charlemagne as an exemplary proto-crusader signalled a dramatic attempt to distance peninsular crusading activity from its direct connections with, and its origins in, the Jerusalem pilgrimage tradition. However, the fact that attempts were being made to associate penitential warfare in Iberia with another cult centre – Santiago de Compostela – suggests that ideas of pilgrimage continued to be of deep importance to the development of crusading thought. In this respect, the themes contained within the *miracula sancti Jacobi* and *Historia Turpini* are indicative of the shift towards the localisation of crusading traditions that was to become especially prominent in Iberia as the twelfth century wore on.[160]

'Crusading' in Iberia, c.1113–c.1150

The propagandists working at Santiago de Compostela in *c.*1140 were by no means the only individuals in the first half of the twelfth century to be projecting crusading ideology on to episodes in the history of warfare between Christians and Muslims that had taken place before 1095.[161] Although it is often unclear how far such efforts were conscious attempts to invent a proto-history of crusading warfare, and how far the retrospective application of crusading ideology was an unconscious response to a set of influential new ideas,[162] there can be little doubt that in the wake of the First Crusade a number of pre-existing traditions of struggles against Islam began to be coloured with crusading motifs. Indeed, it is evident that this cultural and textual phenomenon was by no means limited to wars that had been fought against Muslims: in his *Historia regum Britanniae*, for example, Geoffrey of Monmouth, who was writing in *c.*1136, applied crusading imagery to King Arthur's sixth-century campaigns against the pagan Saxons. According to Geoffrey, immediately before the Battle of Bath in *c.*516, the warriors of Arthur's army, who were 'marked with the sign of the Christian faith', were inspired by the words of what, to all intents and purposes, was a crusade sermon. Geoffrey composed the following speech, in which the speaker, Archbishop Dubricius, instructed the arms-bearers of Britain that to fight for the defence of their countrymen and their *patria* was an act of Christo-mimesis. The language that Geoffrey used was clearly influenced by ideas that had proliferated in the narrative histories of the First Crusade:

> Fight for your fatherland, and if you are killed suffer death willingly for your country's sake. That in itself is victory and a cleansing of the soul. Whoever suffers death for the sake of his brothers offers himself as a living sacrifice to God and follows with firm footsteps behind Christ Himself, who did not disdain to lay down His life for His brothers. It follows that if any one of you shall suffer death in this war, that death shall be to him as a penance and an absolution for all his sins.[163]

(Turnhout, 1990), p. 237. It was only after the intervention of the archbishop of Toledo that the individual in question, Muño Alfonso, was 'ordered to wage war continuously on the Saracens [in Spain] as his penance'. See S. Barton, 'From Tyrants to Soldiers of Christ: The Nobility of Twelfth-Century León-Castile and the Struggle against Islam', *Nottingham Medieval Studies*, 44 (2000), pp. 46–7.

[160] See Riley-Smith, *What were the Crusades?*, p. 17.

[161] See Paul, 'Crusade and Family Memory ', pp. 123–217.

[162] See above, pp. 61–3.

[163] Geoffrey of Monmouth, *Historia regum Britanniae*, ed. A. Griscom and R. Ellis Jones (London,

An important and parallel illustration of the process by which medieval writers retrospectively 'invented' crusades is the narrativisation of the Pisan-Catalan campaign to the Balearic Islands of 1113–15,[164] which has been regarded almost universally by modern historians as a crusade.[165] In fact, it seems far more likely that the expedition to the Balearics was but the latest in a long-standing history of conflicts in the western Mediterranean between the Italian maritime republics and their commercial opponents,[166] which came to be depicted as a crusade by later writers who preserved for posterity the deeds of the Christians from Pisa and the county of Barcelona who had united to fight the Muslims of Ibiza and Majorca.

The campaign to the Balearics was initiated in response to the threats posed in the western Mediterranean by the Muslim pirates who lived on the islands, and to the plight faced by the 'more than thirty thousand [Christian] captives' that the Muslims had imprisoned there.[167] The preaching for the expedition had begun in Pisa in March 1113, but its progenitors soon received the blessing of Pope Paschal II, who was represented on the campaign itself from spring 1114 by a papal legate, Cardinal Boso of St Anastasia.[168] Although the Pisan contingent departed for the Balearics on 6 August 1113, it was not until the following month that the campaign came to involve arms-bearers from Iberia. Even then, it would seem that the contribution of warriors from Catalonia, and the Count of Barcelona's assumption of leadership of the combined forces, was a result of fate, because the Pisan fleet was driven to the Spanish mainland by a storm, and it was only after a period of negotiation that Ramon Berenguer III's participation was confirmed.[169] Having wintered on the Catalan coast, the expedition then set out for the Balearics in 1114. Ibiza was taken in August of that year, and the Muslims of Majorca eventually capitulated in the spring of 1115.

No papal correspondence directly relating to this expedition has survived. The main primary sources are the *vita* of St Oleguer (d. 1137)[170] and the *Liber Maiolichinus*, a poem

---

1929), pp. 437–8. Translation from Geoffrey of Monmouth, *The History of the Kings of Britain*, trans. L. Thorpe (London, 1966), p. 216. Cf. C. Tyerman, *The Invention of the Crusades* (Basingstoke, 1998), p. 16, who wrote in reference to this passage that 'it is almost impossible to identify what is old and what new'.

[164] Cf. Tyerman, *Invention of the Crusades*, especially pp. 8–29, 100.

[165] See, for example, Goñi Gaztambide, *Historia*, pp. 68–9; D.W. Lomax, *The Reconquest of Spain* (London, 1978), p. 83; B.F. Reilly, *The Contest of Christian and Muslim Spain, 1031–1157* (Oxford, 1992), p. 176; O'Callaghan, *Reconquest and Crusade*, pp. 35–6; J.S.C. Riley-Smith, *The Crusades: A History*, 2nd edition (London, 2005), p. 116. The best study of this expedition is G.B. Doxey, 'Christian Attempts to Reconquer the Balearic Islands before 1229', unpublished Ph.D. thesis (Cambridge, 1991), pp. 63–190.

[166] For the context, see J.H. Pryor, *Geography, Technology, and War: Studies in the Maritime History of the Mediterranean, 649–1571* (Cambridge, 1988), pp. 102–11; Doxey, 'Balearic Islands', pp. 25–39, 95–6.

[167] *Liber Maiolichinus de gestis Pisanorum illustribus*, ed. C. Calisse (Rome, 1904), v. 26. The economic context for the campaign should not be overlooked, however. See Pryor, *Geography, Technology, and War*, pp. 91–2, who demonstrates that 'the Balearics . . . were the real key to maritime control in the western Mediterranean'.

[168] Goñi Gaztambide, *Historia*, p. 69.

[169] Doxey, 'Balearic Islands', pp. 115–22.

[170] 'Vita sancti Olegarii', *España Sagrada*, 29 (Madrid, 1775), pp. 473–7.

of around 3,500 verses that purports to be the eyewitness testimony of a Pisan cleric, although its exact provenance is still open to considerable debate.[171] It is not entirely clear that the writers of both these accounts saw the expedition within a crusading context.[172] The author of the *vita* recorded how, in 1114, Ramon Berenguer had joined an expedition to the Balearics that had set out *pro liberatione fratrum* at the behest (*ex praecepto*) of Paschal II.[173] The source's author went on to recount how with 'Majorca destroyed, Ibiza overturned, the Balearic Islands laid waste, [and] a countless number of Christian captives set free and raised up out of the prison of the Moors, the count returned to Barcelona with joyous victory'.[174] More substantial evidence for the casting of the expedition as a crusade is contained within the *Liber Maiolichinus*. The text's anonymous author began his account by describing how in 1113 the archbishop of Pisa had proclaimed the expedition in a sermon that was loaded with crusading imagery, the most obvious feature of which was that he had implored his audience to take the sign of the cross as a symbol of their vow to fight the Muslims of the Balearics.[175] The use of the crusade badge subsequently received papal confirmation – Paschal II was said to have bestowed the sign of the cross and *signa romana* upon the Pisan legates that were sent to him[176] – and the pope was also reported to have emphasised the virtue of the expedition, as well as offering spiritual privileges to those who took part.[177] But perhaps even more intriguing were the descriptions of the sacrifices that the expedition's participants had made, which were referred to in language that evoked the ideas of voluntary exile that were prevalent in the narrative histories of the First Crusade.[178] For example, in his description of the preparations that were being made for the expedition's departure in August 1113, the *Liber's* author described how 'out of love of him [Christ], they left behind their parents and relations, riches and homeland of Pisa'.[179] This theme was also revisited in the speech that the expedition's papal legate, Cardinal

---

[171] *Liber Maiolichinus*. On the authorship of this source, see Doxey, 'Balearic Islands', pp. 70–85. The *Liber* survives in three manuscripts: the P manuscript, which dates from the first half of the twelfth century, and the R and B manuscripts, which both date from the fourteenth centuries. It is also speculated that there is a lost autograph manuscript. For a discussion of the manuscript tradition, see *ibid.*, pp. 64–70. The Balearic campaign is also referred to in a number of other twelfth-century sources. See, for example, *Gesta comitum Barcinonensium*, ed. L. Barrau Dihigo and J. Masso Torrents, *Croniques catalanes*, 2 (Barcelona, 1925), pp. 8, 37–8; 'Gesta triumphalia per Pisanos facta de captione Hierusalem et civitatis Maioricarum et aliarum civitatum et de triumpho habito contra Ianuenses', ed. M. Lupo Gentile, *Raccolta degli storici italiani*, 6.2 (Bologna, 1936), pp. 90–4. The *Gesta triumphalia* recounted Pisan victories in 1099 (in reference to their contribution to the First Crusade), 1112 (a campaign against Henry V of Germany in Lombardy), 1114 (the Balearic expedition), and 1119 (a campaign against the Genoese). See *ibid.*, pp. 89–96.

[172] See Doxey, 'Balearic Islands', pp. 98–103, 106–8.

[173] 'Vita sancti Olegarii', p. 474.

[174] *Ibid.*, pp. 473–4.

[175] *Liber Maiolichinus*, vv. 30–48.

[176] *Ibid.*, vv. 71–5. *Signa romana* perhaps refers to the symbol of the papal keys. For another reference to the papal influence on the campaign, see *ibid.*, vv. 2761–4.

[177] *Ibid.*, vv. 76–81. Doxey, 'Balearic Islands', p. 102, notes that these privileges were not directly equated to those offered to crusaders.

[178] See above, pp. 39–41, 74, 79–81.

[179] *Liber Maiolichinus*, vv. 156–9.

Boso, was reported to have delivered during the siege of Majorca in 1114, where he praised the soldiers because they had 'abandoned native borders, parents, wives, status and whatever seemed sweet to human senses',[180] and reminded them that those who died on the expedition were blessed.[181]

At first glance, the appearance of these crusading motifs – papal authorisation of a war of liberation that was as an act of fraternal charity, whose participants adopted the sign of the cross, embraced of acts of self-denial, and hoped for spiritual rewards – would suggest that the expedition to the Balearics of 1113–15 was one of the earliest, if not the first, occasions on which a crusade was launched without expectation that its achievements would directly contribute to the defence of the Holy Land. However, a few notes of caution should be sounded. First of all, it is striking that at no point in the *Liber Maiolichinus* did the author draw a parallel between the undertaking of those arms-bearers who fought in the Balearics in 1113–15 and those who had fought in the Levant in 1096–1102.[182] Indeed, this oversight – if it is to be regarded as such – is all the more remarkable for the fact that the *Liber*'s author *did* see a connection between those who fought the Muslims of the Balearics in 1113–15 and those who had fought in wars against the Muslims of Sardinia (1015–16), Bona (1034), Palermo (1063–4), and Mahdia (1087), all campaigns that had been waged in the century that had preceded the First Crusade.[183] This suggests that the *Liber*'s author believed that the Balearics expedition was to be regarded as part of a continuum of activity in the western Mediterranean rather than in the context of the more recent and 'miraculous' victory in the Holy Land.[184]

But perhaps the most signal omission in the sources for the Balearic 'Crusade' is the absence of reference to ideas of pilgrimage. It has been argued above that in the early years of the twelfth century what distinguished crusading from other forms of penitential warfare, such as the military campaigns that were waged against the political opponents of the papacy during the Investiture Contest,[185] was the ideological connection with the Holy Land. It would seem that there was a common understanding amongst contemporaries that crusading was a form of armed Jerusalem pilgrimage, and it has been shown that even when crusades came to be projected in Iberia in the 1120s the goal of the Holy Sepulchre remained central to the strategists' thinking. In this context, it therefore seems highly improbable that in c.1113, at such an early stage in the development of the crusading ideal, a 'crusade' could be preached without reference to the Holy Land or to pilgrimage; there is nothing in the sources directly

---

[180] *Ibid.*, vv. 2208–12. On this sermon, see Doxey, 'Balearic Islands', p. 151.

[181] *Liber Maiolichinus*, vv. 2225–6.

[182] Doxey, 'Balearic Islands', p. 95.

[183] *Liber Maiolichinus*, vv. 30–8, 921–74. See also H.E.J. Cowdrey, 'The Mahdia Campaign of 1087', *English Historical Review*, 92 (1977), pp. 1–29; Doxey, 'Balearic Islands', pp. 38–9.

[184] Although cf. P. Rassow, 'La cofradía de Belchite', *Anuario de historia del derecho español*, 3 (1926), p. 225, where connections are drawn between the conquest of Majorca (1115) and the liberation of Jerusalem (1099), the reconquest of Zaragoza (1118) and the activities of the confraternity of Belchite (from 1122).

[185] See Riley-Smith, *First Crusaders*, pp. 51–2. See also N. Housley, 'Crusades against Christians: Their Origins and Early Development, c.1000–1216', *Crusade and Settlement: Papers Read at the First Conference of the Society for the Study of the Crusades and the Latin East and Presented to R.C. Smail*, ed. P.W. Edbury (Cardiff, 1985), pp. 17–36; Tyerman, *Invention of the Crusades*, p. 15.

relating to the Balearic campaign to indicate, for example, that an analogy was drawn between the spiritual rewards offered to those who fought in the Balearics and those that had been offered to first crusaders.[186] Consequently, it seems possible that the sources for the conquest of the Balearics may well represent something that is all the more intriguing: the later reconstruction of an earlier penitential war using (somewhat loosely and inconsistently) terminology that was related to, or inspired by, crusading. In this respect, it would appear that the sources for the 'Balearic Crusade' are comparable with the texts referred to above that projected crusading ideology onto the activities of Charlemagne and King Arthur.

A prominent example of this process is shown in the language that was attributed to the archbishop of Pisa, who was responsible for launching the expedition in a sermon delivered on Easter Sunday, 29 March 1113. In the earliest surviving manuscript of the *Liber*, which dates from the first half of the twelfth century and which, it should be remembered, was possibly at least one remove from a lost autograph,[187] it was recorded that the Pisans had been urged, somewhat ambiguously, 'to take up the signs of heaven (*signa celestia*)'; it was only in the later fourteenth-century redactions that the passage was rewritten to show that the archbishop was explicitly said to have preached the cross (*signa crucis*).[188] Similarly, although the *Liber* recorded that Pope Paschal had confirmed that the cross was to be conferred upon the expedition's participants, it is notable that during the expedition itself the 'crusaders' were reported to have fought under *vexilla sancte Marie*[189] and *vexilla sedis apostolice* rather than *vexilla Christi* or *vexilla crucis*.[190] Furthermore, the only surviving reference for the count of Barcelona taking the cross is not contemporary to the expedition itself. It appears in a treaty that was drawn up between King Jaime I of Aragón and representatives of Pisa in 1233, and in securing this thirteenth-century alliance it is clear that the drafters of the text were looking to recount the events of 1114 as a precedent for an alliance between Catalans and Pisans;[191] as Jaime I had taken the cross himself for his expedition to the Balearics of 1229,[192] it may have seemed plausible that his great-great-grandfather, Ramon Berenguer III, had done the same a century earlier. And finally, and perhaps most importantly, it is significant that when Paschal II wrote to Ramon Berenguer in 1116 in praise of his efforts in the Balearics, there was no suggestion whatsoever that the pope viewed that campaign within a broader context of crusading activity, and no indication that he equated Ramon Berenguer's efforts in the Mediterranean with an expedition to the Holy Land.[193]

---

[186] Cf. Housley, 'Crusades against Christians', p. 20–3.

[187] Doxey, 'Balearic Islands', p. 66, believed that the original text was written 'within living memory of the Balearic war'. See also *ibid.*, pp. 83–5, where the *Liber* is placed within the context of other contemporary 'victory poems', which were composed shortly after the events that they described.

[188] *Liber Maiolichinus*, vv. 39–48.

[189] Cf. 'Gesta triumphalia', p. 92.

[190] *Liber Maiolichinus*, vv. 1684–9. Cf. 'Gesta triumphalia', p. 94.

[191] For the text of the treaty, see *Liber Maiolichinus*, Appendix I, pp. 137–40. Cf. Doxey, 'Balearic Islands', p. 117, who wrote that 'it is impossible to be sure . . . [but] the treaty appears to be based on the genuine record'.

[192] See O'Callaghan, *Reconquest and Crusade*, pp. 89–92.

[193] F. Fita, 'Renallo Gramático y la conquista de Mallorca por el conde de Barcelona don Ramón Berenguer III: Apéndice de documentos', *BRAH*, 40 (1902), no. 11, pp. 70–4. See also Bernardo Maragone, 'Gli Annales pisani', ed. M. Lupo Gentile, *Raccolta degli storici italiani*, 6.2 (Bologna,

In sum, the idea that the expedition to the Balearics of 1113–15 was a crusade appears
to be based on insecure evidence, and as such it should be regarded as something of a
red herring in the history of the development of crusading in Iberia. Indeed, as the
analogies that were drawn by the author of the *Liber Maiolichinus* himself would suggest,
the Balearic campaign had more in common with pre-existing traditions of conflict
with Islam in the western Mediterranean, such as the conquest of Corsica and Sardinia
by 1015[194] and the expedition to Mahdia in 1087, than it did with the First Crusade.[195]
It was only after later writers had revised their histories of the expedition under the
pervasive influence of crusading ideology that the 'Balearic Crusade' came to exist.[196]
Consequently, if this analysis of the erroneous characterisation of the expedition as a
crusade is accurate, it would seem to have more to do with the way the ideology of
crusading in Iberia was developing around the middle of the twelfth century than it does
with the actual circumstances of the 1110s.

By the time that the Second Crusade was being preached across Europe in the middle of
the 1140s, it is clear enough that the Iberian peninsula was regarded as another possible
theatre for both penitential and crusading warfare. Subsequent to the proclamation of
Pope Calixtus II's crusade in 1123, the Council of Clermont had decreed in November
1130 that the appropriate penance for an arsonist would be to spend a year 'in Jerusalem
or in Spain, in the service of God', and this declaration was to be repeated by church
councils in 1131 and 1139.[197] Furthermore, the Order of the Temple had also begun
to acquire property across the peninsula, and in November 1143 the count of Barcelona granted it a number of strategically important castles. The wording of the relevant
charter makes it clear that he believed that the fight against Islam in Iberia was directly
analogous to that which was taking place in the Holy Land:

> I Ramon Berenguer . . . moved by the strength of the Holy Spirit, have decided to
> establish a militia in the power of the heavenly army for the defence of the western
> Church which is in Spain, for the suppression, defeat and expulsion of the Moorish
> people, the exaltation of the faith and religion of Holy Christendom, according to the
> example of the knighthood of the Temple of Solomon in Jerusalem which defends the
> eastern Church.[198]

Reference has already been made to the fact that a number of military campaigns that

1936), p. 8, which, aside from the fact that Paschal II is credited with playing a role in instigating
the expedition, contains nothing to suggest that its writer, Bernardo Maragone (c.1108–c.1188),
regarded the campaign as a crusade. See also *ibid.*, p. 7, for a comparable explanation for the Pisan
contribution to the First Crusade.
[194] Reilly, *The Contest of Christian and Muslim Spain*, p. 72
[195] Cowdrey, 'Mahdia Campaign', p. 17, shows that, like the participants in the Balearic expedition,
by c.1140 it was believed that those Pisans and Genoese who had fought at Mahdia in 1087 had been
rewarded with a remission of their sins.
[196] Cf. Doxey, 'Balearic Islands', pp. 106–7.
[197] F. Fita, 'Actas del Concilio de Clermont (18 Noviembre 1130): revisión crítica', *BRAH*, 4 (1884),
p. 365. For the repetitions, see Goñi Gaztambide, *Historia*, p. 77.
[198] *Cartulaire général de l'ordre du Temple 1119?–1150*, ed. Marquis d'Albon (Paris, 1913), no. 314, p.
204.

were taking place in Iberia in the mid-1140s were understood by contemporaries to be included within the scope of the Second Crusade.[199] It is therefore salutary to conclude this analysis on the early development of crusading in the peninsula by considering how the ideas associated with these campaigns relate to the broader ideological frameworks of crusading considered throughout this book. In this respect, it is striking that by the mid-1140s crusading in Iberia appears to have been moving away from its roots in the Jerusalem pilgrimage tradition and the ideas of Christo-mimesis that had proved so potent a generation earlier.

One of the triumphs of the Second Crusade was the conquest of Lisbon in 1147 by a combined force of Portuguese arms-bearers and northern crusaders who hailed from England, Flanders and the Empire.[200] Scrutiny of the relevant sources suggests, however, that the significance of this event to the history of the development of crusading in Iberia has been overstated. As has already been described above,[201] it is clear that the northern crusaders who fought in Portugal were ultimately bound for the Holy Land,[202] and that many of their number questioned the legitimacy of delaying their arrival in the East by fighting at Lisbon; these men cannot therefore be regarded as having vowed to crusade against the Muslims of Iberia.[203] There is, moreover, very little evidence to suggest that the Portuguese arms-bearers themselves should be considered to be crusaders. There is no indication that Afonso Henriques's men had taken any kind of vow, and only an oblique reference in a letter from Bernard of Clairvaux appears to indicate that they expected to enjoy spiritual privileges.[204] Indeed, Matthew Bennett has recently drawn attention to a passage from *De expugnatione Lyxbonensi* that shows that the majority of the Portuguese arms-bearers abandoned the siege before it had been completed,[205] and he has suggested that by this late stage of the siege the Portuguese forces 'had fulfilled their campaigning obligation',[206] which would indicate that their presence had more to do with secular commitments than any spiritual ones. Consequently, although it is undeniable that the conquest of Lisbon was the result of the efforts of both Portuguese arms-bearers *and* a contingent of second crusaders, it would appear that of those who fought in Portugal in 1147 only the northern Europeans can categorically be termed as crusaders. The accuracy of referring to this campaign as the 'Lisbon crusade', as Charles

---

[199] See above, pp. 94–6.

[200] See O'Callaghan, *Reconquest and Crusade*, pp. 41–4; J.P. Phillips, *The Second Crusade: Extending the Frontiers of Christendom* (New Haven and London, 2007), pp. 244–68.

[201] See above, pp. 77–8.

[202] See G. Constable, 'A Note on the Route of the Anglo-Flemish Crusaders of 1147', *Speculum*, 28 (1953), pp. 525–6; G. Constable, 'A Further Note on the Conquest of Lisbon in 1147', *Experience of Crusading, Volume One*, pp. 39–44.

[203] See also A.J. Forey, 'The Siege of Lisbon and the Second Crusade', *Portuguese Studies*, 20 (2004), pp. 1–13.

[204] Bernard of Clairvaux, 'Epistolae', *SBO* 8, no. 308, p. 228. O'Callaghan, *Reconquest and Crusade*, p. 42, argued that the closing phrase of Bernard's letter to Afonso was 'probably an allusion to papal bulls granting crusading indulgences', but I believe this interpretation stretches credulity.

[205] *De expugnatione Lyxbonensi*, ed. and trans. C.W. David, with a new foreword and bibliography by J.P. Phillips (New York, 2001), pp. 140–1.

[206] M. Bennett, 'Military Aspects of the Conquest of Lisbon', *The Second Crusade: Scope and Consequences*, ed. J.P. Phillips and M. Hoch (Manchester, 2001), p. 80.

Wendell David did,[207] must therefore be called into question.

Whilst most of the northern crusaders who fought at Lisbon immediately went on to complete their journeys to the Holy Land, there is some evidence to indicate that a number of them chose to join campaigns that were being waged elsewhere in the peninsula before fulfilling their vows.[208] For example, the annalist Caffaro recorded that during the siege of Tortosa in 1148 the count of Barcelona was not only fighting alongside troops from Genoa, but also 'the English, along with the knights of the Temple and many other foreigners'.[209] Indeed, the siege of Tortosa was but one in a series of initiatives directed against Muslim-held territories along the east coast of the peninsula for which there is unequivocal evidence of crusading ideology.[210] The expeditions that targeted Almería, Tortosa, and possibly Jaén, contrasted with the Lisbon campaign in that crusade privileges were offered to all participants, regardless of whether they were ultimately bound for the Holy Land; for example, to the crusaders who fought against 'the infidels and enemies of the cross of Christ' alongside the count of Barcelona at Tortosa, Pope Eugenius III offered 'that [same] remission of sins which . . . Pope Urban established for all those going abroad for the liberation of the eastern Church'.[211]

The earliest indication that Eugenius saw the military activities in eastern Iberia as being analogous to the campaigns that were being waged at the same time in the Holy Land and in the Baltic can be found in *Divina dispensatione II* (April 1147).[212] In this letter, Eugenius wrote of Alfonso VII of León-Castile that 'the King of Spain is powerfully arming against the Saracens of those regions, over whom, through the grace of God, he has already frequently triumphed'.[213] In a letter written a year later, the pope also remarked that he had 'willingly allowed . . . [the king] to make an expedition against the tyranny of the infidels',[214] a statement that probably refers to the privileges that had been offered to those Spaniards and Genoese who had participated in the successful campaign that had been directed against the Muslims of Almería in 1147.[215] The sources that describe the siege of Almería confirm that the expedition had received papal support from the outset; according to Caffaro (who was writing before 1164), the citizens of Genoa had sworn to contribute to the campaign as a result of being 'instructed and called by God

---

[207] *De expugnatione*, pp. xxxvii, 16 and *passim*.

[208] See Constable, 'Route of the Anglo-Flemish Crusaders', pp. 525–6.

[209] Caffaro, *De captione Almerie et Tortuose*, ed. A. Ubieto Arteta, *Textos medievales*, 34 (Valencia, 1973), p. 32.

[210] See especially N. Jaspert, '*Capta est Dertosa, clavis Christianorum*: Tortosa and the Crusades', *Second Crusade*, pp. 90–110.

[211] *Colección de documentos inéditos del Archivo general de la Corona de Aragón*, ed. P. de Bofarull y Mascaró et al., 41 vols. (Barcelona, 1847–1910), vol. 4, no. 128, pp. 314–15.

[212] Connections between the peninsular and eastern Mediterranean theatres were also drawn in a contemporary troubadour song, *Chevalier, mult estes guariz*, which referred to the challenge posed to the second crusaders by 'the Turks and the Almoravids'. See *Les chansons de croisade avec leurs mélodies*, ed. J. Bédier and P. Aubry (Paris, 1909), pp. 8–11.

[213] Eugenius III, 'Epistolae et privilegia', *PL* 180, no. 166, cols. 1203–4.

[214] *Ibid.*, no. 295, col. 1346.

[215] Simon Barton has argued that this phrase refers to Alfonso VII's campaign for Jaén in 1148, but if this were the case Eugenius would surely have been speaking in the present tense. See S. Barton, 'A Forgotten Crusade: Alfonso VII of León-Castile and the Campaign for Jaén', *Historical Research*, 73 (2000), pp. 312–20.

through the Apostolic See'.[216] The author of the *Poem of Almería* (which was probably composed 1147x57)[217] was more verbose in his description of the campaign's origins:

> All the bishops of Toledo and León, taking out both the physical and the spiritual sword, entreat the adults and summon the young, so that all may go bravely and safely to battle. Raising their voices to the heavens, they offer release from sins (*crimina persolvunt*), and give assurance to all that they will be rewarded in this life and the next. They promise gifts of silver and crowns of glory, and guarantee [the army] that whatever gold the Moors have will be theirs. Such was the influence and the pious ardour of the bishops, at one time making promises, at another crying out loud, that the young could hardly now be restrained by their mothers.[218]

This passage was not the only one to refer to the spiritual rewards that the expedition's participants might expect to receive. In describing the preaching for the campaign in terms that echoed the crusade letters of Abbot Bernard of Clairvaux, the *Poem's* author wrote that 'the trumpet of salvation rings out across all the regions of the world',[219] and in a sermon delivered before actual conflict began, the bishop of Astorga was reported to have instructed each one of the troops to confess 'correctly and sufficiently (*bene et eque*)' so that they might 'recognise that the sweet doors of paradise are open'.[220] Similarly, the author of the *Chronica Adefonsi imperatoris* wrote that those who joined the siege of Almería did so 'for the redemption of their souls',[221] and the Genoese who fought at Almería and went on to assist the count of Barcelona at the siege of Tortosa in 1148 were described by Caffaro as *bellatores Dei*.[222]

Yet although the Almerían campaign had been authorised by the papacy as a crusade and was described using the vocabulary of penitential warfare, there are several passages in the two main sources that offer a striking contrast to more traditional representations of crusading activity. In particular, neither Caffaro nor the author of the *Poem of Almería* held back in their descriptions of the wealth and luxury in which the armies set out. The Genoese author revelled with pride at the extent of his fellow-citizens' preparedness:

> The consuls ordered all the people of the district of Genoa . . . to gather quickly all of the things necessary [for the expedition]: a large amount of food, so that they would not want for more, many arms, splendid tents, beautiful and handsome banners, as well as all the other things necessary for such an undertaking . . . Not in a thousand years was such a beautiful and handsome fleet seen or heard of.[223]

Those who fought under Alfonso VII were glorified in much the same way:

---

[216] Caffaro, *De captione Almerie et Tortuose*, p. 21.

[217] For the date, see S. Barton and R. Fletcher, *The World of El Cid: Chronicles of the Spanish Reconquest* (Manchester, 2000), p. 157.

[218] 'Prefatio de Almaria', ed. J. Gil, *Chronica Hispana saeculi XII*, p. 256.

[219] *Ibid.*, p. 256.

[220] *Ibid.*, p. 267.

[221] 'Chronica Adefonsi imperatoris', p. 247.

[222] Caffaro, *De captione Almerie et Tortuose*, p. 32.

[223] *Ibid.*, p. 22.

> Their camps shine just like stars in the sky. They glitter with gold, and they carry only silver military equipment. There is no poverty among them, only great wealth . . . They are incredibly proud and overflowing with riches.[224]

The portrayal of crusade armies in these terms was extraordinary, given the fact that in *Quantum praedecessores* Eugenius III had decreed that:

> Since those who fight for the Lord ought never to care for precious clothes, or a refined appearance, or dogs or hawks or other things that might indicate lasciviousness, we impress upon your good sense, in the [name of the] Lord, that those who resolve to begin such a holy work ought to take no interest in multi-coloured clothes or minivers or golden or silver arms.[225]

This injunction was also echoed in the preaching of Bernard of Clairvaux who, in his letter to the Bohemians, wrote that 'It has been decreed that no one shall wear any multi-coloured clothes or minivers or silks, and neither gold nor silver may be used on the livery of horses'.[226]

It is clear, therefore, that the Spanish and Genoese troops were not setting out in the spirit that Eugenius and Bernard believed was appropriate for a penitential campaign. In this way, the descriptions offered of the crusaders by Caffaro and the author of the *Poem* were breaking with the earlier traditions of twelfth-century crusade writers, who, as has been stressed above,[227] often went to great lengths to emphasise the virtue of the crusader setting out in voluntary poverty in imitation of Christ. Indeed, there is such a contrast between the descriptions of the armies of the Almería campaign and established crusading rhetoric that one is forced to question whether those who took part in this expedition saw themselves as 'crusaders' at all. Even though he had been a first crusader,[228] Caffaro did not mention the sign of the cross once in his account, writing instead that the Genoese bore the *vexilla Ianuensium* into battle.[229] As far as Caffaro's work goes, however, it has recently been demonstrated that the involvement of the Genoese in the campaigns to Almería and Tortosa, although ultimately costly and commercially unrewarding, was thought by contemporaries to have been extremely honourable and integral to the development of the commune's identity.[230] The evident pleasure with which Caffaro described the 'beautiful' Genoese troops should therefore perhaps be seen as a manifestation of this civic pride, and should not necessarily be viewed as detracting from the expedition's 'crusading' credentials; the Genoese were, after all, believed to have fought 'with the help and favour of God'.[231] Perhaps it is simply

---

[224] 'Prefatio de Almaria', pp. 259–60.

[225] Eugenius III, 'Quantum praedecessores', ed. P. Rassow, 'Der Text der Kreuzzugsbulle Eugens III. vom. 1. März 1146', *Neues Archiv*, 45 (1924), p. 304.

[226] *SBO* 8, Ep. 458, p. 436. See also *De expugnatione*, pp. 56–7, where it is recorded that the northern crusaders who fought at the siege of Lisbon 'forbade all display of costly garments'.

[227] See above, pp. 39–41, 74, 79–81.

[228] See Riley-Smith, *First Crusaders*, p. 202.

[229] Caffaro, *De captione Almerie et Tortuose*, pp. 31, 34.

[230] J.B. Williams, 'The Making of a Crusade: The Genoese Anti-Muslim Attacks in Spain, 1146–1148', *Journal of Medieval History*, 23 (1997), pp. 29–53.

[231] Caffaro, *De captione Almerie et Tortuose*, pp. 25, 28.

the case that Caffaro, as a historian who did not have a clerical background,[232] expressed Genoese crusade piety in different terminology to that used by other writers. Although his description of the Genoese progression from Almería to Tortosa has clear parallels with the ideas of self-imposed exile that were commonplace in early crusade narratives – 'Although separated from their wives, children and homes for a year, they remained there for the winter for the honour of God and the city of Genoa'[233] – it is possible that Caffaro was being influenced by (and no doubt influencing) Genoese traditions of crusading that were distinct from those expressed in other western sources.

A more pronounced example of the influence of developing localised crusading traditions can be seen in the lines of the *Poem of Almería*, whose composer had possibly come into contact with the ideas expressed in the *Liber sancti Jacobi*. Although the issue of the authorship of the *Chronica Adefonsi imperatoris* (the chronicle to which the *Poem* was appended) cannot be resolved beyond doubt, the most likely candidate is Bishop Arnaldo of Astorga (1144–52), an individual who – according to the *Poem* – played a key role in recruiting for and offering spiritual guidance to the crusaders who besieged Almería.[234] As a prominent figure in the court of Alfonso VII, Arnaldo might well have been influenced by the efforts being made at Compostela to create a foundation legend for crusading in Iberia, and this would certainly explain a number of the references that appear in the text of the *Poem*. For example, in describing the forces as they were setting out for Almería, the *Poem* recorded that:

> The leader of them all was the king of the Empire of Toledo. This man, Alfonso, who holds the title of emperor, was following the deeds of Charlemagne (*facta Caroli*), with whom he is rightly compared. They were equal in courage and in strength of arms, and equal was the glory of the achievements of their wars.[235]

Similarly, the *Poem*'s author wrote of Alvar Fáñez, the ancestor of one of Alfonso VII's senior nobles, Alvaro Rodríguez, that 'if Alvar had been the third man after Oliver in the time of Roland, whom I grant was truly beyond reproach, the Hagarene people would have been brought under the yoke of the Franks, and his dear comrades would not have been overcome by death'.[236]

Whilst these references to the deeds of Charlemagne and his warriors do not provide wholly convincing proof for the influence of Pseudo-Turpin – the *Chanson de Roland* was also in widespread circulation by this time[237] – the *Poem*'s author also went on to make use of ideas that were specific to the *Historia Turpini* and *Liber sancti Jacobi*. In particular, the *Poem* alluded to the patronage and protection that was believed to be offered by St James of Compostela to those who fought the Muslims of Iberia; the troops from Galicia

---

[232] See R.D. Face, 'Secular History in Twelfth-Century Italy: Caffaro of Genoa', *Journal of Medieval History*, 6 (1980), pp. 169–84.

[233] Caffaro, *De captione Almerie et Tortuose*, p. 30.

[234] For the authorship of the *Chronica Adefonsi imperatoris*, see Barton and Fletcher, *World of El Cid*, pp. 155–61. For references to the role of Bishop Arnaldo, see 'Chronica Adefonsi imperatoris', p. 247; 'Prefatio de Almaria', p. 267.

[235] 'Prefatio de Almaria', p. 255.

[236] *Ibid.*, p. 262.

[237] See M. Routledge, 'Songs', *The Oxford Illustrated History of the Crusades*, ed. J.S.C. Riley-Smith (Oxford, 1995), pp. 91–3.

were described as setting out only after they had received a blessing from St James.[238] Indeed, this theme was in evidence in a number of the descriptions within the *Chronica Adefonsi imperatoris* of Christian-Muslim warfare. Before one encounter with the Muslims in 1132, for example, the Christians of León-Castile had 'called out in prayer to the God of heaven and earth, and to St Mary and to St James, so that they would support and defend them [in battle]'.[239] The soldiers of the army were later reported to have been 'crying out with all their hearts to the Lord God, the Blessed Mary and St James, so that they would take pity on them and forget their sins and those of their kings and their parents'.[240] Similarly, in 1143, Christian arms-bearers were reported to have made the following prayer on the eve of battle:

> O Jesus of Nazareth, who was hung on the cross for us and who shed your blood for us, behold the Moabites and the Hagarenes, your enemies and ours. They have come together against us so that they might destroy us. But you can take pity on us and rescue us. O great Virgin of Virgins, intercede for us before your son and our Lord, Jesus Christ. If you deliver us from all dangers, we will faithfully give to your church in Toledo the tithes of all that you have given or will give to us. St James, apostle of Christ, defend us in battle so that we may not perish by the terrible judgement of the Saracens.[241]

The evidence within the *Chronica Adefonsi imperatoris* and the *Poem of Almería* might therefore demonstrate an early success for those individuals who sought to propagate peninsular warfare against Islam by establishing an ideological framework for crusading in Iberia that would see it distanced from the Jerusalem pilgrimage tradition.

Conclusion

The Second Crusade represents a period of transition for the development of crusading thought in the Iberian peninsula. On the one hand, the presence of northern crusaders at the siege of Lisbon demonstrates that fighting the Muslims of Spain and Portugal was perceived by some to be meritorious, albeit unsatisfactory for those who had vowed to complete a journey to the Holy Sepulchre. However, the involvement of these crusaders from England, Flanders and the Empire should also be viewed within a broader context of northern European contributions to military campaigns against both Muslims and Christians along the western coast of Iberia, the history of which Charles Wendell David drew attention to in 1936.[242] In addition, as there is very little to suggest that the Portuguese who fought at Lisbon were 'crusaders', one is forced to conclude that the conquest of Lisbon is of less significance for the development of crusading ideology in Iberia than has previously been suggested.

Conversely, events on the peninsula's east coast were of the utmost importance. It can be proved beyond doubt that crusades were undertaken in 1147–8 against the

---

[238] 'Prefatio de Almaria', p. 257.
[239] 'Chronica Adefonsi imperatoris', p. 205.
[240] *Ibid.*, p. 207.
[241] *Ibid.*, p. 227.
[242] *De expugnatione*, pp. 16–21. See also the report of the remarks of a Muslim elder, *ibid.*, p. 120.

Muslims of Almería and Tortosa, and possibly against those of Jaén,[243] for which the participants were to be rewarded with the same spiritual privileges offered to those who set out for the Holy Land.[244] Moreover, these expeditions involved not only crusaders from Iberia, but also from Genoa, Montpellier and England. It is clear, therefore, that by the mid-1140s, Christians from all over western Europe perceived crusades in Iberia as being not only meritorious undertakings in themselves, but also attractive in spite of the fact that the expeditions were no longer overtly propagated as being directed towards the Holy Sepulchre. That a crusade in Iberia no longer had to be justified solely in terms of an advance to the Levant was the most fundamental difference between the preaching for the Second Crusade in Iberia and the preaching for the campaigns Alfonso of Aragón had led in the 1120s. Indeed, the evidence from the Occitan troubadour Marcabru's *Vers del lavador* (1149) highlights the growing importance of Spain as 'a washing-place such as never existed before, apart from over there near the valley of Josaphat in Outremer'.[245] Linda Paterson has argued that the genesis for this song lay in the failure of the crusade in the East,[246] and she has suggested that Marcabru's intention was to boost the morale of returning crusaders by demonstrating the legitimacy and equivalence of fighting the Muslims of Spain:

> We ought to wash night and morning, according to what is right, I assure you. Each has the opportunity to wash; he ought to go to the washing-place while he is still fit and well, for it is a true medicine for us, because if we go to death beforehand, instead of a lofty mansion we shall have lowly lodgings.[247]

In this way, crusading in Spain was depicted as offering arms-bearers from across Europe an opportunity to secure the remission of sins that they may have felt had eluded them because of the disastrous results of the expedition to the Holy Land.

There is also evidence to suggest that some of those crusaders fighting in Spain in the 1140s were beginning to be influenced by the foundation legend that had been developed by crusade propagandists at Santiago de Compostela to encourage recruitment for campaigns in the peninsula. The longer-term effect of this St James-based propaganda, and also that of the idea of the *iter per Hispaniam*, is beyond the scope of this book.[248] However, one has the impression that both themes were to be used repeatedly to describe subsequent crusading activity in Iberia, and there is at least one example of them being used simultaneously. In 1172, a confraternity from Avila became affiliated

---

[243] See Barton, 'A Forgotten Crusade', *passim*.

[244] Jaspert, 'Tortosa and the Crusades', pp. 95–6, believed that the campaigns conducted by the count of Barcelona in the aftermath of the fall of Tortosa 'generally lacked the crusading lustre of . . . [that] expedition'.

[245] *Marcabru: A Critical Edition*, ed. S. Gaunt, R. Harvey and L. Paterson (Woodbridge, 2000), no. 35, pp. 438–9.

[246] See L. Paterson, 'Syria, Poitou and the *Reconquista* (or Tales of the Undead): Who was the Count in Marcabru's *Vers del lavador*?', *Second Crusade*, pp. 133–49.

[247] *Marcabru*, ed. Gaunt et al., pp. 438–9.

[248] It is striking, as is pointed out by S. Barton, *The Aristocracy in Twelfth-Century León and Castile* (Cambridge, 1997), p. 156, that 'we hear of few [Iberian] laymen travelling to the Holy Land after c.1150'. Efforts to persuade Iberian arms-bearers of the merits of peninsular warfare against Islam might therefore have been fruitful in the longer term.

with the recently established military order of Santiago.[249] In doing so, the members of this confraternity had chosen to take 'the habit and sign of the Military Order of St James, to serve God and, just as the Order itself, to fight without cease in defence of the Church against the enemies of the cross of Christ'. Furthermore, the relevant charter recorded that:

> If it so happens that the Saracens are expelled from Spain beyond the sea, [and] the master and chapter [of the Order of Santiago] should propose to go into the land of the Moroccans, they [the *confratres* of Avila] will not hesitate from aiding them like brothers. Similarly, and if it is necessary, [they will continue on] to Jerusalem.[250]

The appearance of the idea of the *iter per Hispaniam* in a document that relates to the Order of Santiago – an Order whose very existence is testimony to the success of the propaganda from Compostela – illustrates the necessity for further research to be undertaken on the later development of crusade ideology in Iberia. Nevertheless, it seems clear enough that by the mid-1140s it was no longer felt that crusading in Spain had to be legitimised solely in terms of its connections to the Jerusalem pilgrimage tradition. In this context, it is perhaps less surprising that the motifs of *imitatio Christi* that were so prevalent in the narrative sources that recorded the experiences of the second crusaders who fought in the East had all but disappeared in the works that described crusading in Iberia.

In conclusion, the preceding two chapters have suggested that the early development of crusading ideology in Spain can be understood as follows. There was an opening period (1095–c.1120) in which the arms-bearers of Iberia were discouraged by the papacy from abandoning the peninsula for the Holy Land and reassured that any crusade vows they had taken could be commuted by fighting for their native soil. This was followed by an intermediate period (from c.1120), which tacitly acknowledged that that (often unsuccessful) policy of containment could not be maintained, saw the introduction of the idea of liberating an alternative *iter* to the Holy Sepulchre through Spain, and the establishment of full crusading privileges for those who fought in the peninsula. This in turn gave way to a later period (from c.1130) wherein crusading ideology became more rooted in the peninsula and was increasingly associated with more local traditions,[251] such as the idea that those who fought against the Muslims of the peninsula might benefit from the patronage of St James of Compostela because they were working for the liberation of his *iter* and his *terra*, or the related idea that crusaders in Iberia were following the example of the legendary Charlemagne by participating in a penitential conflict that stretched back for generations, and that was even presented as being a precursor to the First Crusade itself.

---

[249] For the foundation of national military orders, see O'Callaghan, *Reconquest and Crusade*, pp. 52–5.

[250] J.L. Martín, *Origenes de la Orden Militar de Santiago (1170–1195)* (Barcelona, 1974), no. 53, pp. 226–7.

[251] See also the concluding remarks of Jaspert, 'Tortosa and the Crusades', pp. 98–100.

Conclusion

Shortly after his release from a Cairo gaol, probably in the summer of 1103, the first crusader Odo Arpin of Bourges was travelling home to France with a number of years of campaigning and later incarceration in the East behind him. According to Orderic Vitalis, Odo Arpin had stopped *en route* for an audience with Paschal II, where he had sought the pope's advice about his future spiritual welfare. Paschal was said to have acknowledged the penitential value of Odo Arpin's endeavours in the Holy Land and described how the crusade had acted as a spiritually cleansing experience, but he also enjoined Odo Arpin not to return to the 'muddy road' of secular life:

> Look into your heart, my son . . . and apply [yourself] to the correction of your life. You have been cleansed by confession and penance, and girded with the raiment of holiness through your difficult pilgrimage and the agonies of martyrdom . . . Secular life is a muddy road, which you should shun at all costs for fear of becoming spattered and losing the crown of the sufferings by which you are glorified. Take care, therefore, not to be like the dog returning to his own vomit or the sow that was washed to her wallowing in the mire. Never again bear arms against Christians, but shun worldly pomps like one of the true poor of Christ. So as a follower in the footsteps of Christ (*imitator vestigiorum Christi*) in works of justice, renouncing your own will through hope of a heavenly reward, you will find bliss in winning the prize of your heavenly calling with the faithful in Abraham's bosom.[1]

Odo Arpin subsequently followed the pope's advice, 'or rather Christ's',[2] by becoming a Cluniac monk, and later probably the prior of La Charité-sur-Loire.[3] He was by no means the only returning first crusader who decided to abandon the world completely by entering a monastery,[4] but his is a particularly clear example of the spirituality that was believed to be associated with recruitment to the religious life in the early twelfth century. In fact, it may even be possible to infer from other surviving evidence about his life how his desire to 'follow in the footsteps of Christ' in 1103 was influenced by his earlier response to Pope Urban II's preaching of the First Crusade itself. It is striking that, prior to his departure for the Holy Land in 1100, Odo Arpin is known to have sold his viscounty of Bourges and his lordship of Dun to the king of France to raise the cash to

---

[1] OV 5, pp. 352–3.

[2] OV 5, pp. 352–3.

[3] J. Shepard, 'The "Muddy Road" of Odo Arpin from Bourges to La Charité-sur-Loire', *The Experience of Crusading, Volume Two: Defining the Crusader Kingdom*, ed. P.W. Edbury and J.P. Phillips (Cambridge, 2003), pp. 11–28.

[4] See J.S.C. Riley-Smith, *The First Crusaders, 1095–1131* (Cambridge, 1997), pp. 154–5.

fund his crusading ambitions.[5] Although impossible to prove, it is certainly tempting to think that, in 1100, Odo Arpin had faithfully responded to the Gospel verses that Pope Urban was believed to have declaimed at the Council of Clermont in 1095 by 'selling all his possessions' and taking the cross to follow in the footsteps of Christ, and that on returning to the West, his crusade vow fulfilled, had sought to continue his pursuit of *imitatio Christi*, which, as the report of Pope Paschal's guidance clearly indicates, necessitated that he 'shun worldly pomps like one of the true poor of Christ' and enter full religious profession.[6]

In this book it has been argued that the ideas of the imitation of Christ that were associated with both monasticism and crusading by writers such as Orderic Vitalis were fundamental to the origins and early development of crusading spirituality. It has been shown that the 'taking of the cross' was understood by contemporaries to be a literal fulfilment of Christ's instruction to his disciples (Matthew 16:24), and emphasised that in 1095 this symbolic act was revolutionary because the idea of taking Christ's cross had previously been inextricably linked with recruitment to the religious life, and because the wearing of crosses was unprecedented in the Jerusalem pilgrimage tradition. Consequently, it has been demonstrated that crusaders were believed to be embracing voluntary poverty and self-imposed exile by following the *via Christi* and by fighting to liberate '*the place in which his feet have stood*', and in so doing were prepared to die for Christ in the Holy Land as he had died there for mankind. It has also been indicated that the ideas of unanimity and religious activity associated with the apostolic life of the primitive Church were widely used by those who described the experience of crusading, and it has been suggested that the application of these concepts might well be traced back to the preaching of Pope Urban II himself. It has also been contended that the potency of Pope Urban's innovative use of *imitatio Christi*, and possibly of *vita apostolica*, may explain why certain professed religious from across western Europe were moved to respond positively to his preaching of the First Crusade in 1095–6. In its own way, this response is illustrative of the fact that the crusade was regarded by many contemporaries as being a quasi-monastic devotional undertaking, which suggests that Jean Leclercq was correct in thinking that crusaders were inspired by much the same spirituality as that which motivated the hermits and monastic reformers who were their contemporaries.[7]

Having established that *imitatio Christi* and *vita apostolica* were central to the foundations of crusading spirituality, the book went on to analyse how these aspects of the crusade ideal developed during the first century of the movement's history. Although ideas surrounding the crusader's adoption of an apostolic life appear to have faded from use reasonably quickly, it has been shown that crusading remained intimately associated with the Jerusalem pilgrimage tradition, and that the idea that the crusade was an act of

---

[5] *Ibid.*, p. 76.

[6] G. Constable, 'The Three Lives of Odo Arpinus: Viscount of Bourges, Crusader, Monk of Cluny', *Religion, Text, and Society in Medieval Spain and Northern Europe: Essays in Honor of J.N. Hillgarth*, ed. T.E. Burman, M.D. Meyerson, and L. Shopkow (Toronto, 2002), pp. 183–99, argues that Odo's patronage of religious houses prior to his departure for the East 'suggests that he already had some sympathy for [the] monastic life'.

[7] J. Leclercq, F. Vandenbroucke and L. Bouyer, *The Spirituality of the Middle Ages* (London, 1968), p. 130.

Christo-mimesis continued to prove popular in the twelfth century. Indeed, it has been suggested that the First Crusade had an important legacy for the piety of the penitential pilgrimage to the East in general, not only because it restored the Holy Land to the custody of western Christians, but also because it introduced a new Christo-mimetic aspect to the devotions of those who set out to worship at the actual sites of the Gospel narratives. However, the book has made pains to stress that not all contemporaries continued to understand the spirituality of crusading in the framework that was established in the 1090s. In particular, it has been argued that two Cistercians, Pope Eugenius III and Abbot Bernard of Clairvaux, played a hitherto unrecognised role in the theological development of crusading in the twelfth century. They were not as beholden to the ideas of Pope Urban II as has often been suggested, but were in fact attempting to institute a radical new understanding of the crusade badge by preaching it as a *signum vitae* rather than a *stigma passionis dominicae*, a symbol of the indulgence that was offered to those who responded to the call to crusade rather than a mark of the bearer's *imitatio Christi*. It has been suggested that the thinking behind such a drastic theological shift may lie in the fact that the Cistercians believed that the imitation of Christ could only be pursued by those who had sworn themselves to full religious profession, and that in this respect crusading was too elementary an undertaking because crusaders were more focused on the earthly than the heavenly Jerusalem. Furthermore, it was demonstrated that, for Bernard, it was the brethren of the Order of the Temple who were understood to have inherited the Christo-mimetic spirituality of the first crusaders, because the Templars lived a life that combined action with contemplation and were thus believed to be committed to going beyond the 'fleshly' knowledge of Christ that was engendered by their physical presence in the Holy Land. Finally, it was argued that one important consequence of the move away from *imitatio Christi* in crusading spirituality in the middle of the twelfth century was that propagandists from Eugenius III onwards were beginning to use other *exempla* to inspire recruitment for expeditions to the East, and the importance of the idea of the *strenuitas patrum* within the language of crusade preaching in the period 1145–87 was highlighted. In this respect, the arguments within this book suggest that Jonathan Riley-Smith was correct in his impression that 'crusading was becoming markedly less monastic by 1200', at least at the theoretical level on which crusades were conceived and promoted by the papacy and other senior churchmen.[8] Furthermore, the conclusions of the present work also indicate that Riley-Smith was accurate in believing that the establishment of the military orders 'channelled the monastic impulses away from ordinary crusading',[9] although once again it would seem that the foundation of the Templars had more effect on the ideas of the theoreticians than it did on those of the individuals who participated in or wrote histories of crusades to the East, for whom crusading and Christo-mimesis appear to have remained closely related.

In considering the impact of crusading in Iberia, it has been argued that the ideas of *peregrinatio* and *imitatio* that were so widespread at the turn of the twelfth century meant that it was initially difficult to persuade arms-bearers from the peninsula of the efficacy of having their crusade vows commuted by engaging in penitential warfare with the Muslims of al-Andalus. On this basis, it was suggested that it is of critical importance that when Pope Calixtus II eventually proclaimed a crusade for Iberia in the early 1120s

---

[8] J.S.C. Riley-Smith, *The First Crusade and the Idea of Crusading* (London, 1986), p. 155.

[9] *Ibid.*, p. 155.

the strategists propagated the idea of opening an alternative route to the Holy Sepulchre via Spain and North Africa. Although it is clear that the idea of the *iter per Hispaniam* did not disappear from the language of crusade preaching in Iberia altogether, the evidence also suggests that by the time of the Second Crusade a more local ideology of crusading activity was beginning to take root. It has been shown how the propagandists for the cult centre of Santiago de Compostela were beginning to develop a militaristic identity for St James the Great, who was presented as being a patron saint of those who fought against Muslims both in the peninsula and further afield, and the attempts to invent a kind of foundation legend for crusading in Iberia that delineated a history of peninsular warfare against Islam that stretched back to the time of Charlemagne, and thus distinguished the origins of crusading in Spain from the Jerusalem pilgrimage tradition, have been described. Nevertheless, the fact that this pseudo-history closely related proto-crusading in Spain to ideas of liberating the *iter* to Compostela and of defending the *terra* of St James suggests that the relationship between pious violence and penitential pilgrimage was retained, albeit in a modified form. Although it is not yet fully clear what impact these new ideas had on the arms-bearers of Iberia themselves, it has been argued that it is obvious from a number of the sources for the Second Crusade that some of the ideas associated with the campaigns that were waged in the peninsula were quite distinct from the Christo-mimetic spirituality that was integral to crusading to the East, and it was suggested that this may show that crusading ideology in Spain was beginning to move away from its Jerusalem-centric roots to reflect more local concerns.

These conclusions have a number of wider implications. First of all, they suggest that the importance of ideas of pilgrimage to twelfth-century understandings of the crusade ideal perhaps ought to be lent a greater significance by historians of the movement's origins and early development. It is clear that for most of the period covered by this book, pilgrimage ideology played a crucial part in the attempts of contemporaries to frame their understanding of crusading, regardless of whether the expeditions took place in the Holy Land or in another theatre of war such as Iberia. It is not the case that crusaders in the late eleventh and twelfth centuries were simply understood to be benefiting from the spiritual rewards associated with penitential pilgrimage: crusades were also widely regarded as acts of pilgrimage in themselves, or were at least closely associated with pilgrimage cult centres such as Jerusalem and Santiago de Compostela. In this respect, it is interesting to note that the characterisation in *c*. 1140 of Iberia as the *terra* of St James bears comparison not only with the way contemporaries understood the Holy Land to be the patrimony of Christ, but also with how Livonia was later presented as being the land of the Blessed Virgin Mary.[10] Nevertheless, it is clear that as crusading developed in the thirteenth century as a distinct form of holy war that could be prosecuted against the enemies of Christ both within and without western Europe, not all crusades could be associated with a pilgrimage shrine or a cult centre.[11] It would

---

[10] See J.S.C. Riley-Smith, *The Crusades: A History*, 2nd edition (London, 2005), pp. xxx, 161–2, 173. With respect to the northern theatre, it is striking that from as early as the first decade of the twelfth century advocates for campaigns against the pagans of the Baltic region were attempting to apply modified ideas of Jerusalem pilgrimage to inspire recruitment: see J.P. Phillips, *The Second Crusade: Extending the Frontiers of Christendom* (New Haven and London, 2007), pp. 230–2.

[11] See, for example, Riley-Smith, *The Crusades*, pp. 166–7. See also N. Housley, 'Crusades against Christians: Their Origins and Early Development, *c*. 1000–1216', *Crusade and Settlement: Papers Read at*

therefore be interesting to explore under what specific circumstances the word *peregrinus* gave way to *crucesignatus* as the normative term used to describe crusaders.[12]

Perhaps more importantly though, the arguments in this book indicate that the range of ideas associated with the 'preaching of the cross', and the response of the crusaders themselves to those ideas, ought to be subjected to a closer scrutiny. In a recent essay in which he reflected on the motivations of first crusaders, Marcus Bull argued that in order to understand the positive response to crusade preaching it is imperative 'to identify in particular any elements [of the crusade message] that lent themselves to effective transmission across boundaries of geography, language and to some extent class', and he considered how two particular motifs might encourage widespread recruitment: 'the circumstances in which the Holy Land, and especially Jerusalem, found itself, and the actions and characteristics of Muslims there'.[13] The conclusions of the present work suggest that alongside 'Jerusalem' and 'Saracen', 'the cross' ought to be ranked amongst the most important trigger ideas in early crusade preaching.[14] It is clear that Pope Urban II's presentation of the crusade badge as a symbol of *imitatio Christi* had an almost universal appeal, and that even when Bernard of Clairvaux tried to distance the sign of the cross from ideas of Christo-mimesis many of his contemporaries failed to notice the shift in emphasis. On this basis, even though many crusaders may have understood themselves to be 'taking Christ's cross', it cannot be assumed that the relationship between the crusade badge and ideas of Christo-mimesis was endemic to crusading spirituality.[15] Consequently, it would be salutary to examine how the theology of the crusader's cross developed after 1187,[16] and to see how quickly the idea of *imitatio Christi* was reused by those who preached crusades after the fall of Jerusalem, particularly because, as Jonathan Riley-Smith has demonstrated, the idea that crusading was a Christo-mimetic act was certainly revived during the pontificate of Innocent III.[17]

It is hoped, moreover, that the arguments put forward in this book may have a significance not only for the history of the crusading movement, but also for the study of medieval spirituality in general and for understanding the trend towards a devotional attachment to Christ's humanity in particular. In an important article published in 1994, Bernard Hamilton suggested that the emphasis in thirteenth-century piety on Christ's human life and sufferings, particularly as was embodied by St Francis of Assisi and his followers, was a direct consequence of the fact that between 1099 and 1187 the holy

the *First Conference of the Society for the Study of the Crusades and the Latin East and Presented to R.C. Smail*, ed. P.W. Edbury (Cardiff, 1985), pp. 17–36.

[12] See M. Markowski, '*Crucesignatus*: Its Origins and Early Usage', *Journal of Medieval History*, 10 (1984), pp. 157–65; C. Tyerman, *The Invention of the Crusades* (Basingstoke, 1998), pp. 49–55.

[13] M. Bull, 'Views of Muslims and of Jerusalem in Miracle Stories, c.1000–c.1200: Reflections on the Study of First Crusaders' Motivations', *The Experience of Crusading, Volume One: Western Approaches*, ed. M. Bull and N. Housley (Cambridge, 2003), p. 23.

[14] Cf. Riley-Smith, *The Crusades*, pp. 183–4, who believed that 'for the first eighty years of the movement . . . [the cross] appears to have been less significant in the words of preachers and the minds of crusaders . . . than the reality of Christ's Tomb in Jerusalem', and argued that it was not until the thirteenth century that the sign of the cross became of paramount importance.

[15] Cf. the comments of N. Housley, *Contesting the Crusades* (Oxford, 2006), p. 20.

[16] See now M. Phillips, 'The Thief's Cross: Crusade and Penance in Alan of Lille's *Sermo de cruce domini*', *Crusades*, 5 (2006), pp. 143–56. See also Tyerman, *Invention of the Crusades*, pp. 76–83.

[17] J.S.C. Riley-Smith, 'Crusading as an Act of Love', *History*, 65 (1980), pp. 179–80.

city of Jerusalem had been in the custody of Christians from western Europe, and that as a result 'it had been possible for the pilgrims who visited it to appreciate the Gospel narratives on a literal level because the whole ethos gave them every encouragement to do so'.[18] In this respect, the arguments that have been presented above are consonant with Hamilton's thinking, but they suggest that his thesis can perhaps be pushed out further still. When Pope Urban II established crusading as a Christo-mimetic activity in 1095, he demonstrated that the idea of 'taking the cross to follow Christ' did not just have to be interpreted allegorically, but could also be seen to have a literal meaning as well. There was still some distance between the Christo-mimetic piety of the first crusaders and that of the Franciscans, but it seems possible that Urban II's literalisation of the ideal of *imitatio Christi* at the Council of Clermont may represent the beginning of a transitional stage in the development towards the devotion to Christ's human life, which was so characteristic of medieval Christian spirituality from the latter half of the twelfth century onwards.

[18] B. Hamilton, 'The Impact of Crusader Jerusalem on Western Christendom', *Catholic Historical Review*, 80 (1994), pp. 712–13.

Bibliography

Primary Sources

'Un acte de l'évêque Pierre de Limoges (1101)', ed. J. Becquet, *Bulletin de la Société Archéologique et Historique du Limousin*, 112 (1985), pp. 14–19.

Adrian IV, 'Epistolae et privilegia', *PL* 188, cols. 1361–1640.

Albert of Aachen, *Historia Ierosolimitana*, ed. and trans. S.B. Edgington (Oxford, 2007).

Alexander III, 'Epistolae et privilegia', *PL* 200, cols. 69–1518.

The Anglo-Norman Pseudo-Turpin Chronicle *of William de Briane*, ed. I. Short (Oxford, 1973).

The Anglo-Saxon Chronicle, trans. and ed. M.J. Swanton (London, 1996).

'Annales sancti Disibodi', *MGH SS* 17, pp. 4–30.

An Anonymous Old French Translation of the Pseudo-Turpin Chronicle, ed. R.N. Walpole (Cambridge, MA, 1979).

Anselm of Canterbury, 'Epistolae', *S. Anselmi Cantuariensis archiepiscopi opera omnia*, ed. F.S. Schmitt, vols. 3–5 (Edinburgh, 1946–51).

Baldric of Bourgueil, 'Historia Jerosolimitana', *RHC Oc.* 4, pp. 1–111.

Bartolf of Nangis, 'Gesta Francorum Iherusalem expugnantium', *RHC Oc.* 3, pp. 487–543.

Bernard of Clairvaux, 'De consideratione ad Eugenium papam', *SBO* 3, pp. 379–493.

Bernard of Clairvaux, 'Epistolae', *SBO* 7–8.

Bernard of Clairvaux, 'Letter to the English People', *The Letters of St Bernard of Clairvaux*, trans. B. Scott James (Sutton, 1998), pp. 460–3.

Bernard of Clairvaux, 'Liber ad milites Templi de laude novae militiae', *SBO* 3, pp. 205–39.

Bernard of Clairvaux, 'Sermones', *SBO* 4–6.

Bernard of Clairvaux, 'Sermones super Cantica Canticorum', *SBO* 1–2.

Bernardo Maragone, 'Gli annales pisani', ed. M. Lupo Gentile, *Raccolta degli storici italiani*, 6.2 (Bologna, 1936), pp. 1–74.

Bernold of St Blasien, 'Chronicon', *MGH SS* 5, pp. 385–467.

Caesarius of Heisterbach, *Dialogus miraculorum*, ed. J. Strange, 2 vols. (Ridgewood, NJ, 1966).

Caffaro, *De captione Almerie et Tortuose*, ed. A. Ubieto Arteta, *Textos medievales*, 34 (Valencia, 1973).

Caffaro, 'De liberatione civitatum orientis', ed. L.T. Belgrano, *Annali genovesi*, 1 (Genoa, 1890), pp. 95–124.

Calixtus II, *Bullaire*, ed. U. Robert, 2 vols. (Paris, 1891).

Cartulaire de l'abbaye cardinale de la Trinité de Vendôme, ed. C. Metais, 5 vols. (1893–1904).

Cartulaire de l'abbaye de Saint-Père de Chartres, ed. B.E.C. Guérard, 2 vols. (Paris, 1840).

'Cartulaire de l'abbaye de Saint-Sulpice-la-Forêt', ed. P. Anger, *Bulletin et mémoires de la Société Archéologique d'Ille-et-Vilaine*, 35 (1906), pp. 325–88.

Cartulaire de la commanderie de Richerenches de l'ordre du Temple (1136–1214), ed. Marquis de Ripert-Monclar (Avignon and Paris, 1907).

Cartulaire général de l'ordre du Temple 1119?–1150, ed. Marquis d'Albon (Paris, 1913).

Cartulaire de Marmoutier pour le Dunois, ed. E. Mabille (Châteaudun, 1874).

Les chansons de croisade avec leurs mélodies, ed. J. Bédier and P. Aubry (Paris, 1909).

'Chronica Adefonsi imperatoris', ed. A. Maya Sánchez, *Chronica Hispana saeculi XII, CC:CM* 71 (Turnhout, 1990), pp. 109–248.

'Chronicon Altinate', ed. A. Rossi, *Archivio storico italiano*, 8 (1845), pp. 20–228.

La Chronique de Morigny (1095–1152), ed. L. Mirot, *Collection de textes*, 41 (Paris, 1909).

La Chronique de St Maixent, 751–1140, ed. and trans. J. Verdon (Paris, 1979).

Chroniques des églises d'Anjou, ed. P. Marchegay and É. Mabille (Paris, 1869).

Colección diplomática de Alfonso I de Aragón y Pamplona (1104–1134), ed. J.A. Lema Pueyo (San Sebastian, 1990).

Conciliorum oecumenicorum decreta, ed. J. Alberigo et al. (Freiburg, 1962).

Crónica de San Juan de la Peña, ed. A. Ubieto Arteta, *Textos medievales*, 4 (Valencia, 1961).

Crusade Charters, 1138–1270, ed. C.K. Slack (Tempe, AZ, 2001).

Decreta Claromontensia, ed. R. Somerville, *The Councils of Urban II. I.* (Amsterdam, 1972).

'Un document sur les débuts des Templiers', ed. J. Leclercq, *Revue d'histoire ecclésiastique*, 52 (1957), pp. 81–91.

'Un document sur Saint Bernard et la seconde croisade', ed. J. Leclercq, *Revue Mabillon*, 43 (1953), pp. 1–4.

'Documents', ed. C. Riant, *Archives de l'Orient latin*, 2 vols. (Paris, 1881–4), vol. 1, pp. 374–614.

Documents para el estudio de la reconquista y repoblación del valle del Ebro, ed. J.M. Lacarra, 2 vols., *Textos medievales*, 62–3 (Zaragoza, 1982–5).

'Documents pour l'histoire de Saint-Hilaire de Poitiers', ed. L. Rédet, *Mémoires de la Société des Antiquaires de l'Ouest* (1847), pp. 1–362.

'Documents relatifs à la croisade de Guillaume Comte de Ponthieu', ed. S. Löwenfold, *Archives de l'Orient latin*, 2 (1884), pp. 251–5.

Domenico Laffi, *A Journey to the West: The Diary of a Seventeenth-Century Pilgrim from Bologna to Santiago de Compostela*, trans. J. Hall (Leiden, 1997).

Ekkehard of Aura, 'Hierosolymita', *RHC Oc.* 5, pp. 1–40.

'Epistola A. Dapiferi militiae Templi', *RHGF* 15, pp. 540–1.

Eugenius III, 'Epistolae et privilegia', *PL* 180, cols. 1013–1606.

Eugenius III, 'Quantum praedecessores', ed. P. Rassow, 'Der Text der Kreuzzugsbulle Eugens III. vom. 1. März 1146', *Neues Archiv*, 45 (1924), pp. 300–5.

De expugnatione Lyxbonensi, ed. and trans. C.W. David, with a new foreword and bibliography by J.P. Phillips (New York, 2001).

Fulcher of Chartres, *Historia Hierosolymitana (1095–1127)*, ed. H. Hagenmeyer (Heidelberg, 1913).

Gelasius II, 'Epistolae et privilegia', *PL* 163, cols. 487–514.

Geoffrey *Grossus*, 'Vita Bernardi Tironiensis', *PL* 172, cols. 1363–1446.

Geoffrey of Le Chalard, 'Dictamen de primordiis ecclesiae Castaliensis', *RHC Oc.* 5, pp. 348–9.

Geoffrey of Monmouth, *Historia regum Britanniae*, ed. A. Griscom and R. Ellis Jones (London, 1929); trans. L. Thorpe, *The History of the Kings of Britain* (London, 1966).

Geoffrey of Vendôme, 'Epistolae', *PL* 157, cols. 33–212.

'Zur Geschichte des Investiturstreites (englische Analekten II)', ed. W. Holtzmann, *Neues Archiv*, 50 (1935), pp. 280–2.

'Gesta Ambaziensium dominorum', ed. L. Halphen and R. Poupardin, *Chroniques des comtes d'Anjou et des seigneurs d'Amboise* (Paris, 1913), pp. 74–132.

Gesta comitum Barcinonensium, ed. L. Barrau Dihigo and J. Masso Torrents, *Croniques catalanes*, 2 (Barcelona, 1925).

Gesta Francorum et aliorum Hierosolimitanorum, ed. and trans. R. Hill (Oxford, 1962).

'Gesta triumphalia per Pisanos facta de captione Hierusalem et civitatis Maioricarum et aliarum civitatum et de triumpho habito contra Ianuenses', ed. M. Lupo Gentile, *Raccolta degli storici italiani*, 6.2 (Bologna, 1936), pp. 87–96.

Gilo of Paris, *Historie Vie Hierosolimitane*, ed. and trans. C.W. Grocock and J.E. Siberry (Oxford, 1997).

Guibert of Nogent, 'Dei gesta per Francos', ed. R.B.C. Huygens, *CC:CM* 127 A (Turnhout, 1996), pp. 76–352.

Helmold of Bosau, 'Chronica Slavorum', *MGH SS* 21, pp. 1–99.

Henry of Huntingdon, *Historia Anglorum*, ed. T. Arnold, *Rolls Series*, 74 (London, 1879).

Histoire générale de Languedoc, 3rd edition, ed. J. Vaissète, C. Devic and A. Molinier, 16 vols. (Toulouse, 1872–1904).

Historia Compostellana, ed. E. Falque Rey, *CC:CM* 70 (Turnhout, 1988).

'Historia ducum Veneticorum', *MGH SS* 14, pp. 72–97.

'Historia peregrinorum euntium Jerusolymam', *RHC Oc.* 3, pp. 165–229.

'Historia de translatione sanctorum magni Nicolai . . . ejusdem avunculi alterius Nicolai, Theodorique . . . de civitate Mirea in monasterium S. Nicolai de Littore Venetiarum', *RHC Oc.* 5, pp. 253–92.

James of Vitry, *Sermones ad fratres minores*, ed. H. Felder, *Spicilegium Franciscanum*, 5 (Rome, 1903).

Jerusalem Pilgrimage 1099–1185, ed. and trans. J. Wilkinson, J. Hill and W.F. Ryan (London, 1988).

Jerusalem Pilgrims before the Crusades, ed. and trans. J. Wilkinson, 2nd edition (Warminster, 2002).

John Canaparius, 'Vita S. Adalberti', *MGH SS* 4, pp. 581–95.

Die Kreuzzugsbriefe aus den Jahren 1088–1100, ed. H. Hagenmeyer (Innsbruck, 1901).

Landulf the Younger, 'Historia Mediolanensis', *MGH SS* 20, pp. 17–49.

Les légendes de l'Hôpital de Saint-Jean de Jérusalem, ed. A. Calvet (Paris, 2000).

Lettres des premiers Chartreux, 2 vols. (Paris, 1962–80).

Libellus de diversis ordinibus et professionibus qui sunt in aecclesia, ed. and trans. G. Constable and B.S. Smith, revised edition (Oxford, 2003).

Liber Maiolichinus de gestis Pisanorum illustribus, ed. C. Calisse (Rome, 1904).

Liber sancti Jacobi: Codex Calixtinus, i. *Texto*, ed. W.M. Whitehill (Santiago de Compostela, 1944).

Liber sancti Jacobi: Codex Calixtinus de la catedral de Santiago de Compostela (Madrid, 1993).

Liber sancti Jacobi: Codex Calixtinus, ed. K. Herbers and M. Santos Noia (Santiago de Compostela, 1998).

'The Lisbon Letter of the Second Crusade', ed. S.B. Edgington, *Historical Research*, 69 (1996), pp. 328–39.

The Little Flowers of Saint Francis: With Five Considerations on the Sacred Stigmata, trans. L. Sherley-Price (London, 1959).

Louis VII, 'Epistolae', *RHGF* 16, pp. 1–170.

Marcabru: A Critical Edition, ed. S. Gaunt, R. Harvey and L. Paterson (Woodbridge, 2000).

'Narratio Floriacensis de captis Antiochia et Hierosolyma et obsesso Dyrrachio', *RHC Oc.* 5, pp. 356–62.

Nicholas of Clairvaux, 'Epistolae in persona S. Bernardi', *PL* 182, cols. 671–4.

Odo of Deuil, *De profectione Ludovici VII in Orientem*, ed. and trans. V.G. Berry (New York, 1948).

Orderic Vitalis, *Historia aecclesiastica*, ed. and trans. M. Chibnall, 6 vols. (Oxford, 1969–80).

Otto of Freising, *Chronica sive historia de duabus civitatibus*, ed. A. Hofmeister, *MGH SSRG* 45 (Hanover and Leipzig, 1912).

Otto of Freising, *Gesta Friderici I imperatoris*, ed. G. Waitz and B. de Simson, *MGH SSRG* 46 (Hanover and Leipzig, 1912).

Papsturkunden für Kirchen im Heiligen Lande, ed. R. Hiestand (Göttingen, 1985).

Papsturkunden für Templer und Johanniter, ed. R. Hiestand, 2 vols. (Göttingen, 1972–84).

'Papsturkunden in Florenz', ed. W. Wiederhold, *Nachrichten von der Gesellschaft der Wissenschaften zu Götingen, Phil.-hist. Kl.* (1901), pp. 306–25.

'Papsturkunden in Malta', ed. P. Kehr, *Nachrichten von der Gesellschaft der Wissenschaften zu Götingen, Phil.-hist. Kl.* (1899), pp. 369–409.

Papsturkunden in Sizilien, ed. P. Kehr (Göttingen, 1899).

Papsturkunden in Spanien: I. Katalonien, ed. P. Kehr (Berlin, 1926).

Paschal II, 'Epistolae et privilegia', *PL* 163, cols. 31–448.

Paulinus of Nola, *Epistolae*, ed. G. de Hartel, *Corpus scriptorum ecclesiasticorum Latinorum*, 29 (Vienna, 1999).

Peter Damian, 'Vita Dominici Loricati', *PL* 144, cols. 1009–24.

Peter Tudebode, *Historia de Hierosolymitano itinere*, ed. J.H. and L.L. Hill (Paris, 1977).

Peter the Venerable, *The Letters of Peter the Venerable*, ed. G. Constable, 2 vols. (Cambridge, MA, 1967).

Peter the Venerable, 'Petri Venerabilis Sermones tres', ed. G. Constable, *Revue bénédictine*, 64 (1954), pp. 224–72.

The Pilgrim's Guide to Santiago de Compostela: A Critical Edition, ed. A. Stones, J. Krochalis, P. Gerson and A. Shaver-Crandell, 2 vols. (London, 1998).

'Prefatio de Almaria', ed. J. Gil, *Chronica Hispana saeculi XII, CC:CM* 71 (Turnhout, 1990), pp. 249–67.

The Pseudo-Turpin, edited from Bibl. Nat. Ms. 17656, ed. H.M. Smyser (Cambridge, MA, 1937).

Ralph of Caen, 'Gesta Tancredi', *RHC Oc.* 3, pp. 602–716.

Raymond of Aguilers, *Liber*, ed. J.H. and L.L. Hill (Paris, 1969).

Recueil des chartes de l'abbaye de Cluny, ed. A. Bernard and A. Bruel, 6 vols. (1876–1903).

Reginald of Durham, *Libellus de vita et miraculis S. Godrici, heremitae de Finchale*, Surtees Society, 20 (London, 1847).

La règle du Temple, ed. H. de Curzon (Paris, 1886).

Robert of Rheims, 'Historia Iherosolimitana', *RHC Oc.* 3, pp. 717–882.

Robert of Torigni, *Chronica*, ed. R. Howlett, *Rolls Series*, 82 (London, 1889).

Sancti Eusebii Hieronymi epistulae, ed. I. Hilberg, *Corpus scriptorum ecclesiasticorum Latinorum*, 54 (Vienna and Leipzig, 1910).

Sigebert of Gembloux, 'Chronica', *MGH SS* 6, pp. 268–374.

'Sigeberti continuatio Gemblacensis', *MGH SS* 6, pp. 385–90.

'Sigeberti continuatio Praemonstratensis', *MGH SS* 6, pp. 447–56.

Bibliography

'Sigeberti continuatio Valcellensis', *MGH SS* 6, pp. 458–532.

Suger of St Denis, 'Epistolae', *Oeuvres complètes de Suger*, ed. A. Lecoy de la Marche (Paris, 1867), pp. 239–317.

Suger of St Denis, 'Epistolae', *RHGF* 15, pp. 483–532.

Suger of St Denis, *Vita Ludovici Grossi regis*, ed. and trans. H. Waquet (Paris, 1929).

Die Traditionsbücher des Benediktinerstiftes Göttweig, ed. A.F. Fuchs (Vienna, 1931).

Urban II, 'Epistolae et privilegia', *PL* 151, cols. 283–558.

Die ursprüngliche Templerregel, ed. G. Schnürer (Freiburg, 1903).

'Vita Altmanni episcopi Pataviensis', *MGH SS* 12, pp. 226–43.

'Vita sancti Olegarii', *España Sagrada*, 29 (Madrid, 1775), pp. 472–91.

Wibald of Stavelot, 'Epistolae', *RHGF* 15, pp. 532–40.

William of Tyre, *Chronicon*, ed. R.B.C. Huygens, *CC:CM*, 63, 63A (Turnhout, 1986).

Secondary Works

Alphandéry, P., and Dupront, A., *La chrétienté et l'idée de croisade*, 2 vols. (Paris, 1954–9).

Antonsson, H., 'Insigne Crucis: A European Motif in a Nordic Setting', *The North Sea World in the Middle Ages: Studies in the Cultural History of North-Western Europe* (Dublin, 2001), pp. 15–32.

Asbridge, T., *The Principality of Antioch, 1098–1130* (Woodbridge, 2000).

d'Avray, D., 'Popular and Elite Religion: Feastdays and Preaching', *Elite and Popular Religion*, ed. K. Cooper and J. Gregory, *SCH*, 42 (Woodbridge, 2006), pp. 162–79.

Baker, D., 'Crossroads and Crises in the Religious Life of the Late Eleventh Century', *The Church in Town and Countryside*, ed. D. Baker, *SCH*, 16 (Oxford, 1979), pp. 137–48.

Barber, M., *The New Knighthood: A History of the Order of the Temple* (Cambridge, 1994).

Barber, M., 'The Charitable and Medical Activities of the Hospitallers and Templars', *A History of Pastoral Care*, ed. G.R. Evans (London, 2000), pp. 148–68.

Barton, S., *The Aristocracy in Twelfth-Century León and Castile* (Cambridge, 1997).

Barton, S., 'A Forgotten Crusade: Alfonso VII of León-Castile and the Campaign for Jaén', *Historical Research*, 73 (2000), pp. 312–20.

Barton, S., 'From Tyrants to Soldiers of Christ: The Nobility of Twelfth-Century León-Castile and the Struggle against Islam', *Nottingham Medieval Studies*, 44 (2000), pp. 28–48.

Barton, S., 'Traitors to the Faith? Christian Mercenaries in al-Andalus and the Maghreb, c. 1100–1300', *Medieval Spain: Culture, Conflict and Coexistence. Studies in Honour of Angus MacKay*, ed. R. Collins and A. Goodman (New York, 2002), pp. 23–45.

Barton, S., 'Spain in the Eleventh Century', *The New Cambridge Medieval History*, vol. 4.2, ed. D. Luscombe and J.S.C. Riley-Smith (Cambridge, 2004), pp. 154–90.

Barton, S., and Fletcher, R.A., *The World of El Cid: Chronicles of the Spanish Reconquest* (Manchester, 2000).

Bennett, M., 'Military Aspects of the Conquest of Lisbon', *The Second Crusade: Scope and Consequences*, ed. J.P. Phillips and M. Hoch (Manchester, 2001), pp. 71–89.

Berman, C.H., *The Cistercian Evolution: The Invention of a Religious Order in Twelfth-Century Europe* (Philadelphia, PA, 1999).

Berry, V.G., 'Peter the Venerable and the Crusades', *Petrus Venerabilis 1156–1956: Studies and Texts Commemorating the Eighth Centenary of his Death*, ed. G. Constable and J. Kritzeck, *Studia Anselmiana*, 40 (Rome, 1956), pp. 141–62.

Birch, D.J., *Pilgrimage to Rome in the Middle Ages: Continuity and Change* (Woodbridge, 1998).

Birch, D.J., 'Jacques de Vitry and the Ideology of Pilgrimage', *Pilgrimage Explored*, ed. J. Stopford (Woodbridge, 1999), pp. 79–93.

Bishko, C.J., 'The Spanish and Portuguese Reconquest, 1095–1492', *A History of the Crusades*, vol. 3, ed. H.W. Hazard (Madison, WI, 1975), pp. 396–456.

Blake, E.O., 'The Formation of the "Crusade Idea"', *Journal of Ecclesiastical History*, 21 (1970), pp. 11–31.

Blake, E.O., and Morris, C., 'A Hermit Goes to War: Peter and the Origins of the First Crusade', *Monks, Hermits and the Ascetic Tradition*, ed. W.J. Sheils, SCH, 22 (Oxford, 1985), pp. 79–107.

Blumenthal, U.-R., *The Investiture Controversy: Church and Monarchy from the Ninth to the Twelfth Century* (Philadelphia, PA, 1988).

Bolton, B.M., '"Paupertas Christi": Old Wealth and New Poverty in the Twelfth Century', *Renaissance and Renewal in Christian History*, ed. D. Baker, SCH, 14 (Oxford, 1977), pp. 95–103.

Bolton, B.M., *The Medieval Reformation* (London, 1983).

Bolton, B.M., 'The Cistercians and the Aftermath of the Second Crusade', *The Second Crusade and the Cistercians*, ed. M. Gervers (New York, 1992), pp. 131–40.

Bousquet, J., 'La fondation de Villeneuve d'Aveyron (1053) et l'expansion de l'abbaye de Moissac en Rouergue', *Annales du Midi*, 75 (1963), pp. 538–42.

Bredero, A.H., *Christendom and Christianity in the Middle Ages: The Relations between Religion, Church and Society*, trans. R. Bruinsma (Grand Rapids, MI, 1994).

Brooke, C.N.L., 'Approaches to Medieval Forgery', *Medieval Church and Society* (London, 1971), pp. 100–20.

Brooke, C.N.L., 'Monk and Canon: Some Patterns in the Religious Life of the Twelfth Century', *Monks, Hermits and the Ascetic Tradition*, ed. W.J. Sheils, SCH, 22 (Oxford, 1985), pp. 109–29.

Brown, E.A.R., 'Saint-Denis and the Turpin Legend', *The Codex Calixtinus and the Shrine of St. James*, ed. J. Williams and A. Stones, *Jakobus-Studien*, 3 (Tübingen, 1992), pp. 51–88.

Brown, E.A.R., and Cothren, M.W., 'The Twelfth-Century Crusading Window of the Abbey of Saint-Denis', *Journal of the Warburg and Courtauld Institutes*, 49 (1986), pp. 1–40.

Brundage, J.A., '*Cruce Signari*: The Rite for Taking the Cross in England', *Traditio*, 22 (1966), pp. 289–310.

Brundage, J.A., *Medieval Canon Law and the Crusader* (Madison, WI, 1969).

Brundage, J.A., 'A Transformed Angel (X 3.31.18): The Problem of the Crusading Monk', *Studies in Medieval Cistercian History Presented to Jeremiah F. O'Sullivan*, vol. 1, Cistercian Studies Series, 13 (Spencer, MA, 1971), pp. 55–62.

Brundage, J.A., 'Prostitution, Miscegenation and Sexual Purity in the First Crusade', *Crusade and Settlement: Papers Read at the First Conference of the Society for the Study of the Crusades and the Latin East and Presented to R.C. Smail*, ed. P.W. Edbury (Cardiff, 1985), pp. 57–65.

Brundage, J.A., 'St. Bernard and the Jurists', *The Second Crusade and the Cistercians*, ed. M. Gervers (New York, 1992), pp. 25–33.

Brundage, J.A., 'Crusades, Clerics and Violence: Reflections on a Canonical Theme', *The Experience of Crusading, Volume One: Western Approaches*, ed. M. Bull and N. Housley (Cambridge, 2003), pp. 147–56.

Bull, M., *Knightly Piety and the Lay Response to the First Crusade: The Limousin and Gascony, c.970–c.1130* (Oxford, 1993).

Bull, M., 'Origins', *The Oxford Illustrated History of the Crusades*, ed. J.S.C. Riley-Smith (Oxford, 1995), pp. 13–33.

Bull, M., 'The Capetian Monarchy and the Early Crusade Movement: Hugh of Vermandois and Louis VII', *Nottingham Medieval Studies*, 40 (1996), pp. 25–46.

Bull, M., 'The Diplomatic of the First Crusade', *The First Crusade: Origins and Impact*, ed. J.P. Phillips (Manchester, 1997), pp. 35–56.

Bull, M., *The Miracles of Our Lady of Rocamadour: Analysis and Translation* (Woodbridge, 1999).

Bull, M., 'Views of Muslims and of Jerusalem in Miracle Stories, c.1000–c.1200: Reflections on the Study of First Crusaders' Motivations', *The Experience of Crusading, Volume One: Western Approaches*, ed. M. Bull and N. Housley (Cambridge, 2003), pp. 13–38.

Bulst-Thiele, M.L., 'The Influence of St. Bernard of Clairvaux on the Formation of the Order of the Knights Templar', *The Second Crusade and the Cistercians*, ed. M. Gervers (New York, 1992), pp. 57–65.

Bynum, C.W., *Docere verbo et exemplo: An Aspect of Twelfth-Century Spirituality* (Missoula, MT, 1979).

Bynum, C.W., *Jesus as Mother: Studies in the Spirituality of the High Middle Ages* (Berkeley, Los Angeles and London, 1982).

Callahan, D.F., 'Jerusalem in the Monastic Imaginations of the Early Eleventh Century', *Haskins Society Journal*, 6 (1994), pp. 119–27.

Cantor, N.F., 'The Crisis of Western Monasticism, 1050–1130', *American Historical Review*, 66 (1960–1), pp. 47–67.

Carlson, D., 'The Practical Theology of St Bernard and the Date of the *De laude novae militiae*', *Erudition at God's Service*, ed. J.R. Sommerfeldt, *Studies in Cistercian Medieval History*, 11 (Kalamazoo, MI, 1987), pp. 133–47.

Cerrini, S., 'A New Edition of the Latin and French Rule of the Temple', *The Military Orders: Welfare and Warfare*, ed. H. Nicholson (Aldershot, 1998), pp. 207–15.

Cerrini, S., 'La fondateur de l'ordre du Temple à ses frères: Hugues de Payns et le *Sermo Christi militibus*', *Dei gesta per Francos: Crusade Studies in Honour of Jean Richard*, ed. M. Balard, B.Z. Kedar and J.S.C. Riley-Smith (Aldershot, 2001), pp. 99–110.

Chenu, M.-D., *Nature, Man and Society in the Twelfth Century: Essays on New Theological Perspectives in the Latin West*, ed. and trans. J. Taylor and L.K. Little (Toronto, 1968).

Coffey, T.F., Davidson, L.K., and Dunn., M., *The Miracles of Saint James: Translations from the Liber sancti Jacobi* (New York, 1996).

Cohn, N., *The Pursuit of the Millennium: Revolutionary Millenarians and Mystical Anarchists of the Middle Ages*, revised edition (New York, 1970).

Cole, P.J., *The Preaching of the Crusades to the Holy Land, 1095–1270* (Cambridge, MA, 1991).

Cole, P.J., '"O God, the heathen have come into your inheritance" (Ps. 78.1): The Theme of Religious Pollution in Crusade Documents, 1095–1188', *Crusaders and Muslims in Twelfth-Century Syria*, ed. M. Shatzmiller (Leiden and New York, 1993), pp. 84–111.

Comte, F., *L'abbaye Toussaint d'Angers des origines à 1330: étude historique et cartulaire* (Angers, 1985).

Constable, G., 'A Note on the Route of the Anglo-Flemish Crusaders of 1147', *Speculum*, 28 (1953), pp. 525–6.

Constable, G., 'The Second Crusade as Seen by Contemporaries', *Traditio*, 9 (1953), pp. 213–79.

Constable, G., 'A Report on a Lost Sermon by St Bernard on the Failure of the Second Crusade', *Studies in Medieval Cistercian History Presented to Jeremiah O'Sullivan* (Spencer, MA, 1971), pp. 49–54.

Constable, G., 'Opposition to Pilgrimage in the Middle Ages', *Studia Gratiana*, 19 (1976), pp. 123–46.

Constable, G., 'Monachisme et pèlerinage au Moyen Âge', *Revue historique*, 258 (1977), pp. 3–27.

Constable, G., '*Nudus nudum Christum sequi* and Parallel Formulas in the Twelfth Century: A Supplementary Dossier', *Continuity and Discontinuity in Church History: Essays Presented to George Hunston Williams on the Occasion of his 65th Birthday*, ed. F. Forrester Church and T. George, *Studies in the History of Christian Thought*, 19 (Leiden, 1979), pp. 83–91.

Constable, G., *Attitudes toward Self-Inflicted Suffering in the Middle Ages* (Brookline, MA, 1982).

Constable, G., 'The Financing of the Crusades in the Twelfth Century', *Outremer: Studies in the History of the Crusading Kingdom of Jerusalem Presented to Joshua Prawer*, ed. B.Z. Kedar, H.E. Mayer and R.C. Smail (Jerusalem, 1982), pp. 64–88.

Constable, G., 'Forgery and Plagiarism in the Middle Ages', *Archiv für Diplomatik*, 29 (1983), pp. 1–41.

Constable, G., 'Papal, Imperial and Monastic Propaganda in the Eleventh and Twelfth Centuries', *Prédication et propagande au moyen âge: Islam, Byzance, Occident*, ed. G. Makdisi, D. Sourdel and J. Sourdel-Thomine (Paris, 1983), pp. 179–99.

Constable, G., 'The Diversity of Religious Life and Acceptance of Social Pluralism in the Twelfth Century', *History, Society and the Churches: Essays in Honour of Owen Chadwick*, ed. D. Beales and G. Best (Cambridge, 1985), pp. 29–47.

Constable, G., 'Medieval Charters as a Source for the History of the Crusades', *Crusade and Settlement: Papers Read at the First Conference of the Society for the Study of the Crusades and the Latin East and Presented to R.C. Smail*, ed. P.W. Edbury (Cardiff, 1985), pp. 73–89.

Constable, G., 'The Ceremonies and Symbolism of Entering Religious Life and Taking the Monastic Habit, from the Fourth to the Twelfth Century', *Settimane di studio del Centro italiano di studi sull'alto medioevo*, 33 (Spoleto, 1987), pp. 771–834.

Constable, G., 'Past and Present in the Eleventh and Twelfth Centuries: Perceptions of Time and Change', *L'Europa dei secoli XI e XII fra novità e tradizione: sviluppi di una cultura* (Milan, 1989), pp. 135–70.

Constable, G., *Three Studies in Medieval Religious and Social Thought* (Cambridge, 1995).

Constable, G., *The Reformation of the Twelfth Century* (Cambridge, 1996).

Constable, G., 'The Crusading Project of 1150', *Montjoie: Studies in Crusade History in Honour of Hans Eberhard Mayer*, ed. B.Z. Kedar, J.S.C. Riley-Smith and R. Hiestand (Aldershot, 1997), pp. 67–75.

Constable, G., 'The Place of the Crusader in Medieval Society', *Viator*, 29 (1998), pp. 377–403.

Constable, G., 'Jerusalem and the Sign of the Cross (with Particular Reference to the Cross of Pilgrimage and Crusading in the Twelfth Century)', *Jerusalem: Its Sanctity and Centrality to Judaism, Christianity, and Islam*, ed. L.I. Levine (New York, 1999), pp. 371–81.

Constable, G., 'The Historiography of the Crusades', *The Crusades from the Perspective of Byzantium and the Muslim World*, ed. A.E. Laiou and R.P. Mottahedeh (Washington, DC, 2001), pp. 1–22.

Constable, G., 'The Three Lives of Odo Arpinus: Viscount of Bourges, Crusader, Monk of Cluny', *Religion, Text, and Society in Medieval Spain and Northern Europe: Essays in honor of J.N. Hillgarth*, ed. T.E. Burman, M.D. Meyerson, and L. Shopkow (Toronto, 2002), pp. 183–99.

Constable, G., 'A Further Note on the Conquest of Lisbon in 1147', *The Experience of Crusading, Volume One: Western Approaches*, ed. M. Bull and N. Housley (Cambridge, 2003), pp. 39–44.

Constable, O.R., 'Muslim Spain and Mediterranean Slavery: The Medieval Slave Trade as an Aspect of Muslim–Christian Relations', *Christendom and Its Discontents: Exclusion, Persecution, and Rebellion, 1000–1500*, ed. S.L. Waugh and P.D. Diehl (Cambridge, 1996), pp. 264–84.

Coupe, M.D., 'Peter the Hermit – A Reassessment', *Nottingham Medieval Studies*, 31 (1987), pp. 37–46.

Cowdrey, H.E.J., 'Pope Urban II's Preaching of the First Crusade', *History*, 55 (1970), pp. 177–88.

Cowdrey, H.E.J., 'The Mahdia Campaign of 1087', *English Historical Review*, 92 (1977), pp. 1–29.

Cowdrey, H.E.J., 'Pope Gregory VII's "Crusading" Plans of 1074', *Outremer: Studies in the History of the Crusading Kingdom of Jerusalem Presented to Joshua Prawer*, ed. B.Z. Kedar, H.E. Mayer and R.C. Smail (Jerusalem, 1982), pp. 27–40.

Cowdrey, H.E.J., 'Martyrdom and the First Crusade', *Crusade and Settlement: Papers Read at the First Conference of the Society for the Study of the Crusades and the Latin East and Presented to R.C. Smail*, ed. P.W. Edbury (Cardiff, 1985), pp. 46–56.

Cowdrey, H.E.J., 'Pope Urban and the Idea of Crusade', *Studi medievali*, 36 (1995), pp. 721–42.

Cowdrey, H.E.J., 'Pope Gregory VII and the Bearing of Arms', *Montjoie: Studies in Crusade History in Honour of Hans Eberhard Mayer*, ed. B.Z. Kedar, J.S.C. Riley-Smith and R. Hiestand (Aldershot, 1997), pp. 21–35.

Cowdrey, H.E.J., 'Pope Gregory VII and Martyrdom', *Dei gesta per Francos: Crusade Studies in Honour of Jean Richard*, ed. M. Balard, B.Z. Kedar and J.S.C. Riley-Smith (Aldershot, 2001), pp. 3–11.

Cowdrey, H.E.J., 'Christianity and the Morality of Warfare during the First Century of Crusading', *The Experience of Crusading, Volume One: Western Approaches*, ed. M. Bull and N. Housley (Cambridge, 2003), pp. 175–92.

Cushing, K.G., *Reform and the Papacy in the Eleventh Century: Spirituality and Social Change* (Manchester, 2005).

Davidson, L.K., and Dunn-Wood, M., *Pilgrimage in the Middle Ages: A Research Guide* (New York and London, 1993).

Davis, R.H.C., *The Normans and their Myth* (London, 1976).

Delaruelle, É., 'Essai sur la formation de l'idée de croisade', *Bulletin de littérature ecclésiastique*, 42 (1941), pp. 24–45, 86–103; 45 (1944), pp. 13–46, 73–90; 54 (1953), pp. 226–39; 55 (1954), pp. 50–63.

Delaruelle, É., 'L'idée de croisade chez Saint Bernard', *Mélanges Saint Bernard* (Dijon, 1953), pp. 53–67.

Díaz y Díaz, M.C., *Visiones del mas alla en Galicia durante la alta edad media* (Santiago de Compostela, 1985).

Díaz y Díaz, M.C., *El Códice Calixtino de la catedral de Santiago: estudio codicológico y de contenido* (Santiago de Compostela, 1988).

Dickinson, J.C., *The Origins of the Austin Canons and their Introduction into England* (London, 1950).

Doxey, G.B., 'Christian Attempts to Reconquer the Balearic Islands before 1229', unpublished Ph.D. thesis (Cambridge, 1991).

Dozy, R., *Recherches sur l'histoire et la littérature de l'Espagne pendant le Moyen Âge*, 3rd edition, 2 vols. (Paris, 1881).

Dunbabin, J., 'Discovering a Past for the French Aristocracy', *The Perception of the Past in Twelfth-Century Europe*, ed. P. Magdalino (London, 1992), pp. 1–14.

Dupront, A., 'La spiritualité des croisés et des pèlerins d'après les sources de la première croisade', *Pellegrinaggi e culto dei santi in Europa fino alla Ia crociata* (Todi, 1963), pp. 51–83.

Dutton, M.L., 'Intimacy and Imitation: The Humanity of Christ in Cistercian Spirituality', *Erudition at God's Service*, ed. J.R. Sommerfeldt, *Studies in Cistercian Medieval History*, 11 (Kalamazoo, MI, 1987), pp. 33–69.

Edgington, S.B., 'The First Crusade: Reviewing the Evidence', *The First Crusade: Origins and Impact*, ed. J.P. Phillips (Manchester, 1997), pp. 55–77.

Erdmann, C., *The Origin of the Idea of Crusade*, trans. M.W. Baldwin and W. Goffart (Princeton, NJ, 1977).

Face, R.D., 'Secular History in Twelfth-Century Italy: Caffaro of Genoa', *Journal of Medieval History*, 6 (1980), pp. 169–84.

Farmer, D., *The Oxford Dictionary of Saints*, 4th edition (Oxford, 1997).

Ferreiro, A., 'The Siege of Barbastro, 1064–5: A Reassessment', *Journal of Medieval History*, 9 (1983), pp. 129–44.

Ferzoco, G., 'The Origin of the Second Crusade', *The Second Crusade and the Cistercians*, ed. M. Gervers (New York, 1992), pp. 91–9.

Fita, F., 'Actas del Concilio de Clermont (18 Noviembre 1130): revisión crítica', *BRAH*, 4 (1884), pp. 360–6.

Fita, F., 'Sobre un texto del arzobispo don Rodrigo', *BRAH*, 4 (1884), pp. 367–88.

Fita, F., 'El concilio nacional de Palencia en el año 1100 y el de Gerona en 1101', *BRAH*, 24 (1894), pp. 215–35.

Fita, F., 'Renallo Gramático y la conquista de Mallorca por el conde de Barcelona don Ramón Berenguer III', *BRAH*, 40 (1902), pp. 50–80.

Fletcher, R.A., *St James's Catapult: The Life and Times of Diego Gelmírez of Santiago de Compostela* (Oxford, 1984).

Fletcher, R.A., 'Reconquest and Crusade in Spain, c.1050–1150', *Transactions of the Royal Historical Society*, 5th ser., 37 (1987), pp. 31–47.

Fletcher, R.A., *The Quest for El Cid* (London, 1989).

Flori, J., 'Mort et martyre des guerriers vers 1100. L'exemple de la prèmiere croisade', *Cahiers de civilisation médiévale*, 34 (1991), pp. 121–39.

Flori, J., 'Faut-il réhabiliter Pierre l'Ermite? Une réévaluation des sources de la première croisade', *Cahiers de civilisation médiéval*, 38 (1995), pp. 35–54.

Flori, J., *La guerre sainte: la formation de l'idée de croisade dans l'Occident chrétien* (Paris, 2001).

Flori, J., 'Ideology and Motivations in the First Crusade', *Palgrave Advances in the Crusades*, ed. H.J. Nicholson (Basingstoke, 2005), pp. 15–36.

Fonnesberg-Schmidt, I.M., *The Popes and the Baltic Crusades, 1147–1254* (Leiden, 2007).

Forey, A.J., *The Templars in the Corona de Aragón* (London, 1973).

Forey, A. J., 'The Will of Alfonso I of Aragón and Navarre', *Durham University Journal*, 73 (1980), pp. 59–65.

Forey, A. J., 'The Military Orders and the Spanish Reconquest in the Twelfth and Thirteenth Centuries', *Traditio*, 40 (1984), pp. 197–234.

Forey, A. J., 'The Emergence of the Military Order in the Twelfth Century', *Journal of Ecclesiastical History*, 36 (1985), pp. 175–95.

Forey, A. J., *The Military Orders from the Twelfth to the Early Fourteenth Centuries* (Basingstoke, 1992).

Forey, A. J., 'The Siege of Lisbon and the Second Crusade', *Portuguese Studies*, 20 (2004), pp. 1–13.

France, J., *Victory in the East: A Military History of the First Crusade* (Cambridge, 1994).

France, J., 'The Destruction of Jerusalem and the First Crusade', *Journal of Ecclesiastical History*, 47 (1996), pp. 1–17.

France, J., 'The Anonymous *Gesta Francorum* and the *Historia Francorum qui ceperunt Iherusalem* of Raymond of Aguilers and the *Historia de Hierosolymitano itinere* of Peter Tudebode: An Analysis of the Textual Relationship between Primary Sources for the First Crusade', *The Crusades and their Sources: Essays Presented to Bernard Hamilton*, ed. J. France and W. Zajac (Aldershot, 1998), pp. 39–69.

France, J., 'The Use of the Anonymous *Gesta Francorum* in the Early Twelfth-Century Sources for the First Crusade', *From Clermont to Jerusalem: The Crusades and Crusader Societies, 1095–1500*, ed. A. V. Murray (Turnhout, 1998), pp. 29–42.

France, J., 'Holy War and Holy Men: Erdmann and the Lives of the Saints', *The Experience of Crusading, Volume One: Western Approaches*, ed. M. Bull and N. Housley (Cambridge, 2003), pp. 193–208.

France, J., 'Two Types of Vision on the First Crusade: Stephen of Valence and Peter Bartholomew', *Crusades*, 5 (2006), pp. 1–20.

Freeman, E., *Narratives of a New Order: Cistercian Historical Writing in England, 1150–1220* (Turnhout, 2002).

Garrisson, F., 'A propos des pèlerins et de leur condition juridique', *Études d'histoire du droit canonique dédiées à Gabriel le Bras* (Paris, 1965), pp. 1165–89.

Geary, P. J., *Furta Sacra: Thefts of Relics in the Central Middle Ages*, revised edition (Princeton, NJ, 1990).

Gieysztor, A., 'The Genesis of the Crusades: The Encyclical of Sergius IV (1009–12)', *Medievalia et humanistica*, 5 (1948), pp. 3–23, and 6 (1950), pp. 3–34.

Goñi Gaztambide, J., *Historia de la bula de la cruzada en España* (Vitoria, 1958).

Graboïs, A., 'Anglo-Norman England and the Holy Land', *Anglo-Norman Studies*, 7 (1984), pp. 132–41.

Graboïs, A., 'The Crusade of King Louis VII: A Reconsideration', *Crusade and Settlement: Papers Read at the First Conference of the Society for the Study of the Crusades and the Latin East and Presented to R. C. Smail*, ed. P. W. Edbury (Cardiff, 1985), pp. 94–104.

Graboïs, A., 'Louis VII Pèlerin', *Revue d'histoire de l'église de France*, 74 (1988), pp. 5–22.

Graboïs, A., 'Le concept du "contemptus mundi" dans les pratiques des pèlerins occidentaux en terre sainte à l'époque des croisades', *Mediaevalia Christiana, XIe–XIIe siècles: hommage à Raymond Foreville de ses amis, ses collègues at ses anciens élèves*, ed. C. E. Viola (Paris, 1989), pp. 290–306.

Graboïs, A., 'Militia and Malitia: The Bernardine Vision of Chivalry', *The Second Crusade and the Cistercians*, ed. M. Gervers (New York, 1992), pp. 49–56.

Grafton, A., *Forgers and Critics: Creativity and Duplicity in Western Scholarship* (Princeton, NJ, 1990).

Grundmann, H., *Religious Movements in the Middle Ages*, trans. S. Rowan (Notre Dame, IN, 1995).

Hamilton, B., 'The Cistercians in the Crusade States', *One Yet Two: Monastic Tradition, East and West*, ed. M.B. Pennington (Kalamazoo, MI, 1976), pp. 405–22.

Hamilton, B., 'Rebuilding Zion: The Holy Places of Jerusalem in the Twelfth Century', *Renaissance and Renewal in Christian History*, ed. D. Baker, SCH, 14 (Oxford, 1977), pp. 105–16.

Hamilton, B., *The Latin Church in the Crusader States: The Secular Church* (London, 1980).

Hamilton, B., 'The Impact of Crusader Jerusalem on Western Christendom', *Catholic Historical Review*, 80 (1994), pp. 695–713.

Hamilton, B., 'Ideals of Holiness: Crusaders, Contemplatives, and Mendicants', *International History Review*, 17 (1995), pp. 693–712.

Hamilton, B., '"God Wills It": Signs of Divine Approval in the Crusade Movement', *Signs, Wonders, Miracles: Representations of Divine Power in the Life of the Church*, ed. K. Cooper and J. Gregory, SCH, 41 (Woodbridge, 2005), pp. 88–98.

Hamilton, S., *The Practice of Penance, 900–1050* (Woodbridge, 2001).

Hamilton, S., 'Penance in the Age of Gregorian Reform', *Retribution, Repentance and Reconciliation*, ed. K. Cooper and J. Gregory, SCH, 40 (Woodbridge, 2004), pp. 47–73.

Hehl, E.-D., *Kirche und Krieg im 12. Jahrhundert: Studien zu kanonischem Recht und politischer Wirklichkeit* (Stuttgart, 1980).

Hendrix, S.H., 'In Quest of the *Vera Ecclesia*: The Crises of Late Medieval Ecclesiology', *Viator*, 7 (1976), pp. 347–78.

Herbers, K., 'The Miracles of St. James', *The Codex Calixtinus and the Shrine of St. James*, ed. J. Williams and A. Stones, *Jakobus-Studien*, 3 (Tübingen, 1992), pp. 11–35.

Hiestand, R., 'The Papacy and the Second Crusade', *The Second Crusade: Scope and Consequences*, ed. J.P. Phillips and M. Hoch (Manchester, 2001), pp. 32–53.

Hillenbrand, C., *The Crusades: Islamic Perspectives* (Edinburgh, 1999).

Hohler, C., 'A Note on *Jacobus*', *Journal of the Warburg and Courtauld Institutes*, 35 (1972), pp. 31–80.

Housley, N., 'Crusades against Christians: Their Origins and Early Development, c.1000–1216', *Crusade and Settlement: Papers Read at the First Conference of the Society for the Study of the Crusades and the Latin East and Presented to R.C. Smail*, ed. P.W. Edbury (Cardiff, 1985), pp. 17–36.

Housley, N., 'Jerusalem and the Development of the Crusade Idea, 1099–1128', *The Horns of Hattin: Proceedings of the Second Conference of the Society for the Study of the Crusades and the Latin East*, ed. B.Z. Kedar (Jerusalem, 1992), pp. 27–40.

Housley, N., *Contesting the Crusades* (Oxford, 2006).

Hunt, E.D., 'The Itinerary of Egeria: Reliving the Bible in Fourth-Century Palestine', *The Holy Land, Holy Lands, and Christian History*, ed. R.N. Swanson, SCH, 36 (Woodbridge, 2000), pp. 34–54.

Jaspert, N., '*Capta est Dertosa, clavis Christianorum*: Tortosa and the Crusades', *The Second Crusade: Scope and Consequences*, ed. J.P. Phillips and M. Hoch (Manchester, 2001), pp. 90–110.

Jensen, J.M., '*Peregrinatio sive expeditio*: Why the First Crusade was not a Pilgrimage', *Al-Masaq: Islam and the Medieval Mediterranean*, 15 (2003), pp. 119–37.

Jones, C.P., '*Stigma*: Tattooing and Branding in Graeco-Roman Antiquity', *Journal of Roman Studies*, 77 (1987), pp. 139–55.

Joranson, E., 'The Great German Pilgrimage of 1064–1065', *The Crusades and Other Historical Essays Presented to Dana C. Munro by his Former Students*, ed. L.J. Paetow (New York, 1928), pp. 3–43.

Joranson, E., 'The Problem of the Spurious Letter of Emperor Alexius to the Count of Flanders', *American Historical Review*, 55 (1949–50), pp. 811–32.

Jotischky, A., *The Perfection of Solitude: Hermits and Monks in the Crusader States* (University Park, PA, 1995).

Jotischky, A., 'Greek Orthodox and Latin Monasticism around Mar Saba under Crusader Rule', *The Sabaite Heritage in the Orthodox Church from the Fifth Century to the Present*, ed. J. Patrich (Leuven, 2001), pp. 85–96.

Jotischky, A., *The Carmelites and Antiquity: Mendicants and their Pasts in the Middle Ages* (Oxford, 2002).

Kahl, H.-D., 'Crusade Eschatology as Seen by St. Bernard in the Years 1146 to 1148', *The Second Crusade and the Cistercians*, ed. M. Gervers (New York, 1992), pp. 35–47.

Katzenellenbogen, A., 'The Central Tympanum at Vézelay, its Encyclopaedic Meaning and its Relation to the First Crusade', *Art Bulletin*, 26 (1944), pp. 141–51.

Katzir, Y., 'The Conquests of Jerusalem 1099 and 1187: Historical Memory and Religious Typology', *The Meeting of Two Worlds: Cultural Exchange between East and West during the Period of the Crusades*, ed. V.P. Goss (Kalamazoo, MI, 1986), pp. 103–13.

Katzir, Y., 'The Second Crusade and the Redefinition of *Ecclesia*, *Christianitas* and Papal Coercive Power', *The Second Crusade and the Cistercians*, ed. M. Gervers (New York, 1992), pp. 3–11.

Kedar, B.Z., 'Gerard of Nazareth, a Neglected Twelfth-Century Writer in the Latin East: A Contribution to the Intellectual History of the Crusader States', *Dumbarton Oaks Papers*, 37 (1983), pp. 55–77.

Kedar, B.Z., 'A Second Incarnation in Frankish Jerusalem', *The Experience of Crusading, Volume Two: Defining the Crusader Kingdom*, ed. P.W. Edbury and J.P. Phillips (Cambridge, 2003), pp. 79–92.

Kedar, B.Z., 'The Jerusalem Massacre of July 1099 in the Western Historiography of the Crusades', *Crusades*, 3 (2004), pp. 15–75.

Kelly, J.N.D., *The Oxford Dictionary of Popes* (Oxford, 1986).

Kemp, B., 'The Miracles of the Hand of St James', *Berkshire Archaeological Journal*, 65 (1970), pp. 1–19.

Kemp, B., 'The Hand of St James at Reading Abbey', *Reading Medieval Studies*, 16 (1990), pp. 77–96.

Kenaan-Kedar, N., and Kedar, B.Z., 'The Significance of a Twelfth-Century Sculptural Group: Le retour du croisé', *Dei gesta per Francos: Crusade Studies in Honour of Jean Richard*, ed. M. Balard, B.Z. Kedar and J.S.C. Riley-Smith (Aldershot, 2001), pp. 29–44.

Knight, G.R., *The Correspondence between Peter the Venerable and Bernard of Clairvaux: A Semantic and Structural Analysis* (Aldershot, 2002).

Koziol, G., *Begging Pardon and Favor: Ritual and Political Order in Early Medieval France* (Ithaca and London, 1992).

Labande, E.R., 'Recherches sur les pèlerins dans l'Europe des XIe et XIIe siècles', *Cahiers de civilisation médiévale*, 1 (1958), pp. 159–69, 339–47.

Labande, E.R., '*Ad limina*: le pèlerin médiéval au terme de sa démarche', *Mélanges offerts à René Crozet*, ed. P. Gallais and Y.-J. Riou, 2 vols. (Poitiers, 1966), vol. 1, pp. 283–91.

Lacarra, J.M., 'Los franceses en la reconquista y repoblación del valle del Ebro en tiempos de Alfonso el Batallador', *Cuadernos de historia*, 2 (1968), pp. 65–80.

Lacarra, J.M., 'La conquista de Zaragoza por Alfonso I (18 diciembre 1118)', *Al-Andalus*, 12 (1974), pp. 65–96.

Lacarra, J.M., *Alfonso el Batallador* (Zaragoza, 1978).

Ladner, G.B., '*Homo Viator*: Medieval Ideas on Alienation and Order', *Speculum*, 42 (1967), pp. 233–59.

Lawrence, C.H., *Medieval Monasticism: Forms of Religious Life in Western Europe in the Middle Ages*, 3rd edition (Harlow, 2001).

Leclercq, J., 'Saint Bernard et ses secrétaires', *Revue bénédictine*, 61 (1950), pp. 208–29.

Leclercq, J., 'Monachisme et pérégrination du IXe au XIIe siècle', *Studia monastica*, 3 (1961), pp. 33–52.

Leclercq, J., 'L'encyclique de saint Bernard en faveur de la croisade', *Revue bénédictine*, 81 (1971), pp. 282–308, and 82 (1972), p. 312.

Leclercq, J., 'The Monastic Crisis of the Eleventh and Twelfth Centuries', *Cluniac Monasticism in the Central Middle Ages*, ed. N. Hunt (Glasgow, 1971), pp. 217–37.

Leclercq, J., 'Pour l'histoire de l'encyclique de saint Bernard sur la croisade', *Études de civilisation médiévale, IXe–XIIe siècles: mélanges offerts à Edmond-René Labande par ses amis, ses collègues, ses élèves* (Poitiers, 1974), pp. 479–90.

Leclercq, J., Vandenbroucke, F., and Bouyer, L., *The Spirituality of the Middle Ages* (London, 1968).

Leyser, H., *Hermits and the New Monasticism: A Study of Religious Communities in Western Europe, 1000–1150* (New York, 1984).

Licence, T., 'The Templars and the Hospitallers, Christ and the Saints', *Crusades*, 4 (2005), pp. 39–57.

Licence, T., 'The Military Orders as Monastic Orders', *Crusades*, 5 (2006), pp. 39–53.

Linehan, P.A., 'Religion, Nationalism and National Identity in Medieval Spain and Portugal', *Religion and National Identity*, ed. S. Mews, *SCH*, 18 (Oxford, 1982), pp. 161–99.

Little, L.K., *Religious Poverty and the Profit Economy in Medieval Europe* (London, 1978).

Livermore, H., 'The "Conquest of Lisbon" and its Author', *Portuguese Studies*, 6 (1990), pp. 1–16.

Lomax, D.W., *The Reconquest of Spain* (London, 1978).

Loud, G.A., *The Age of Robert Guiscard: Southern Italy and the Norman Conquest* (Harlow, 2000).

Loud, G.A., 'Some Reflections on the Failure of the Second Crusade', *Crusades*, 4 (2005), pp. 1–14.

Lourie, E., 'The Will of Alfonso I, "El Batallador", King of Aragon and Navarre: A Reassessment', *Speculum*, 50 (1975), pp. 635–51.

Lourie, E., 'The Confraternity of Belchite, the Ribat, and the Temple', *Viator*, 13 (1982), pp. 159–76.

Lourie, E., 'The Will of Alfonso I of Aragon and Navarre: A Reply to Dr. Forey', *Durham University Journal*, 77 (1984), pp. 165–72.

McCluskey, R., 'Malleable Accounts: Views of the Past in Twelfth Century Iberia', *The Perception of the Past in Twelfth-Century Europe*, ed. P. Magdalino (London, 1992), pp. 211–25.

McDonnell, E.W., 'The *Vita Apostolica*: Diversity or Dissent', *Church History*, 24 (1955), pp. 15–31.

McGinn, B., '*Iter sancti Sepulchri*: The Piety of the First Crusaders', *Essays on Medieval Civilization*, ed. B.K. Lackner and K.R. Philp (Austin, TX, 1978), pp. 33–71.

McGinn, B., *Visions of the End: Apocalyptic Traditions in the Middle Ages* (New York, 1979).

MacKay, A., *Spain in the Middle Ages: From Frontier to Empire, 1000–1500* (London, 1977).

Maitland, S.R., *The Dark Ages*, 5th edition, ed. F. Stokes (London, 1890).

Markowski, M., '*Crucesignatus*: Its Origins and Early Usage', *Journal of Medieval History*, 10 (1984), pp. 157–65.

Marshall, C., 'The Crusading Motivation of the Italian City Republics in the Latin East, 1096–1104', *The Experience of Crusading, Volume One: Western Approaches*, ed. M. Bull and N. Housley (Cambridge, 2003), pp. 60–79.

Martín, J.L., *Orígenes de la Orden Militar de Santiago (1170–1195)* (Barcelona, 1974).

Mayer, H.E., *The Crusades*, trans. J. Gillingham, 2nd edition (Oxford, 1988).

Mayr-Harting, H., 'Odo of Deuil, the Second Crusade and the Monastery of Saint-Denis', *The Culture of Christendom: Essays in Medieval History in Memory of Denis L. T. Bethell*, ed. M.A. Meyer (London, 1993), pp. 225–41.

Medieval Iberia: An Encyclopaedia, ed. E.M. Gerli (New York and London, 2003).

Meschini, M., *San Bernardo e la seconda crociata* (Milan, 1998).

Moisan, A., 'Aimeri Picaud de Parthenay et le "Liber sancti Jacobi"', *Bibliothèque de l'École des Chartes*, 143 (1985), pp. 5–52.

Morin, G., 'Rainaud l'ermite et Ives de Chartres: un épisode de la crise du cénobitisme aux XIe–XIIe siècle', *Revue bénédictine*, 40 (1928), pp. 99–115.

Morris, C., 'Christ after the Flesh: 2 Corinthians 5.16 in the Fathers and in the Middle Ages', *The Ampleforth Journal*, 80 (1975), pp. 44–51.

Morris, C., 'Propaganda for War: The Dissemination of the Crusading Ideal in the Twelfth Century', *The Church and War*, ed. W.J. Sheils, *SCH*, 20 (Oxford, 1983), pp. 79–101.

Morris, C., 'Policy and Visions: The Case of the Holy Lance at Antioch', *War and Government in the Middle Ages: Essays in Honour of J.O. Prestwich*, ed. J. Gillingham and J.C. Holt (Woodbridge, 1984), pp. 33–45.

Morris, C., *The Papal Monarchy: The Western Church from 1050 to 1250* (Oxford, 1989).

Morris, C., 'The *Gesta Francorum* as Narrative History', *Reading Medieval Studies*, 19 (1993), pp. 55–71.

Morris, C., 'Martyrs on the Field of Battle before and during the First Crusade', *Martyrs and Martyrologies*, ed. D. Wood, *SCH*, 30 (Oxford, 1993), pp. 93–105.

Morris, C., 'Memorials of the Holy Places and Blessings from the East: Devotion to Jerusalem before the Crusades', *The Holy Land, Holy Lands, and Christian History*, ed. R.N. Swanson, *SCH*, 36 (Woodbridge, 2000), pp. 90–109.

Morris, C., *The Sepulchre of Christ and the Medieval West: From the Beginning to 1600* (Oxford, 2005).

Murray, A.V., '"Mighty against the Enemies of Christ": The Relic of the True Cross in the Armies of the Kingdom of Jerusalem', *The Crusades and their Sources: Essays Presented to Bernard Hamilton*, ed. J. France and W.G. Zajac (Aldershot, 1998), pp. 217–38.

Nelson, L.H., 'Rotrou of Perche and the Aragonese Reconquest', *Traditio*, 26 (1970), pp. 113–33.

O'Banion, P.J., 'What has Iberia to do with Jerusalem? Crusade and the Spanish Route to the Holy Land in the Twelfth Century' (Forthcoming).

O'Callaghan, J.F., *Reconquest and Crusade in Medieval Spain* (Philadelphia, PA, 2003).

Olsen, G., 'The Idea of the *Ecclesia Primitiva* in the Writings of the Twelfth-Century Canonists', *Traditio*, 25 (1969), pp. 61–86.

Paterson, L., 'Syria, Poitou and the *Reconquista* (*or* Tales of the Undead): Who was the Count in Marcabru's *Vers del lavador?*', *The Second Crusade: Scope and Consequences*, ed. J.P. Phillips and M. Hoch (Manchester, 2001), pp. 133–49.

Paul, N.L., 'Crusade and Family Memory before 1225', unpublished Ph.D. thesis (Cambridge, 2005).

Pellegrin, E., 'Membra disiecta Floriacensia', *Bibliothèque de l'École des Chartes*, 117 (1959), pp. 5–56.

Phillips, J.P., 'Hugh of Payns and the 1129 Damascus Crusade', *The Military Orders: Fighting for the Faith and Caring for the Sick*, ed. M. Barber (Aldershot, 1994), pp. 141–7.

Phillips, J.P., *Defenders of the Holy Land: Relations between the Latin East and the West, 1119–1187* (Oxford, 1996).

Phillips, J.P., 'St Bernard of Clairvaux, The Low Countries and the Lisbon Letter of the Second Crusade', *Journal of Ecclesiastical History*, 48 (1997), pp. 485–97.

Phillips, J.P., 'Ideas of Crusade and Holy War in *De expugnatione Lyxbonensi (The Conquest of Lisbon)*', *The Holy Land, Holy Lands, and Christian History*, ed. R.N. Swanson, SCH, 36 (Woodbridge, 2000), pp. 123–41.

Phillips, J.P., 'Papacy, Empire and the Second Crusade', *The Second Crusade: Scope and Consequences*, ed. J.P. Phillips and M. Hoch (Manchester, 2001), pp. 15–31.

Phillips, J.P., *The Crusades, 1095–1197* (Harlow, 2002).

Phillips, J.P., 'Odo of Deuil's *De profectione Ludovici VII in Orientem* as a Source for the Second Crusade', *The Experience of Crusading, Volume One: Western Approaches*, ed. M. Bull and N. Housley (Cambridge, 2003), pp. 80–95.

Phillips, J.P., *The Second Crusade: Extending the Frontiers of Christianity* (New Haven and London, 2007).

Phillips, M., 'The Thief's Cross: Crusade and Penance in Alan of Lille's *Sermo de cruce domini*', *Crusades*, 5 (2006), pp. 143–56.

Porter, J.M.B., 'Preacher of the First Crusade? Robert of Arbrissel after the Council of Clermont', *From Clermont to Jerusalem: The Crusades and Crusader Societies, 1095–1500*, ed. A.V. Murray (Turnhout, 1998), pp. 43–53.

Powell, J.M., 'Myth, Legend, Propaganda, History: The First Crusade, 1140–ca.1300', *Autor de la première croisade: actes du colloque de la Society for the Study of the Crusades and the Latin East 1995*, ed. M. Balard (Paris, 1996), pp. 127–41.

Pryor, J.H., *Geography, Technology, and War: Studies in the Maritime History of the Mediterranean, 649–1571* (Cambridge, 1988).

Purkis, W.J., 'Stigmata on the First Crusade', *Signs, Wonders, Miracles: Representations of Divine Power in the Life of the Church*, ed. K. Cooper and J. Gregory, SCH, 41 (Woodbridge, 2005), pp. 99–108.

Queller, D.E., and Madden, T.F., *The Fourth Crusade: The Conquest of Constantinople*, 2nd edition (Philadelphia, PA, 1997).

Raedts, P., 'St Bernard of Clairvaux and Jerusalem', *Prophecy and Eschatology*, ed. M. Wilks, SCH Subsidia, 10 (Oxford, 1994), pp. 169–82.

Rassow, P., 'La cofradía de Belchite', *Anuario de historia del derecho español*, 3 (1926), pp. 200–26.

Reilly, B.F., 'The *Historia Compostelana*: The Genesis and Composition of a Twelfth-Century Spanish *Gesta*', *Speculum*, 44 (1969), pp. 78–85.

Reilly, B.F., *The Contest of Christian and Muslim Spain, 1031–1157* (Cambridge, MA, and Oxford, 1992).

Remensnyder, A.G., *Remembering Kings Past: Monastic Foundation Legends in Medieval Southern France* (Ithaca and London, 1995).

Reuter, T., 'The "Non-Crusade" of 1149–50', *The Second Crusade: Scope and Consequences*, ed. J.P. Phillips and M. Hoch (Manchester, 2001), pp. 150–63.

Riant, P., *Expéditions et pèlerinages des Scandinaves en Terre Sainte au temps des croisades* (Paris, 1865).

Richard, J., 'La confrèrie de la croisade: à propos d'un épisode de la prèmiere croisade', *Études de civilisation médiévale, IXe–XIIe siècles: mélanges offerts à Edmond-René Labande par ses amis, ses collègues, ses élèves* (Poitiers, 1974), pp. 617–22.

Richard, J., '1187: point de départ pour une nouvelle forme de la croisade', *The Horns of Hattin: Proceedings of the Second Conference of the Society for the Study of the Crusades and the Latin East*, ed. B.Z. Kedar (Jerusalem, 1992), pp. 250–60.

Richter, H., '*Militia Dei*: A Central Concept for the Religious Ideas of the Early Crusades and the German *Rolandslied*', *Journeys toward God: Pilgrimage and Crusade*, ed. B.N. Sargent-Baur (Kalamazoo, MI, 1992), pp. 107–26.

Riley-Smith, J.S.C., *The Knights of St John in Jerusalem and Cyprus, c.1050–1310* (London, 1967).

Riley-Smith, J.S.C., 'Government in Latin Syria and the Commercial Privileges of the Foreign Merchants', *Relations between East and West in the Middle Ages*, ed. D. Baker (Edinburgh, 1973), pp. 109–32.

Riley-Smith, J.S.C., 'Peace Never Established: The Case of the Kingdom of Jerusalem', *Transactions of the Royal Historical Society*, 5th ser., 28 (1978), pp. 87–102.

Riley-Smith, J.S.C., 'Crusading as an Act of Love', *History*, 65 (1980), pp. 177–92.

Riley-Smith, J.S.C., 'The First Crusade and St. Peter', *Outremer: Studies in the History of the Crusading Kingdom of Jerusalem Presented to Joshua Prawer*, ed. B.Z. Kedar, H.E. Mayer and R.C. Smail (Jerusalem, 1982), pp. 41–63.

Riley-Smith, J.S.C., 'Death on the First Crusade', *The End of Strife*, ed. D.M. Loades (Edinburgh, 1984), pp. 14–31.

Riley-Smith, J.S.C., *The First Crusade and the Idea of Crusading* (London, 1986).

Riley-Smith, J.S.C., 'The Venetian Crusade of 1122–1124', *I comuni italiani nel regno crociato di Gerusalemme*, ed. G. Airaldi and B.Z. Kedar (Genoa, 1986), pp. 339–50.

Riley-Smith, J.S.C., 'Family Traditions and Participation in the Second Crusade', *The Second Crusade and the Cistercians*, ed. M. Gervers (New York, 1992), pp. 101–8.

Riley-Smith, J.S.C., 'The Crusading Movement and Historians', *The Oxford Illustrated History of the Crusades*, ed. J.S.C. Riley-Smith (Oxford, 1995), pp. 1–12.

Riley-Smith, J.S.C., *The First Crusaders, 1095–1131* (Cambridge, 1997).

Riley-Smith, J.S.C., 'Raymond IV of St Gilles, Achard of Arles and the Conquest of Lebanon', *The Crusades and their Sources: Essays Presented to Bernard Hamilton*, ed. J. France and W.G. Zajac (Aldershot, 1998), pp. 1–8.

Riley-Smith, J.S.C., *What were the Crusades?*, 3rd edition (Basingstoke, 2002).

Riley-Smith, J.S.C., *The Crusades: A History*, 2nd edition (London, 2005).

Riley-Smith, J.S.C., 'An Army on Pilgrimage' (Forthcoming).

Roby, D., '*Stabilitas* and *Transitus*: Understanding Passage from One Religious Order to Another in Twelfth Century Monastic Controversy', unpublished Ph.D. thesis (Yale, 1971).

Routledge, M., 'Songs', *The Oxford Illustrated History of the Crusades*, ed. J.S.C. Riley-Smith (Oxford, 1995), pp. 91–111.

Rowe, J.G., 'Paschal II, Bohemund of Antioch and the Byzantine Empire', *Bulletin of the John Rylands Library*, 49 (1966), pp. 165–202.

Rowe, J.G., 'The Origins of the Second Crusade: Pope Eugenius III, Bernard of Clairvaux and Louis VII of France', *The Second Crusade and the Cistercians*, ed. M. Gervers (New York, 1992), pp. 79–89.

Rowe, J.G., 'Alexander III and the Jerusalem Crusade: An Overview of Problems and Failures', *Crusaders and Muslims in Twelfth-Century Syria*, ed. M. Shatzmiller (Leiden and New York, 1993), pp. 112–32.

Rubenstein, J., 'How, or How Much, to Reevaluate Peter the Hermit', *The Medieval Crusade*, ed. S.J. Ridyard (Woodbridge, 2004), pp. 53–69.

Rubenstein, J., 'Putting History to Use: Three Crusade Chronicles in Context', *Viator*, 35 (2004), pp. 131–68.

Rubenstein, J., 'What is the *Gesta Francorum* and who was Peter Tudebode?', *Revue Mabillon*, 16 (2005), pp. 179–204.

Runciman, S., 'The Pilgrimages to Palestine before 1095', *A History of the Crusades*, vol. 1, ed. K. Setton (Madison, WI, 1969), pp. 68–78.

Schaller, H.M., 'Zur Kreuzzugsenzyklika Papst Sergius IV', *Papsttum, Kirche und Recht im Mittelalter: Festschrift für Horst Fuhrmann zum 65. Geburtstag*, ed. H. Mordek (Tübingen, 1991), pp. 135–53.

Schein, S., *Gateway to the Heavenly City: Crusader Jerusalem and the Catholic West (1099–1187)* (Aldershot, 2005).

Schuste, B., 'The Strange Pilgrimage of Odo of Deuil', *Medieval Concepts of the Past: Ritual, Memory, Historiography*, ed. G. Althoff, J. Fried and P.J. Geary (Cambridge, 2002), pp. 253–78.

Sclafert, C., 'Lettre inédite de Hughes de Saint-Victor aux chevaliers du Temple', *Revue d'ascetique et de mystique*, 34 (1958), pp. 275–99.

Selwood, D., 'Quidam autem dubitauerunt: The Saint, the Sinner, the Temple and a Possible Chronology', *Autor de la première croisade: actes du colloque de la Society for the Study of the Crusades and the Latin East 1995*, ed. M. Balard (Paris, 1996), pp. 221–30.

Shepard, J., 'Cross-purposes: Alexius Comnenus and the First Crusade', *The First Crusade: Origins and Impact*, ed. J.P. Phillips (Manchester, 1997), pp. 107–29.

Shepard, J., 'The "Muddy Road" of Odo Arpin from Bourges to La Charité-sur-Loire', *The Experience of Crusading, Volume Two: Defining the Crusader Kingdom*, ed. P.W. Edbury and J.P. Phillips (Cambridge, 2003), pp. 11–28.

Shepkaru, S., 'To Die for God: Martyrs' Heaven in Hebrew and Latin Crusade Narratives', *Speculum*, 77 (2002), pp. 311–41.

Short, I., 'A Study in Carolingian Legend and its Persistence in Latin Historiography (XII–XVI Centuries)', *Mittellateinisches Jahrbuch*, 7 (1972), pp. 127–52.

Siberry, E., *Criticism of Crusading, 1095–1274* (Oxford, 1985).

Siberry, E., 'The Crusading Counts of Nevers', *Nottingham Medieval Studies*, 34 (1990), pp. 64–70.

Smalley, B., 'Ecclesiastical Attitudes to Novelty, c.1100–c.1250', *Church, Society and Politics*, ed. D. Baker, SCH, 12 (Oxford, 1975), pp. 113–31.

Smith, R.D., *Comparative Miracles* (St Louis, MO, 1965).

Somerville, R., 'The Council of Clermont (1095) and Latin Christian Society', *Archivum Historiae Pontificae*, 12 (1974), pp. 55–90.

Somerville, R. 'The Council of Clermont and the First Crusade', *Studia Gratiana*, 20 (1976), pp. 325–37.

Southern, R.W., 'The English Origins of the "Miracles of the Virgin"', *Mediaeval and Renaissance Studies*, 4 (1958), pp. 176–216.

Southern, R.W., *Western Society and the Church in the Middle Ages* (Harmondsworth, 1970).

Spiegel, G., 'The Cult of St. Denis and Capetian Kingship', *Journal of Medieval History*, 1 (1975), pp. 43–69.

Spiegel, G., *Romancing the Past: The Rise of Vernacular Prose in the Middle Ages* (Berkeley, CA, 1993).

Stalls, C., *Possessing the Land: Aragon's Expansion into Islam's Ebro Frontier under Alfonso the Battler, 1104–1134* (Leiden, New York and Cologne, 1995).

Sumption, J., *Pilgrimage: An Image of Mediaeval Religion* (London, 1975).

Throop, S., 'Vengeance and the Crusades', *Crusades*, 5 (2006), pp. 21–38.

Thurston, H.J., *The Physical Phenomena of Mysticism* (London, 1952).

Tinsley, E.J., *The Imitation of God in Christ: An Essay on the Biblical Basis of Christian Spirituality* (London, 1960).

Tyerman, C., *The Invention of the Crusades* (Basingstoke, 1998).

Ubieto Arteta, A., 'La participación navarro-aragonesa en la primera cruzada', *Príncipe de Viana*, 8 (1947), pp. 357–84.

Ubieto Arteta, A., 'La creación de la cofradía militar de Belchite', *Estudios de edad media de la corona de Aragón*, 5 (1952), pp. 427–34.

van Engen, J., 'The "Crisis of Cenobitism" Reconsidered: Benedictine Monasticism in the Years 1050–1150', *Speculum*, 61 (1986), pp. 269–304.

van Herwaarden, J., 'The Origins of the Cult of St. James of Compostela', *Journal of Medieval History*, 6 (1980), pp. 1–35.

van Herwaarden, J., 'Saint James in Spain up to the 12th century', *Wallfahrt kennt keine Grenzen*, ed. L. Kriss-Rettenbeck and G. Möhler (Munich and Zurich, 1984), pp. 235–47.

Vauchez, A., *The Laity in the Middle Ages: Religious Belief and Devotional Practices*, ed. D.E. Bornstein (Notre Dame and London, 1993).

Verdon, J., 'Une source de la reconquête chrétienne en Espagne: la Chronique de Saint-Maixent', *Mélanges offerts à René Crozet*, ed. P. Gallais and Y.-J. Riou, 2 vols. (Poitiers, 1966), vol. 1, pp. 273–82.

de Waha, M., 'La lettre d'Alexis I Comnène à Robert I le Frison', *Byzantion*, 47 (1977), pp. 113–25.

Ward, B., *Miracles and the Medieval Mind: Theory, Record and Event, 1000–1215* (Aldershot, 1987).

Watkins, C.S., 'Sin, Penance and Purgatory in the Anglo-Norman Realm: The Evidence of Visions and Ghost Stories', *Past and Present*, 175 (2002), pp. 3–33.

Webb, D., *Medieval European Pilgrimage, c.700–c.1500* (Basingstoke, 2002).

Willems, E., 'Cîteaux et la seconde croisade', *Revue d'histoire ecclésiastique*, 49 (1954), pp. 116–51.

Williams, J.B., 'The Making of a Crusade: The Genoese Anti-Muslim Attacks in Spain, 1146–1148', *Journal of Medieval History*, 23 (1997), pp. 30–53.

Yarom, N., *Body, Blood and Sexuality: A Psychoanalytic Study of St Francis' Stigmata and their Historical Context* (New York, 1992).

Index

For primary sources, either the author (where known) or the title has been cited, but not both.

St Père de Chartres, abbey of 16
St Reparata, abbey of 15
St Romain, abbey of 158
Saladin, sultan of Egypt and Syria 111
Samson, archbishop of Rheims 114
Santiago, Order of 177–8
Santiago de Compostela: *see* Compostela
Saracens: *see* Muslims, Islam
Sardinia 168, 170
Saxony 163
Schein, S., historian 4
Sergius IV, pope 45–7
Short, I., historian 151 n.86
Sibylline Books 79
Sicily 146
Sidon 67
Sigebert of Gembloux, chronicler 13, 26, 49, 123 n.22
Sigurd, king of Norway 67–8
Simeon, Greek patriarch of Jerusalem 42, 106
Simon of Cyrene 34, 66
Smith, R.D., theologian 36 n.47
Somerville, R., historian 13 n.6
Southern, R.W., historian 8, 52 n.180, 56–7, 85, 141 n.14, 144 n.36
Spain: *see* Iberia
Spanish crusades: *see under* crusading spirituality, definition of 7–8
stabilitas 14–15, 27–8, 100
Stephen, anchorite 148
Stephen of Blois, crusader 16, 124 n.28
Stephen of Neublans, crusader 42
Stephen, St 71
stigmata, stigmatics: *see under* imitation of Christ
strenuitas patrum: see family honour, as a theme in crusade preaching
Suger, abbot of St Denis 68, 69, 111–13
Syria 74

Tancred Marchisus, crusader 20, 22, 33, 57, 72 n.115
Tarragona 19, 122, 123, 125
Templars 27, 66, 74, 83–4, 100–11, 114, 115, 117–18, 133–4, 136–7, 170, 172, 181; as defenders of the Holy

Land 97, 101–3, 104–8; as exponents of the apostolic life 83–4; historiography of 3–4; as imitators of Christ 11, 104–11, 117–18, 181; *Primitive Rule* of 84, 101, 103, 105, 107, 108; *see also under* Bernard, St, abbot of Clairvaux
Theoderic, pilgrim 62, 63
Theodosius, *Topography of the Holy Land* 61
Thomas of Canterbury, St 144
Tiberias 147
Timothy, St 53
Tinsley, E.J., theologian 8, 22, 56
Toledo 123, 132, 146, 164, 173, 175, 176
Tortosa 127, 172–5, 177
Toulouse 126; council of (1118) 127–8, 136
transitus 10, 27–9, 100
Troyes, council of (1129) 101, 103, 107
Tunisia 156
Turks 18, 19, 50, 64, 68, 70, 76, 84, 125, 147, 172 n.212
Turpin of Rheims, archbishop: *see Historia Turpini*
Tyerman, C., historian 4–5, 118 n.224, 166 n.163
Tyre 74

Uclés, battle of (1108) 126 n.46
Ulger, bishop of Angers 108
Urban II, pope: and the apostolic life 52–6; and the liberation of Tarragona 19, 122–5; preaching of the First Crusade 10, 11, 12–14, 15–17, 19, 20, 28, 30–4, 35, 39–40, 41, 42, 45–7, 48, 52–6, 57–8, 59–60, 66, 69, 72, 73, 74, 75, 82, 85, 86–7, 88, 92, 94, 98, 104, 105, 117, 121–6, 155, 160–1, 162–3, 164, 172, 179–80, 181, 183, 184
Urraca, queen of León-Castile 131

Vallombrosans 12–13, 15, 28
Vasconia 156
Vauchez, A., historian 8
Vélay 94
Venice, Venetians 46, 73–4
Vézelay 76, 89

CPSIA information can be obtained at www.ICGtesting.com
Printed in the USA
BVOW04s1041110914

366347BV00005B/14/P